REMOVABLE *Type*

REMOVABLE
Type

HISTORIES *of the* BOOK *in* INDIAN COUNTRY,
1663–1880

Phillip H. Round

THE UNIVERSITY OF NORTH CAROLINA PRESS
Chapel Hill

Designed and set in Adobe Caslon Pro and Monticello by Rebecca Evans

The paper in this book meets the guidelines for permanence
and durability of the Committee on Production Guidelines for
Book Longevity of the Council on Library Resources.

The University of North Carolina Press has been a
member of the Green Press Initiative since 2003.

Library of Congress Cataloging-in-Publication Data
Round, Phillip H., 1958–
Removable type: histories of the book in Indian
country, 1663–1880 / Phillip H. Round.
p. cm.   Includes bibliographical references and index.
ISBN 978-0-8078-3390-2 (alk. paper)—ISBN 978-0-8078-7120-1 (pbk.: alk. paper)
1. Indians of North America—Books and reading. 2. Books and reading—United States—
History. 3. Indians of North America—Government relations. 4. Literacy—Social
aspects—United States. 5. Indians of North America—Cultural assimilation. I. Title.
E98.B65R68 2010   028.089'97073—dc22   2010006644

cloth   14 13 12 11 10   5 4 3 2 1
paper   14 13 12 11 10   5 4 3 2 1

An earlier version of chapter 8 appeared as "Indigenous Illustration: Native American
Artists and Nineteenth-Century U.S. Print Culture," *American Literary History* 19,
no. 2 (2007): 267–89; reprinted by permission of Oxford University Press.

Excerpts from Delphine Red Shirt, *Bead on an Anthill: A Lakota Childhood*,
© 1998 The University of Nebraska Press, are reprinted by
permission of the University of Nebraska Press.

Excerpts from Ray A. Young Bear, *Black Eagle Child*, are reprinted
by permission of the University of Iowa Press.

For Antonio

When they arrived they had only the Book and we had the land;
now we have the book and they have the land.

VINE DELORIA JR.,
Custer Died for Your Sins

Contents

Illustrations

Acknowledgments

FIRST THANKS GO TO MY FAMILY — to Teresa for reading every word and to Antonio for being the happy genius of our household. I would also like to acknowledge the many scholars, students, and friends who have influenced my study of book history in Indian Country over the past seven years. This project began as a short paper for Kate Shanley's Lannan Summer Institute in Native American autobiography at the D'Arcy McNickle Center for American Indian History at the Newberry Library, Chicago. In addition to Kate's kind guidance, I owe a debt of gratitude to all my fellow seminar participants for their kind support that summer, and to Rob Galler, who was acting director of the McNickle Center during the seminar.

An American Indian Studies (AIS) Consortium Faculty Fellowship from the Committee on Institutional Cooperation (CIC) helped bring my research into sharper focus, and again the staff at the McNickle Center and the Newberry Library were exceptionally generous with their support. I would like to thank especially James R. Grossman, vice president for research and education; Brian Hosmer, then director of the D'Arcy McNickle Center for American Indian History; and John S. Aubrey, Ayer collections librarian. Among the many CIC AIS faculty who helped me out along the way, I want to acknowledge the collegiality of Jean O'Brien, Joseph Gone, Robert Dale Parker, and John M. McKinn. I would also like to thank the students who took my seminar at the Newberry in 2005. Their conversations during class pushed this book in new and exciting directions.

My colleagues at the Society of Early Americanists who have offered constructive advice on several parts of this book deserve many thanks as well. Joshua Bellin, Joanna Brooks, Kristina Bross, Sandra Gustafson, Laura Mielke, Gordon Sayre, Laura Stevens, Ivy Schweitzer, and Hilary Wyss all contributed substantial support as I worked on this project. At the University of Iowa, I was blessed to have two incredibly patient and helpful colleagues in American Indian and Native Studies, Jacki Rand and Michelene Pesantubbee. Each inspired me to work harder and to sharpen my research and teaching in American Indian Studies. In the English Department, Matthew Brown and Kathleen Diffley offered invaluable insights into the history of the book and answered my many pestering questions with patience and good cheer. Finally, my work on this book could never have been completed without the constant encouragement of my former colleague at Iowa, Susie Phillips. I would also like to thank the Office of the Vice President for Research at the University of Iowa, which provided a subvention for this book. Royalties from the sale of this book will go directly to the American Indian College Fund.

REMOVABLE *Type*

Prologue

SOMETIME BETWEEN 1838 AND 1841 IN ROME, a young Native American man worked patiently on a manuscript entitled "Conversión de los Luiseños de Alta California." The story was part of an assignment he had been given by his teacher, Giuseppe Caspar Mezzon Fanti (1774–1849), chief custodian of the Vatican Library. The young man, Pablo Tac (1822–41), was studying at the Urban College after having been taken from his California homeland in 1832. Tac's manuscript, written in Spanish, tells the story of his people, known in their own language as the Quechnajuichom. Although intended for a European audience, the central story of the author's conversion at times gives way to the sentiments of a seventeen-year-old whose pride in his tribal community equals his sense of duty to his new overseers. After two paragraphs of mission history, Tac launches into a description of his community's most fearsome enemies, the Quichamcauchom (Kumeyaay)—their surprise attacks and their war regalia and weaponry. In the end, his nation turns to the Spanish for protection, and—as Tac approvingly relates—"merciful God freed us of these miseries through Father Antonio Peyri, a Catalan."[1]

Tac's little-known manuscript is interesting for many reasons. For one, it voices resistance even as it celebrates Christian conversion. In the paragraph after his panegyric to Father Peyri, Tac relates how his tribal leader, upon first meeting the Spaniards, challenged them, "What is it you seek? Get out of our Country,"[2] thus undercutting the triumphant tale of conversion. For another, it is but one of hundreds of such manuscripts produced by the Native peoples of North America during the eighteenth and nineteenth centuries that scholars have yet to explore for the richness and variety of American Indian interactions with alphabetic literacy, manuscripts, and print during the period. Tac's manuscript features not only an alphabetically literate Luiseño man's narrative but also his drawings. At one point when describing a tribal dance, he produces an image of Luiseño ceremonial life that is striking for its immediacy (figure 1). The "Indians" in this sketch are not seen through an

Figure 1. Pablo Tac, "Luiseño Dancers," in his "Conversión de los Luiseños de Alta California" (ca. 1838–41). Courtesy of Santa Barbara Mission Archive-Library.

outsider's ethnographic gaze. They evoke no stereotypical stoicism, no demonic irrationality. They appear happy, dancing with the joy that ceremony and celebration bring to those who commune together in such dances.

Thirty years later, another group of American Indians was offered help by the representative of another non-Indian group, this time in the form of lined ledger books and colored pencils. The man offering them was a prison warden, Colonel Richard Pratt. It was 1875, and the men, mostly Cheyenne and Kiowa warriors, were serving extended sentences in a special prison at Fort Marion, Florida. The colonel believed that the paper and pencils might help raise his prisoners' self-esteem. Perhaps their drawings could even be sold as souvenirs to help defray the cost of their upkeep. Although the beautiful drawings of the Fort Marion prisoners have been studied for some time, they have rarely been examined in light of their portrayal of yet another American Indian community coming to terms with the book—not the book-as-Bible, emphasized in so much of the scholarship of Native life during the period—but the "blank book." These ledger books were printed and bound codices intended for business record keeping and personal journal writing. Viewed from the perspective of book history, these warriors created not only what has come to be known as "ledger art," a term that refers to the transfer to bound blank books of traditional Plains pictorial art, but also a place for books in a Plains society that had never had a need for them before.

Figure 2. Ledger book cover (Blair's Tablet, Blair's Keystone Stationery Co., ca. 1870s), "Tablet Containing 21 Drawings . . . by Samson Kelly (Cheyenne), and Carl Sweezy (Arapaho)" (ca. 1904). Courtesy of National Anthropological Archives, Smithsonian Institution (MS 2531).

The cover illustration of one such book, captured by American troops from Cheyenne leader Dull Knife's village in 1876, speaks volumes about the complex cultural dynamics at play in the use of books in Indian Country (figure 2). Two stock figures from American nineteenth-century popular culture, the frontiersman and the African bondsman, dramatize the blank book's place in the colonization of America. The backwoods teacher points to a printed map on the wall, while a printed book lies casually on a chair in the background. Anyone using this book had to enter its pages through this colonial portal, an illustration that offers a shorthand synopsis of nineteenth-century colonization strategies. Although there were many maxims that captured this image's formula, perhaps Richard Pratt's infamous phrase serves best here: "Kill the Indian . . . and save the man."[3] This man, the same Pratt who had given his Native prisoners pencils and paper, later advocated "industrial" boarding schools for Native peoples as the best engine to drive the progress envisioned in his succinct aphorism.

The tablet found at Dull Knife's village shows that by the 1870s books were entering Indian Country in surprising and often secular ways. It is the volume's subsequent history, however, that encapsulates the real complexities of the role European codices played in the diverse tribal worlds of nineteenth-century America. This particular tablet would remain empty until 1904, when James Mooney of the Bureau of American Ethnology commissioned some drawings from the Arapaho artist Carl Sweezy, who used its pages to fulfill Mooney's request. The circuitous journey of this single book—produced in the eastern United States during the 1870s, acquired by Cheyenne people on the Plains soon thereafter, and then captured as war booty by American troops, only to be returned to Native hands and filled with drawings at the behest of an ethnographer—reflects in microcosm the complex story behind the Vine Deloria quotation that serves as epigraph to my study: "When they arrived they had only the Book and we had the land; now we have the book and they have the land."

Between 1840, when Pablo Tac sketched the Luiseño dancers, and 1876, when Dull Knife's community was raided by American troops, Native peoples in North America had begun to devise hundreds of ways to exploit the European technologies of alphabetic literacy and printed books for their own ends. Although we often think of Indian books as a "modern" phenomenon, the reality is very different. In the following pages, the reader will discover a heretofore-unrecorded history of almost two centuries of American Indian life among books.

Introduction

TOWARD AN INDIAN BIBLIOGRAPHY

IN THE OPENING PAGES OF *The Experiences of Five Christian Indians*, Pequot author and activist William Apess (1798–1838) informed readers that he would soon be "publishing a book of 300 pages, 18 mo. in size, and there the reader will find particulars respecting my life." The resulting work, *A Son of the Forest* (1831), became a classic "first" in American Indian autobiography—a self-authored, copyrighted text.[1]

Apess's conception of his life story in terms of bibliographic/print culture detail ("a book of 300 pages, 18 mo. [octodecimo] in size") would be shared by several generations of Native American writers for whom the material properties of texts, as well as the manner in which they were produced and consumed, would become an important component of their creative and expressive efforts. *Removable Type* explores the ways in which print provided these Native authors and their communities with a much-needed weapon in their battles against relocation, allotment, and cultural erasure. It traces the interaction of Native Americans and print culture over the period from 1663 to 1880 by surveying the emerging semiotic practices that inflected print in the many tribal societies that comprised "Indian Country" during this period.

The historical scope of *Removable Type* (1663–1880) is determined by the interplay of two timelines in North American political and cultural history. The first follows the development of print culture. In 1663, Puritan missionary John Eliot, with the help of a Nipmuck convert whom the English called James Printer, produced the first Bible printed in North America. It was also one of the first books printed in a Native language.[2] Thus, the trajectory of print history in America has been from the beginning intimately tied to the indigenous cultures of this continent, even if it was another hundred years before a Native author published a work of his own here.

From this foundational moment in American printing history, print culture developed in a colonial world very much tethered to the logic of English mercantilism, until the Revolution created liberated colonies that produced printed materials under the auspices of an emerging national ethos. With the establishment of copyright in 1790, "the very meaning of public writing was transformed" in the United States.[3] Literature became property, and authors, "proprietors." During the same decade, what Patricia Crain has called "the alphabetization of America" unfolded, as spellers and primers "fueled . . . an explosive print marketplace, and [created] . . . readers, writers and consumers of print."[4] Meanwhile, for Euro-Americans across the continent, reading became "a necessity of life."[5] The 1830s thus witnessed a "golden age of local publishing." For the first time in America there emerged a "fluid and multi-layered marketplace for books."[6] By the 1870s, a national market for magazines made authorship part of a new mass culture of machine-reproduced words and images.

The second timeline traces relations between the U.S. federal government and the numerous American Indian nations. From the first publication of Eliot's Indian Bible (*Mamusse wunneetupanatamwe up biblum God*) in 1663, through the ratification of the U.S. Constitution in 1788, the Removal Act of 1830, the establishment of the western reservations in the 1870s, and the forced relocation of Indian children into boarding schools in the 1880s, the history of Indian Country has been tied to legal documents, deeds, autobiographical writings, and polemical treatises printed by diverse Indian nations. Osage scholar Robert Warrior has argued that "modern" American Indian intellectual history began in 1880 with the federal government's decision to forcibly relocate Indian children to schools. This move to codify learning had the unexpected consequence of producing the first generation of intertribal activists and scholars. Lakota artist Battiste Good verbally glossed that year on his Winter Count calendar as "sent-the-boys-and-girls-to-school-winter" (figure 3).

Forced education—especially at boarding schools located in the East—brought additional hardships to most Indian communities, but it also coincided with an upsurge in Native-language literacies. Natives and non-Natives alike produced syllabaries (non-alphabetic symbols systems used for writing) and Roman alphabet orthographies in the nineteenth century. It was during the 1880s that Lakota men like George Sword began to write down autobiographical Native-language narratives in manuscript books that would later also include ceremonial and cosmological materials. It was also during

Figure 3. Battiste Good (Wapostangi), Brulé Winter Count for
the years 1851–80 (ca. 1880). Courtesy of National Anthropological
Archives, Smithsonian Institution (MS 2372).

this period that Ho-Chunk (Winnebago) people adopted a syllabic written
form of their language that spread to the Meskwaki of present-day Iowa.[7]
Works written in the Ho-Chunk syllabary and the Lakota Roman type orthographies (along with several others), derived from alternate literacies and
substitute codices, have led anthropologist Ray DeMallie to postulate the
emergence of "new Native genre[s]" in the period.[8]

In 1772, Samson Occom became the first Native American to publish his
work; in 1828, Cherokee author Elias Boudinot became the first indigenous
editor of a newspaper whose audience was both Native and non-Native. By
the 1880s, the first generation of professional Indian writers was just entering school — Zitkala Sa at White's Manual Institute in Indiana and Carlos
Montezuma at Carlisle. Soon after these writers graduated, there emerged a
mass market for books by American Indians, and Native writers like Charles
Eastman, Sa, and Montezuma were able to showcase their work in national
publications like the *Atlantic Monthly* and *Harper's.*

Given the great diversity of Native nations in the United States, the geographic and social range of my study is harder to define than its historical
scope, but it too derives from specific historical and political forces and events.

These historical and political contexts have become codified in federal Indian policy and everyday Native American life by the phrase "Indian Country." In this book I employ "Indian Country" as a heuristic term that enables me to conceptualize the cultural field within which Native production and consumption of manuscript and printed texts took place during the period under study. It is a phrase taken from the familiar language used by Native peoples in the United States today. Two of the major Native American newspapers in the United States employ it on their mastheads (*Indian Country Today* and *News from Indian Country*). Scholarly articles use it in titles. Tribal community members rely on it in day-to-day conversation to locate themselves geographically within their respective homelands, politically within their shared legal status with other indigenous peoples, and imaginatively within the spiritual homelands of their hearts and minds.

The phrase is also used extensively in federal Indian law. In 1948, the U.S. Congress gave the concept of Indian Country its present legal definition:

- All land within the limits of any Indian reservation under the jurisdiction of the United States government, notwithstanding the issuance of any patent, and including rights-of-way running through the reservation;
- all dependent Indian communities within the borders of the United States, whether within the original or subsequently acquired territory thereof; and
- all Indian allotments, the Indian titles to which have not been extinguished, including rights-of-way running through the same.[9]

Here the term is focused on land and on the history of dispossession sedimented in that land—reservations, "dependent Indian communities," allotments of tracts to individuals. But even in its legal usage, the term conjoins the land base of Native identity and cultures to textual discourse. Interwoven into all of these meanings of Indian Country are the texts of laws, treaties, autobiographies, and migration stories. Most of these, in turn, have been codified in the form of printed books.[10]

My use of the term "Indian Country" thus combines Native, idiomatic usage with federal policy so as to create a conceptual category to aid in our understanding of the "place" of American Indian cultural production. It is akin to a conceptualization found in the Euro-American critical canon to describe spaces of cultural production in the African diaspora—Paul Gilroy's "Black Atlantic." In Gilroy's work on cultural formation among Africans dispersed across the early modern Atlantic world by the slave trade, the geography of human displacement also maps a cultural field of radical political potential that, in effect, gave rise to modernity as a countercultural discourse against the enslaving forces. Gilroy describes this geographic space of Atlantic black life as a set of deep "structures of feeling, producing, communicating, and remembering." Within this sphere of cultural production, there emerged "a complex pattern of antagonistic relationships with the supra-national and imperial world for which the ideas of 'race,' nationality, and national culture produce the primary . . . indices."[11] As Jonathan Elmer observes in a review essay on the continuing relevance of Gilroy's idea, the "Black Atlantic" "remains a powerful model of thinking," precisely because it moves us "beyond the self-serving narratives of the nation state . . . to transcend both the structures of the nation state and the constraints of ethnicity and national particularity."[12]

The term "Indian Country" in this book's subtitle, like the term "Black Atlantic," refers to a specific geographical location ("any Indian reservation, dependent Indian community, [and] all Indian allotments") during the specific historical period of about 1663 to 1880—that is, from the time of the first "Indian Book" to the decade that produced the 1887 Dawes Act (the "severalty act," which created land allotments on reservations)—and to a cultural "place" characterized by specific structures of "feeling, communicating, producing, [and] remembering" across the Indian nations of North America.

For contemporary Native peoples, the "feeling . . . and remembering" that constitutes Indian Country is often a complex weave of deep-felt contradictions, like those Meskwaki writer Ray A. Young Bear enunciates in *Black Eagle Child*:

> Although we were together as Indians
> . . . throughout
> the country—related in dialects and customs—
> we were like rural farmsteads separated
> from each other by infinite miles.
> That was the frightening reality.
> Being compartmentalized but always
> Being apart.[13]

Yet I use the term "Indian Country" not only to expose such contradictions, especially those surrounding printing and books, but also to point out the structures in this geographic space of cultural encounter that bring Indian people together.

As Craig Womack (Muskogee) has demonstrated, the notion of nationhood has been a unifying trope for indigenous peoples in North America, working to bind together the disparate elements of Indian Country in an effort to prevent the kind of alienation expressed in the Young Bear poem. Womack writes:

> The concept of nationhood itself is an intermingling of politics, imagination, and spirituality. Nationhood encompasses ongoing treaty relationships with the U.S. government. Nationhood has to do with federal Indian law, and tribes' testing of the sovereignty waters through new economic development and other practices. Nationhood is affected by imagination in the way the citizens of tribal nations perceive their cultural and political identity. Nationhood recognizes spiritual practices, since culture is part of what gives people an understanding of their uniqueness, their difference, from other nations of people. Literature plays a vital role in all of this, since it is part of what constitutes the idea of nationhood; people formulate a notion of themselves and an imagined community through stories.[14]

The term "Indian Country" therefore engages both Young Bear's sense of the colonial "compartmentalization" of Indian lives and Womack's belief in nationhood's constitutive power within distinct tribal communities. In the following study, I focus on the importance of books to Indian Country, on the central role they play in the ongoing, constitutive discourse of resistance in which "the translation of land into property and of orality into alphabetic writing are linked."[15]

In this way, *Removable Type* participates in a recent trend in American Indian studies that aims to describe "Native literature's place in Indian Country." It opens to view a new and expanded Native canon, what one critic has called that heretofore-unrecognized "large body of written and oral works authored and spoken by Indian people, both primary literatures and commentaries on those literatures in written and oral forms."[16] In the following pages, I explore the relationship of this canon to Euro-American print culture in the nineteenth century.

The "Problem" of Native Literacy

Any description of the place of books in Indian Country must first grapple with the "problem" of Indian literacy. Native literacy has been a particularly vexing issue in the historiography of early America because, as literary scholar

Laura Donaldson reminds us, "its function as a colonial technology has remained obscure." "Writing," she observes, "worked alongside . . . more overt weapons of conquest." But Native North Americans, as Donaldson argues, "were [not] always only victims of Western literacy."[17] The historical records, both oral and written, reveal something very different. A reexamination of Native literacy is therefore necessary before we begin to build a more general model of Native American interaction with books.

The critical role of literacy in colonial Native subject formation has been in part obscured by oversimplified representations of Native peoples' fascination with print's supposed "magical qualities." The original inhabitants of the eastern woodlands were so impressed by European books and literacy, ethnohistorian James Axtell explains, that communicating at a distance with print and manuscript books was viewed as "an awe-inspiring spiritual feat."[18] Anthropologist Peter Wogan cautions against overgeneralizing Axtell's version of the Native experience of print. In particular, Wogan warns against the assumption that print had a universal appeal for Native people. Instead, he urges us to deploy "ethnographic approaches to literacy" that take into account the kind of sociocultural factors that "mediate and determine the uses of literacy of any given culture."[19]

To follow Wogan, then, we must first acknowledge that two main sets of cultural practices mediated Native use of and reaction to European print. First, the oral traditions of tribal communities—even though they differed in distinctive ways—shared many of the paralinguistic and performance features of Euro-American discursive practices in the period. Such traditions would come to mediate the circulation, use, and production of print in Native communities. Second, many precontact forms of graphic communication held sway across North America. From the eastern woodlands, where wampum circulated in beaded belts imbued with spiritual Manitou and rhetorical power, to the Great Plains, where tepee covers and buffalo robes detailed personal, family, and communal identities in pictographs and graphic designs, Native people were already employing a wide array of sign systems prior to the arrival of Europeans.[20]

In one of the earliest descriptions of the Algonquian peoples by an English writer, Thomas Harriot focused on the Powhatan reaction to the Bible he carried to Virginia in 1585–86: "Manie times and in every towne where I came, according as I was able, I made declaration of the contents of the Bible . . . and although I told them the book materially and of itself was not of any such vertue, as I thought they did conceave, but only the doctrine therein

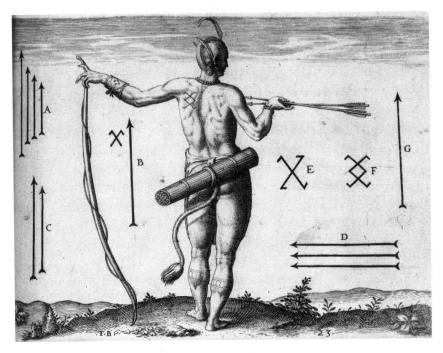

Figure 4. Theodore DeBry, "The Marks of Sundry of the Chief Men," in Thomas Harriot, *A Brief and True Report of the New Found Land of Virginia* (1590). Courtesy of Edward E. Ayer Collection, Newberry Library, Chicago.

contained; yet would many be glad to touch it, to embrace it, to kisse it, to hold it to their breasts and heades, and stroke it over all their bodies with it."[21] Like the compasses and burning glasses he showed them, the book seemed to Harriot to "farre exceed [the Native peoples'] capacities to comprehend." In another section of his book, however, Harriot illustrates the Powhatan use of tattoos, graphic markings that were just one part of an elaborate semiotic system that included verbal and materials signs (figure 4). These tattoos, representing clan affiliation and other designations of individual and collective identity, struck Harriot as interesting examples of a sort of Native "heraldry." Yet he was unwilling or unable to make the leap to consider these signs as a form of "written" expression. In his mind, the Powhatan were and would remain "very simple, and rude."[22]

All across Indian Country, signs and symbols like those of the Powhatan performed something akin to the role of written language, extending semiotic production deep into the material culture of the various tribes, as well as into the natural world in which their communities flourished. In 1790, after a victory over the Euro-American settlers of the near frontier, intertribal nativists built "a large painted encampment" one-quarter to one-half mile in length in a place called the Glaize in the Ohio River Valley. In "stripping all the saplings in the area, [and] painting them red with hieroglyphics," the encamped tribes made the forest itself a script of Indian-white interaction.[23] Across Indian Country in the eighteenth and nineteenth centuries, Euro-Americans observed and discussed phenomena they actually called "Indian Writing." "The visible or written language of these people," one author observed, "consists principally of significant signs and gestures, by which they communicate their ideas to strangers, and a limited method of picture writing, which they have in common use among themselves: such as are often seen engraved on their war clubs, or wooden cases of their looking glasses, and also such as are painted on trees, grave posts, and the walls of their dwellings."[24]

As Lisa Brooks explains in her study of indigenous writing in the Northeast, European writing and print entered and circulated in Native communities via already established channels of communication. Just as wampum and Mi'kmaq hieroglyphs traveled up and down river ways and through woodlands, both physically and symbolically "circulating," so too alphabetic print and manuscript text would follow well-trodden paths. This complex "network of relations and waterways," beaded belts and birch-bark scrolls, came together with imported European written materials to produce what Brooks calls the "Common Pot," the "native place" where Indian writing transpired as a *new* field of cultural production within the frame of encounter. Brooks terms this intersection of literacy and landscape in Indian Country a "spatialized writing tradition," and she carefully traces "the ways in which writing that came from Europe was incorporated into this spatialized system." It is in this sense of syncretic literacy practices—from within the Native spaces of communicative performance—that I discuss alphabetic literacy and print in Indian Country.[25]

In addition to reexamining Native discursive contexts for an emerging semiotic that would expand to include writing, manuscripts, and print, we must also consider Native literacy practices from the perspective of a broader "ideology of the book." In *The Darker Side of the Renaissance* (1990), Walter Mignolo points out that "the spread of Western literacy . . . did not only take the form of reading and writing." He argues that we must consider the book as an object in and of itself, as a material thing in its own right, beyond the words it contains. The book-as-object (called simply the "book object" in book studies) circulates in a social world that "does not respect limits either linguistic or national"[26] and serves as an agent of European colonization. Mignolo describes this book-based aspect of the colonial literacy project as "a massive operation in which the materiality and the ideology of Amerindian semiotic interactions were intermingled with or replaced by the materiality and ideology of Western reading and writing cultures." For the Europeans who came to the Americas, the content of the book was sometimes less important than its ideological function as "*the* object in which a set of regulations and metaphors was inscribed, giving to it the special status of Truth and Wisdom."[27]

In fact, there exists a persistent undercurrent within the discourse of colonization and contact in which the book figures prominently as "an agent of change" for both Europeans and Native peoples. Timothy Alden's account of an eighteenth-century Christian mission among the Seneca exemplifies this mind-set. He quotes a Six Nations chief as saying, "I have often told my people that we must be wrong, that you must be right, because you have the words of the Great Spirit written in a book." The leader then "[drew] the finger of his right hand across his left, repeatedly, to give an idea of the disposition of the lines on the page of the Bible," performing the semiotic difference that Alden believed obtained between European and Indian sign systems.[28]

Native peoples, however, could just as easily turn the discourse of book conquest on its head. Samuel Kirkland reported that Onoongwandekha in the 1760s counseled the Oneida against accepting Kirkland's mission because the Bible, a "White people's book[,] . . . was never made for Indians." The "Great Spirit gave us a book," Onoongwandekha continued, but "he wrote it in our hands, and in our minds."[29] In yet another tribal context, Claudio Saunt reports that some Muskogee who were in favor of appeasing the Americans during the first decade of the nineteenth century adopted writing and "branded their stock with the same marks they drew on written documents." In the Muskogee language, Saunt notes, "'branded' and 'written' are . . . the same word."[30]

To understand the diverse responses to books and writing in Indian Country, then, it is important to heed the call of contemporary Native scholars like Craig Womack who urge us to "break down the oppositional thinking that separates orality and literacy wherein the oral constitutes the authentic culture and the written contaminated culture." In many tribal settings, Womack contends, "books were used as a complement of oral tradition rather than [as] a replacement."[31] The goal of my study is to uncover the nature and extent of these uses, viewed, to the greatest extent possible, from the perspective of the tribal members themselves.

An "Indian Bibliography"

Because my history of the book in Indian Country focuses especially on the transmission of texts produced by and for Native Americans from 1663 to 1880, it belongs to a curious genre of American textual study called "Indian Bibliography." This is the phrase used by Thomas Field, whose *Essay towards an Indian Bibliography* (1873) is a landmark in the collation of works by Indian authors. Although Field's text is little more than a catalog, its title resonates within the long-standing discourse of "book conquest." Field's title brings to mind, for example, Cotton Mather's name for the religious tracts that John Eliot and other Puritan missionaries produced in seventeenth-century New England—the "Indian Library." Its ideological thrust is present in Samuel Drake's *Book of the Indians* (1833), Henry Rowe Schoolcraft's *Bibliographical Catalogue* (1849), and Daniel Brinton's *Aboriginal American Authors and Their Productions* (1883). Each of these works combines a catalog of Native texts with a narrative of contact in which the meeting of Europeans and indigenous peoples is essentially determined "by and through books."

Schoolcraft's bibliography is particularly revealing about the role of early book history in federal Indian policy and European colonization. "The true history of the Indian tribes and their relations" Schoolcraft writes, "must rest . . . upon the light obtained from their languages. To group and classify them into families on philosophical principles, will be to restore these ancient relations. Their traditions and historical activities, so far as they reach, will generally attest the truth of the facts denoted by language. In our future policy, they should be removed or colonized in reference to this relationship, and foreign groups not be commingled with cognate tribes."[32] Like European educators and missionaries before and after him, Schoolcraft employs books—in the form of a bibliographic listing of codices in Indian languages—to control the Native population. They will be "colonized in reference" to their bibliographic and linguistic relationships.

In my version of an "Indian bibliography," however, in order to tease out the complex interactions between alphabetic literacy, Native graphic sign systems, and the ideology of the book, I employ the techniques of book studies (*histoire du livre*). D. F. McKenzie, one of the founders of modern Anglo-American book studies, was the first to recognize the applicability of *histoire du livre* to "the contact between the representatives of a literate European culture and those of a wholly oral indigenous one." In *Bibliography and the Sociology of Texts*, McKenzie observes that the history of the book provides a theoretical framework for moving from simple questions of textual authority "to those of dissemination and readership as matters of economic and political motive." Such questions are paramount in the case of Native American cultures because of the central role played by "oral, manuscript, and printed texts in determining the right of indigenous peoples . . . subjected . . . to the commercial and cultural impositions of the powerful technologies of print."[33] Many scholars continue to fall back on literary critic Arnold Krupat's now hackneyed phrase "bi-cultural composite composition" to refer to texts produced by American Indians with the help of Euro-American editors, printers, and publishers.[34] In reexamining such works from the point of view of current book studies theory, however, I insist that *all* texts are produced in a composite way, and that *all* texts, Euro-American and Native American alike, are the products of complex networks of publishers, printers, editors, audiences, and authors. By adopting a book studies approach to Native literacy, we may better recognize "the continuing reciprocities of speech and print in the evolution of [Indian] texts," even as we acknowledge that this "reciprocity" was neither evenhanded nor equal for Native Americans.[35]

Removable Type also employs the methodology of book history to dispel simplistic characterizations of American Indian authors as individual, often quaintly "romantic," writers and instead to foster an appreciation for the sociological complexity of their work. "The book historian," Canadian book studies scholar Germaine Warkentin observes, "is grounded in the same solid materiality" as are the various sign systems of the indigenous peoples of North America. Thus, "book history assumes the basic bibliographic requirement of *marks made upon a material base for the purpose of recording, storing, and communicating information.*"[36]

In the following pages, I focus particularly on Native peoples' self-conscious application and adaptation of Anglo-American ideologies of print, on the many competing notions of print literacy that were emerging in their societies, and on the interpenetration of oral, manuscript, and printed forms of "publication." As I examine Indian authors and readers from this perspective, many interesting questions arise. What do the physical properties of Native-authored print texts (the size, typography, frontispiece illustrations, editorial matter, and bibliographic information) reveal about their production, circulation, and consumption? What do Indian manuscripts look like? How were such texts composed? Is there evidence of outside editorial intervention? Where does print (in its largest sense — the pressed word on the page in a typographic script) fit into the many competing forms of communication extant in early Native America?

CHAPTERS I AND 2 EXPLORE the ideological centrality of the book to Indian conversion projects of the seventeenth and eighteenth centuries, especially those of New England, and their legacies to subsequent generations of Native peoples in North America. Chapter 3 extends these explorations into the nineteenth century and beyond strictly religious publishing contexts. With a title borrowed from Jedidiah Morse's explanation of his vision for nineteenth-century missionary enterprises to the Indians, chapter 3 examines both the changing nature of Native literacy and education and the transformed nature of book publishing in the first half of the nineteenth century. It then moves on to examine the material processes by which written words became physical objects in Indian Country. Using disparate sources from the eighteenth and nineteenth centuries, it weaves together details regarding the production, circulation, and consumption of works like the co-authored translation of the *Book of Common Prayer* produced by the Reverend John Stuart and Mohawk leader Joseph Brant in 1787, and the Native-language works published by missionary Jotham Meeker, together with several Native translators and pressmen at the Shawanoe Mission press in Kansas Territory. The result is a composite story of the making of Indian books that reveals the labor of Native peoples often overlooked in histories of the book in America.

Chapters 4 through 8 take up McKenzie's call to embrace a form of bibliography whose principal goal is recovery of the "wealth of human experience" that is involved in reading, writing, producing, and consuming books. McKenzie calls those recovered human experiences the "sociology of texts." This section of *Removable Type* thus focuses on "the social, economic, and political motivations of publishing, the reasons why texts were written and read as they were, why they were rewritten and redesigned, or allowed to die." Following McKenzie, I explore "the full range of social realities which the medium of print had to serve, from receipt blanks to bibles," always keeping in view "the human motives and interactions which texts involve at every stage of their production, transmission, and consumption." In the process, I uncover "the roles of institutions, and their own complex structures, in affecting the forms of social discourse, past and present."[37] In these chapters, I ask questions of print similar to those anthropologist Keith Basso has asked of writing in general: What is the distribution of print in nineteenth-century Indian Country?

What demographic factors—age, gender, and socioeconomic status—hold sway in Native communities' relationship with print? What activities are associated with print? In what setting is it accomplished? How does print information differ from that which is disseminated through alternate channels? And, finally, "What position does . . . [print] occupy in the total communicative economy of the society under study and what is the range of its cultural meanings?"[38]

In my exploration of these many and varied instances of reading, writing, and printing among Native people over the course of two centuries, several axioms emerge. The first is that print mattered in Indian Country—both in external U.S. political relations and within local communities. The second is that Native people self-consciously manipulated print and were integral members of the composite body that is American print culture. Taken together, these observations affirm that Native American "ideologies of the book" were quite diverse and expansive, reflecting a wide range of tribal/national political positionings, from "republicanism" to entrepreneurialism, from nativist to assimilationist.

Because my study takes a "big picture" perspective on the history of books in Indian Country, I have had to exclude some tribal communities from extended study. By focusing almost exclusively on the Anglophone print tradition, I leave undiscussed the fascinating story of literacy among the Diné (Navajo), the many Pueblo nations, the Western Apache, the Tohono O'Odham, and others whose influence in present-day American Indian literature is substantial. Despite these limitations, however, I hope my work will instill in the reader a new appreciation for the American Indian men and women who wrote and published before 1880—the date used by most historians of Indian writing as the beginning of "modern" Native literature. The fact is that Native people have been writing for a long time. Whether penning memorials, autobiographies, "myths and legends," or "sketches of Indian life," they were exploring new, nontraditional public and political modes of expression that, over time, were often integrated with other, time-honored forms of sociability like storytelling, wampum belts, pictographic inscription, midewiwin scrolls, beadwork, and hide painting. These new modes of communication in turn made up what Robert Warrior has called the "intellectual tradition" that informs so much of life in Indian Country today.

I close with a contemporary Ojibwe account of the role played by books and print in the revitalization of one American Indian community. While visiting Anishinaabe poet Al Hunter in his Canadian community, Louise Erdrich discovers something "very striking" about books in Indian Country:

> [Hunter] says that when he returned home after his education, to work, there were many terrible and pressing needs to address on his reserve— poverty, alcoholism, despair—so he called a meeting. At this meeting, he needed to tell people there was something that their reserve greatly needed. A library.
>
> Books. *Why?*
>
> Because they are wealth, sobriety, hope.[39]

One

THE COMING OF THE BOOK

TO INDIAN COUNTRY

FROM THE VERY BEGINNING, Native peoples and Europeans in British North America related to each other by and through the book. In early English contact literature, the figure of the book as an agent of conquest is ubiquitous, as are myriad fantasies about Native codex production and consumption. The official seal of the Society for the Propagation of the Gospel, one of the most influential missionary bodies in early America, features a ship arriving to the shores of the New World, a missionary at its bow waving a book at the Native people gathered there (figure 5).

For this study, we can pinpoint the exact year the book may be said to have "come" to Indian Country in British North America. In 1663, John Eliot (ca. 1604–90), Puritan missionary pastor to the indigenous nations of southern New England, published an Algonquian translation of the Christian Bible. Looking back at over a hundred years of proselytizing efforts in America, nineteenth-century missionary Samuel Bartlett focused on the primacy of Eliot's Indian Bible for all future evangelical endeavors. It was, he believed, "the index and monument of [Eliot's] achievements," having been the "first and long the only, Bible printed in America."[1]

Bartlett's 1876 narrative of the Christian evangelization of Native peoples in North American is structured as the story of how print came to the New World's "unlettered" masses. In this retelling, Eliot's book project leads seamlessly to the work of Eleazar Wheelock, founder of Moor's Charity School (1754), the first sustained "Indian School" in the colonies. Wheelock oversaw the education into alphabetic literacy of Native luminaries such as Joseph Brant and Samson Occom. He was also responsible for the distribution of a great deal of print—especially primers and spellers—throughout New England and New York. From Wheelock, Bartlett moves to John Sergeant,

Figure 5. Seal of the Society for the Propagation of the Gospel. Courtesy of John Carter Brown Library at Brown University.

minister to the Housatonic in the eighteenth century, and so on, down to his nineteenth-century contemporaries' evangelization of the Cherokee and Choctaw Nations. A traveler to the western country in 1830, Bartlett assures his readers, "would have found half the Cherokees in Georgia able to read." Between 1816 and 1860, Bartlett continues, missionaries and Cherokees collaborated in producing more than 14 million pages of printed vernacular text. During the same period, the Choctaw produced 11 million. To Bartlett, as to many of his readers and contributors to the missionary project of gospel propagation, the history of redemption *was* a history of the book.[2]

Bartlett's account indicates the staying power of an ideology of book conquest that began with John Eliot's mission and remained foremost in the Anglo-American imagination throughout the eighteenth and nineteenth centuries. It was from within this ideology of the book that most literacy projects in Indian Country took shape. But Bartlett's outline of the progress of Native literacy is only part of the story. In this chapter, I outline how Eliot's literacy mission served not only as the cornerstone of later book-centered Euro-American ideologies of conquest but also as the starting point for several powerful alphabetic literacy complexes built and maintained by Native peoples in the eighteenth century. The coming of the book to Indian Country was a dialogic process. Books arrived in the New World and transformed it forever. Yet, just as significant, books were themselves transformed in the process. American books like those produced at Eliot's New England Mission press were often the result of bicultural cooperation and relied heavily on Indian compilers, translators, and editors. In the hands of these indigenous craftsmen, polemicists, writers, and readers, the European ideology of the book was put to the service of Native nation building in ways that far surpassed the expectations of the colonizers.

The "Indian Library"

Native conversion and education was the rhetorical centerpiece of the English colonists' propaganda about the New England Way, the name given to the peculiar form of church and civil government that reigned in the colonies throughout the seventeenth century. From early works like *New England's First Fruits* (1643) to Increase Mather's *A Brief History of the War with the Indians* (1676), New England writers framed their settlement of the New World as narratives about the "progress of the gospels" to the "heathen" peoples living there. In practice, however, the Massachusetts Bay and Plymouth colonies were inconsistent in implementing educational opportunities for Native communities. When the metropolitan Parliament finally established its American missionary society, called the Society for the Propagation of the Gospel in New England (known to most people simply as the New England Company) in 1649, it institutionalized and centralized missionary efforts. It also permanently linked them to the English imperial administrative system and to a print culture formation that would come to be known as the "Indian Library," a series of texts in the Massachusett language. It was a logical step for a Protestant missionary society deeply rooted in a Christian humanist ideology of the book in which "true writing [was] alphabetic writing and . . . indistinguishable from the book."[3] In the New England Company's view, writing was synonymous with civility and took the specific material form of the European codex. The hundreds of English men and women who contributed monetarily to the New England Company in order to propagate books in the New World shared these beliefs. In fact, it would seem that most people in the mother country thought that books were what the Indians needed most. One London bookseller, for example, bewailed the fact that "the poor Indians" lacked "the treasures of knowledge contained in books."[4] The society thus made books its first priority and set out to provide Indian peoples with a bibliographic foundation for the creation of "schools, and nurseries of learning for the education of the children of the Natives."[5]

Book history scholar Matthew Brown argues that for New England's Reformed Protestants the ideology of the book was grounded in "a literary culture predicated on the religious socialization of readers through the materiality of the written record." John Eliot's Indian Library thus provided "instructional works intended to transmit Christian doctrine, the Massachusetts primers and catechisms sought to displace oral modes of communication [and] . . . the presence of the written record in the Eliot mission demoted oral knowledges and promoted the book as a sign of English superiority."[6]

The book remained ideologically central to New England Indian conversion through 1676, when full-scale war erupted between New England's allied Native tribes and the English settlers. Colonists treated Native survivors harshly after the war, selling many into slavery. Yet, even then, Increase Mather assured his readers that "the main design of the fathers of this colony [remains] to Propagate the Gospel and the Kingdom of Christ among these Indians." As evidence, Mather pointed to John Eliot, the most famous missionary to the Native peoples of Massachusetts, and his translation of "the whole Bible into the *Indian Language*. In which respect *New England* . . . hath outdone all other places."[7] As Mather's comments indicate, New English exceptionalism was often a bibliographic exceptionalism, a *translatio librii*, in which the Native peoples figured crucially as the exemplary site of the revelation of the word through the literacy they had been granted by their colonizers.

Mather and his Puritan predecessors were particularly touchy about Indian literacy and conversion because they were invariably questioned about these topics back in London. Routinely accused of "intolerance" and "irregular" church discipline, New Englanders often found themselves on the defensive when it came to explaining their role in Christianizing the Indians. More than one Englishman pointedly suggested that such missions were founded "[not] in pitty to mens soules, but in hope to possesse the land of those Infidels, or of gaine by Commerce."[8] John Eliot fueled the fire of these suspicions when he tried to explain to a British correspondent that "[the Indians] must have visible civility . . . before they can rightly enjoy visible sanctity in ecclesiastical community."[9] In putting civil society ahead of Church and doctrine, he exacerbated the mercantile qualms of some metropolitans. Was all this missionizing really about trade?

Back in the 1660s, however, Eliot's argument prevailed among the commissioners of the New England Company, and vernacular texts in Massachusett became the material culture centerpiece of their vision of an Indian civil society. Many discussions of this aspect of Eliot's ministry focus on translation and language issues.[10] In their stubborn materiality and monumental presentation, however, books were also useful signs of the "visible civility" Eliot demanded from his Native parishioners. Matthew Brown has observed that this "visible" culture of the book in Puritan New England provides us with ample opportunities to explore Euro-American settlers' representations of imagined Native peoples, sentimentalized and idealized in now-familiar tropes like that of the "melancholic Praying Indian." Brown, however, is unwilling to view the books in the Indian Library as "ethnographic facts drawn from the contact zone or as neutral sources of Algonkian expression."[11] I believe that they did indeed become part of the fabric of Native life in southern New England, inspiring new forms of cultural production and a revitalization of Native belief systems, particularly in the 1660s. They in fact formed the discursive basis upon which emerging new civil institutions like the Praying Towns and land allotments depended. Ultimately, books provide an important backdrop for understanding cultural revitalization in New England Native communities during the late seventeenth century.

Though Eliot promoted his Indian books as Eurocentric, visible signs of civility, the Indian Library actually grew out of a fundamentally unstable bicultural communicative field. In describing the New England missions, Eliot's colleague Thomas Shepard (1605–49) was fairly frank about the missionaries' uneven facility with Native languages. In *The Clear Sunshine of the Gospel Breaking Forth Upon the Indians* (1648), Shepard describes how Eliot employed a special discourse of the middle ground—using simple concepts, familiar metaphors, and exaggerated gesture as part of a rhetorical complex he considered essential to cross-cultural communication. Eliot explained doctrinal concepts by "demonstrations," which—according to him—the Native peoples "delight[ed] in." Using "circumlocutions and variations of speech and the helpe of one or two Interpreters," Eliot spoke and gestured his way to Indian conversion.[12]

In this haphazard rhetorical setting, Eliot reasoned, Indian books could serve some very practical purposes. First, they offered to stabilize unregulated linguistic slippage and rhetorical play (unruly language use unleashed by unsure translators and skeptical Native auditors). They grounded ministerial utterance in the material form of the codex, an object treated with reverence by Eliot and his colleagues and believed to safeguard unvarying meaning from one reading to the next. Textual, material stability was especially important in Indian Country, a Puritan missionary astutely observed, precisely because "a few words from the Preacher were more regarded then many from the Indian Interpreter."[13] Because Native peoples seemed to privilege the authority of the speaking subject, Eliot sought to cut out the middle man, replacing the interpreter with his culture's own recognized authoritative site of gospel speaking—the book. Second, because the missionaries were far from fluent in the local languages, a printed version of the texts allowed them to pronounce Massachusett words syllabically. This afforded them more cultural authority and (they hoped) more doctrinal accuracy in their evangelical performances.[14]

Between 1649 (when he first broached the subject of publishing a Bible in Algonquian to the Plymouth Colony's Edward Winslow) and 1653 (when the first, fragmentary Algonquian works reached print), John Eliot enlisted the help of Christian Indians to work up a syllabic orthography of the Massachusett language. This orthography would function for several decades as a crucial mediating semiotic in New England's colonial middle ground. Most historians agree that the orthographic language we see on the pages of Eliot's Indian Library is not spoken Massachusett but rather a kind of approximation or "trade language" in print.[15] At first the "books" Eliot used were produced in manuscript only, but slowly, over the period from 1653 to 1655, he moved into print. In 1653, Eliot's first text in Algonquian, a one-volume primer/catechism, was published by the Society for the Propagation of the Gospel and printed by Samuel Green in Cambridge, the only village in New England with a press. Two years later, the book of Genesis and part of Matthew were printed as an experiment. In 1656, journeyman printer Marmaduke Johnson was hired in England and shipped to New England, along with a new printing press, to assist in the project. By 1661, Johnson, Green, and their Native translators were able to print a run of 1,500 copies of the New Testament. In 1663, complete translations of the Old and New Testaments were printed together in a single 1,180-page volume.[16]

At a time when Michael Wigglesworth's extremely popular *Day of Doom* (1662) was produced in a print run of 1,800 copies, Eliot's 1,500 impressions of a folio Bible (which few Englishmen could read) reflected a substantial outlay of time and effort. The production of the Indian Library would thus have an important ripple effect on the New England book market in general during its earliest years. First, it brought to the country a very experienced journeyman printer who would later return to the colonies to work for a rival press. Second, because the vernacular language editions required eighty pounds of new type, including "extra Os and Ks to accommodate Eliot's transcription of

Algonquian phonemes," the typographic capacity of the New England press was greatly expanded. Finally, as the only press licensed to print the Bible in British America, Eliot's operation was instantly elevated to an especially sacred and politically charged level. As Brown remarks, "These material practices had an indirect though crucial effect on the history of publication in New England. The missionary's intentions to supply 'many books' for natives resulted in the revitalization of the *colony's* print-house, producing titles for a second generation *Anglo-American* audience. . . . [Thus] Eliot's promotional efforts underwrote a second-generation white archive of jeremiad textuality."[17]

Brown, however, may be too quick to dismiss the role that writing and print began to play in Native cultures across southern New England as a direct result of Eliot's Indian Library. By employing the first Native American artisans (like Nipmuck convert James Printer) to work as translators, compilers, and printers, the press inaugurated the collaborative, bicultural enterprise that would shape the history of the book in Indian Country down through the nineteenth century. The text produced by this press, as an article of production and consumption known as "Eliot's Bible," has long been viewed as the work of John Eliot alone, and therefore as a colonial and Christian imposition from "outside" Native societies. Yet to regard the Indian Bible in this way is, as Kristina Bross points out, to erase "the participation of the praying Indians in its production."[18] In addition to James Printer, Eliot relied heavily on Job Nesuton, a Massachusett-speaking convert who joined Eliot's mission in 1646 and probably did most of the translating.

The physical properties of the 1663 *Mamusse wunneetupanatamwe up biblum God* (known as "Eliot's Bible" or the "Indian Bible") reveal the collaborative, bicultural social horizon from which the Native print vernacular emerged. A comparison of the title page of the Indian Bible with that of a contemporary English-language edition printed in London reveals slight differences in typography, layout, and translation — those "visual and tactile features" of books that lie beyond their content but yet "render [a book] perceptible and accessible to others" (figure 6).[19] The Algonquian Bible follows the layout conventions of the English Bible in most details. In both editions, the text appears in two columns of Roman type preceded by an elaborate initial. Both also include glosses, and the Algonquian version even includes the English-language overview of the chapter that the English text provides. The Massachusett Bible is, however, more ornate than the average English Bible of the 1660s, employing typographic ornamentation instead of rules and rule frames to separate text from title. It opens with a fairly literal translation of the En-

Figure 6. Title page of *Mamusse wunneetupanatamwe up biblum God* (1685).
Courtesy of Edward E. Ayer Collection, Newberry Library, Chicago.

glish Bible's original heading ("The First Book of Moses, Called Genesis"), using the Algonquian word "negonne" (literally, "first") and following the English edition's practice of italicizing the word "Moses."[20] A cursory reading of the entire text reveals that literal translation and slightly more elaborate typography and ornamentation extend throughout the work, making it both a useful, "practical" text, and an attractive gift book. In the 1660s, copies were sent across the Atlantic to both Robert Boyle and Charles II.

Yet the Algonquian vernacular cannot stretch to accommodate many of the underlying ideological principles of either Protestant doctrine or book culture that inform the Bible's production. The table of contents from the

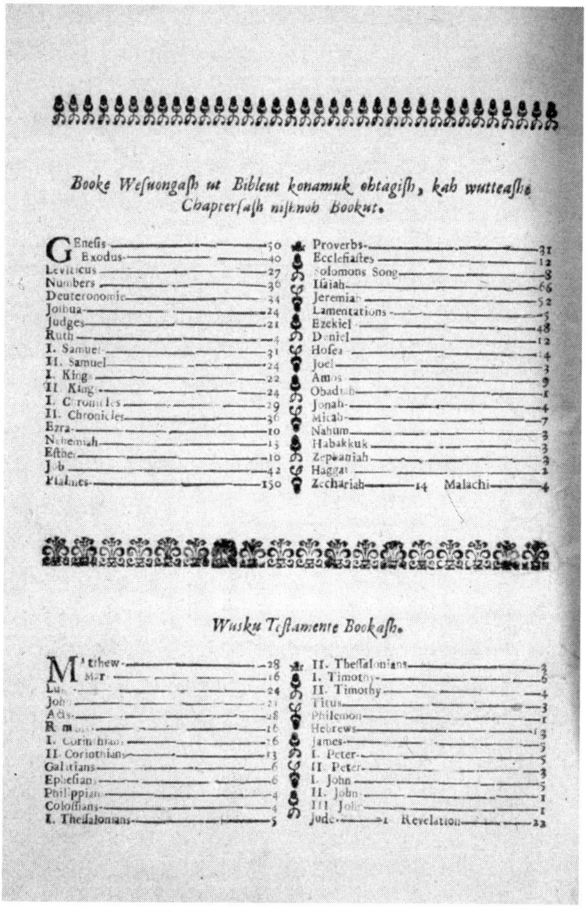

Booke Weſuongaſh ut Bibleut konamuk ohtagiſh, kah wutteaſh Chapterſaſh niſhnoh Bookut.

Geneſis	50	Proverbs	31
Exodus	40	Eccleſiaſtes	12
Leviticus	27	Solomons Song	8
Numbers	36	Iſaiah	66
Deuteronomie	34	Jeremiah	52
Joſhua	24	Lamentations	5
Judges	21	Ezekiel	48
Ruth	4	Daniel	12
I. Samuel	31	Hoſea	14
II. Samuel	24	Joel	3
I. Kings	22	Amos	9
II. Kings	24	Obadiah	1
I. Chronicles	29	Jonah	4
II. Chronicles	36	Micah	7
Ezra	10	Nahum	3
Nehemiah	13	Habakkuk	3
Eſther	10	Zephaniah	3
Job	42	Haggai	2
Pſalmes	150	Zechariah 14 Malachi	4

Wusku Teſtamente Bookaſh.

Matthew	28	II. Theſſalonians	3
Mark	16	I. Timothy	6
Luke	24	II. Timothy	4
John	21	Titus	3
Acts	28	Philemon	1
Romans	16	Hebrews	13
I. Corinthians	16	James	5
II. Corinthians	13	I. Peter	5
Galatians	6	II. Peter	3
Epheſians	6	I. John	5
Philippians	4	II. John	1
Coloſſians	4	III. John	1
I. Theſſalonians	5	Jude 1 Revelation	22

Figure 7. Table of contents of *Mamusse wunneetupanatamwe up biblum God* (1663). Courtesy of Edward E. Ayer Collection, Newberry Library, Chicago.

Up biblum God vividly illustrates how a particular Protestant ideology of the book cleared a typographic space for itself within the long syllabic phrases of the Massachusett language (figure 7). The signifier "God," for example, resists translation because the missionaries believed that the Algonquian dialect itself was "by no means sufficient to convey . . . the knowledge of Divine things."[21] This seems to have held true for concepts of a distinctly print culture origin as well. Thus the words "Booke," "Bibleut," "Chaptersash," "Bookut," and "Bookash" dominate the page. In the Algonquian edition, the concept of "book" itself is untranslatable. The editors of the Eliot Bible appear to have felt obliged "to supply that defect in the Native tongue" by "introducing English words."[22] Thus the Eliot Bible serves both as a "supplement" to the presumed inadequacies of Indian language and as an introduction to an ideology of the book in which printed words are wholly "other" to Native life.

Thus far, it would seem that Eliot's book project was indeed the disciplinary technology that most scholars have made it out to be, and that "the Eliot mission demoted oral knowledges and promoted the book as a sign of English superiority."[23] Yet, as Kristina Bross has recently pointed out, "the vernacular Bible made Indian readers possible."[24] Furthermore, the work of Bross, Hilary Wyss, and Jill Lepore highlights the importance of alphabetic literacy to the colonial subject formation of New England's Native converts. Caught in the amorphous gap between English and traditional ways, these peoples lived, in Wyss's words, "as cultural half-breeds inhabiting that dangerous no-man's-land between identifiable cultural positions."[25] Bross, Wyss, and Lepore have all demonstrated how converts like James Printer employed "cross-cultural mediations, appropriations, and translations" drawn from the commingling of missionary discourse and Algonquian cultural practices to negotiate the divide.[26] None of these scholars, however, has adequately dealt with the *printedness* of Native vernacular literacy. Converts were not only invested in literacy as reading and writing but also as material practice. And the material culture of Eliot's Indian Library grew steadily around them during the 1660s and 1670s. In addition to Eliot's 1663 Bible, converts had at their disposal four other works that were intended to shape Native literacy in a special, bookish, and printed way. These included Eliot's first Algonquian book, *The Indian Grammar* (1660); *The Indian Primer* (1669); a compilation of catechistic exercises to aid converted Indians called the *Indian Dialogues* (1671); and *The Logic Primer* (1672).

In fact, the Indian Library's effects on seventeenth-century Native literacy practices were substantial. Ives Goddard and Kathleen Bragdon have discovered that the literacy rate in Native language syllabary texts (both manuscript and print) was nearly 30 percent among Massachusett-speaking people by the first decade of the eighteenth century. In communities like Mashpee, Natick, and Gays Head, texts printed and written in Massachusett were "produced in the normal course of conducting the daily affairs of the Indian communities." The documents that have survived from the period reveal uses of writing and print that range from sacred to secular, public to private. Deeds are most common, but Bragdon and Goddard have also cataloged "records of town meetings, . . . depositions, wills, petitions, letters, notes, arrest warrants, a power-of-attorney, a notice of banns, . . . [and] marginalia in books."[27]

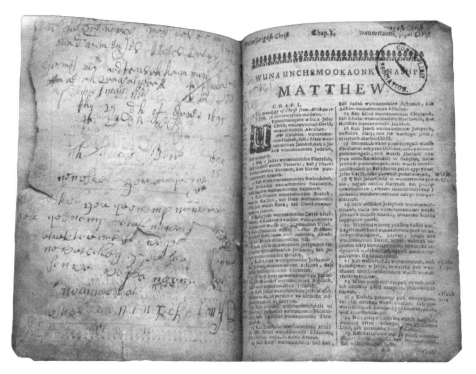

Figure 8. Annotated page from *Mamusse wunneetupanatamwe up biblum God* (1663). Courtesy of Congregational Library, Boston, Massachusetts (RBR EL 4.48).

Profound anxiety was woven into this new possibility of print literacy for many Indian readers. Marginalia penned in Massachusett in several extant copies of the Indian Bible show that, although vernacular print provided a protected space in which to express oneself and affirm community, it could also tap into emerging doubts and self-loathing. Some converts, interacting with print for the first time, would proudly write, "This is my hand," or "This book is right." Others, however, found the experience daunting. "I do not like very much to read," one wrote, "for I am too pitiful in this world"[28] (figure 8).

At the same time, David Silverman has shown that the Wampanoag Christians on Martha's Vineyard actually began to experience a Native cultural revitalization through the new teaching of the Christian missionaries. In a process Silverman calls "religious translation," these Native people "filtered Christian teachings through Wampanoag religious ideas and terminology." "By the mid-1660s," Silverman observes, "Christian services took place at every corner of the island, and by 1674 all but one of the Vineyard's three hundred or so families called themselves Christian." The success of the mission in this location, according to Silverman, was due specifically to the new printed vernacular: "Print runs large enough to supply a Bible to every Christian Indian family, combined with public readings by literate Wampanoags, brought these works to the eyes and ears of nearly everyone on the islands."[29]

More direct evidence of the impact of printed matter on the religious lives of Southern Algonquians may be found in the questions Native converts put to missionaries in the 1660s. On several occasions, converts posed queries directly related to a printed work in the Indian Library. "What is meant," one asked John Cotton Jr., "by that Phrase in Mr. Eliots Catechism, when a man dyes, his soule goes into a Strange Country?"[30]

After completing the Algonquian Bible, Eliot carefully considered what other kinds of books to print for Indians. Writing to Richard Baxter, he confided, "I am meditating what to do next for these Sons of this our Morning: they having no books for their private use, of ministerial composing."[31] Eliot seems to have detected an emerging body of intensive readers in convert communities who would be interested in consuming books in "private." Bibles in Eliot's day were considered communal, public books, neither portable nor self-explanatory enough to be used wholly in "private." Reformed Protestants in both England and the Massachusetts Bay Colony moved quickly to fill this "private" reading niche with a new genre of book object, the tract. A portable, brief, and easily consumable form of theological exposition, the tract (or "pious affordable handbooks," as Matthew Brown so aptly defines them) was produced for "circulation among ordinary readers" and was perhaps of "greater influence than even Bibles."[32] To fill the void created by his new and growing Native readership, Eliot decided to produce his own Indian tract, a translation of Baxter's *Call to the Unconverted* (1652). Eliot clearly believed he was witnessing the emergence of "ordinary" readers in the Indian convert communities. He thus argued that "though the word of God be the best of Books, yet Humane Infirmity is, you know, not a little helped, by reading the holy Labours of the Ministers of Jesus Christ."[33]

Viewed from the perspective of book history, Eliot's dilemma as he searched for a follow-up text also reflects typical marketing concerns. He now had an eye out for that most important of all Protestant book ventures in early modern British America, the "steady seller." David D. Hall and Matthew Brown argue that the constant presence of a body of popular religious tracts in the New England colonies, republished and imported generation after generation, suggests that a "Protestant vernacular" culture flourished there. This culture depended upon the symbiotic relationship between a "mass" pub-

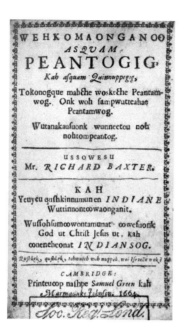

Figure 9. Title pages of John Eliot, *Wehkomaonganoo* (1664), and Richard Baxter, *A Call to the Unconverted* (1652). Courtesy of Huntington Library, San Marino, California (63563), and © The British Library Board (c.30a.31), respectively.

lic of intensive readers and a "mass" market for books that appealed to them.[34] Thus Eliot's reworking of Baxter's *Call* for an Indian audience may be seen to exhibit many of the characteristics that book historian Roger Chartier claims are typical of a work that is being repackaged for a "broader" (and in this case, culturally different) audience. Popular reprinting, Chartier argues, often calls for "shortening texts, [and] simplifying them." Reprinted works often feature more "visible signals [such] as anticipatory headings, recapitulative summaries . . . or woodcuts." Certainly Eliot's Indian reprint represents an attempt to draw on its readers' "previous knowledge" of conventions and codes.[35]

The "typographic transformations" performed by the Cambridge press on Baxter's *Call* offer insights into its target audience and their imputed reading practices (figure 9).[36] The edging of the Algonquian *Call* is fancier than the original, with type ornaments replacing the rule frame, suggesting that even though Eliot printed it for "private" Indian use he was keeping open the possibility of the pamphlet's having a ceremonial, gifting function. Although intended as a "popular" reprint, a potential "steady seller" in the Algonquian language, Eliot's *Call* remained "exotic" to non-Indians.

The Coming of the Book (33)

The title page of the Algonquian tract, like Eliot's Bible translation, is basically a literal rendering of the Baxter text. The Massachusett words "wehkomaonganoo," "asquam," and "peantogig" all are roughly equivalent to the English words "call," "not yet," and "converted." Yet, unlike the English edition, which highlights the word "call," the missionary printers chose to single out the word "peantogig" in a larger typeface. The substitution is illuminating, for the Algonquian word not only puts more emphasis on the "unconverted" nature of its readership, but it also presents its Native readers with local language shadings not present in the English original. According to John Trumbull's *Natick Dictionary* (1909), *peantogig* is a word that refers both to supplication and to the act of speaking quietly.[37] It appears to be written in a third-person form that suggests that "they are supplicant." The other obvious change the colonial printers made is the introduction of the words "Indiane" and "Indiansog" in the portion of the text that translates Baxter's "To be read in families where any are unconverted." Here, the Native language edition appears to be either labeling Indian peoples in general as heathens or appealing to a whole new sort of audience — Indian readers. More than a mere translation, the New England title page thus signals cultural difference while acknowledging an emerging Indian public, for whom the nuanced word "peantogig" might have more appeal than the straightforward European "call." In a further move away from its English counterpart, Eliot's text inserts an italicized Algonquian rendering of Ezekiel 33:11 ("Turn Ye, Turn Ye, from your evil ways"), thus underscoring a millenarian dimension to his book-centered brand of Native evangelization.[38]

A look inside the two books points to other socially derived points of contact and divergence in the New England colonial book world that Eliot's hoped-for steady seller would help construct. The Algonquian text appears slightly more elaborate than its English counterpart. It is more tightly set, presenting the reader with a denser body of type — partly due to the phrase-length sets of type that result from syllabic translation. The Indian Library book again duplicates the English original's elegant initial and imitates its use of a horizontal rule to separate the title from the text. The Algonquian version as a whole, however, is pared down by many pages. Much of Baxter's prefatory material is excised.

The result is a much tighter work, and upon closer inspection, a book that typographically may highlight its role as a template for oral recitation or performance (figure 10). The method of typographical bracketing employed here (which does not appear in English editions) was likely designed with the

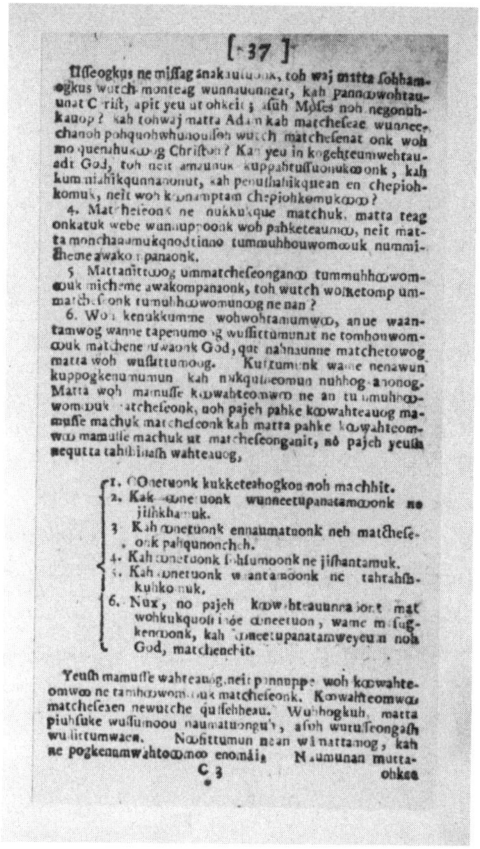

[37]

Uſſeogkus ne miſſag anakauſuonk, toh waj matta ſohhamogkus wutch monteag wunnauunneat, kah pannꝏwohtauunat Criſt, apit yeu ut ohkeit; aſuh Moſes noh negonuhkauop? kah tohwaj matta Adam kah matcheſeae wunneechanoh pohquohwhunouſſeh wutch matcheſenat onk woh mo quenahukꝏog Chriſtum? Kah yeu in kogehteumwehtauadt God, toh neit amaunuk kuppahtuſſuonukꝏonk, kah kumniahikqunnaonut, kah penuſhahikquean en chepiohkomuk, neit woh kounamptam chepiohkomukꝏ?

4. Matcheſeonk ne nukkukque matchuk, matta teag onkatuk webe wunnuppoonk woh pahketeaumꝏ, neit matta monchaaamukqnodtinno tummuhhouwomꝏuk nummiſheme awakompanaonk.

5. Mattanittꝏog ummatcheſeonganꝏ tummuhhꝏwomꝏuk nicheme awakompanaonk, toh wutch woſketomp ummatcheſeonk tumuhhꝏwomunꝏg ne nan?

6. Woh kenukkumme wohwohtamumwꝏ, anue waantamwog wanne tapenumoog wuſſittumunat ne tomhouwomꝏuk matchene uwaonk God, qut nahnaunne matchetowog matta woh wuſittumoog. Kuttumunk wame nenawun kuppogkenumumun kah nukquineomun nuhhog anonog. Matta woh mamuſſe kꝏwahteomwꝏ ne an tumuhhꝏwomꝏuk matcheſeonk, noh pajeh pahke kꝏwahteauog mamuſſe machuk matcheſeonk kah matta pahke kꝏwahteomwꝏ mamuſſe machuk ut matcheſeonganit, nó pajeh yeuſh nequtta tahſhinaſh wahteauog,

1. Onetuonk kukketeahogkon noh machhit.
2. Kah onetuonk wunneetupanatamꝏonk ne jiſhkhamuk.
3. Kah onetuonk ennaumatuonk neh matcheſeonk pahqunonchch.
4. Kah onetuonk ſohſumoonk ne jiſhantamuk.
5. Kah onetuonk wantamoonk ne tahtahſhkuhkonuk.
6. Nux, no pajeh kꝏwahteaunnaionk mat wohkukquoh inoe onneetuon, wame miſugkenꝏonk, kah onneetupanatamweyeuun noh God, matchenehit.

Yeuſh mamuſſe wahteauog, neit pannuppe woh kꝏwahteomwꝏ ne tamhꝏwomꝏuk matcheſeonk. Kꝏwahteomwꝏ matcheſeaen newutche quſſehheau. Wuhhogkuh, matta piuhſuke wuſſumoou naumatuonguh, aſuh wutuſſeongaſh wuſittumwaen. Nꝏſittumun nean wi nattanog, kah ne pogkenumwahtoꝏmꝏ enomaia. Naumunan mutta-

C 3 ohkea

Figure 10. Page from John Eliot, *Wehkomaonganoo* (1664). Courtesy of Huntington Library, San Marino, California (63563).

Native missionary or pastor in mind. The layout offers rhetorical guidelines for underscoring the text's main points to a culturally "other" audience. It is perhaps the typographic trace of what Eliot called the "circumlocutions," "demonstrations," and "familiar similitudes" that were required of the missionary preacher in his dealing with the Native peoples of New England.[39]

If we consider the Cambridge press's techniques in republishing Baxter's *Call* for an Indian audience, together with its handling of the Bible, the differences we have noted above begin to exhibit a pattern of emendation that we might tentatively begin to call "Indian print." "Indian print" is first characterized by literal translation, simplification, and a direct importation of "hard" words from the English language to correct the supposed "defects" of the Algonquian dialects. In his Bible and tracts, Eliot was concerned first and foremost with simplifying doctrine and sacred writ. In a letter to Baxter, he spoke about the need to popularize Christian doctrine, focusing on his free translation of Baxter's tracts as an example of how dissenting doctrine "shall be made to speak in their own Ears, in their own language, that you may preach unto our poor Indians." Eliot admitted that he found "a great difference" in translating a steady seller from his "former Translations" of the Gospels. In translating the Bible, Eliot had been "strict." But whereas he felt theologically obliged to perform literal translations of Bible passages, with the Baxter tract he felt free to "alter the Phrase, for the facilitating and fitting it to our language."[40]

This is the second hallmark of "Indian print," an underlying structural principle of "free" translation when cultural difference threatens the assumed transparency of meaning in the English original. The difference in approach was thus dictated not only by the needs of a "popular" text but also by cultural distinction. Indeed, Eliot found that "some things which are fitted for English people, are not fit for [Native readers], and in such cases, I make bold to fit it for them."[41] Although he never specifies which changes fall into this category, his emphasis of the word "peantogig" on the title page of *Call* would appear to be one example of making Baxter's work a better "fit" for the social and cultural world of Native converts in New England.

Indian print, however, is not a phenomenon that flows only from the printed work outward, as a matter of editorial intention. We also find that Native readers of these books reacted to them in a number of complex ways, thus constructing their own "Native" books from works intended to strip them of their traditional ways. Such reactions ranged from writing marginalia (both anxious and mundane) in copies of the Bible, to quoting from tracts when engaging European ministers over points of doctrine, to suggesting turns of phrase that would appeal to Algonquian speakers, to accepting books as profoundly powerful gifts, gifts that functioned across a cultural array of meanings from "amulet" to "trade good."[42] Native readers of Indian print took the literacy they gained from the specifically Christian context of religious practice and applied it to other important interactions with whites, writing and signing land deeds, town meeting books, and letters of indenture.

In describing his vision for how the Indian Library would further the Algonquian peoples' conversion, John Eliot abstracted the morphology of Native literacy into a simple formula: "*Legendo, scribendo, Loquendo.*"[43] But what did the vernacular texts mean to seventeenth-century Native converts? As Roger Chartier has observed, "Reading is always a practice embodied in acts, spaces, and habits." It "brings the body into play, it is inscribed in a space, and a relationship with oneself or with others."[44] Certainly one of the ways these

Figure 11. Page from John Eliot, *The Indian Primer* (1720). Courtesy of Edward E. Ayer Collection, Newberry Library, Chicago.

Native converts read was within the disciplinary framework set forth by the missionary himself. Eliot's printed matter attempted to control Native bodies as well as their minds. His missionizing imposed a set of textual practices borrowed from the English common school and its textbooks. To read in this system, using these primers, was to recite the alphabet, to move into the pronunciation of printed syllables, and finally to intone the words of the Westminster Assembly's catechism. Viewing a page of Eliot's *Indian Primer* with these disciplinary procedures in mind, we can imagine the reading practices and tacit ideologies it actuated in a seventeenth-century mission classroom. Figure 11 shows a page from a later edition of the *Indian Primer* (printed in Boston in 1720). Its participation in the larger, ongoing colonial education project Patricia Crain calls "the alphabetization of America" is clear. Yet the image also exemplifies how Eliot's vernacular Massachusett print guided Native readers toward the subtler forms of literacy entailed in typography. Like the European education manual it emulates (*The New England Primer*), the *Indian Primer* begins with an array of alphabets in Roman, italic, and black letter type. The facing page "translation" not only shows the Native reader how to form letters in the Massachusett syllabic alphabet, but also how to shape the typographic tone of his or her utterance to master European typographic convention. In this way, the *Indian Primer* served as a specialized disciplinary educational technology, "introducing the alphabet into a nonalphabetized culture and to a nonprint audience."[45]

Yet, within these disciplinary confines, many Native communities in early New England approached Euro-American literacy education as a means of achieving status in the emerging bicultural colonial society. Jennifer Monaghan observes that on Martha's Vineyard, "social cachet was attached to literacy education."[46] Hiacoombes, the first convert on the Vineyard, appears to have used his new religion and literacy to acquire higher status in the community than he had enjoyed prior to missionization. After the initial contact of missionaries with Southern Algonquians interested in pursuing the new faith and its accompanying technology of the book, moreover, literacy tended to run in families. Members of literate families, in turn, took up positions of authority within Praying Towns, and leadership lineages appear to have formed around literacy practices.[47] There was also a definite Native method that informed how individual converts progressed through their literacy education. As Monaghan discovered in a careful reading of Experience Mayhew's *Indian Converts* (1727), although most Native converts were taught to read, writing instruction was limited primarily to men, and mainly in a school setting.[48] Writing was an institutional practice tied to the colonial power structure; as a result, this aspect of Native literacy was especially status laden. Therefore, while the Indian Library produced readers across genders and communities, it produced *writers* in a slightly different way, emphasizing the role of men and underscoring written literacy's role in the emerging colonial power structure.

Taken together, Native language texts like the Bible, the *Primer*, and Baxter's *Call*, along with manuscript, printed works, and marginalia, found meaning in Massachusett communities by supplementing and extending existing cultural values. In societies in which "skilled speech and status were interrelated," written and printed rhetorical style and formal protocols were practiced as extensions of these modes of sociability. Kathleen Bragdon finds that in Native New England "writing was inherently social, . . . [and] reading and writing were 'inextricably' linked to speech." As a result, such works were far more than mere "remnants of the oral mode that survived into writing." They describe a print literacy that embodies "the ongoing sociability and orality of literacy among the Massachusett speaking people."[49]

By 1675, the Native peoples of southern New England who embraced some form of Christianity—together with some modes of vernacular literacy and print culture experience—lived in a world separated by institutional and material cultures from Native neighbors who had opted for a more traditional life. Most of the Christianized Native population was settled in "Praying Towns," some fourteen villages set aside by colonial authorities for their particular use. Eliot described the villages as located "some what remote from the English, where they must have the word constantly taught, and government constantly exercised . . . [and a] means of instructing them in Letters, Trades, and Labours."[50] In these separate communities, alphabetic literacy in the Massachusett vernacular was coupled with theological and civil instruction to create distinct syncretic cultural spaces that mediated the converts' interactions with both backcountry traditional Native life and the colonial world being established by English settlers.

As historian Jean O'Brien remarks, such Native settlements produced "remarkable histories" that belie the adage common in nineteenth-century histories that the Indians of New England had "disappeared." To the contrary, O'Brien demonstrates, "the Mashpee and Gay Head Wampanoag and the Nipmuck in Massachusetts, the Mashantucket Pequot and Mohegan in Connecticut, the Narragansett in Rhode Island, the Abenaki in Vermont and western Maine, and the Passamaquoddy and Penobscot in Maine" all live creative lives to this day.[51] In every one of these cases, books played a major role in the innovative techniques these communities employed to preserve themselves. By the end of the seventeenth century, many of these books had become as "Indian" as they were European. From the Eliot Bible buried with a parishioner in Natick to the Mi'kmaq prayer book printed with inverted alternate pages to match traditional, precontact elder/student educational protocols, writing and print circulated across the Native Northeast along time-honored circuits of kinship and geography, adopted when necessary and cast off when a threat to community survival.[52]

"Carried Away, Burned, or Destroyed"

In 1675, war broke out between the pan-tribal allied forces of Wampanoag leader Metacom (known to the English as King Philip) and the British. As a result, the story of the coming of the book to Indian Country veered off in a direction very different from the one John Eliot had imagined in 1663. King Philip's War became a watershed moment in the history of New England

Native life "by and through the book." In the military campaign between allied Wampanoag and Nipmuck warriors and the English, some 5,000 Native and 2,000 English lives were lost. When the war ended in 1676, an all-out ideological struggle ensued over the hearts and minds of the New England reading public. At issue was whether Eliot's literacy mission had "civilized" Indians at all. In nearly every account of the war written by the English, the Christian and literate members of Praying Towns were singled out for special abuse. At the height of the hostilities, nearly all of John Eliot's Indian Library was destroyed. Scholars have yet to determine whether responsibility for this lay with Metacom's army, that of the English, or both. Afterward, Jill Lepore observes, the English printed more than 15,000 books in an effort to justify their side of the story.[53] These postwar apologies "descended on a very small Anglo-American book market between 1675 and 1682," thus establishing a disproportionate English-language bibliomania to counteract the former print cultural dominance of the Indian Library.[54]

In the early nineteenth century, Timothy Dwight voiced the view that "King Philip's War put an end both to the efforts and the hopes of our ancestors concerning this subject [literacy education], and destroyed all disposition on the part of the Indians to receive the benefits intended."[55] Dwight's critique targets Native peoples in an attempt to restore moral clarity to his ancestors' missionary effort. Yet his observation was correct in one respect—the war forever changed the dynamics of Native literacy in New England. From a book history point of view, King Philip's War, and the explosion of English-language print that followed in its wake, produced a fascinating postwar cultural battle that was waged by and through books. A comparison of the book exploits of New England colonist and war captive Mary Rowlandson and Native convert-turned-conspirator James Printer will serve to illustrate the state of Native print literacy as the region entered the eighteenth century.

James Printer, both as New-England-government-sponsored prewar pressman and wartime propagandist for Metacom's anti-English forces, is a complex exemplum of Native colonial subjectivity achieved in part through literacy. The son of a deacon of the Praying Town of Grafton, Printer was educated at the short-lived Indian School at Harvard. His father was also a Nipmuck sachem, and it may be that this dual lineage informed Printer's social roles in both Native and English communities. It is certain that when the war broke out he abandoned his position as printer at Samuel Green's shop and joined the Native warriors allied under Metacom. Increase Mather summed up his feelings about Printer in one scathing sentence: "[He] could not only read and write but had learned the art of printing, notwithstanding his apostasy."[56] The last phrase is quintessentially Mather in its ambiguity. *Notwithstanding his apostasy.* Did Mather mean that Printer's literacy, extending beyond reading and writing to typesetting, was useful to the English and so in some measure excused his treason? Or was he expressing surprise that Printer had mastered the art of printing in spite of being at heart an apostate? Books were so highly valued as an outward manifestation of religiosity in New England that Printer's desertion must have been truly hard to fathom.

As a Praying Indian, Printer's literacy made him a particular focus of wrath and suspicion. Wyss points out that Praying Indians during King Philip's War were "valuable to both sides as translators and scribes, yet [their] liminal identity left them mistrusted by both."[57] The picture of Printer that emerges from Wyss's careful study, *Writing Indians* (2000), is of someone who used his literacy both to support Metacom's cause and then, when it became clear it could not prevail, to save his own neck. In Mary Rowlandson's captivity narrative, *The Sovereignty and Goodness of God* (1682), Printer appears as one of many shadowy Indian figures whose "conversions" are clever ploys to disguise the devil's work. Wyss's depiction, however, allows us to see the Nipmuck convert as a genuine historical agent, one for whom alphabetic and print literacy were central both to self-fashioning and to cultural affiliation during the confusion of war.

Printer authored two ransom demands on behalf of Indian commanders holding white hostages during the war. The rhetorical approach is different in the two notes, indicating, in Hilary Wyss's view, Printer's shifting relationship to the pan-tribal cause over time. In a "note that was left after a February 21 [1675] attack on Medfield," Printer used the plural "we" to indicate "his sense of unity with Philip's Algonquian alliance." Subtle clues in the note suggest that Printer nursed some bitterness over his indenture to John Eliot. Boasting that the Indians will "war this twenty-one years if you will," Printer spends much of the short paragraph justifying the Algonquians' aggression. They have been "provoked to wrath and anger" and are far from "vanishing," as white people had hoped. In fact, Printer notes, the Medfield warriors numbered 300 men. He also clearly and scornfully articulates his understanding of how the English were affected by their material losses in the early days of the war, while stressing that the Native perspective was not nearly so materialistic: "The Indians lost nothing but their life; you must lose your fair houses and cattle."[58]

In his second letter to the colonial establishment, written just before the end of the war, Printer adopts a much more conciliatory tone. The "we," Wyss notes, now becomes "I." Printer apologizes for the part he played in the hostilities ("I am sorry that I have done much wrong") and submits himself to the colony's punishment. Although he is still speaking for Native captors who hold non-Indian hostages, he appears to leave the door open for reconciliation with the English. For Printer, writing and books gave entrée into both sides of the conflict, and he therefore mobilized them cautiously to carefully controlled effect.

For her part, Mary Rowlandson used alphabetic literacy to produce a narrative of the war that thematizes a newly reenergized Protestant ideology of the book at century's end. Her tale of captivity thus becomes a devotional manual on the proper practice of intensive reading. Captured in August 1675 by Nipmuck and Wampanoag forces led by Quinnapin, Rowlandson was ransomed for twenty pounds (and the promise of some tobacco) in 1676. After being reunited with her minister husband and resettling in Wethersfield, Connecticut, Rowlandson published an account of her captivity in 1682.

The book-centered and book-devotional nature of her narrative becomes apparent early on in the story. In chapter 3, Rowlandson describes witnessing returning Native warriors celebrating over "English scalps" and dividing up the spoils taken from storehouses and dwelling places: "One of the Indians that came from the Medfield fight, had brought some plunder, came to me, and asked me, if I would have a Bible, he had got one in his basket. I was glad of it, and asked him, whether he thought the Indians would let me read? He answered, Yes: So I took the Bible, and in that melancholy time, it came to my mind to read first the 28th Chapter of Deuteronomy."[59]

It is significant that the Bible is identified as "plunder," part of the stuff of conquest. As James Printer had observed in his defiant note to the English, settlers like Mary Rowlandson had—just prior to the start of the war—seemingly become more enamored with their "fair houses and cattle" than with their souls. Throughout the narrative, Rowlandson herself alludes to the many material things that had led her away from proper devotional practices in the period just before the Indian attack. In addition to mentioning hours wasted in frivolity (instead of in pious tract reading), Rowlandson also pointedly mentions her tobacco smoking as a sign of her backsliding faith. Taken as war booty, as yet another sign of English materialism, the Bible itself needed to be "redeemed" by the trials of Indian bondage. Books are, after all, things, and by 1675, they had become perhaps less godly things than they had been for New England's earlier generations. Although Rowlandson's Native captors deny her many elements of "civilization," they do not deprive her of her reading. Indeed, throughout the narrative, she is free to read the Bible as she pleases. Her reading practices in captivity are revealing. Suffering from hunger and hard labor, Rowlandson nevertheless takes time to read. Her reading usually takes the form of "bibliomancy," an act of divination in which a Bible verse is selected at random and then applied to the experience at hand. In this usage, the Bible becomes less a mundane object and more a talisman endued with great power.

From this point on in the narrative, Rowlandson's story becomes an ever-more-explicit instructional manual in the practices of devotional reading and the allusive power such reading formations had for second-generation European New Englanders. On several important occasions—when she is separated from her friends and children at different points in her captivity—Rowlandson pulls out her Bible and asks a fellow captive "whether he would read." Each time, the two readers "light" upon a comforting bit of scripture that transforms their experience into something understandable and thus more bearable. During the book's twelfth chapter, Rowlandson describes an especially interesting bicultural interchange by and through the book: "My mistress, before we went, was gone to the burial of a papoose, and returning, she found me sitting and reading my Bible; she snatched it hastily out of my hand, and threw it out of doors; I ran and caught it up, and put it into my pocket, and never let her see it afterward."[60] Her Algonquian captor's violent response to books and reading is emblematic of the tensions over alphabetic literacy that informed the cultural context for the Native nations at war with the English. It is reflected in their response to Natick convert John Sassamon's literacy, which Lepore outlines in *The Name of War*. Lepore argues that Metacom had Sassamon (a Praying Indian engaged in shuttle diplomacy between the two sides) killed because his literacy suggested an abandonment of Indian ways.[61] The Algonquian woman's reaction to Rowlandson's reading is consonant with the nativist belief that such seminal European cultural activities were "impure" and threatened to infect the spiritual fabric of Algonquian society.

After Metacom's defeat in 1676, many Native people tried to negotiate a postwar settlement through the medium of alphabetic writing. Sagamore Sam, a rebel Native leader, wrote a letter to colonial authorities pleading for clemency for his family and nation. Although he wielded his literacy with skill, his appeals were rejected and he was executed for his part in the uprising. Fate was kinder to James Printer. Perhaps because of his particular skills (and thus his patent usefulness), Printer was allowed to return to his job in Samuel Green's print shop. Increase Mather's remarks on this are notable, for they suggest that Printer was disciplined through print and word. When faced with an English warrant outlining his offenses, Printer "did venture himself upon the mercy and truth of the English declaration which he had seen and read."[62] In the final analysis, it was literacy, not faith, that spared the life of James Printer.

As a result of the war and the intense scrutiny it brought to Native literacy, the colonial authorities lost interest in promoting Native vernacular print. Most New England missionary efforts in the eighteenth century shifted their focus to English language education. As Lepore has argued, racial lines hardened and group identities became more fixed.[63] In the minds of Euro-Americans, Native literacy in New England became permanently associated with dissembling. The death of John Eliot in 1690 furthered this literacy trend in the region. In her study of the Praying Town of Natick, Jean O'Brien quotes Increase Mather on the subject as an indication of the untenable position of postwar Native converts: "'Here has bin a signal blast of heaven on ye Indian work, very many of the most pious Indians . . . being dead also.'"[64]

Nevertheless, in 1709 James Printer teamed with Benjamin Green to print *The Massachusetts Psalter*, his last known work and the final installment of the Indian Library. As the last officially sanctioned Massachusett print text, the *Psalter* reveals the state of Native vernacular print literacy at the dawn of the eighteenth century. Subtitled "An Introduction for Training Up the Aboriginal Nations, in Reading and Understanding the Holy Scriptures," the book embodies its own biblical epigraph from John 39: "Search the scriptures." The Gospel of John was printed along with the Psalter but was sometimes bound separately. The book's format is interesting in that it is a bilingual edition of two columns with facing translation. In its physical properties, the Gospel shows some signs of being the last gasp of the Indian-run press. Its columns are reversed from the Psalter, so that, when bound together, the book's facing page translations shift confusingly, and the Algonquian text is set in type so small as to be almost unreadable. In some ways, this text points out the direction of Native literacy that would be advanced in the new century by Increase and Cotton Mather. At best, the Algonquian print literacy so hard won by seventeenth-century converts would be a Native gloss on the English-language text of Christianity that was now in ascendance.[65]

Despite this major adjustment in approach to Native literacy instruction, Algonquian speakers in southern New England would continue to engage in the literacy practices established by their seventeenth-century ancestors. Native families and villages that had adopted literacy as part of their cultural revitalization in the postcontact years would, in the eighteenth century, develop "proprietary lineages" in an effort to mediate the rapid alienation of Indian lands through recourse to a blending of cultural practices.[66] And even though John Eliot's Indian Library was virtually wiped out during King Philip's War, it lived on as an ideological construct for generations of Euro-American missionaries who, like Samuel Bartlett, would construct visions of the Native American missionary enterprise based on the concept of book conquest that John Eliot had introduced two centuries before.

In the next chapter, we will examine the shift in New England Indian missionary policy away from vernacular language syllabary texts and toward literacy education in English. When Eleazar Wheelock founded Moor's Charity School for Native children in 1754, he had in mind its role in furthering the imperial interests of Britain. "There is good reason to think," Wheelock wrote his British benefactors, "that if one half which has been, for so many Years past expended in building Forts, manning and supporting them, had been prudently laid out in supporting faithful Missionaries, and School Masters among [the Indians], the instructed and civilized Party would have been a far better Defense than all our expensive fortresses."[67] He too thought in terms of the ideology of book conquest when he thought of evangelization. For Wheelock, God's displeasure at New England's failure to missionize her Native population was "inscribed in Capitals, on the very Front of divine Dispensation, from Year to Year, in permitting the Savages to be such a sore Scourge to our Land."[68] Within this reactionary climate of English-only attitudes and imperial conquest, Massachusett-language literacy rates fell. Although never completely extinguished during the eighteenth century, many tribal communities faced what Jean O'Brien has called a "dispossession by degrees," not only of their land base, but of their linguistic foundations as well. Yet, thanks to the interactions between missionaries like John Eliot and the Mayhews and Native translators and compilers like James Printer, Hiacoombes, and Jacob Nesuton, books qua books had become a permanent fixture in the Native landscape. Native peoples *had* found a role for printed matter in their everyday lives. Books formed a material presence in the seventeenth-century Native Northeast and carved out a discursive space that was one place among many in which bicultural communication and cultural production could flourish in the eighteenth century.

CHAPTER

Two

BEING AND BECOMING LITERATE
IN THE EIGHTEENTH-CENTURY
NATIVE NORTHEAST

IN 1773, MOHEGAN MISSIONARY Joseph Johnson (1751–77) wrote in a letter meant for public circulation, "Be it known to all in general, that I am Properly an Illiterate man."[1] Johnson was apologizing in advance for his writing style to anyone who might one day happen upon his manuscripts. This was a man who read the Bible and religious tracts regularly, turning often to Richard Baxter's *Saint's Everlasting Rest* after long days of teaching and working in the fields. He was fluent in two languages and working on a third (Oneida). In the years following this letter, he would write many public petitions to government officials. Yet, in speaking to an imagined Anglo-American public, Johnson felt the need to depict himself as unskilled with the written word.

This chapter offers an explanation of Johnson's puzzling statement about his literacy by relating it to the two sets of material practices out of which it arose—Native communicative protocols and those of an emerging Euro-American public culture. By focusing on the writings of Joseph Johnson and his elder mentor, Samson Occom (1723–92), I map the Native performance, literacy, scribal, and print practices surfacing in the Northeast during the eighteenth century. These shared practices reveal that Johnson's anxiety about literacy is symptomatic of a whole generation of Native writers. As Christian converts under the sway of British and American colonialism, such writers uneasily adopted aspects of the emerging public culture taking shape across British America. At the same time, they worked to preserve and revivify traditional rhetorical protocols from within their own tribal communities. In the process, Native intellectuals like Joseph Johnson found themselves performing literacy in ways that differed from their seventeenth-century ancestors.

Readers and writers of texts in the Massachusett language had engaged Eliot's Indian Library through a Native print vernacular that aided them in establishing what David Silverman has called "religious translation" of Puritan literacy practices into hybrid Euro-Algonquian societies. In contrast, the Mohegans and allied Niantics of Connecticut, the intertribal groups settled at Stockbridge in western Massachusetts, and the Mohawks and Oneida in Iroquoia were encouraged to perform a very different set of literacy and material practices by their eighteenth-century missionary mentors. First, they found that English-only literacy was the order of the day. Second, they discovered that a new model of devotional practice was coming to dominate sectors of the Anglo-American community during the evangelical Great Awakening of the 1730s and 1740s. This model, which encouraged extemporaneous performance from the pulpit and from within the congregation as a necessary complement to Bible reading and explication, offered traditional Native performative practices a chance to reassert themselves against the previous century's book-centered ideology of conquest. Sandra Gustafson has described this new discursive model as a "performance semiotic" in which "speech and text" were viewed as "symbolic and performative forms of language rather than discrete and hierarchical entities."[2]

Finally, as European depredations of their homelands increased while their own social standing as individuals waned, men like Joseph Johnson were forced to explore a much wider range of literary genres and scribal and print practices. In manuscript autobiographies they surveyed their progress to Christian salvation, their struggles with Native and non-Native skeptics, and their personal doubts about the efficacy of the very literacy practices they were employing. In handwritten letters, they petitioned royal governors and legislators on behalf of their tribal communities, requesting greater sovereignty and firmer commitment to treaty obligations. When missionary society funds were low, as they generally were, they hand-copied important tracts and hymnals, stitching together manuscript books for tribal congregations in the backcountry. Often, they used no script at all, performing their evangelical exhortations extemporaneously, sometimes in their Native languages and sometimes in English.

As Joseph Johnson's public pronouncement about his literacy shows, however, these newfound spaces in the public culture of eighteenth-century colonial America were not without their anxieties for the indigenous journal writer, epistolary correspondent, or government petitioner. Indian writers from this period found themselves caught up in a European-wide "civilizing process" in which "communal identity brought into being by speech acts or writing" was profoundly marked by new rules concerning "discursive manners."[3] In this world, the old Protestant vernacular embodied in the published tracts and sermons of New England's clergy was increasingly being challenged by an authoritative new body of discourse composed of belletristic verse, satires, and essays that circulated in cosmopolitan manuscript coteries. Writers like Joseph Johnson, viewed by Euro-Americans as "Indians," were ideologically constrained both in their performance of nonscripted exhortation and in their belletristic literary output. During this period of Euro-American "refinement" (1720–90), Native peoples remained trapped by dominant culture representations that placed them in the untenable and contradictory position of being simultaneously noble and "republican" in their traditional oratory, but essentially "unlettered" and anti-intellectual in their grasp of alphabetic literacy.[4]

Following Lisa Brooks, I argue that Joseph Johnson's anxious literacy practices were very much a function of a dynamic eighteenth-century "Native space," which stretched geographically from Montauk villages on Long Island to Mohegan towns in Connecticut, Narragansett settlements in Rhode Island, and on up the Connecticut River Valley to Deerfield and Stockbridge, then west to the upper Ohio River, where Mohawk and Oneida communities staked claim to the western "door" of the Iroquois confederacy. The dynamism of this northeastern portion of Indian Country was not only geographic but also intercultural. Brooks reminds us that a profound intermingling of tribal ethnicities "had become a prominent feature of Native space."[5] Perhaps most important, Brooks's examination of texts produced in this part of eighteenth-century Indian Country show that "writing was operating as a tool of communication and delineation in Native space, independent of colonial institutions and even in direct opposition to the colonial project."[6] All of these factors must be taken into account when we evaluate Joseph Johnson's self-conscious critique of his own literacy, for he was among the generation of "literate Mohegans [who] banded together, using writing to reconstruct the body politic, re-member their collective history, and reclaim their 'Native rights.'"[7]

Although Euro-Americans stubbornly continued to depict Indian people as "unlettered" and uncivilized well into the nineteenth century, Mohegan converts like Samson Occom and Joseph Johnson were able to engage intercultural communication practices that at once affirmed their Christian identities, asserted their rights as indigenous peoples, and addressed their concerns about the dispossession of traditional lands and the fragmentation of local communities. At the end of his life, after he had left Mohegan lands to lead a new intertribal convert settlement in Oneida country, Samson Occom still had a love for books and would write letters requesting fine editions for his Brotherton tribal library. He also kept in touch with his sister Lucy, who never left Mohegan and never adopted alphabetic literacy as her primary mode of self-expression. Writing to her after years of separation, Occom sent along a traditional wood-splint basket as a sign of his connection to her. It was a potent and heartfelt gesture from a man who had reluctantly given up his homeland. But, more important for our study, the Mohegan bark box reminds us, as Joanna Brooks points out, "that English language literacy did not cancel out other forms of Native writing"—even for this famous man credited with being the first Native American to publish a book in America.[8]

Native Literacy and Colonial Cohesion, 1676–1720

Jean O'Brien's study of the Natick community of Praying Indians during the crucial post–King Philip's War period offers important insights into the nature of the social transformations that were imbricated in Native literacy practices during the eighteenth century. From the outset, Christian evangelization in New England paired textual materiality with a kind of geographic isolation that, O'Brien argues, created cultural spaces of "convergence . . . between English colonial ideology, which could envision a place for Indian people as religious and cultural converts fixed in bounded geographic places, and Indian resistance to crushing English colonialism." This dualistic nature of Praying Indian cultural production—at once bounded and literate, yet Native and resistant—framed the fundamental social tensions that would shape Native English language literacy and the use of printed texts during the period. Just as Native converts in Praying Towns employed "knives, combs, scissors, guns, [and] hatchets" to annex themselves more firmly to English material culture, so too did they adopt books and writing as material practices that gave them some purchase in negotiating with the European colonial power structures.[9] Praying Town communities employed not just Bibles and tracts, but also hundreds of other kinds of texts—town meeting records, depositions, wills, petitions, letters, notes, arrest warrants, and power-of-attorney documents— which Ives Goddard and Kathleen Bragdon have collected in *Native Writings in Massachusett.*

As a result of King Philip's War, British policy toward Native peoples in New England became more restrictive. From that time forward only four Praying Towns were officially recognized by the English: Natick, Punkapoag,

Hassanmisco, and Wamesit. O'Brien's research also shows that New England colonial authorities employed a whole host of other social control mechanisms to "unambiguously stabilize" Indian life. Rules were imposed "regulating Indian residency in towns, confining them there during military conflicts, monitoring Indian indentured servitude, controlling their use of firearms, and supervising Indian trade at the Boston market." It was this increased supervisory bureaucracy that produced the corresponding paper trail that Goddard and Bragdon document. Laws were even written to require "hunting Indians to lay down their arms and present certificates upon demand in the woods."[10] By 1720, New England Indian life was inexorably intertwined with books.

Land was at the center of the evolution of Native literacy practices in eighteenth-century New England. Increasingly under pressure from English colonists to sell off portions of their Praying Town grants, Native communities turned to the literate members among them to represent them in the complex legal maneuvers entailed in land tenure. At Natick in 1677, John Wompas was entrusted by the community with power of attorney "because he spake English well and was well aged with the English."[11] Unfortunately, Wompas turned out to be unreliable, making profits on land transfers and illegally representing the community in several unauthorized transactions. After 1682, the Massachusetts colonial government decreed that "no Indian shall sell any land belonging to yr towns without the unanimous consent of every proprietor," and there was slow movement toward corporate ownership of towns like Natick.

While this steady alienation of Indian land was under way, colonial authorities moved to supplement material acculturation with linguistic acculturation. O'Brien cites Samuel Sewell's recommendation—"the best thing we can do for our Indians is to Anglesises them in all agreeable Instances; and in that of Language as well as others"—as evidence of the literacy dimensions of this cultural transformation. By 1721, when an English minister arrived at Natick to replace the recently deceased Native Christian leader John Neesnumin, the community had moved quite far from its seventeenth-century Native-language literacy roots. Although Native community members "continued to use the Massachusett language, acquisition of literacy (for some) resulted in the recording of community actions in both Massachusett and English."[12] As mentioned earlier, O'Brien has characterized this process as a "dispossession by degrees." Yet nineteenth-century Anglo-American claims regarding the demise of the Native people of New England were greatly exaggerated. Wampanoag, Narragansett, Pequot, and others lived, worked, read, and wrote in dispersed settlements in southern New England well into the twentieth century.

The Great Awakening and Native Literacy

In 1730, at the height of this colonial dispossession project, the Great Awakening—that "great stir of religion in these parts," as Samson Occom called it—swept across New England. It brought with it a further shift in Euro-American attitudes toward Indian literacy and Christianization. As Sandra Gustafson has shown, this tension between competing ideologies of the book (cast as a battle between "New Light" theologians, who embraced evangelical fervor, and "Old Lights," who disdained it) did not mean that books or literacy were disparaged by the New Lights and embraced by the Old. Rather, it signaled a redeployment of the "performance semiotic" that had previously obtained in New England Reformed Protestant culture. Whereas the earlier New England Protestants had sought to employ books and print as technologies of social boundary maintenance and political hegemony, Great Awakening theologians like Solomon Stoddard questioned the "literary orientation" of the older literacy practices. Extemporaneous explication of biblical texts and divinely inspired exhortations about the uses and applications of those texts were welcomed as a necessary supplement to formal, print exposition and the sometimes deadly dull practice of reading from the printed page.

For Native peoples leaning toward Christian conversion, this reorientation of the Protestant performance semiotic seemed more in keeping with traditional religious and social systems of expression, especially given the "prominence and symbolic value afforded oral performance" in the New Light system.[13] Although Native "civility" was still reckoned in terms of alphabetic literacy by most non-Natives, some converts—like Samson Occom—were able to enunciate and perform an intercultural version of a performance semiotic that fused alphabetic literacy with Native orature. Gustafson writes that Occom created a "hybridized, evangelical, savage persona, whose liminal position between cultures permitted a range of identifications across cultures."[14] Converts like Occom, however, soon learned just how tethered to the old ideology of the book their utterances remained. As Joseph Johnson, a fellow Mohegan missionary, recalled in 1773, "If an Indian appears in publick he is looked upon with disdain, and in the hearts of the spectators is despised."[15]

Gustafson focuses on how Indian ministers like Occom effectively moved between speech and text to harness the power of a hybridized rhetorical position, but I wish here to underscore the role material practices rooted in print and manuscript texts continued to play in Native Christian life, even as New Light theologies beckoned to converts with the promise of "a new mode for the continuation of orality."[16] Books and print were becoming increasingly important modes of political and social struggle, even for illiterate or semi-literate Native converts. The missionary diary of Joseph Fish, who recorded his ministrations to the Narragansett between 1765 and 1776, describes how Native people of southern New England used print even if they could not always read it.

Like many Indian communities in the region, the Narragansett converts were divided in their loyalties between the traditional sachem of their group, Thomas Ninigret, who subscribed to Fish's preaching, and the local Native Christian lay leader, Samuel Niles. Christianity was not the source of the rift, for both men were Christians. It was rather their relationship to print and learning. Fish lamented that Niles "has a good deal of the Scriptures by ear, and professes a regard for the Bible, But his unhappiness is this, He *cannot read a word*, and so is wholly dependant upon the (too Seldom) Reading of others."[17] Time and again in his journal, Fish criticizes the Niles faction for being under the sway of the Baptists and uninterested in reading and learning. All of Niles's Native charges were "of the separate [that is, Baptist] stamp," Fish reported. "Very Ignorant:—Scarce any of them able to read a Word." Yet their ignorance did not prevent these nonreaders from developing knowledgeable anti-Fish opinions, thanks to their immersion in Baptist printed polemics performed verbally: "Jno Shattock informed me that Mr. Baccus's Books against me were plenty among them, and supposed that was one Reason why so few attended the Lecture." And it was not only Baptist print that was causing mischief. Fish's own printed sermons against the Baptists also came back to haunt him: "Saw danger of the Indians being disaffected toward Me, on Account of my Late printed Sermons upon the subject of Separations." Someone was reading Fish's and Baccus's printed works aloud and inciting the Niles faction to dissent.[18]

The Missionary Literacy Complexes

Mohegan missionary Samson Occom emerged as the first published Indian author in British North America out of this cultural war over Native literacy. His own literacy education was especially significant in determining how he would go about negotiating the tricky balance between his participation in the Old Light's "Protestant vernacular" and the emerging New Light performance semiotic, not to mention his personal and political identity as a Mohegan leader.[19]

Consider one formative moment from Occom's career. In December 1765, Occom sat disconsolately on a ship in Boston harbor waiting to set sail for England. He and Nathaniel Whittaker, a Connecticut clergyman, were being sent across the Atlantic to drum up contributions for Eleazar Wheelock's Indian Charity School. Like all things involving Indians and religion in New England, Occom's mission was fraught with controversy. On the eve of his departure, he was questioned publicly about his "fitness" for such an assignment, and, as was usual for a Native convert, that questioning was weighted toward his "Indianness." "Some say I cant talk Indian," Occom lamented to Wheelock; "others say I cant read."[20] In what would become a familiar story for American Indians active in the Euro-American political public sphere, Occom's ethnicity was the crux of the conflict. Yet the words he used to describe the attack on his character are telling. They focus on literacy and oral performance—both Native language and European print—as indices of Occom's identity.

Occom's response to these charges is equally revealing. He penned his answers in a manuscript autobiography titled "A Short Narrative of My Life." We have two drafts of Occom's life story. One is a single sheet apparently written on the scene in 1765; the other, a more extensive recitation, was drafted in 1768. Occom states his reason for this "self-life-writing" in the manuscript's first sentence: "Since there is great miss Representations by Some Concerning my Life and Education; I take this opportunity to give the world a few Words—the true Account of my Education."[21] Scribal manuscript practice rather than overt public condemnation of his accusers in print or speech became a way for Occom to face "the world."

Occom's choice of manuscript publication offers us insight into his process of being and becoming a Christian Mohegan in the 1750s, and it also underscores the thematic focus of his autobiographical account. Occom's narrative recounts how he began ministering to Native converts when he was twenty-seven years old, and he was ordained in 1758. Although he started out in life "a Heathen in Mmoyanheeunnuck," by the age of seventeen he had begun "to think about religion." It was because of this that he "began to learn to read." At nineteen, he went to live with Eleazar Wheelock, where he spent three years. Occom ends his first draft here, with a desire for Christian conversion to be realized through a "weakly [weekly]" course in "reading." Literacy, faith, and identity are inextricably intertwined in this simple, page-long description of Occom's education.

In his second, more polished, "Short Narrative," Occom describes his educational trajectory as both self-motivated and underwritten by Euro-American colonialism. He also pointedly notes that not all missionary education systems were effective, and that not all Native people wanted outside help. Occom is especially critical of the state of Indian education during his youth, a time when seventeenth-century Puritan missionary John Eliot's program had fallen into disfavor and the political will of New Englanders for educating Indians was at an all-time low.[22] In the 1730s at Mohegan, Occom recalled, "there was a sort of a school kept . . . but I believe there never was one [there] that ever learned to read anything."[23] Occom was saved from such neglect when the Reverend Eleazar Wheelock took him into his own home for literacy education between 1753 and 1755.

Unlike Eliot's mission schooling in the seventeenth century, Wheelock's brand of Indian education was founded on a fairly strict ethnocentrism. A treatise written by one of Wheelock's fellow missionaries, John Sergeant's *A Letter from the Revd. Mr. Sergeant* (1743), set forth the assumptions and goals behind this new system.[24] Sergeant, missionary to the Housatonic converts in western Massachusetts, proposed a method "as shall in the most effectual manner change their whole habit of thinking and acting" and thus transform them into "a civil industrious and polished people." His plan differed from older models like Eliot's in that he insisted on introducing "the English language among them instead of their own imperfect and barbarous dialect." Sergeant's program was progressive in that he included "Girls as well as Boys," believing that "the cultivation of both the sexes has a natural tendency to improve each other." Yet his metaphors are revealing. Sergeant's Native learners merge with the metaphoric language of an idealized agricultural economy: "The need there is of cultivating a Soil so barren, a soil so overrun with hateful weeds, and pricking Thorns."[25]

Indeed, Sergeant's pastoralization of Native converts became one of the most important image patterns in the many set pieces of Indian education that eighteenth-century New Englanders produced in their effort to solicit contributions from fellow colonists and metropolitans. Minister Theophilous Chamberlain's description of a visit to the Indian school at Kanjohare (in northern New York), for example, exploits the picturesque contrast between the Native students' "orderly salute" and the school's romantic surroundings of "small groves" and "gliding stream." Chamberlain especially revels in the

Figure 12. Masthead of *The Mental Elevator* (1841), Native-language newspaper of the Buffalo Creek Mission School for Seneca students. Courtesy of Edward E. Ayer Collection, Newberry Library, Chicago.

sonorous hum that wafts over from the school—the "sound of them beginning to pronounce syllables."[26] The young Indian children's recitation serves as a bridge between their disciplinary educational practices and their "wild" natural setting.

Engravings and woodcuts produced to enhance these glowing descriptions of Native education also idealize literacy education as a passage between civilization and wilderness, often placing a book at the focal point of the illustration. This pictorial trope, made famous in the Dartmouth College seal, was perfected in the 1840s, when the Buffalo Creek Mission School for Seneca students published a Native language newspaper whose masthead vignette formalized the role of literacy education in transforming the Indian hunter into the gentleman property owner (figure 12).

Native perspectives on literacy practices were decidedly different. Indian converts chronicled similar scenes in their own narratives, but with different emphasis. Joseph Johnson, describing his school at Farmington, reported that when "This day Came the Indians for to see what Proficiency their Children made in the 10 Weeks Past . . . the Hearts of the Parents were not little Effected to see their Children stand in Order, like a row of willow."[27] Johnson focuses on the parents' hearts, rather than the missionary's "affections," suggesting that for Native communities literacy education encompassed motivations beyond property ownership and rational enlightenment.

Indeed, the historical record suggests that many Native parents viewed relinquishing their children to European schools as an important way of rebuilding community in the face of Euro-American colonization. Often, "giving" a child to a missionary for education was understood as part of well-established practices of alliance building. During the seventeenth century, Native sons and daughters were "given" to Euro-American missionaries and teachers in much the same way that Pocahontas was "married" to John Rolfe. The practice continued well into the eighteenth century. In 1761, Joseph Brant and two other young Mohawk men were sent to Wheelock's school in a deal struck between Wheelock, Commissary for Indian Affairs Sir William Johnson, and Mohawk leaders. Brant's schooling was cut short by the French and Indian War, but Johnson's later expulsion of missionary Samuel Kirkland and his refusal to send more Indian children to the school underscores that he and the tribal council viewed education as primarily a diplomatic strategy and a reciprocal ceremonial endeavor.[28]

Moreover, from the very beginning Native communities in New England approached Euro-American literacy education as a means of achieving status in the emerging bicultural colonial society. As outlined in chapter 1, with education came "social cachet," and certain Native families gained political power through their cultivation of literacy. Other eighteenth-century Native people, those more on the economic margins of this new colonial world, took literacy education as a form of "repayment" for the indenture of their children. Ezra Stiles noted in his diary that in 1782 his son "brought home an Indian Boy from Killingworth bound to me till aet. 21." Ruth Waukeet, identified in the indenture as an Indian widow, asked in return for her son's service that "Stiles agree[s] to learn the said Aaron to read and to give him a Bible."[29]

Tribal communities, however, often entertained very different views about the relationship between alphabetic literacy and the profession of Christianity from their Euro-American schoolmasters. Some demanded that Christian catechism and literacy education be decoupled. Samuel Kirkland's report on the Haudenosaunee in this regard is typical: "[Some] they would wish to be taught in the English language, to read and write the same. The other kind of schooling they would have to be in their own language and in their respective villages."[30] Samson Occom recalled that in his youth the Mohegan community remained ambivalent about education, and that the missionaries' efforts appeared either half-hearted or threatening. He also alleged that many of his neighbors showed up at services only for the blankets handed out there. During his ten-year stay (1749–59) on Long Island, Occom found that although the Montauk "can read, write, and cipher well," they are "not so zealous in religion," indicating that the two sets of practices could be (and were often) kept separate in Native communities.[31]

Within the complex set of desires for and demands regarding literacy education in Native communities, Occom's account of his own pedagogical practices demonstrates a bicultural blend of Anglo-American print pedagogy and sensitivity to cultural difference and local needs. Most school days began, Occom recalled, "as soon as the Children got together, and took their proper seats." Occom "prayed with them, then began to hear them, I generally began . . . with those that were yet in their Alphabets, so around, . . . and I obliged them to study their Books, and to help one another. . . . As Soon as they could Spell, they were obliged to Spell when ever they wanted to go out."[32] Occom noticed that some of the children could "say over their letters" but that "their eyes can't distinguish the Letter." He then sought "to Cure em" by transforming the primer's two-dimensional alphabet into a more tactile experience.

"Making an Alphabet on Small bits of paper," Occom "glued them on small chips of cedar, after this manner, A B &c. I put these on letters in order on a Bench, then point to one letter and bid a Child to take notice of it, and then I order the Child to fetch me the letter from the Bench, if it brings the Letter, it is well, if not it must go again and again till it brings the right Lr When they can bring any Letters, this way, then I Just Jumble them together, and bid them to Set them in Alphabetical order, and it is a Pleasure to them; and they soon Learn their Letters this way." Occom's classroom thus became a bicultural environment, mixing material practices borrowed from tribal communities with print culture objects from Euro-American schools. When Occom catechized his students from the *Assembly's Shorter Catechism*, he often posed questions in his "own tongue."[33] But in order to teach them how to read the *Catechism* on their own, he employed primers much like the one Eliot had used a century before, only this time in English. Occom's use of printed primers and readers taught his students another important cultural lesson, namely, that the English alphabet and typography were the universal linguistic representational medium. Books like the *Indian Primer* had been instructing Native students about the expressive potential of typography and the power relations of alphabetic literacy since the seventeenth century. Occom's English language textbooks were different in only one respect. They had erased the Native language's printedness altogether.

Oral Native language performance and English print literacy went hand in hand in Occom's school, with Native material practices working to "supplement" printed texts and Euro-American concepts. Occom's cedar alphabet, for example, mediated the children's experience of the English language by doing what Roger Chartier suggests all reading practices do, which is to "bring . . . the body into play."[34] Occom's classroom "embodied" literacy by making the letters of the alphabet tactile, thus bringing Native bodies into play with the alphabet quite literally. By allowing his students "recess" time outside if they correctly arranged the alphabet, Occom instituted another important literacy practice, one that exploited the fact that alphabetic reading occurs "inscribed in a space, and [within] a relationship with oneself or with others."[35] Occom thus employed literacy as a means of allowing his students to shuttle back and forth between play and discipline, the woods and the schoolroom.

But even as Occom's classroom embodied a bicultural literacy experience, there were important features of the school system that could not be assimilated into the Native worldview. Corporal punishment, a routine part of Euro-American education at the time, took on a troubling significance in the Indian classroom. Occom recounts that one young Native man said of a teacher, "I believe he beats me . . . because I am an Indian." The Mohegan missionary also had occasion to pass along to colonial authorities the complaints of the Mohegan community against Anglo missionary Robert Clelland, who appeared to seat only white students near the school stove in wintertime.[36] Joseph Wolley, a Delaware missionary, reported that Montauk tribal member David Fowler (another of Wheelock's Native protégés) "beat his scholars very much . . . which the Indians don't like."[37] Thus, despite the fact that Joseph Johnson and Samson Occom gave lip service to the formula that remains at the core of Western education ("Read, write, and cipher"), their literacy education practices were far from simple and engaged cultural concerns quite different from their Anglo-American counterparts.

Scenes of Reading

Once they were taught to read, Native students like Occom's employed their skill in a number of ways. Like their non-Indian Christian counterparts, reading religious tracts became a form of devotional practice, and giving or receiving such books further served as a symbolic affirmation of their membership in a larger Christian, literate community. Within the books Native converts read, they often encountered what book historian David Shields has called "discursive manners."[38] These readers then learned to copy passages they liked as models of the best "humane composure."[39] In this way, Native readers became skilled at writing persuasive arguments in the petitions they submitted to government authorities. This was perhaps the most important role their literacy education played in their developing new social roles in the transformed Native spaces of the eighteenth century.

Like most literate eighteenth-century Euro-Americans, Indian converts read only after the day's physical labors were done, and then they read "intensively," a mode of reading characterized by its "devotional and ritualistic function."[40] For example, when he had the time, Joseph Johnson poured over Richard Baxter's steady seller, *Saint's Everlasting Rest* (1652). He read and re-read the book over a period of several weeks, returning many times to a section that recommends "the necessity of diligently seeking of the Saints rest." Around the same time, Johnson remarked in a letter that he "went out along to seek favour from God and Carried a Bible and found a convenient place for retirement."[41] By taking the book into the woods, Johnson turned the act of reading into a devotional ritual.

Not all of Johnson's reading habits, however, fell into this category. Some of his reading was spur of the moment, making the most of the few opportunities for leisure available to an overworked missionary teacher. In one diary entry, Johnson relates that on one particular night he found when retiring to his room after a long day that it was "so light [he could] read by the moon light through a window." During bad weather, Johnson spent "the chief of the time reading." Through the view offered by Johnson's journal we also find that not all of his reading was strictly spiritual. On Christmas Day, 1772, Johnson whiled away the hours with Isaac Frasier's *Brief Life* (1768), the sensational tale of a highwayman.[42]

To arrive at this point—an intensive reader of religious texts and an opportunistic reader of secular ones—Joseph Johnson, like many Native converts, had moved through a series of stages from an oral vernacular literacy into print literacy. Occom described one such aspiring Native reader's travails in a 1760 letter of reference: "He never had but little Instruction in reading and he can read English books well, in his way, he can't pronounce many English words proper."[43] In this convert's case, reading was an internalized activity, while the recitation of the text deemed necessary both to rudimentary reading education and to Christian congregational membership was still lacking. Observing an eighteenth-century Anglo-American mission school, Jonathan Edwards Jr. complained about this "Indian" way of reading. "Children learn, after a sort, to read," he noted, before judging that they were really only learning "to make such sounds on the sight of such marks" but not knowing what they read.[44]

Part of the problem was that reading was a leisure-time activity that ran counter to most Native lifestyles. Although eighteenth-century Euro-American minister/scholars like Ezra Stiles routinely read for thirteen hours in a day—and his children had "read through the Bible in course" at least six times by the time they reached maturity—most Indian converts had little time for reading.[45] Occom's "Personal Narrative" focuses on how overworked and underpaid he is. He notes that he "was obliged to Contrive every way to Support [his family]" and could often be found "whoeing . . . Corn some time Before Sun Rise and after . . . school is dismist." Joseph Johnson's letters and journal entries are punctuated with scenes of manual labor. More than once Johnson laments that he could sit down to read or write only "between school" or after making ladles and caning chairs. Yet Indian readers like Occom and Johnson were a particularly motivated group. Occom recalled that his first reading experience did not take place in school but occurred when he found himself "a Primmer and used to go to . . . English neighbors frequently for Assistance in Reading."[46]

Occom's earlier description regarding one Indian convert's reading formation (that he read "in his way") therefore becomes a particularly salient example of what Roger Chartier calls the "specific mechanisms" that distinguished Christian Indian readers from their Anglo-American counterparts.[47] It echoes Jonathan Edwards Jr.'s comments about the Stockbridge school, suggesting a pattern shared by many Native readers. This halting reading style, in which the Native reader struggled to articulate text, was usually accompanied by a high level of spoken fluency in the Native vernaculars. Occom's follow-up comment about the aspiring reader points out that "he is a good speaker of Indian." Though he goes on to shape this fellow's future into a hopeful "civilizing" narrative ("a good speaker of Indian like a wild tree in the Wilderness; but we hope, he is cut down now"), present-day scholarship confirms that literacy in at least two languages was the norm for such readers. Occom in 1760 could "read" belts of wampum concerning the Shawnee uprising in Virginia. He was presented with these and other tokens of Native expression and idiom throughout his career. At one point on his fund-raising trip to England, Occom and Whittaker requested that a wampum belt be sent from the Oneidas because it "would be of great use to us as [Occom] remembers the Speech." He also preferred to catechize his students in his native language.[48]

In spite of their often ad hoc approach to English-language printed texts and their busy, overfilled schedules, Native converts had a striking array of books available to them. Occom mentions reading and distributing Testaments "printed in Oxford by Thomas Baskett." He also often suggested other books to prospective donors that he felt would work well with Native literacy skills and spiritual needs. In this vein, he lobbied his English patrons for copies of Benjamin Keach's *Tropologia* (1683), a text that he considered "the best

Book for the Instruction of the Indians of Humane Composure I ever saw."[49]
He also recommended Alexander Cruden's *A Complete Concordance to the Holy Scriptures* (1738) and was given Matthew Poole's *Annotations upon the Holy Bible* (1683) by one of Wheelock's correspondents. In his own library, Occom had works like Thomas Horton's *Forty-six Sermons* (1674) and a 1685 edition of Eliot's Indian Bible. Joseph Johnson later bought some of these books from Occom, and we already have seen that he was an avid reader of Baxter's *Saint's Everlasting Rest* and Frasier's *Brief Life*. Many of these titles remained staples of Native converts' libraries into the nineteenth century. Mohawk missionary Eleazar Williams reported that when Jacob Jemison died of brain fever off the coast of Algiers in 1830, his trunk of belongings included Jeremy Taylor's *The Rules and Exercises of Holy Dying* (1670), Baxter's *Call to the Unconverted* (1652), and a pocket Testament. When Jemison's books were later given to Williams, he noted that "some of them had been used much."[50]

For his parishioners and prospective converts, Occom drew on a rapidly growing body of evangelical tracts created specifically for American Indian and African readers and circulated by the Society for the Propagation of the Gospel. Wealthy benefactors supplied Occom with "Several Sorts of Hymn and Psalm books" to distribute to Indian towns. Occom reported back to his patrons that "they continue to Come to me from all Quarters for Books, even to the Distance of 60 miles." He specifically requested "Little Hymn Books Design's for the Negroes, Printed by John Oliver," and commented that "Mr. Mason's songs and Penitential Hymns are very Pleasing to the Indians."[51] The society also sent him 200 copies of *Sin and Danger of Slighting Christ and the Gospel*.[52]

Occom's and Joseph Johnson's letters suggest that the demand for good quality print among Native converts was greater than the society could meet. The two men frequently pleaded for small print favors—"half a Dozen of Smal Quarto Bibles, With good Paint and Papers and Binding"—that might carry a fledgling Christian community through its first tentative stages of formation. When Occom and his parishioners made the move to Oneida country in 1785 to settle the intertribal community of Brotherton, he sent the society yet another letter that signals the importance of books to these fledgling Native Christian communities: "Our most Humble Petition and Request is, this once, to help us a little, in our settling, in this wilderness, we extreamly want a grist mill and saw mill and we very Destitute of all manner of Husbandry Tools and we should be glad and thankfull for a little Liberary."[53]

Within this circuit of printed materials in the eighteenth-century Native

Northeast, books functioned as valuable and valued material objects, often cementing relationships as symbols of affection and esteem, as well as providing a useful form of capital. On his trip to England, Occom received books as gifts on more than one occasion; he carefully noted those like the ones a Mr. Dilley offered him "for my own use." When he visited missionaries or others interested in the mission cause, Occom often accepted both donations and books, as, for example, when he "went to seen the Rev. Graves, and he gave me 9 books and one dollar." On his later travels in upstate New York, he received a "Mohawk book" from a priest, and a Native woman showed him a book he had given her when she was a little girl. Increasingly, the Native spaces of the near frontier were knit together, for Christian converts at least, by the ligaments of book exchange.

The many handwritten inscriptions in Occom's books also tell the tale of a reader whose economic marginality made books a valuable source of capital when times were tough. In 1776, Joseph Johnson bought a book from Occom, one that his mentor had received as a gift. Lemuel Haynes bought Horton's *Sermons* from Occom, and Thomas Shaw is recorded as having purchased Occom's copy of the Eliot Bible in 1790. We know, too, that Occom bound books to supplement his meager missionary wages.[54]

To read "in his way," then, a Native convert in the eighteenth century engaged in bicultural and bilingual reading practices that highlighted reading as a devotional act, often performed in a communal setting. Even when a group of Native people could not read well, they were surrounded by printed texts donated by individuals and missionary societies. Native converts liked to read not only steady sellers but also exciting stories about highwaymen. They stole time from their long days of physical labor to read, sometimes by moonlight. They traded books with Anglo-American missionaries, begged for them from missionary societies in London, and sold them when their wages failed to cover the expenses of life on the frontier. As books circulated in ever-increasing networks across the Native spaces of the eighteenth-century Northeast, the "discursive manners" they exhibited also took their place among Native communicative protocols as important parts of the performative gestures that knit indigenous communities together.

Scenes of Writing

Native writing—both as a complement to reading and as a specialized skill in its own right—was considered by Euro-American missionaries to be the

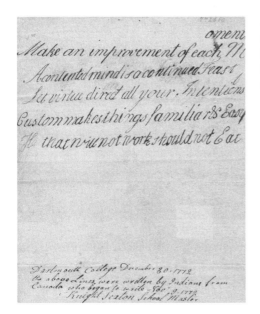

Figure 13. Samples of Native student handwriting collected by Eleazar Wheelock (1772). Courtesy of Dartmouth College Library.

crowning achievement of Indian education. Eleazar Wheelock routinely included samples of Native student writing in his fund-raising missives to British benefactors. Among the Wheelock Papers at Dartmouth are practice aphorisms common to English writing schools around the Atlantic world.[55] What makes these particular examples special, Wheelock's handwritten note observes, is that they "were written by two Indians from Canada, who had the advantage of learning to write only five weeks" (figure 13).

Evidence drawn from the mission schools at Stockbridge, Oneida, and Mohegan, as well as from the diaries and letters of both Anglo and Indian missionaries, however, suggests that eighteenth-century Indian students' experience with writing was something quite different. Although "words on paper held less weight for Native people than oral communication and material exchange in council," written documents and printed publications continued to grow in importance in most Native communities in the Northeast.[56] By the time Samson Occom began to study with Eleazar Wheelock in 1755, writing for Christian Indians in New England "held a meaning that was both more personal and more generalized [than reading]. It was used for making notes for sermons, for keeping records, and for preserving the last words of loved family members. But it was also used in broader political and legal contexts."[57] As with reading, the writing experiences of eighteenth-century Native converts in the Northeast were tied to missionization, revitalization, and diplomacy. Native writers, already marked as "uncivilized" because they were Indian, were forced to use their literacy first and foremost as a performative practice that validated their entry into Anglo-American public culture. As often-underpaid missionaries, they were also sometimes forced to use their writing skills to copy whole books that their congregations could not afford. Finally, as the primary agents of literacy in their communities, they employed their writing skills in petitions and letters to governmental authorities concerning land tenure disputes and treaty violations.

For most Indian writers, the practice of writing was initially authorized by a performance of scribal worth before an assembly of Euro-American elites. Thus Indian writing, like Indian reading, was constantly under surveillance. Before Joseph Johnson could teach at Farmington, he "read and wrote before several," including Governor Timothy Pitkin. Once men like Johnson had performed successfully for the authorities, they were shipped off to the frontier to preach to Native communities. In these communities, writing became a difficult "frontier" task, performed far from the libraries and studies in which Anglo-American clerics did their writing. Many of the young men who served in Wheelock's missions in Oneida country, for example, were rushed into missionary service on the frontier. Once there, they had to continue their writing education on their own. They were a highly motivated group, albeit handicapped by their "wilderness" settings. A typical journal entry from Joseph Johnson highlights this challenging context for Indian writing: "It is too dark for me to write much more, but I believe I can read my own writing."[58]

Like Anglo-Americans, Native Americans relied on the written word to replace or supplement printed texts that were either unavailable or too expensive. Wheelock wrote to English evangelist George Whitfield in 1756 that Occom had "scarce any book but what he borrowed."[59] We find Joseph Johnson typically spending part of his day "in writing out Hymns," mostly because his community was "so poor that [it] cant purchase Bibles and books."[60] A Euro-American scholar might choose to copy manuscript books from the collections of other pastors, but such copying for Native converts was an essential part of literacy and devotional practice. During the winter of 1772 in Farmington, Connecticut, Joseph Johnson stitched together eight gamuts, or singing books, some for impoverished members of the congregation, others as gifts for the more well-to-do.[61] Paper on which to copy these printed works was in short supply. Johnson's and Occom's letters and diaries are filled with requests for quires of paper and lamentations about the expense.

Writing as copying had another important function in Native communities—it served as a way of modeling the rhetorical structures of power and the "polished manners" of civility. Early in Occom's journal, we find him copying down an especially rhetorically stylish letter of transit he received in 1761 from Jeffery Amherst, the military commander of British forces in North America. Apparently Occom found Amherst's formal language inspiring and potentially useful for his own future writing needs. Joseph Johnson borrowed a "copy plate" from Occom and dutifully practiced his writing by imitating the words and phrases he found there. When a Euro-American commentator wished to praise a literate Native writer, he or she often noted that the individual "wrote as good a hand as myself."[62]

Of the several written genres that literate Native writers produced in the eighteenth century, handwritten autobiographies and journals represent a particularly vexed conjunction of institutional duty and self-revelation. Journal writing was required of Indian missionaries by the various societies as evidence of how funds were being spent and what progress was being made. The written work required a complex marshaling of manual dexterity, rhetorical flourish, and self-examination. It was often an anxiety-ridden task. When Mohawk cleric Eleazar Williams looked over his manuscript autobiography, written not long after he left Moor's Charity School, he observed that it "was written at a time after I just begin to write . . . [and] was written with no alterations." Although he believed that "many places ought to be corrected," he decided that since it was only for in-house use, he would "let them be just as it is."[63] This kind of self-consciousness about written performance followed Indian writers into the public sphere. When Joseph Johnson addressed the Connecticut government, he felt obliged to remark, "I hope you will look indulgent upon us, and upon this Writing, as I am but an indifferent Scribe."[64]

Such scribal writing demanded much of men like Johnson, but it was at the same time one of the most fruitful cultural performances by which literate Native people could achieve a voice in colonial British affairs. The letters exchanged between Eleazar Wheelock and his Indian students epitomize the shifting power dynamics at work in eighteenth-century indigenous epistolarity. During the 1750s, Wheelock printed many of his students' letters under the auspices of different metropolitan missionary groups—the Society for the Propagation of the Gospel and the Society in Scotland for the Propagation of Christian Knowledge, among others—in order to raise money for his mission. Through a skillful manipulation of Native voices, Wheelock produced a body of Indian epistles that seemed to repeat the motto of the Massachusetts Bay Colony seal, which depicted a Native American calling to Europe, "Come over and help us." However, as Laura J. Murray explains, Wheelock's Indian correspondents "still maintained circles in which they could speak and act outside of his knowledge or control." Murray shows how the letters of one convert, David Fowler, actually shuttle between "complex emotion or negotiation and formulaic obedience."[65]

Letters like these were important to Native peoples because their very survival was bound up in written legal contests over land and sovereignty. In his own correspondence, Occom underscored the important role literacy played in this struggle. Writing to the Reverend Samuel Buell in 1773, Occom observed, "I am afraid the Poor Indians will never Stand a good chance with the English, in their Land controversies because they are very poor . . . and the Indians have no Learning, no Wit nor Cunning the English have."[66] Land tenure disputes, like the long-standing Mason Controversy in which Occom himself was involved (over Mohegan land claims in Connecticut), became in essence a war of written words.

During the second half of the eighteenth century, literacy practices like those detailed above were repeated in Native villages up and down the eastern seaboard. From the Six Nations country of present-day New York to the Muskogee Nations of Alabama, books, print, and paper had become a fact of Indian life. When John Parrish journeyed from Philadelphia to Indian Country for the great Indian councils of 1793 and 1794, he found that in the process of negotiation, "the Indians produced a bundle of papers as reasons and ratifications." Joseph Johnson's own father kept a "pocket book" containing written copies of important treaties, land sales, and the like. Sometime before 1750, the Cherokee created a repository of "letters, and other documents given to them by the British" at their "mother town" of Chota in present-day Tennessee. American forces captured this collection of manuscript texts, now known as the "Cherokee Archive," during the Revolutionary War when they burned Chota to the ground, in 1781.[67]

In addition to manuscript notebooks and loose papers, Native communities increasingly looked to the printed word as well. By the turn of the nineteenth century, books like those that Samson Occom and Joseph Johnson identify as common texts for Native converts could be found in dispersed villages throughout the near frontier. Perhaps more important, the Protestant tracts and basic primers that had appeared in the eighteenth century were increasingly being supplemented by geographies, arithmetics, and natural histories, as educational practices and local publishing concerns adapted to an emerging reading public.

"Thankful for a Little Library"

Samson Occom's literary, ministerial, and activist careers all derive from his transformation of Eleazar Wheelock's literacy complex (Eurocentric, obsessed with self-promotion, demeaning to Native peoples) into a genuinely Native set of material practices that merged traditional performance with scribal and print media. From his critique of the inherently racist ideologies underpinning Indian conversion and performance in his "Personal Narrative" to his scathing admonition against Wheelock's giving over Moor's Charity School (now Dartmouth College) to white students, Occom grew over time into the epitome of the literate Native intellectual. As the creator of two printed books—*Sermon, Preached at the Execution of Moses Paul* (1772) and *A Choice Collection of Hymns and Spiritual Songs* (1774)—he entered the print public sphere of colonial America as both author and Indian. As the writer of manuscript journals that cover the amazing span of 1748 to 1790, he engaged the scribal world of Protestant self-examination through the experiences of colonial marginalization, mapping a lifelong journey of personal spiritual struggle intertwined with collective action. As an itinerant minister, he marshaled every tool of the New Light performance semiotic—providing extemporaneous sermons to mixed congregations, reading from manuscript outlines when more formality was required, and entertaining his hosts on his long circuit rides with Christian card games, hymns, and question-and-answer sessions. Between 1774, when Occom began negotiating on behalf of an intertribal group of Native believers for a plot of land in Oneida country, and 1785, when the group finally founded the community of Brotherton in upstate New York, a nexus of manuscript and printed books, writing, and reading served as one foundation of the community's effective reconstitution of Indian identity and sociability in the Native Northeast.

Occom's *A Sermon, Preached at the Execution of Moses Paul*, first published by Timothy Green in New London, Connecticut, in 1772, marks a crucial point in the history of Indians and print in America. In this work, the varied experiences of Native people in the Northeast finally coalesced with European print to produce the first "Indian" book. As we have seen, Occom's breakthrough into Anglo-American print culture did not come out of nowhere. A close reading of the physical properties of this text shows that the

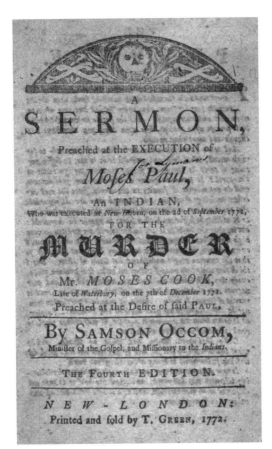

Figure 14. Title page of Samson Occom, *A Sermon, Preached at the Execution of Moses Paul* (1772). Courtesy of Edward E. Ayer Collection, Newberry Library, Chicago.

technology of movable type was becoming an integral part of the emerging broader practices of cultural literacy. The title page of an early edition of Occom's *Sermon* announces its subject not only through its content but also through typography (figure 14).

The death's-head motif at the top of the page locates the pamphlet in an established Puritan literary genre: the execution sermon. The words *Sermon, Moses Paul,* and *Murder* leap from the page, the typography imparting to each word a special meaning beyond its semantic signification. Black letter type sets off *Murder* from the rest of the page in a gothic effort to sensationalize the pamphlet. Although the modern reader might prefer to think that it was Occom's "Indian" identity that sold this work to popular readers, the typography of the title page does not support this notion. Murder, after all, always sells. Occom's title page sets up his sermon to be a steady seller with an irresistible blend of prurience and piety.

Only the introduction, which follows the title page, exposes the author's vexed relationship (ethnic, political, racial) to this material object (the book), which has effectively signaled its own authority and sensationalism (read: "steady sellerness") in typographical ways. Here Occom writes, "The world is already full of books. . . . What folly and madness it is in me to suffer anything of mine to appear in print, to expose my ignorance to the world." Hesitation and doubt notwithstanding, Occom's text goes on, both in material form and in rhetorical structure, in exemplary execution sermon style, with typography—especially italic type—underscoring crucial points in the orally delivered address and adding emphasis and immediacy to the printed work. When, for example, Occom addresses his fellow Native Americans directly as "*my poor kindred,*" the type is set off in italic, as is his later apostrophe to Paul himself.

In addition to the way the sermon is set on the page, the text exposes the role of print in forging social relationships between Indian converts and Anglo-American Christians in early America. Marginal notations written here and there on this particular copy of the 1772 edition, along with title page autographs, show how such texts were disseminated, who read them, and how readers reacted to them. Joseph Lyman, a Connecticut cleric and supporter of missionary work among the Indians, first owned this edition. On the last page, a handwritten exclamation brackets the printed text: "*Amambam Audiebam*" (O Everlasting Love! O Hearken unto this Everlasting!).[68] Lyman's marginal interjection suggests the powerful interactive response that the printed text could engender in late eighteenth-century readers.

Evidence drawn from outside the printed work suggests that it also enjoyed popularity among Native American Christian converts. In 1772, Joseph Johnson convened a group of fellow Christians in Farmington, Connecticut, "that [he] might read the Revd. Samson Occoms Sermon." The work so affected Johnson that he wrote and published his own response, *Letter from J—h J—n . . . to Moses Paul* (1772). Later, on a missionary trip to the Mohawk, Johnson again gathered a group together to hear him read the sermon. Johnson's diary notation suggests that this reading may have been at the request of the Mohawk community: "I being desired to make a short stop here, in order to read unto these Indians the Sermon."[69]

By 1774, when Occom produced *A Choice Collection of Hymns and Spiritual Songs*, he appears to have begun to see print as a way to "to forge a corporate identity."[70] Occom initially produced the book to remedy a "hymnal shortage" across the Native Northeast. This shortage resulted in "different tribal communities rel[ying] upon an assortment of donated, secondhand, and hand-made hymnbooks representing song traditions from competing missionary societies and denominations." Yet Joanna Brooks argues that "the Collection served as the base text for a new, common Christian Indian culture." According to Brooks, Occom's hymns weave Euro-American Christology with Mohegan sacred migration traditions so as to effect "reconciliation between the individual and the community, the dead and the living, the past and the present." In one hymn, which Occom probably wrote himself, the book ideology of the Protestant vernacular comes through loud and clear: "I read my bible, it was plain,/The sinner must be born again."[71]

Occom's surviving twenty-odd manuscript sermons further dramatize how his emergent Native performance semiotic struck a unique balance of print, manuscript, and oral performance. An early sermon from 1759, dedicated to explicating Matthew 22:42 ("What think ye of Christ? Whose son is he?"), is really an outline of prompts for extemporaneous preaching.[72]

These hybrid exhortations, drawn from textual sources and everyday life, from print conventions and oral performance, come together in Occom's 1760s version of "Saying What Think Ye of Christ." This sermon demonstrates how Occom used the written word to complement oral presentation in such a way as to make the "extemporaneous" in-dwelling of the spirit reproducible on the many long circuits he rode around the rural Northeast. When we compare the completed sermon with its 1759 outline, what emerges is a much bolder and more provocative speech act. In the earlier version, Occom merely set out to explain the Christological significance of the lines from Matthew. In the later draft, he personalizes the gospel text, turning the very performance of the sermon into its own application: "It looks to me Some like a Dareing presumption that I should stand before you this Day as a Teacher, What can I say to you, you that are highly Priviledge'd of the Lord of Hosts . . . and you that are refin'd with Literature and all kinds of Science, Who am I Should that I Stand before this Great Congregation this Day, . . . for I have not the Wisdom of the Wise nor knowledge of the Learned nor Eloquence of an Orator."[73] Occom exploits the inherent irony in his social position as an Indian minister, using it as the basis for building to a rhetorical crescendo in which his words and the words of the apostle become a univocal exhortation to spiritual action.[74]

In addition to using manuscript texts in a variety of ways, Occom also at times had recourse to a print culture formation little discussed in most histories of his ministry. At one of his circuit stops in 1785, Occom noted in his

1

JACOB WRESTLING.

And Jacob was left alone ; and there wrestled a man
with him until the breaking of the day. And when he saw
that he prevailed not against him, he touched the hollow
of his thigh ; and the hollow of Jacob's thigh was out of
joint, as he wrestled with him. Genesis 32 : 24, 25.

Come, O thou traveler unknown,
Whom still I hold, but cannot see !
My company before is gone,
And I am left alone with thee :
With thee all night I mean to stay,
And wrestle till the break of day.

Mass. S. S. Society, Depository 25 Cornhill, Boston.

Figure 15. Massachusetts Sabbath School Society, Bible verse card (Boston, n.d.). Courtesy of American Philosophical Society.

diary, "After supper we had little exercise, with my Printed, Versified Notes of Christian Cards."[75] He is probably referring to professionally printed excerpts from the Psalms and other parts of the Bible, which were circulated in the late eighteenth and early nineteenth centuries. A card found in the archives of the American Philosophical Society is probably very similar to the ones Occom used in his missionary travels (figure 15). Throughout the 1760s, Occom's journal entries are punctuated with comments about the kind of Christian sociability such cards afforded him. Playing a Christian card game and drinking tea with his congregants, Occom performed the very same social activities that historians have outlined as framing the refinement of Anglo-American society in the eighteenth century.

By the time Samson Occom died, in 1797, a new generation of Native converts educated in the Wheelock literacy complex were coming into their own across the American backcountry.[76] To these inhabitants of newly formed Native communities in upstate New York—places like Oneida Castle, Brotherton, and New Stockbridge—print had become much more than a European-inspired technology for archiving land claims and treaty rights. Print was part of the constitutive process of community formation, joining nonalphabetic forms of signification like wampum belts and wood-splint baskets to bind together intertribal groups of refugees and converts alike. Leaders like Mahicans Hendrick Aupaumut (1775–1829) and John W. Quinney (1797–1855) and Mohawk Eleazar Williams (1787–1858) had begun to use writing and print to negotiate with the U.S. government and others for their right to distinctly Native spaces across the frontier. By the 1820s, Aupaumut and Quinney's Stockbridge-Munsee community would emigrate from upstate New York to present-day Wisconsin. So too would a portion of the Oneida community that Williams ministered to. Fighting unfair, forc-ible removal along the way, these literate Native advocates transplanted the literacy practices developed by pioneers like Occom and Johnson to the Great Lakes region, where they would in turn influence many subsequent genera-tions of Native peoples.[77]

To missionaries and other Anglo-Americans engaged in the circulations of books and literacy to Native peoples, the westward flow of print deeper into Indian Country represented factual and codifiable "results," proof that the long-sought-after reclamation of the Indians to Church history was under way. Nineteenth-century Native converts, following the path blazed by Samson Occom and Joseph Johnson, nevertheless remained "thankfull for the little library" they had been granted through the efforts of such men. It would provide them with an added weapon in their battles for sovereignty and identity on into the nineteenth century.

CHAPTER

Three

NEW AND UNCOMMON MEANS

CHRISTIAN MISSIONS CONTINUED TO BE the single most important source of print media in Indian Country during the nineteenth century. But unlike John Eliot and Eleazar Wheelock, the missionaries who fanned out across an ever-expanding territory to the west of the original thirteen states used what geographer, clergyman, and "friend of the Indian" Jedidiah Morse (1761–1826) called "new and uncommon means" to produce and circulate religious books to their Native charges. With modern printing technologies like steam presses and stereotype plates and emerging marketing strategies that guaranteed mass circulation, this new generation of missionary print providers looked forward to a time when "every family" would have access to "a competent supply of common Bibles, and catechisms, a good reference Bible, concordance, and commentary."[1] Of course, these evangelical dreams focused most often on "*the* Book," the Bible. In reality, however, the new Christian print missions that spread among the tribal communities of the Great Lakes, the Plains, the Columbia Plateau, and the Southeast distributed a wealth of other printed materials—tracts, primers, hymnals, geographies, and spellers—to their Native parishioners. Missionary presses produced not only Bibles but also "school cards," treaties, and laws, often in Native languages. Sometimes they engaged in job printing to make ends meet. One missionary printer's diary noted that along with hymnals and tracts he produced horse bills and trade licenses.[2]

On the surface, it would appear that the ideology of the book that John Eliot had established in seventeenth-century New England sustained nineteenth-century missionaries as well. In theory, much had remained unchanged in the nineteenth century, despite the rapid transformation in print technologies and the establishment of tract societies dedicated to circulating religious books to the unconverted. The pages of many new missionary magazines, monthlies published to report the success of Christian evangelical enterprises, were filled with conversion narratives depicting the ongoing "book conquest" of Indian Country into the West.

A typical narrative appearing in the *Baptist Missionary Magazine* of 1849 presents the case of Ah-sho-wis-sa (described as "the speaker" of the Ottawa Nation) in singularly bookish terms. Ah-sho-wis-sa sought solace in Christian conversion after being bilked of his community's land base by unscrupulous whites who forced him to sign a deed while drunk. His missionary teacher detailed the role literacy played in the Native man's conversion for the edification of the magazine's subscribers: "He now, thirsting after religious knowledge, desired to be taught to read. After purchasing for him a pair of spectacles, I taught him the Ottawa alphabet. He soon, by perseverance, read fluently in the Ottawa translations, learned to write and cipher, kept his own accounts, and corresponded frequently with me and others by writing. While on his death-bed, I occasionally visited him; generally found his scripture translations on his pillow."[3] We do not know whether the Ottawa "translations" were manuscript or print, but the seeming profusion of alphabetic materials around Ah-sho-wis-sa, his use of eyeglasses, and the scriptural materials at his bedside are indicative, if nothing else, of the continuing centrality of the ideology of the book in Christian missionization into the nineteenth century.

Yet this apparent continuity of the book as agent of conversion across the eighteenth and nineteenth centuries concealed a subtle but significant change of emphasis. For the readers of journals such as the *Baptist Missionary Magazine* and the *Panoplist*, book conquest was now tied to an emerging nationalism, and success in Indian conversion meant success in American nation building. As historian Steven Conn explains, cultural forces were at work in the period that eventually established the stereotyped figure of the vanishing Indian to make room for the rise of the Euro-American nation. By the 1820s, Jacksonian America's "expansion minded ... progress-minded stance" reduced indigenous North Americans to mere obstacles to be "removed" or assimilated. Thus real indigenous peoples were increasingly replaced by invented ones.[4]

This nationalist turn in the ideology of book conquest gave rise to an elaborate fantasy discourse surrounding the seemingly magical appearance of books in the wilderness, of hidden scrolls and complex orthographies that predated European contact. Coming together mysteriously in Indian Country, books and "vanishing" Indians inspired a new discourse of American nationalist nativism, expanding on a tradition stretching back to John Eliot that equated Native peoples to the Lost Tribes of Israel. One exponent of this trend, writing in the *Chronicles of the North American Savages* in 1835, epitomized its thrust by equating Native pictographs with "Isreale's symbols in Joshua."[5] By the middle of the nineteenth century, elaborate hoaxes gave these primitivist book fantasies life where historical evidence was wanting.[6]

For Native peoples, however, the Euro-American books that came to Indian Country in the nineteenth century were often viewed in complex and conflicted ways. In many cases, prospective converts saw little use for Christian books. As one Wyandot leader explained to a missionary, "The Son of God came among the white people and preached to them, and left his words written in a book, that they when he was gone, might read and learn his will concerning them; but he left no book for the Indians, and why should he, seeing that we red people know nothing about books? If it had been the will of the Great Spirit that we should be instructed out of this book, he would have provided some way for us to understand the art of making and reading the books that contain his words."[7]

Missionary Stephen Riggs reported a similar ambivalence among the Dakota. For some converts, "a book was a marvelous thing. It was a *wowape*," a Dakota word for objects containing spiritual power.[8] To these tribal members, books were both sacred and artful objects. Riggs describes a vivid moment of the coming of the book to the Long Hollow Native congregation in Minnesota: "I took a few copies of nicely bound books in my satchel and went to the . . . church to spend the Sabbath. Solomon, the native pastor of that church, selected a book for himself. It was a beautiful book—morocco, gilt, with a clasp. They all admired it very much, and he wrapped it up carefully and laid it away."[9] According to Riggs, Solomon was so taken with the book that he exclaimed, "I feel just like a little boy who has got a new bow." Not all the Dakota were so enamored, however. In another report, Riggs noted that many "were bitterly disappointed that no magic resulted after such a laborious learning process" in learning to read such books.[10]

By the 1860s in Cherokee country, manuscript books written in the Sequoyah syllabary had become a sacred staple of medicine people, archiving the written formularies of ancient tradition. In fact, across Indian Country by this period, manuscript and printed books had become similarly essential parts of the ritual paraphernalia of ceremonial practice. Meanwhile, they had also become integral to the emerging political economies of the modern Indian nations, in the form of treaties, legal codes, tribal constitutions, and memorials. For both whites and Indians, the uneasy juxtaposition of mission publishing with imperial conquest created unusual strains and opportunities in the material practices of book conquest during the nineteenth century.

Indian Books, the Backcountry, and the Atlantic World

Missionary groups such as the Society for the Propagation of the Gospel had always made "fix[ing] parochial libraries" and circulating "a considerable number of little books" part of their core mission.[11] At the turn of the nineteenth century, however, dedicated mission publishing houses truly began to flourish in the United States. The 1816 founding of the American Bible Society, followed by the 1825 establishment of the American Tract Society, meant that Bibles and religious pamphlets began flowing into Indian Country at an extraordinary rate. In 1841, the *Baptist Missionary Magazine* announced that the American Tract Society had put into circulation some 59,383,711 publications, "including 1,598 volumes." Although not all of these were destined for Native communities, a substantial number were intended specifically for circulation in Indian Country.[12]

Although Christian missionary evangelization envisioned the circulation of mostly religious publications, this nineteenth-century "coming of the book" to Indian Country actually entailed the diffusion of a range of cultural activities. David Paul Nord has noted that among the many effects of missionary book circulation was the modernization not only of printing technology but also of distribution and even of stylistic presentation. Missionary presses and tract societies like the American Bible Society and the American Tract Society were among the first to adopt "stereotype printing, steam power, and machine made paper."[13] At Stephen Riggs's mission, for example, the "American Bible Society had generously assumed the whole expense of electrotyping and printing the Bible for the Dakotas."[14]

In addition, these organizations revolutionized the way books were put into circulation. They centralized production in major urban areas and localized distribution, particularly through the innovative deployment of colporteurs—itinerant booksellers who were commissioned to circulate tracts and Bibles across the frontier. The tract societies were singularly focused on getting religious pamphlets into as many hands as possible. Their objective reflected a new ideology of mass media: "To have everyone talking about the same thing at the same time." Along with this modern creation of a religious "imagined community," the Bible and tract societies attempted to regularize literary style and textual layout in order to compete with the ever-increasing circulation of secular popular print. According to a popular religious journal of the day, the stylistic goal was to mass-produce texts that were "simple, striking, entertaining, nonsectarian, and full of ideas."[15]

In Indian Country, the work of these tract and Bible societies was even more complicated, more imbricated with "modern" cultural practices due to the fact that printing there was so entangled with Euro-American colonialism. Recent scholarship on Indian Country during this period has clarified the cultural "spaces" occupied by tribal communities within the broader Atlantic world of European economic and political expansion. In addition to the "middle ground," defined by historian Richard White as the place "in between cultures, peoples, and in between empires and the nonstate world of villages,"[16] we now have recourse to the broader term "backcountry" to describe the geopolitical spaces wherein print circulated to Indian communities in the early nineteenth century. James Merrell calls this European/ Indian backcountry of communication and negotiation "the woods." In *Into the American Woods* (2000), he documents the emergence not only of a recognizable geographical space of shuttle diplomacy between "Indian ground" and "English country" but also a discursive "idiom" that was "cacophonous [and] kaleidoscopic."[17] Deep in the American woods, cultural go-betweens "were at best semi-literate" and engaged each other in negotiations that eventually yielded a distinctive body of cultural productions.[18]

In structural terms, America's "backcountry" marked the space not only of intercultural communication between Native and non-Native peoples but also of the confrontation between the European mercantile, imperial Atlantic world and the Western Hemisphere's resource base of natural goods and human agents. It was thus first and foremost a geopolitical region, fundamentally characterized by "the encroachment of the Atlantic economy into peripheral regions."[19] For Native peoples, it was the site of an emerging "new order." Claudio Saunt maintains that "the rapid pace of change around the Atlantic world was overturning earlier political, economic, and social relationships in the Great Lakes and Lower Mississippi Valley."[20]

Christian missions and their books were significant "points of contact" in this Atlantic periphery. Joel Martin reasons that the "missionaries' pulpits . . . depended on underlying economic processes of development that rendered [Native peoples] dependent and vulnerable to cultural imperialism."[21] With the missionaries came roads, farm allotments, and alien horticultural practices.[22] In the first decade of the nineteenth century, Seneca leaders in the

New York backcountry divided into factions over the question of whether missionaries were a bane or a boon. The so-called Pagan Party "charged the Christian Party with selling themselves to be the bond slaves of the ministers 'who would eat up their land and consumer them off the earth.'" Pagan Party leader Red Jacket asked, "What [has] been the result of those numerous tribes who [have] received missionaries among them? What [has] become of them? They are extinct; they are forever gone, so that the name even is no more remembered."[23]

Recognizing Indian Country along the Great Lakes, the Plains, the Columbia Plateau, and the Southeast as a colonial periphery of the Atlantic world allows us to view books in these regions as but one of many commodities in the "new order of things." Like brass kettles, firearms, and rum, books were material objects and trade items. As such, they operated in much more material ways than most missionary accounts of book conquest in the period would suggest. Every mission in Indian Country kept careful records of the commodities that flowed out through its doors and into nearby tribal communities. Listed along with the hundreds of "thread, [and] needles," we find "pamphlets and tracts" and "book, slates, [and] pencils." At the Brainerd Mission among the Cherokee in the 1820s, a box "containing 100 Bibles and 100 NT [New Testaments] . . . 7 Octavo Bibles, 1 doz. Testaments, and 800 tracts" would be stacked alongside ones containing "bonnets, 35 tracts, 6 primers, 1 gross buttons." "Paper, quills, [and] pins" flowed into Indian Country, along with "needle books, work pockets, Bibles, and other small books."[24]

Within this array of objects, books offered a new technology of communication, which simultaneously worked to reinforce certain Euro-American cultural assumptions about social order. Books of laws pouring into Indian Country, for example, not only argued for new forms of private property protections and trade relations but also modeled "civilized" social relations through the physical properties of the codex. Such books often included hierarchic tables of contents and indexes, calendars, and other ordering devices meant to instantiate the ideological perspective implied in European property regulations. At the Buffalo Creek Mission, for example, the press published "a small 16-page pamphlet containing such portions of the Revised Statues as related to gambling, horse racing, profanity, disturbance of the peace, etc." Its preface states that it had been printed to encourage the Seneca "to act the part of sober and respectable inhabitants of a civilized community."[25] In Indian Territory (now present-day Kansas) in 1839, Jotham Meeker printed the federal Whiskey Law in the Ottawa language. At the Lapwai Mission press in Idaho in 1843, missionaries produced "The Laws and Statues" in the Spokane language. The printers included a calendar in this volume, apparently to educate the local population about the Euro-American system of marking time, which underwrote nearly all aspects of colonial rule—from treaty rights to jurisprudence and land tenure.[26]

Despite the overwhelming evidence of a book revolution going on in Indian Country during the nineteenth century, it is important to remember that book culture was never, in and of itself, a totalizing cultural force among Native peoples *or* Euro-Americans. As William Gilmore has argued, the United States was only on the verge of becoming a full-fledged book society during the period from 1780 to 1835. Reading would constitute "a necessity of life" for most members of the republic by the 1830s,[27] but the cultural practices of this nascent world of books were still fluid, still susceptible, and influenced by what one historian has described as the backcountry's welter of "rumor mongering, animated discussions, . . . countless anecdotes, and . . . new visions."[28]

Doctrinal divisions among the Christian denominations—especially between Roman Catholics and Protestants—were among the most visible sites of rupture in European ideologies of the book in Indian Country. Disparate missionary groups sparred among themselves for readers from non–alphabetically literate societies. One classic controversy occurred at the Upper Sandusky Mission in Ohio, among the Wyandot Nation. In 1816, John Stewart, an African American Protestant evangelist, began preaching there among the Native communities. After hearing Stewart's sermons and glimpsing his books and tracts, Wyandot leaders became concerned, "finding that Stewart taught doctrines so different from those they had learned from the Romish Priest." After "conclud[ing] that he did not preach from a genuine Bible, or at least that here must be a discrepancy between his Bible and that used by the Priests . . . some of the principal men went to Mr. Walker, sub-agent, for the purpose of hearing his opinion concerning this man and his doctrines, and whether his Bible was really the word of God."[29]

With the help of the Indian agent, the Wyandot elders devised a way to test the validity of Stewart's books. Walker would "summon Stewart to appear before him" and examine "his books in their presence." During this command performance,

> a great silence prevailed. The poor Christian proselytes gazed with deep anxiety on the examiner, to whom it was referred to decide the impor-

tant question whilst the enemies of the cause were not less anxious. At length, Mr. Walker having closed the examination, called the attention of the assembly . . . [and] informed them that he had carefully examined Stewart's Bible, and found . . . that it most certainly was the same kind of those used by the Roman Priests, with only this difference, that those were in Latin and Stewart's was English. . . . He therefore pronounced the Bible and Hymn book to be genuine and good. A visible change appeared in the very countenances of the Christian part of the assembly. New spirits appeared to enliven their hearts, and joy to spring up in their souls on account of the decision in favor of books.[30]

The uneasy mix of oral and print culture in this scene points to a deeper, ideological explanation for the constant tension one encounters in the diaries and government reports from Indian Country at this time, which pit missionaries against traders. At issue was the relative morality of the literacy practices of each group. The political stakes of these rival practices are made clear in the remarks of Eleazar Williams, Mohawk Episcopal minister to the Oneida in the first half of the nineteenth century. Concerning the immoral wielding of literacy in Indian Country, Williams wrote: "I am very sorry to say that I fear too many people stand ready to write and serve the Indians and seem, when serving them that they often put words in their mouths—whether they are friendly or not to the Indians, I cannot say."[31] Williams's comments here may stand in for the scores of others that punctuate missionary accounts of the circulation of literacy and books among Indians peoples at this time.[32]

The uneven flow of political power that Williams and others describe in the written and printed "representation" of Indian interests in governmental and missionary negotiations and interactions was systemic. In part, this reflects a structural transformation in communication practices in the United States at the time. Modernizing forces like the centralization of religious publishing in eastern seaboard cities like Boston and New York and the stereotyping of popular texts to produce printing plates that could be easily transferred to frontier printing establishments were indeed innovative. However, they also effectively reinforced the old center-periphery relations of the backcountry, even as the practitioners of the new communications technologies sought a mass (and unifying) system of book publishing to erase sectional and doctrinal divisions.[33]

Over and against these modern, centralizing structures stood tribal communities and their unerring adherence to the local and the vernacular. Under the strain of federal government colonial expansion, tribal communities found themselves faced with the need to transform their own sense of "national" and ethnic identity. Seizing the opportunities provided by missionaries working in their communities, Native groups began to demand printing presses of their own and books written in their own languages. In response, several of the important missionary societies elected to buck the authority of the urban eastern publishing houses and ship printing presses far into Indian Country. Their decision was made in response to several threats to their authority on the frontier. First, many frontier missionaries found that Native peoples wanted books written in their own languages. Meanwhile, already well-established Roman Catholic Native language presses in Upper Canada and Detroit presented a threat to frontier Protestant evangelicals who had no such frontier establishments. Finally, the ability of print to stabilize the vagaries of interpreters and translators convinced many missionary societies to opt for this more local approach to publishing in Indian Country in the decades leading up to the Civil War.[34]

The Rise of Indian Mission Presses

The surprising nineteenth-century reversal of English-only practices established by the missionary societies a century before reflects a convergence of new ideological realities on the ground in Indian Country and within the new American nation. While Native communities were advocating literacy instruction as a way of coping with the unwieldy and unfair practices of European colonial expansion, American nationalists were busy trying to record Native languages in print to preserve them against the Indians' "inevitable" decay. Local printing and circulation of books in Indian Country was slow and ad hoc at first. The production of syllabic, printed approximations of Native languages had not, by the nineteenth century, progressed much beyond what John Eliot had achieved in his Indian Library. It seemed that every missionary sent to Indian Country after 1776 began to establish his own "peculiar," "original," or "systematic" orthography for recording Native languages in manuscript phrase books and word lists. These were then cobbled together to produce sermons and facilitate general communications with the tribal communities. Such orthographies fell into three basic categories: logographic systems, in which individual symbols signified complete words; syllabary systems, where symbols represented syllables in the Native language; and phonetic systems, in which the sounds of an indigenous language were spelled out with Roman type (à la John Eliot).[35] In 1820, however, an American philologist made a stab at introducing some uniformity to these alphabets. John Pickering's *An Essay on the Uniform Orthography for the Indian Languages of North America* (1820) reflects the subtle interweaving of burgeoning American nationalist ideology with colonialist pragmatism and scientific rationalism, which became an essential part of book production in Indian Country.[36]

Pickering argued that finding "some common and systematic method of writing" American Indian languages was important to the broader Enlightenment project of studying language in order to understand "the constitution and history of its possessor, man." There was also a pragmatic "American" reason for seeking a uniform orthography: to obtain "the means of communicating with the various tribes of our borders, either with a view to the common concerns of life or the diffusion of the principles of our religion among them."[37]

Woven into these scientific goals and pragmatic concerns was an evolving discourse of American nationalism in which Native peoples played a significant, albeit mythical, role. Indian languages in 1820 were, to men like Pickering, "neglected dialects, like the devoted race of men who have spoken them for so many ages, and who have been stripped of almost every fragment of their paternal inheritance except their language." Saving Indian languages with a universal orthography suddenly became an effort to save something truly "American."[38]

Despite Pickering's good intentions (and even though some missionaries did employ his methods), the alphabetic reality on the ground in Indian Country never approached anything like a universal orthography during the nineteenth century. Among the Six Nations of the Iroquois (Haudenosaunee), for example, editions of syllabary tracts and gospel translations with orthographies based on those used by John Eliot appeared irregularly between 1769 and 1790. There was no centralization of the distribution of these orthographies or the books made from them.[39] Local Native converts like Mohawk John Norton (ca. 1760–1825) worked informally with local ministers to write up important sections of the gospel in a Roman type alphabetic version of Mohawk. They then applied to mission society sponsors for funding to produce and distribute their works as books. Norton reported in his diary that 2,000 copies of his translation of the Gospel of John were sent into the countryside at the beginning of the nineteenth century, to supplement some 500 Mohawk Bibles delivered in 1807 by the British Foreign Bible Society.[40] A "case of Bibles" here, 1,000 books there, that was the process by which printed

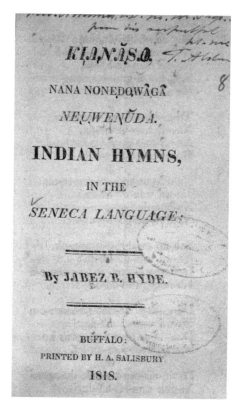

books began to circulate in Indian Country in the decades immediately after the American Revolution.

It was not until 1815, when the American Board of Commissioners for Foreign Missions decided to turn their attention to "the education of the heathen youths" in America, that a systematic distribution of printed syllabic texts took shape in the land of the Haudenosaunee.[41] For the New York Missionary Society, the education of Iroquois children in their local communities would include books printed in their own language. Missionary Jabez Hyde's *Indian Hymns* (1818)—published with the support of the New York Missionary Society—is typical of this kind of in-country missionary publication. Its title page mixture of different fonts indicates that the missionaries had commissioned some special syllabary type for unique Seneca language sounds, mixing them with Roman type in a bicultural and bilingual collage of typefaces (figure 16).[42]

The story of how Jabez Hyde's book came to be printed and how his missionary society came to establish a press in the Six Nations community of

Buffalo Creek is paradigmatic of similar situations across Indian Country in the nineteenth century. First, it is important to note that both Six Nation leaders and non-Indian missionaries selected the location for the mission and the press. They based their decision on the fact that the Buffalo Creek settlement was the nexus of an important "political hub" in the geopolitical world of the eighteenth-century American backcountry. As Alyssa Mt. Pleasant shows in her recent study of the community, "After the Whirlwind," the pantribal villages that were grouped around Buffalo Creek and its American mission were founded in the aftermath of the 1797 Treaty of Big Tree, by which the "contiguous Seneca land base was broken up into eleven reservations."[43]

"De-yoh-ho-gah," the Seneca place-name for Buffalo Creek, means "where the stream is separated into two branches." Embedded within its literal meaning was a migration story. An elder's post-treaty vision had suggested that the Haudenosaunee were destined to inhabit this place once the Treaty of Big Tree sundered the centuries-old covenant chain that had bound Seneca, Cayuga, Oneida, Mohawk, Onandagas, and Tuscaroras together as a political confederacy. Many historians have viewed Buffalo Creek as a "refugee haven" and a place of cultural disintegration, but Mt. Pleasant convincingly argues that it effectively maintained the values of the longhouse, the traditional council fire of the old confederacy. As a geographical place where two streams divided, Buffalo Creek symbolized that most hallowed of all Haudenosaunee beliefs, embodied in the two-row wampum, the *Kaswentha*, a beaded belt that is often referred to today by contemporary members of the Six Nations as their "constitution." This wampum belt of "two parallel purple lines . . . on a background of white beads" stood as a "metaphor for . . . two vessels, each possessing its own integrity, traveling the river of time together."[44] To the Haudenosaunee, the two-row wampum signifies the Six Nation's most sacred obligation—to maintain balance through political consensus. The community of Buffalo Creek embodied the meeting of two peoples (Native and European) in the backcountry, and its subsequent political actions reflected a revitalized cultural approach to managing the social tensions that ensued.

Seneca Christianity and its accompanying print culture grew out of this traditional "two-stream" consensus-building attitude toward cultural conflict. It also reflected a pragmatic response to American encroachment and landgrabbing. "With a growing American settlement only a few miles from their villages," Mt. Pleasant explains, "the people of Buffalo Creek were forced to acknowledge that increased familiarity with American customs and practices was necessary for their continued survival and prosperity."[45] Buffalo Creek's eventual establishment of a Native printing press was thus paradigmatic of Native mission print practices in another respect. Native leaders adopted printing as a way to survive and prosper in the face of American encroachment. But the history of how this community chose to adopt print makes it very clear that it would do so only on its own terms.

From 1803, when missionary societies began lobbying the Haudenosaunee for a mission at Buffalo Creek, through 1841, when they finally installed Asher Wright (1803–75) and a printing press in the central village, the Buffalo Creek community practiced a policy that Mt. Pleasant calls "gradual compliance." The community maintained firm control over every missionary's labors, promoting his efforts to expand the community's alphabetic literacy and numeracy while discouraging his Christian evangelism. They even went so far as to forbid the outright preaching of sermons. By 1818, when Jabez Hyde finally produced his Seneca hymnbook on a job press in the American town of Buffalo, New York, he and his sponsoring organization had pretty much given up on the Native village, saying that a "progress of improvement . . . [was] almost imperceptible."[46]

Ironically, 1818 was a year that witnessed an unexpected revival of spiritual fervor across Haudenosaunee country. The 1815 death of the Seneca prophet Handsome Lake (1735–1815) and increasing pressure from land speculators appears to have reawakened the people to their sense of prophetic mission at Buffalo Creek. A small group of supporters of the Christian mission began to emerge among the Seneca.[47] This revival and the surfacing of a local Christian movement was the Native context out of which Hyde's hymnal finally emerged in 1818. It was followed, in the "gradualist" Haudenosaunee tradition, by the establishment in 1823 of the Seneca Mission Church. After missionary Asher Wright in 1841 purchased a "hand printing press, . . . equipped with fonts of specially prepared type for printing books and papers in the Seneca language," a virtual flood of Seneca language texts followed. Just as printers and print houses were becoming part of the settled infrastructure of the expanding missionary enterprise all across Indian Country, printed books could now be produced in the New York backcountry where prospective converts actually lived. Wright built a school and meetinghouse and was then joined by Benjamin C. Van Duzee, whom he employed as a printer. The Seneca press was "set up in a 'lean-to' attached to the house." During his tenure at the Buffalo Creek Mission, Wright produced *A Spelling Book in the Seneca Language with English Definitions* (1842) and the *Mental Elevator* (1841–50), a Seneca language newsletter.[48]

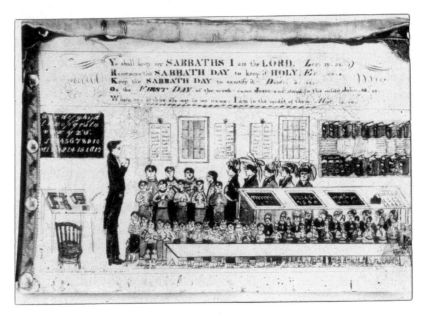

Figure 17. Dennis Cusick, "Seneca Mission School" (1821).
Franklin Trask Library, Andover Newton Theological School.

Tuscarora artist Dennis Cusick (1799–ca. 1822) captured the book culture milieu of the Buffalo Creek schoolhouse that was born of the 1818 revival in a pen-and-ink illustration he produced to adorn one side of a church collection box. At first glance, Cusick's image seems to conform to a classic, assimilationist, book conquest ideology. The students appear in regimented rows; behind them adult women dressed in middle-class finery observe the proceedings. All direct their attention to the black-suited missionary teacher at the front of the room. Writing and printed books dominate the scene around the figures, effectively organizing the space into rectilinear areas of codices and copy plates (figure 17).

Beneath the colonial order implied by Cusick's illustration, however, lies a drawn-out battle between the Haudenosaunee community and the New York Missionary Society over sovereignty and tribal rights. Even though community members sanctioned the schoolhouse, they resisted moving the Sunday school from the council house (the traditional meeting place) in an apparent effort to maintain traditional supervision over missionary activities. When the boarding school that appears in the Cusick image was initially proposed by the missionary society, the Seneca women in favor of it deployed a shrewd rhetorical strategy. They slowed down the process in order to get it approved in the traditional Seneca way—deliberately and through consensus. The scene Cusick illustrates could take place only after the Christian Native community struck a deal with "pagan" party members from the larger Haudenosaunee community outside Buffalo Creek. Among other things, they pledged that the missionary work would be done on "this reservation only." In Mt. Pleasant's view, the "construction of the missionary-run school reflected the goals of the Haudenosaunee people at Buffalo Creek. Their interest in Euro-American–style education sprang from the desire to maintain their land and lifeways."[49]

Even once the schoolhouse was in place, Haudenosaunee history in the region did not become a tale of assimilation or even widespread alphabetic literacy. For the period from 1780 to 1825, Mt. Pleasant did not find "any records created by a Haudenosaunee person in Seneca or another Haudenosaunee language bearing on Buffalo Creek."[50] It was only after 1825, when the Seneca community was fractured by a civil war between those who sought to sell their land and move west and those who wished to stay at Buffalo Creek, that syllabic literacy became fairly commonplace in the nation among the ruling elites. Everyday correspondence was conducted in both English and Seneca, and by the 1840s even the rituals of medicine societies were sometimes written out to supplement yearly oral ceremonial recitation.[51]

Out in the Kansas Territory, a similar project was under way with the Shawanoe Mission, founded in 1831 by Baptist missionary and printer Jotham Meeker (1804–56). Like Buffalo Creek, the Native settlements clustered around Meeker's Shawanoe Mission press near present-day Turner, Kansas, and those around the more powerful Shawnee Methodist Mission nearby, were displaced communities. They were made up of Delaware, Shawnee, and Potawatomi who had suffered removal from their lands east of the Mississippi. Also like Buffalo Creek, the Shawanoe Mission press was located at the center of a political hub, where the convergence of removed tribes, Indian traders, and an emerging territorial government came together to form a powerful imperial nexus. The press was close to the newly established Santa Fe Trail west. The rival Shawnee Methodist Mission would soon become the territorial governor's home and the region's legislative seat. Shawnee Methodist Mission leader Rev. Thomas Johnson (1802–65) was a slaveholding supporter of the Confederacy, and his mission was at the center of the "bloody Kansas" uprisings of the 1850s. In 1865, unknown assailants whose motive may have been political payback for his stance during the prewar years shot him dead on the porch of his mission home.

It was from the center of this political hub that Jotham Meeker began to produce Native-language texts both for his own Baptist mission and for the Methodists. Between 1831 and 1855, Meeker printed Native-language texts with type and a press he had purchased in Cincinnati for 500 dollars. In all, Meeker produced "about ninety pieces of printed matter . . . in the form of small books containing hymns, selections from scripture, translated into various Indian language." Meeker also launched one of the earliest Native-language newspapers west of the Mississippi, the *Siwinowe Kesibwi* [*Shawanoe Sun*] (1835–41), of which there is only one known surviving copy. By 1839, the local Indian agent estimated that there were 15,000 pages of print in Indian languages circulating among Native communities in Kansas.[52] Aided by Native converts like William Turner, Ealmmatah-kah, and David Green, Meeker produced Native-language texts in a bicultural process that was being replicated in Native convert communities across North America.[53]

A missionary printer like Meeker began the process of translating an important Bible passage, hymn, or verse into a Native language by working with a Native speaker. Throughout the translation process, missionaries like Meeker were faced with the daunting task of shaping a syllabic printed version of the Native oral rendition out of the common Roman type available to small presses. An inventive man who had worked as a printer before he became a Baptist missionary, Meeker devised his own personal orthographic system for writing Shawnee. Isaac McCoy, the nineteenth-century historian of the Baptist missions, described Meeker's system as follows: "Every uncompounded sound which can be distinguished by the ear is indicated by a [Roman] character." Using this elementary phonemic method, McCoy declared that "as soon as the learner acquires a knowledge of the uses of the characters, . . . he is capable of reading; because, by placing the organs of speech, or uttering a sound, as is indicated by each character as it occurs, *he is actually reading*."[54] Books like Meeker's often remained in manuscript for a long time before they were published. As such, they were used by missionaries until suitable printed versions could be made. Eleazar Williams, Mohawk missionary to the Oneida, produced a beautiful manuscript of Anglican liturgy for use in the field until a printed one was produced (figure 18).

Frontier missionary manuscripts like Williams's were often eventually printed using the "English types" because, as Isaac McCoy explains of the Meeker orthography, "they answer as well as characters of any other shape, and by so doing the expense of making new types is avoided." English types were also useful "because the English scholar can more easily learn to read

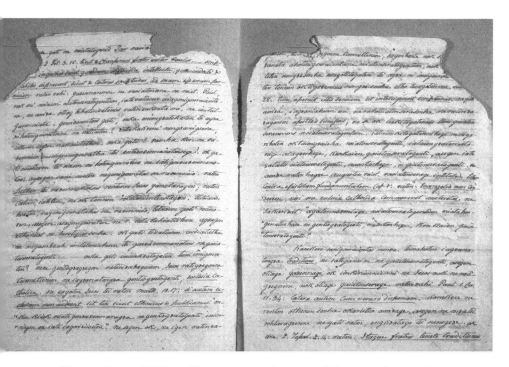

Figure 18. Eleazar Williams, Haudenosaunee-language religious tract (ca. 1820s). Courtesy of Edward E. Ayer Collection, Newberry Library, Chicago.

with these than with newly invented characters." By including an introductory key in the preface, such books allowed English speakers "to read, understandingly, to those acquainted with the language, whether he understands it or not; and he can, without any knowledge of the language himself, teach others to read it."[55] Because of the ad hoc nature of such orthographic systems, however, Native language presses run by missionaries and their Native convert assistants had varying degrees of success in producing alphabetic literacy in their local Native communities.

In a nineteenth-century Cree translation of *The Book of Common Prayer*, for example, the editor included helpful illustrations for the use of schoolmasters who wished to teach their Indian students to read. "Because all Indians learn their mother tongue through the medium of the ear," he reasoned, "there is a great diversity of pronunciation." His proposed solution was a system of body movements that would "quickly and permanently, [fix] upon the memory, the position of the vowels portions of the symbols." The editor of this primer continued: "The teacher should stand with his back to the learners,

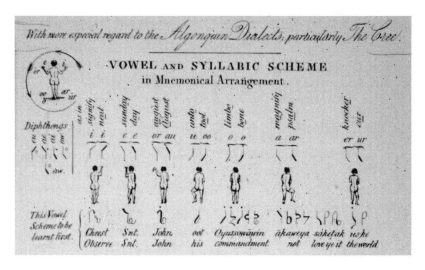

Figure 19. Page from Church of England, *Portions of the Book of Common Prayer . . . in Cree* (1856). Courtesy of Edward E. Ayer Collection, Newberry Library, Chicago.

taking special care that they imitate his actions. As well as repeat the words after him, with mutual emphasis upon the vowel under notice. After a little explanation of what is to be done, he should elevate his right hand while pronouncing the word 'Cheest.'" It was an embodied performative technique that harked back to John Eliot's "gestures" and Samson Occom's cedar-chip alphabet (figure 19).[56]

Once an orthography had been established and taught to a Native assistant, missionary and aide had to carefully check both the translation from the English text and the transcription of the Native words into the orthographic system. In many cases, a Native convert fluent in the language checked the transcription. For the *Wlkr Potrwatome* (*Potawatami First Book*; 1834), Meeker employed Native speaker William Ash, who spent a whole day at the mission house checking the missionary's work before he set it up in type.[57]

H. F. Buckner, missionary to the Muskogee in Alabama, described in his preface to *The Gospel of John* (1860) how he had gone about the process: "My interpreter sat by me, while I explained to him, in the most simple style, the sense of each word in English." Not content with merely explicating the ordinary English significance of the gospel passage, Buckner made reference to the original Greek texts and to works of exegesis like "Bloomfield's Notes." As the two men sat together, the Muskogee assistant would "pronounce slowly and distinctly the Creek rendering while [Buckner] would write it down on waste paper." Buckner would in turn read his syllabic handwritten version back to his Native translator. Bucker read "slowly and distinctly, to see if [he] had made no mistake, at the same time comparing it again with the English." If mistakes were found, Buckner would "re-write it on waste paper until he was fully satisfied that the Creek contained the true sense." The whole lengthy process concluded only once the two men "had gone over the whole book in this way." Buckner would then take the manuscript on his "preaching tours" of Muskogee country, where he would "[read] it to the best judges I could find, [to] solicit their criticisms," which Buckner "carefully noted down."[58]

As was the case at Buffalo Creek, the Shawnee, Delaware, and Potawatomi converts who helped Jotham Meeker produce his Indian books did so with specifically Native agendas in mind. When Meeker noted in his diary that "the Indians seem much delighted at receiving books in their own language,"[59] he may have been observing the reactions of a community that had successfully channeled the outside influence of the missionaries toward their own local goals. We know, for example, that one well-known convert among the Ottawa with whom Meeker worked and published, Ealmmatah-kah, expressed his desire for conversion in terms that suggest he sought both the spiritual and the political power offered by the new linguistic forms of books. At first, Ealmmatah-kah experienced great "difficulty . . . understanding . . . the language" that missionaries used. It appeared to be a new kind of English, one endued with power, and in great contrast to the traders' language that dominated the economics and politics of the backcountry. Ealmmatah-kah dubbed that mercantile discourse "the grocery language."[60] Similarly, at the Shawanoe Mission in Kansas, print production went forward in 1834 only when the Shawnee tribal council "decided to drop the mode of writing used by the Methodists and to adopt the new Indian orthography devised by Meeker."[61] As at Buffalo Creek, literacy (and even orthography) was guided by Native council decisions.

Printing and "getting up" a book was the final stage in the missionary printing process before a text could be circulated to the community. Itinerant journeyman printers were often hired temporarily to help with the actual printing. Meeker's diary mentions the brief tenures of two men—a Mr. Quisinbury and a Mr. Day—who worked for a time at the Shawanoe press. At other times, Native apprentices were contracted to do the presswork. A proof sheet was then struck and again checked against the original—sometimes by a Native helper and sometimes by another missionary familiar with the particular Native language involved. It was a painstaking, laborious process, made more difficult by the bilingual nature of the work and the "frontier" conditions of the press. Meeker's journal during his printing years is punctuated with phrases that shuttle back and forth between print shop and field: "Distributed type, set out cabbage . . . replant corn, set types."[62]

Around the same time, in what is now Idaho, the Lapwai Mission press printed the first book in a syllabic version of the Nez Perce language. The *Nez Perce First Book* (1839) was produced on a Ramage printing press imported from yet another mission in the Hawaiian Islands. This text, the work of missionary Henry Spaulding, employed a phonetic alphabet using Roman type and was sponsored by the American Board of Commissioners for Foreign Missions. In 1839, there were few active printing presses west of the Rockies—one in California, one in New Mexico, and the Lapwai Mission press in Idaho. Spaulding's press was thus intended to cover a wide geographic range and to supply Native-language spiritual reading for a constellation of three Protestant missions in the Columbia River Plateau—the Waiilatpu Mission near Fort Walla Walla, the Tshimikain Mission at Fort Okanogan on the upper Columbia, and Lapwai, on the Clearwater River, near present-day Lewiston, Idaho.[63]

Again, like the missionary printing enterprises at Buffalo Creek and the Shawanoe Mission, the Lapwai Mission press was positioned at the center of an important imperial political and economic hub. The Columbia Plateau was a Native cultural area that had been established by geography and demography long before the arrival of Europeans. Situated on an ancient lava plain and taking in the whole Columbia River drainage, the region was home to the Cayuse, Spokane, Yakima, and Nez Perce. Mapped onto this indigenous cultural region in the nineteenth century was a British imperial network that spread south and east of the Hudson Bay Company at Fort Vancouver in British Canada. After the Anglo-American Convention of 1818, the whole of the Oregon Territory, which included all of the Columbia Plateau, was placed under joint control of American and British merchants. This shared power arrangement quickly created a contested backcountry. By 1821, Fort Boise (under Hudson Bay Company control) had skirmished with the American Fort Hall over the region's fur trade. Adding fuel to this contentious political fire was the battle between rival missionary organizations, as Hudson Bay Company representatives evangelized the Native populations with Roman Catholic doctrine; their American counterparts were Protestant.[64]

As was the case throughout Indian Country in the nineteenth century, the juxtaposition of Christian missions with economic competition warped the book conquest practices of the colonizers. In 1825, Hudson Bay Company officials directed missionaries to recruit young men from local tribal communities to be educated at Fort Garry, near present-day Winnipeg. Two young Native men, renamed Spokane Garry and Kootenai Kelly after Hudson Bay Company officials by the missionaries, later returned to their home communities in the Columbia Plateau with "Bibles and other religious books, and began to preach and demonstrate the power of the white men's learning."[65] Meanwhile, "a chain of mission compounds" grew. By 1840, it extended "along the route Lewis and Clark had traced three decades earlier, [forming] a small but significant rival" to the Hudson Bay Company missions.[66]

This was the cultural context within which Henry Spaulding produced the first books printed in the Oregon Territory. Like Jotham Meeker and Jabez Hyde, his first challenge was to adapt the Roman alphabet to the Columbia Plateau languages. In his characteristically ethnocentric way, Spaulding remarked, "We found it altogether insufficient as a medium by which to communicate to their dark minds the meaning of the gospel." In fact, Spaulding privately believed that "the natives do not possess perseverance sufficient to hold them to study a sufficient length of time to enable them to read the Roman alphabet."[67] In addition to his less-than-successful orthography, Spaulding had to contend with the usual vagaries of backcountry publication. Paper shortages caused short print runs, as did a short supply of type. The print house itself had to be lodged in one of his "living rooms."[68]

Spaulding was eventually replaced by Elkanah Walker (1805–79) and Cushing Ells (1810–93), who steered the Lapwai Mission press toward a more ambitious print campaign. Finding Spaulding's syllabary to be nearly unintelligible to the Native community, Walker and Ells developed yet another new orthography. Their press produced at least seven texts, and missionaries reported large print runs of more than 400 copies each to the American Board of Commissioners for Foreign Missions. What did not follow, however, was a widespread adoption of the texts by the Spokane and Nez Perce communities they were intended to serve.[69] In 1847, a force of Cayuse and Umatilla warriors, driven partly by missionary inflexibility and partly by nativist prophecies that decried the mission as "contagion," attacked the Waiilaptu mission (near present-day Walla Walla), killing thirteen white settlers, including the missionaries Marcus and Narcissa Whitman. This attack, which became known among whites as the Whitman Massacre, put book conquest in the region on hold. That same year, the local missionary group in the Oregon Territory voted to abandon the Roman type orthography and to examine whether the syllabary used by the Roman Catholics among the Cree might better serve their purposes.[70] In a revealing example of the tortuous history of Native-language printed works in the American backcountry, in 1862 a secular newspaper press in Portland eventually reprinted the 1845 Nez Perce vocabulary that the missionaries had produced. This printing was expressly intended to assist Americans in their commercial communications with local peoples during the region's brief gold rush.[71]

Missionary print had a different (and perhaps more lasting) impact among the Dakota of Minnesota. Again during the same period (1830–50), Congregationalist missionaries Samuel W. Pond and Gideon H. Pond devised an orthography for the Dakota language. In 1834, a local distribution system of Native-language printed texts produced in Cincinnati and Boston emerged under the direction of the Reverend Stephen Return Riggs. Riggs was an especially active advocate of Indian-language text publication in Indian Country, bringing into print works like *The Dakota First Reading Book* (1839), *Dakota wowapi wakan kin: The New Testament* (1865), and *Psalm wowapi: The Book of Psalms in the Dakota Language* (1869). In 1851, Gideon Pond started production on a newsletter, *Dakota Tawaxiku Kin* [The Dakota Friend], on a local press in St. Paul, Minnesota. By 1871, in Greenwood, South Dakota, Congregationalist and Presbyterian missionaries began printing another bilingual illustrated weekly, *Iapi Oaye, the Word Carrier*.[72]

The range of the Pond and Riggs publication efforts—from gospel texts and tracts to spellers, geographies, and newspapers—and the effectiveness of the orthography they reproduced, is indicative of how print in Indian Country had moved far beyond "religion" or doctrine and had begun to point to wider social and cultural transformations. Anthropologist Ray DeMallie has remarked on the historical importance of the *Word Carrier*: "This widely circulated monthly paper—which developed into separate native language and English editions, whose contents, in most cases were entirely different—published materials written by individuals from all of the widely scattered Sioux communities. Editorials and letters were printed in the dialect in which they were written, making the *Iapi Oaye* a historical archive representing the diversity of spoken Sioux dialects." DeMallie's work on the Lakota-language manuscripts produced by George Sword (1847–1910) during the period from 1905 to 1910 sheds light on the Native-directed uses to which such imported typographies and syllabaries were put. Examining Sword's original handwritten Lakota narratives in terms of rhetorical style and diction, DeMallie argues that the Sword manuscripts represent "a new genre of Native literature." Texts like Sword's, drawing on missionary-produced print orthographies, "are not . . . simply written versions of oral narratives but are instead a new type of written narrative."[73]

By the time of the American Civil War, books had "arrived" in Indian Country—from the Columbia Plateau in the Northwest to the Indian Territory of present-day Oklahoma and Kansas. Print could be found in Native communities around the Great Lakes, stretching from Lake Erie to Lake Superior and the upper Mississippi. With the exception of those works printed in the Cherokee syllabary and Cree works produced in Canada in the James Evans syllabary (ca. 1840), the books circulating through these regions were in Roman type. Whether in English or in a syllabic approximation of a Native language, most were the products of bicultural interaction between Anglo-American missionaries and Native converts who served as printer's apprentices, translators, and compilers.

These missionary presses dutifully reported their print runs to their eastern headquarters, and writers in the *Panoplist*, the *Baptist Missionary Magazine*, and other publications eagerly cited the numbers. But the bare statistics do not tell the whole story of the impact of books on Native readers. Whatever the reception of missionary books, we can say with some certainty that these presses had lasting effects on many Indian Country communities.

The biography of Spokane Garry, the Native man who first brought books to Columbia Plateau communities in 1827, will serve as a coda to this chapter's survey of print production constellated around imperial political hubs in the American backcountry. As historian Larry Cebula describes Garry's postconversion life, the young man's role in his tribal community, although centered on alphabetic literacy, played out in surprising ways. According to Cebula, "Garry's own status declined precipitously in the era of the missions."[74] The white missionaries who set up the Lapwai Mission press and surrounding meetinghouses disapproved of his syncretic religious practices. Despite becoming a Christian, Garry kept several wives, as was the norm in his community. His preaching espoused a very Native-centered, individual-salvation approach to the gospels and was thus viewed as unacceptably unorthodox by non-Indian missionaries like Elkanah Walker. Scandalized whites rejected Garry on the grounds of lax moral behavior and improper theology. Native traditionalists, on the other hand, viewed him as a traitor, and local tribal communities shunned him. From 1838 to 1870, a disconsolate Garry abandoned his ministry. He returned to a pre-mission traditional life, casting off Euro-American clothes and trappings and following his community into buffalo country when invading Europeans disrupted their traditional foodways.

When the Yakima War broke out in 1856, Garry tried to convince his community to stay above the fray. Drawing on his literacy and familiarity with whites, he counseled fellow tribal members against getting drawn into the conflict. Ultimately, however, Americans overran the Columbia Plateau, and many tribal peoples were consigned to life on a reservation far from their traditional homeland. Then, in 1871, Spokane Garry did another surprising thing. He returned to Christianity and reestablished the Indian school he had abandoned thirty years before. It is within this context, that of Native man returning to the Christian faith—on his own terms—that the 1871 reprinting of the Lapwai Mission press's Native-language Gospel of Matthew is most fruitfully approached. The 1871 reprint demonstrates the kind of Native-centered afterlife that books printed at mission presses often enjoyed. Photographs of Nez Perce converts from the same period show them with books grasped in their hands. Similar stories of Native-centered book culture could be told about Lakotas like George Sword and Black Elk on the Great Plains, Choctaws like David Folsom in Indian Territory, and Ojibwe writers like William Warren and George Copway on the Great Lakes. Stories like these can be told as well of members of the Brotherton, Stockbridge-Munsee, and Oneida communities, who made their way from upstate New York to Wisconsin in the 1830s. Books "arrived," were accepted or rejected on Indian terms, and were then incorporated into the lives of community members. Some individuals, like Sword and Copway, even attempted to revitalize their local communities through recourse to the new technology the European empires had brought to their homelands.

When Jedidiah Morse spoke of the "new and uncommon means" that nineteenth-century missionaries would have available, he was thinking of stereotype printing, colportage, and centralized production. In Indian Country, however, the "new and uncommon means" of the printing and distribution of books came to mean preserving tribal sovereignty, protecting traditional religions, and mediating imperial power by turning back upon them the very tools the colonizers had brought to subordinate the Native nations.

Four

PUBLIC WRITING I

"To Feel Interest in Our Welfare"

THE PERIOD FROM 1774, when Samson Occom's *Several Hymns* appeared in print, to 1871, when Spokane Garry returned to his school house on the Columbia Plateau, was notable for more than the influx of alphabetic literacy and print into Indian Country. For the same material practices that embodied the "new and uncommon means" of print missionization also served as the wellspring of a transformation in the public, performative discursive spaces within which tribal, intertribal, and intratribal communications flourished. In this chapter and the next, I examine the creation of discursive spaces that I call "Indian publics." I argue that the circulation of books and manuscripts went hand in hand with a revolution in Native polities across Indian Country. These changes created vexing choices between direct political action and more mediated forms of discourse often cloaked in the rhetorics of Christian conversion.

The career of Samson Occom is a perfect illustration of how such Indian publics were forged out of tough decisions concerning political action and print and manuscript mediation. Occom, after all, managed to become the first Native American published in North America in part by publicly abjuring his right to be a political figure. About to depart for England on his 1764 fund-raising mission, Occom put his signature on this apology for his participation in Mohegan tribal business: "Although, as a member of the Mohegan tribe, and for many years, one of their council, I thought I had not only a natural and civil right, but that it was my duty, to acquaint myself with their temporal affairs, Yet I am, upon serious and close reflection, convinced, that as there was no absolute necessity for it, it was very imprudent of me, and offence to the *Public*, that I should so far engage, as, of late, I have done, in the Mason Controversy: which has injured my Ministerial Character, hurt my Usefulness, and brought Dishonour upon Mr. Wheelock's school and the Correspondents. . . . I am heartily sorry."[1]

Occom's apology for getting involved in the land tenure dispute between the Mason family, the colony of Connecticut, and the Mohegan Nation, like most of his public writing, ironically exposes the hypocrisy of the missionary institution even as he apparently acquiesces to its demands.[2] Although Occom may have been theoretically justified in feeling that he had both a "natural and civil" right to use his literacy to benefit the Mohegan people, this passage reminds us that, in practice, such rights were generally not available to American Indians. As a result, most eighteenth- and nineteenth-century Native intellectuals found that European alphabetic literacy was most safely wielded from the position of "ministerial character." In the public writing produced by men like Joseph Johnson and Samson Occom, it is thus the "Christian" persona that most often seems to authorize their entry into public debate.

By the last decades of the eighteenth century, however, Native diplomats and intellectuals had available a variety of rhetorical practices through which to make themselves and their communities "visible" in the print-culture–dominated world of early U.S. government Indian policy. At the same time, within tribal communities, nativist prophets began to employ counterdiscourses to the dominant culture's print public sphere, pointing to books, print, and alphabetic literacy—even to Christianity itself—as the main signs of "declension" in their societies. Native prophets proffered alternative "books" and "publics" as cures for their communities' many ills: loss of traditional lands, rising alcoholism, and overall subjugation by the newly established United States. Public writing by Native people in the period from 1790 to 1850 is this chapter's focus. I argue that Indian publics—as distinct from Anglo-American publics—took form within a profound tension between those who advocated discursive practices that treated alphabetic literacy, manuscripts, and print as media that could be appropriated and made suitable for Indian public expression and those who decried such practices as "impure," as signs of dangerous contagion from an unsettled spirit world.

Indian Publics

By the end of the American Revolution, Native discourse was already deeply intertwined with Euro-American public writing. Treaties and land grants are perhaps the best-known examples of this fact.[3] But, in a broader sense, Native peoples began increasingly to engage in many forms of communication designed to address "the public." This imaginary "public" was itself the product of European intellectuals' conceptualization of a communicative space for the circulation of manuscript and print that was relatively free of and unencumbered by church and state. Some called this space a "republic of letters," and to them it signaled the serendipitous convergence of individual liberty, civic humanism, and communicative practice that epitomized the era Immanuel Kant called the "Enlightenment." Frankfurt School sociologist Jürgen Habermas coined the term "public sphere" to describe this eighteenth-century space of communicative interchange. He argued that civil society itself came into being as a result of this revolution in communication and was constituted by "private people coming together as a public." As this new public began to openly debate issues like political governance, social relations, and labor rights, it produced a body of texts that came to be known as "public opinion." For later scholars of early American public culture, like Michael Warner, print was the "decisive mark" (to use Habermas's phrase) of this emergent public sphere and the public opinion it engendered.[4]

Subsequent critics (Sandra Gustafson, in particular) have criticized Warner for "overemphasiz[ing] the role that print plays in defining public discourse . . . [by] assuming a sharp divide between printed texts and oral performances."[5] Nevertheless, the basic shape of his description of the early American public sphere remains a powerful explanatory model for understanding how writers positioned their work for public consumption in the first century of full-scale printing and distribution in America. Warner's most recent work is especially salient in this regard, seeking to introduce the notion of "counterpublic" discourse into scholarship on the public sphere. His definition informs my discussion of emergent Indian publics in the nineteenth century. According to Warner, a counterpublic "is usually related to a subculture, but there are important differences between these concepts. A counterpublic, against the background of the public sphere, enables a horizon of opinion and exchange; its exchanges remain distinct from authority and can have a critical relation to power; its extent is in principle indefinite, because it is not based on a precise demography but mediated by print, theater, diffuse networks of talk, commerce, and the like."[6]

There is no question that the many tribal communities that made up nineteenth-century Indian Country constituted subcultures within the dominant Euro-American political/structural framework supported by federal Indian policy and print culture. Yet my argument regarding Indian publics does not rest with merely calling them "subcultures," thus implying a simplistic and subservient relation to a "dominant culture." As Warner makes clear, a true counterpublic must reflect "a critical relation to power." Nineteenth-century Indian publics, although profoundly mediated by the material culture of the print and manuscript media they were wielding with increasing sophistication, sought to perform these mediations within special tribal cultural practices and languages. Their "critical relation to power," as Robert Warrior has defined it, was one of *intellectual* sovereignty. This form of sovereignty (as opposed to purely political or land-tenure usages) is "a praxis." Native diplomacy took the form of a discursive praxis that was performed within a communicative space where Native speakers, writers, and readers shared "the wide array of pain, joy, oppression, celebration, and spiritual power of . . . American Indian community existence."[7]

Most descriptions of early America's public sphere—whether they consider counterpublics or not—barely mention Indian peoples.[8] Yet there is ample evidence to show that Native Americans, as surely as their Euro-American contemporaries, were grappling with the new modes of communication and affiliation that scholars such as Warner and Gustafson have described. American Indians conceptualized and used these phenomena differently, however. Although the story of the Native conception of the public sphere often parallels that of Euro-American writers and intellectuals, there are many cases in which the tribal context inflects a sense of "public" that diverges significantly from that of the United States.[9]

The preface to one of the most famous early Native American texts gives a sense of the kind of modification that Indian peoples introduced into the public sphere. In introducing his *Sermon, Preached at the Execution of Moses Paul* (1772), Samson Occom reflects on the nature of the "public" to which his work is addressed: "The people of God are abundantly furnished with excellent books upon divine subjects. . . . And when I come to consider [this], I am ready to say with myself, what folly and madness is it . . . to expose my ignorance to the world."[10] Critics commonly interpret these lines as the self-deprecating abasement required of Occom in his public position as an Indian; but in so doing, they may overlook a more obvious point. The force of Occom's comments seems directed toward the overabundance of theological niceties in most printed religious tracts of the period. Reading his comments about his sermon's position in light of the way he imagines his public, we can understand his performance semiotic as part of the New Light's disparagement of learning for the sake of learning and of books for books' sake. A world full of books does not need more books unless those books are somehow different.

Indeed, Occom's next paragraph suggests how his book will be different. Its "service to the world" will come from its "plain, everyday talk" issuing from "an uncommon quarter."[11] In other words, its distinction lies in its Indianness. Internal evidence in the sermon suggests that Occom did indeed conceive of an "Indian public" and of himself as an "Indian" speaker (he often addressed his readers/listeners as "brethren" when speaking of specifically Native concerns). The famous discussion in a 1765 letter to his missionary sponsor, Eleazar Wheelock, of how others questioned his Indianness prior to his departure for the English fund-raising tour ("Some say, I cant talk Indian") provides further background for Occom's statements about the sermon's origination in an "uncommon quarter" of the public sphere.[12] Finally, when read against the twenty other manuscript sermons that Joanna Brooks has collated in *Collected Writings of Samson Occom*, it becomes clear that Occom's "everyday talk" included phrases and metaphors meant to appeal to everyone from working carpenters to African slaves and Native tribal members.[13]

Occom's insistence on the Indianness of his public performance represents a technique of Native self-representation that would become increasingly common during the eighteenth and nineteenth centuries. As late as 1858, long after several Native authors had copyrighted their printed works, Narragansett writer and hymnodist Thomas Commuck wrote that he was "fully aware of the difficulties attendant upon an attempt to appear successfully as an author before a scrutinizing and discerning public, especially . . . being descended from that unfortunate and proscribed people, the Indians." He confesses to "appear[ing] at the bar of public opinion," with "great diffidence."[14]

Mohawk theorist Taiaiake Alfred helps non-Native readers appreciate the depth of Native discursive difference that both Thomas Commuck and Samson Occom were demonstrating as the new colonial public sphere took hold across North America. First, he points out that Native people's reality is, and always has been, communal.[15] Unlike the anonymous print format that Michael Warner argues was essential to the eighteenth-century public sphere, Native discursive space was profoundly collective, grounded, and "known." Alfred further suggests that the ultimate goal of indigenous diplomacy was to challenge "mainstream society to question its own structure . . . to convince others of the wisdom of the indigenous perspective." With "no separation between society and state" in traditional indigenous social systems, the ideal public sphere was "a non-coercive, participatory, transparent, consensus-based system."[16] As fundamental challenges to liberalism, then, such positions are quintessentially "counterpublics" in the sense Warner has articulated. Thomas Commuck was thus merely underscoring what most Native intellectuals already knew, that sedimented in their engagement with America's new and supposedly democratic public sphere was a long and tortured history of Indian/European discursive interaction that both sharply attenuated Native agency and fundamentally miscast Native public personhood. That history is rooted in the centuries-old intercultural discourse of diplomacy, and it is within this discursive field that the construction of Indian publics first began.

Diplomatic Writing

Native peoples in the Americas have been engaged in diplomatic exchanges with Europeans since contact. In early America, indigenous diplomats presented their political positions with a highly elaborated sense of the "public" with which they were communicating, regardless of whether they were using their own or European languages. Europeans, meanwhile, from the beginning of intercultural diplomacy in the New World, made a concerted effort to portray Native understanding of the emerging colonial public sphere as naive, inferior, and Other. Columbus famously reported that he used Native captives to proclaim to indigenous people "in a loud voice 'Come, come, and you will see the celestial people.'"[17] He thus became the first in a long line of Europeans to claim that the public sphere of diplomatic discourse provided European peoples an opportunity to confound and awe their Native interlocutors by appearing otherworldly, mythic, or immortal. From Columbus's 1493 letter onward, Indian discourse was situated on a very uneven playing field.[18]

By the dawn of the eighteenth century, however, this situation had changed dramatically. Over the course of the next fifty years, especially in North America, Native negotiators would shift the terms of diplomatic engagement, forcing Europeans to accommodate or even adopt traditional tribal practices and protocols. Intercultural discursive performances between Natives and non-Natives, mixing European and indigenous practices, were the bases for Richard White's formulation of the middle ground in the *pays d'en haut*,[19] as well as for James Merrell's analysis of the "cacophonous" and "kaleidoscopic" intermixing of materials, practices, and performances in the eighteenth-century Pennsylvania backcountry.[20] Amid such intercultural protocols, borrowed performative practices like alphabetic literacy began to emerge. Literacy then allowed tribal communities to formulate a nascent set of American Indian "publics" through which they could negotiate with each other, argue with colonial adversaries, and preserve for posterity their motives and deliberations during diplomatic struggles. From about 1750, Cherokee leader Atakullakulla and his successors would maintain what has come to be known as the "Cherokee Archive," a body of diplomatic materials written on paper but treated like ceremonial ritual paraphernalia, to supplement tribal oral negotiations and recitations.[21] In 1761, the Cherokees enlisted the services of English Virginian Henry Timberlake, who served as a sort of scribe/hostage during tense treaty negotiations with the British that year. Timberlake was taken to the Chota "townhouse," the centerpiece of frontier Cherokee life, where he acted as a secretary for the Native "Senate," who employed him in "reading and writing letters."[22]

The emergence of American Indian publics began in earnest in the 1790s, after the Constitution established an officially American political economy and institutions of Indian policy.[23] The new United States began to make intensive diplomatic efforts to appease the Native "Western Nations" in the lands of the Ohio River Valley, where Anglo-American settlers were beginning to venture. In this charged atmosphere, the federal government turned to Native negotiators, some of whom were alphabetically literate, to plead their case before "hostile" tribes. To explore how this process unfolded, I will examine here two texts from the canon of early Native alphabetic manuscript literature, Hendrick Aupaumut's "Journal of a Mission to the Western Tribes of Indians" (1791) and Benjamin Williams's "Life of Governor Blacksnake" (ca. 1854). Through a close reading of their scribal practices, I will investigate the repercussions of this U.S. diplomatic effort on Native identity formation. Works like Aupaumut's and Williams's represent some of the first halting efforts of indigenous nations in the East toward constructing and performing a public, political Indianness. They thus model an emerging indigenous speaking subject in American political discourse. They also mark the beginning of the process of constructing an imagined mixed audience of Native and non-Native auditors in the public sphere of the early republic.

"Journal of a Mission to the Western Tribes of Indians" (1791) was written by Hendrick Aupaumut (1757–1830), grand sachem of the Mahican Nation and an important leader of the Stockbridge people. Aupaumut was educated by the Moravians at Stockbridge in the 1760s, and he enlisted in the Continental Army at the start of the Revolutionary War. When the Stockbridge settlement removed to Oneida country after the war, Aupaumut became an emissary between Indian interests and the U.S. government, traveling at the request of Secretary of War Henry Knox for eleven months in 1790–91 among the Delawares, Miamis, Shawnees, and others in the Ohio River Valley. It was after this journey that he penned his journal.

A different account of these negotiations appears in the as-told-to autobiography collaboratively produced by grand sachem and Seneca elder Chainbreaker and Benjamin Williams, an alphabetically literate Seneca man from Cold Spring on the Allegheny Reservation. Chainbreaker, known to whites as Governor Blacksnake, was an important leader of the Six Nations, his two maternal uncles being Cornplanter and Handsome Lake. He too fought in the Revolutionary War, on the British side, and was involved in complex negotiations with the Americans after the conflict. While Aupaumut was traveling in the Ohio River Valley on behalf of the U.S. government, Chainbreaker was making a similar journey on behalf of the Six Nations. Sometime during the 1840s, Chainbreaker narrated his life story in Seneca to Williams, who transcribed it into English. At the urging of Chainbreaker's son, Williams attempted to sell the manuscript for publication to Wisconsin antiquarian Lyman C. Draper, in whose voluminous collection of manuscripts it remains today.[24]

Both of these texts offer historians a wealth of information about the events that transpired in the Ohio River Valley in the 1790s. Both also detail the indigenous diplomatic protocols that framed negotiations between Indian communities in the postwar period. Perhaps most significant, both texts narrate these events and performances from Native points of view, focusing largely on Native-to-Native interactions. In the process, they articulate varying indigenous perspectives on the 1790s diplomatic mission, allowing us to appreciate the array of American Indian interests at play across the Northeast and the Ohio River Valley. They also help us broaden the ground for our conceptualization of Native public performance in the period, offering us a sense of the diversity of opinion and complexity of motive that informed Indian diplomacy.

Both Aupaumut and Chainbreaker emphasize the performative intricacy of their negotiations by highlighting the Native protocols involved. Their meetings with the Western Nations took place in pre-established, ceremonially prepared forest clearings or creek-side villages. Aupaumut relates how negotiators ritually cleansed each other so that all might "hear plain." One Native diplomat embraces Aupaumut, saying, "I put my hand to take away the dust from your ears." The night before such meetings, Chainbreaker tells us, his party would gather in council to "talk on the subject . . . for to see clear with the Naked eyes and open . . . ears," not wishing to "hold their heads down and see nothing." These rituals, sachem Tautpuhqtheet explains to Aupaumut, are those "our good ancestors did hand down to us [as] a rule or path where we may walk."[25]

Both men also dramatize scenes of political division within their respective negotiating parties. When traveling with his cohort of warriors and diplomats, Aupaumut had a chance encounter with Mohawk sachem Joseph Brant and gave him an overview of his planned arguments. In an ominous sign of dissension to come, Brant "gave him no answer." Later, in the Ohio Valley, Brant would call Aupaumut "a deceiver and a roag [rogue]." Nor is Aupaumut's detailed description of his run-in with the famous Five Nations leader the only time he represents political dissent among Indians. His repeated reflections on the subject suggest that such matters were not merely personal or even bilaterally intertribal (that is, between Mohawks in Canada and Mahicans in the new United States) but rather part of the confusing new discursive matrix within which negotiations were taking place. Aupaumut is careful to delineate the complex political divisions affecting several tribes among the Western Nations, which are the result of imperial pressures from British and American forces as well as of internal social unrest within the tribes themselves. The Wyandots, for example, were "divided" over whether to go to war with the Americans (as the dominant Shawnees were insisting upon), and "only one part of them held the opinion of the Delaware" that war was the right option. In addition, Aupaumut differentiated the main players among the Western Nations (Shawnees, Delawares, Miamis) from those of the "Back Nations" (Wyandots, Ottawas, Chippewas, and Potawatomis), all of whose decision-making processes seem to have been much more grounded in self-interest than in consideration of Euro-Native imperial alliances. The Munsees were so happy to see Aupaumut's party that "they did a dance" for them, but the Shawnees repeatedly refused him audience.[26]

Chainbreaker's narrative is likewise rife with descriptions of discord, particularly between Brant and Cornplanter, Red Jacket, and nearly everybody else. Chainbreaker recalls that warriors in intertribal councils "had great dail of controversy created amongst themselves[.] Some for Brant and some for Cornplanter [and this] appeared to create it in two party."[27] Because both men spend so much time explaining these "controversies," it seems clear that they wished to add political texture to negotiations that Europeans might otherwise have dismissed as merely ceremonial, largely untrustworthy, and (to use a word common in European descriptions of the period) little more than "harangues." It is precisely these political differences that created the "critical relations of power" that in turn make Chainbreaker's and Aupaumut's manuscripts much more than autobiographies or histories of the period — that make them, that is, such significant records and representations of the emerging Indian public sphere.

This process of emergence becomes particularly evident when one notes that the diplomatic negotiations that gave rise to so much rhetorical "controversy" were conducted via the agency of a range of ritual objects — printed texts, treaties written on a "pease of skin," tin boxes stuffed with legal papers, medicine bags filled with ancient wampum, land plats, and even commemorative oil portrait paintings — most of which were not yet fully integrated into Native ceremonial and rhetorical practices. Indeed, this lack of integration could itself become a source of controversy. Chainbreaker describes Joseph Brant's histrionics in 1784 at being handed a sheaf of "receipts," a "written contract, and a letter" in support of an American alliance during a tribal council: "Brand [Brant] took it in his hand and read a few lines and begun to sweare and stamp down and turn right faces round [toward] us."[28] This incident and others like it scattered in journals describing similar negotiations during the period suggest that it was not only the content of the message but its medium that drew Brant's ire. For Brant and others, printed and written paper documents sometimes disrupted oral protocols, driving a material wedge between negotiators.

Nevertheless, as James Merrell so capably documents for the comparable Pennsylvania context, such hybrid negotiating practices and materials were becoming increasingly common in the backcountry during this period.[29] The hybrid performative techniques described in Aupaumut's and Chainbreaker's texts, then, suggest that the formal properties of these two manuscript reports may themselves represent extensions of actual woodland diplomatic performances. That is, the documents may reflect the new materials being integrated, sometimes even ceremonially, into the fabric of traditional autobiographical recollection and historical commemoration. And, as such, these textual performances offer unique insight into the late eighteenth-century processes by which Native political figures constructed an Indian public sphere while demonstrating how the written word came to play a major part in that process.

The original manuscript of Aupaumut's "Journal," housed in the Pennsylvania Historical Society, is bound as a book. Its hand-lettered and framed title page states: "Journal of a Mission to the Western Tribes of Indians by Hendrick Aupaumut, 1791." The chronicle is written both as a journal—a personal reminiscence and therefore constructive of self or identity—and as a report, a political document in the public sphere. This dual purpose may be seen in the ways Aupaumut marked his manuscript to make it easier to "read" as a public document: hand-drawn rules separate the days of the week, tribal groups, and speakers; occasional marginal brackets and other markings denote asides and interjections. The rules also stand out as signs of Native scribal difference when compared with the small bracketed inserts apparently introduced by the editors of the 1827 *Memoirs of the Historical Society of Pennsylvania* edition of Aupaumut's manuscript. These inserts are clearly derived from print culture practice (a typical entry reads: "[Sig.14—fol. 101])." Although Aupaumut's handwriting is quite good and he is very careful to indent for paragraph divisions in his narrative, he is just as likely to use extended dashes and great swaths of white space and brackets to set off ceremonial practices that exceed the conventions of scribal practice.

On page 22 of the manuscript, for example, Aupaumut finishes a paragraph of narration by drawing a vertical line underneath, down the center of the page, and writing on the left side, "Then they rose and shake our hands," while on the right side of the division he comments, "This all I have to say— four strings of wampum of three feet long delivered." Centered below this line and division is a single sentence: "Few minutes after this." The regular narration then resumes with conventional paragraphing, including, however, a hand-drawn marginal bracket that extends over the following two pages of the narrative, indicating the rest of the meeting that day (figure 20).

Although these textual markers indicate how Aupaumut's "book" engaged the Anglo-American public sphere with a critical performance of scribal difference, the first sentence of his report specifically invests the journal with a uniquely indigenous agency. It works to position its speaker in a public space somewhat outside the sphere of influence of the United States. Aupaumut begins by asserting that he has "agreed with the Great Men of the United States to take a tour with their Message of peace to the hostile nations." Calling himself both an "Indian, and a true friend," Aupaumut continues this textual shuttle diplomacy, placing his contemporary colonial activities within an ancestral tribal tradition of peacemaking and peacekeeping. Protocol and family, clan obligations and civility, as essential in the 1790s Ohio River Valley as they are in Indian Country today, are fundamental to Aupaumut's textual performance. He makes it clear that his performance is intended to "reflect in the path of [his] ancestors": "Before I proceed in the business I am upon," he

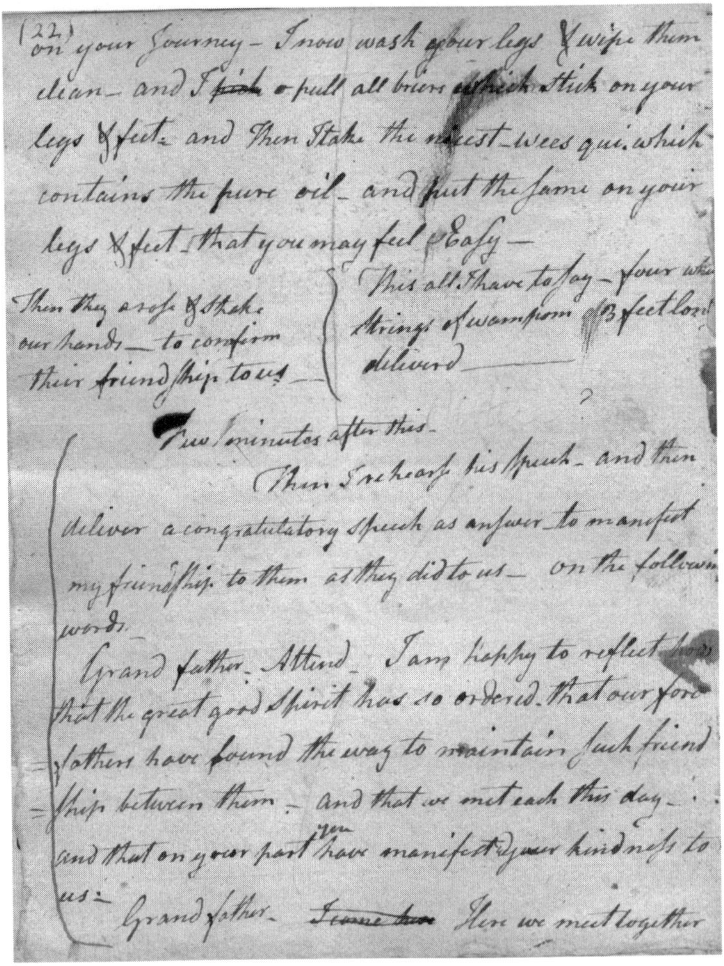

(22) on your Journey — I now wash your legs & wipe them
clean — and I ~~pick~~ pull all briers which stick on your
legs & feet — and then I take the nicest Wees qui. which
contains the pure oil — and put the same on your
legs & feet — that you may feel Easy —

Then they arose & Shake our hands — to confirm their friendship to us —

This all I have to say — four white strings of wampum of 3 feet long delivered —

Two minutes after this.

Then I rehearse his speech — and then
deliver a congratulatory speech as answer to manifest
my friendship to them as they did to us — on the following
words.

Grand father — Attend — I am happy to reflect how
that the great good Spirit has so ordered that our fore
fathers have found the way to maintain such friend
ship between them — and that we met each this day —
and that on your part you have manifest your kindness to
us — Grand father — ~~[illegible]~~ Here we meet together

Figure 20. Page from Hendrick Aupaumut, "Journal of a Mission to the Western Tribes of Indians" (1791). Courtesy of Historical Society of Pennsylvania, Indian Papers (MS 310).

writes, "I think it would be necessary to give a Short Sketch of the friendship and connections our forefathers and we have had with the western tribes."[30] The "connections" Aupaumut describes are familial: the Shawnees, Miamis, Munsees, Wyandots, Ottawas, Potawatomis, Ojibwes, and Kickapoos all stand in relation to the speaker and his journal as so many uncles, cousins, fathers, and younger brothers in a family tree.

Such familial relations are themselves time-honored, and accordingly, they allow Aupaumut to link his written narrative to "time-immemorial" oral tradition. "It was the business of our forefathers to go around the towns of these nations to renew the agreements between them," he states, just as it was his duty to engage in his current diplomatic mission. His ancestors were required to tell the Western Nations "many things which they discover is among the white people in the east." So too it is Aupaumut's lot to write such details down on paper in the form of a report. The medium is modern but the message is rooted in tradition, and the text itself is committed to forging continuity between new and old, between written words and pictographic records on wood, shell, and stone. Aupaumut's allegiance to tribal tradition is especially evident at one crucial moment in the negotiations when it appears that an English officer (a Colonel McKee) is attempting to lure him away from the bargaining table with a spurious "urgent" message requesting his presence at Fort Jefferson. Aupaumut's indignant response marshals all the performative intercultural practices at his disposal: "But I said, I have not seen any token or Message, in strings of wampum, or writing, nor Tobacco, I will not go—I am not to regard emty messages, &c."[31]

Benjamin Williams's biography of Chainbreaker initiates similar claims of continuity with Seneca history in its opening page, anchoring the claims in narrative and scribal practices much like those found in Aupaumut's manuscript. Williams positions Chainbreaker's narration within a tradition "handed down from Generation to generation—we cannot tell the number of years ago, for we have no written account, only what we get from the oldest and good man statements."[32] Williams's text is especially interesting in this regard: the text not only introduces Chainbreaker's memoir by situating it in relation to the Seneca origin story but it also provides his detailed recitation of Handsome Lake's prophecy and code of conduct, thus locating both him and his story within an emergent, modern Seneca nativism. After explaining Chainbreaker's name (this is his "real" name, Williams states, although the whites call him Governor Blacksnake), the manuscript defends its interpretations by arguing that it "can be ascertained fect of the Said Life of governour Blacksnake and others connected with it and the traditions of ancient history—the creation of the world and late prophet [Handsome Lake]." Williams even maintains that some blanks in the old warrior's memory have been filled in through reference to details found "on the head of an ancient pipe."[33]

Williams's text, though less formally marked than Aupaumut's, also opens with a carefully lettered title—"Life of Blacksnake"—and is similarly punctuated by marginal asides and glosses. Williams sometimes uses these corrections and marginalia to set off speeches from the main narrative; at other times they are self-conscious corrections of factual detail, pitched, like Aupaumut's defensive comments, to a Euro-American audience that demands a culturally specific kind of historical accuracy. Still other asides in the Williams text are written in syllabic Seneca and appear to be directed at maintaining communal and cultural integrity for an indigenous audience. Such asides often involve words that cannot readily be translated, or they show how the typical Euro-American phrase is inadequate to explain or perform what really happened.

The process begins almost immediately in the text with Williams's ritual recitation of Chainbreaker's name and ancestry, a paragraph directed at both non-Seneca audiences unfamiliar with the linguistic complexities of the old man's formal title and the Seneca oral tradition's customary way of locating a speaking subject within family and clan lineages. Interestingly, it was this very cross-cultural performance that Williams's contemporary editor, Thomas Abler, an accomplished ethnologist with close ties to the Senecas, relegated to an appendix. Abler dismissed the passage as "a lengthy, confused introduction, not closely related to the story that follows and possibly more difficult to read than any other section of the text."[34] Yet it is precisely its impenetrability to the modern reader that suggests its relevance to another, alternative set of scribal practices. These practices echo those found in the Aupaumut text and are a further illustration of how writing in manuscript and print during the first decades of U.S.-Native diplomacy was (however uncomfortably) being woven into the fabric of Native protocols.

Williams introduces Blacksnake's narrative with this "cacophonous" and "kaleidoscopic" set of sentences: "The birth of governour Blacksnake or more correctly of Ten wr, nyrs—for Such was his Real name—interpretation is Chainbreaker his las name give to him at the time he became a chief warrior . . . but when in Boyhood was then called—Daghgr, yan, Doh—until he became a young man . . . following to according to their custome of their Rules and Traditions . . . this can be asurtained fect of the Said Life of governour Blacksnake, and others connected with it and traditions of their ancient history, account of creation of the world and late prophet, and Sanctuary three times a year."[35] Williams also feels obligated to add conventional Euro-American writing practice in his method of marking time in the old warrior's narrative. When recounting deeds that occurred in 1749, Williams adds a broad-stroked "1749" in the left-hand margin, followed by a bracketed gloss: "What called by the Seneca Language gau, dr, â."[36] This self-conscious marking of time in both the traditional Seneca and European ways continues throughout the manuscript. In other passages, it seems clear that Williams is thinking in Seneca even as he writes the elder's story in English. Given to writing vertical marginal glosses during crucial points in Chainbreaker's story, Williams narrates the Senecas' fight at Fort Stanwix by marking it twice with the marginal gloss "Fort Stanwix." On the third page, however, he writes, "fort Ga, doh, ga, Battle." Like Aupaumut, Williams follows what seems to have become a scribal convention of setting off traditional Native oratory from the main body of the narrative by employing white space, indentation, dashes, and ceremonial salutations (for example, "Brothers—"). On page 113 of the manuscript, he follows Aupaumut's practice exactly when he centers the phrase "Red Jackett given answer," followed by a separate paragraph of oratory beginning, "Brothers we are suppose you are ready to hear."[37]

Neither of these manuscript performances of Indian publics is without its own tension and irony. Thus, when transferred to the page to be performed by the speaking subjects of these written texts, the embodied performances carry with them the marks of "intersubjectivity," the term Greg Sarris has used to describe "the specific social contingencies of the exchange" between Natives and non-Natives. For instance, whenever Aupaumut cites a Native negotiator's speech, he either brackets or indents it and takes care to mention the wampum exchange. At one point, he even pauses to explicate the meaning of an especially important belt. It was a "large belt . . . which contains 15 rows and in the middle there is 15 square marks which denotes 15 united sachems and path of peace goes through these marks." In this manner, he performs his expertise in the Native semiotic system, thereby bridging the gap between the political selves he described earlier as "Indian" and "friend." In a later aside, he bristles that if his Euro-American readers need proof of his loyalty he can "show the wampum of their speech."[38] Here Aupaumut's Indian subjectivity is in danger of being eclipsed by a colonial relation of inequality and a discursive field that immediately marks Indian utterance as suspect.

Yet, in a particularly vivid and assertive moment in the text, Aupaumut suggests a way out of this dilemma. It occurs during his description of Delaware leader Big Cat's diplomatic performances. In trying to help Aupaumut steer the Western Nations away from war, Big Cat articulates his support of some European politics and practices while rejecting others on Native grounds. Questioned by Captain Eliot of the British command about the precise membership of his negotiating committee and their recent comings and goings, Big Cat responds with a furious argument for sovereignty: "Did you ever see me at Detroit or Niagara, in your councils, and there to ask you where such and such white man come from? Or what is their Business? Can you watch, and look all over the earth to see who come to us? Or is what their business? Do you not know that we are upon our own Business? And we have longed to see these our friend." At this, Aupaumut reports, Elliot's "mouth was stopd immediately." In moments such as these and in his final rousing defense of his own character (one he thinks has been "darkened" by rumor and innuendo), Aupaumut represents his diplomacy and that of his Indian allies as a product of specifically Indian publics, never of subaltern obeisance to colonial authority.[39]

The "social contingencies of exchange" are somewhat different in the case of the Chainbreaker manuscript, divided as they are between Chainbreaker's own goals in narrating his life to a fellow Seneca tribal member and Williams's efforts to communicate Chainbreaker's story to a sometimes-skeptical Lyman Draper. Chainbreaker expresses his intersubjective stance when he explains that he is narrating his story as part of his duty to the "welfare" of his people and when he apologizes to an imagined non-Indian readership: "The Readers must Excuse me for I do not Regelect on what month or what Day of the month for I have no larn or to understand English Either I only what I hear from the enterpreter."[40] Williams performs his own intersubjectivity when he inserts vertical marginal glosses that simultaneously explain Seneca things to non-Seneca readers and, perhaps self-consciously, model nineteenth-century print conventions. Marginal glosses were routinely used during this period to mark narrative movement, directing readers' attention to the high points of a story.[41] Yet Williams's marginal asides go beyond even these important functions. At several key points in the narrative, Williams acidly pens ironic marginal critiques of the perfidy surrounding the 1777 negotiations between the Six Nations and the British ("the time the Indians was bribe by the British"),[42] all the while accurately recording Chainbreaker's own recollections of the meeting.

In thus foregrounding the social contingencies of exchange that lay behind their narratives, both authors push toward something Native literary theorist Scott Richard Lyons has termed "rhetorical sovereignty." This kind of sovereignty, related as it is to the political and economic sovereignty that men like Chainbreaker and Aupaumut were seeking to negotiate with the United States in the 1790s, lies in the rhetorical gestures Indian writers make in their texts. Rhetorical sovereignty, Lyons argues, "is the inherent right and ability of *peoples* to determine their own communicative needs and desires . . . to decide for themselves the goals, modes, styles, and languages of public discourse."[43] Toward the end of his journal, Aupaumut pointedly asserts his rhetorical sovereignty when he reports what he *did not* say to the Western nations: "I . . . were oblige to say nothing with regard to the Yorkers. How they cheat my fathers. How they taken our Lands Unjustly—and how my fathers were groaning as it were to their graves In losing their Lands for nothing—although they were faithful friends to the Whites. . . . Had I mention these things to the Indians—it would aggravate their Prejudices against all white people."[44] This comment is, of course, aimed directly at his Euro-American sponsors. But it is also a further example of Aupaumut's complex performance of Native political identity. He is simultaneously someone who "agreed" to be sent west, someone who views himself as both "Indian and friend," and someone whose political power in both Native and non-Native circles derives from the self-conscious (and sometimes ironic) manipulation of what he knows to be true as well as what he deems it prudent to say. Yet, as with most of his narrative, this statement is directed toward reinforcing the sovereignty of his own tribe's position. He is letting his white sponsors know that he sees them for what they are, that is, often untruthful manipulators of Indian public opinion. Throughout the manuscript, the speaking subject of the narrative remains a man who refers to himself as "I, the Muhheuconneew," refusing translation and asserting linguistic and tribal sovereignty.[45]

Chainbreaker, meanwhile, tells us that as a young man he was "nothing but passengers among the warriors . . . to hear all the business going on." He did, however, listen carefully, committing "the business" to memory. He would eventually decide to recite it to Benjamin Williams because "it seem . . . very in Deed important business to be understood on the most important part, and put myself to feel interest in our welfare."[46] The phrase "interest in our welfare" provides a good gloss on the guiding principles of these two texts, firmly locating their production in the space of an emerging Indian public, which both authors perform simultaneously as voice in their text and audience for their words. That is, both narratives manifest their authors' rhetorical sovereignty by placing Native speakers and Native auditors at the center of their manuscript performances. That the "welfare" they seek is *Indian* welfare, and that these political publics are *Indian* publics, is made quite clear in Aupaumut's manuscript, where both pro- and anti-American factions repeat a constitutive rhetorical formula to their Native auditors when they ask for support of their respective positions: "That you may contemplate the welfare of our own colar [color]."[47]

Although print has become the most highlighted aspect of the early republic's public sphere, it is clear from these examples, and from other non-Native cases Sandra Gustafson has explicated in her recent critique of Michael Warner's thesis, that scribal and performative practices shared the stage with print. It is also clear that "these emerging media cannot be mapped neatly onto a binary social geography divided between publics and counterpublics any more than 'print culture' can be meaningfully distinguished from 'oral culture.'" Both Aupaumut's and Williams's scribal practices confirm Gustafson's assertion that focusing "on the semiotic properties of speech and writing and of material artifacts such as maps, baskets, and wampum offers alternative frameworks for understanding that avoid rigid distinctions between media."[48]

Certainly both of these Native manuscripts exhibit efforts to highlight "voice" over script in coming to terms with the new diplomatic discourse of the 1790s. At the conclusion of his failed effort to convince the Shawnees not to enter into war with the United States, Aupaumut writes of the other peaceful nations, that "they will send their voice to the US that the US may know what were the obstacles to the path of peace." The emphasis here is on voice, not treaty document or even journal report, and it is perhaps for this reason that Aupaumut concludes his narrative on a profoundly personal note, vigorously defending his own character and the "occasion of my speaking this sort."[49] The primacy of voice in early Indian publics is found even in the work of Williams, a writer who definitely had print in mind when he transcribed Chainbreaker's oral narrative. What comes through clearly in the tortured letters that trace the negotiations regarding the work's publication is that it may have been the profound orality of Williams's writing style (what Six Nations ethnographer Anthony F. C. Wallace termed "very bad reservation English")[50] that most influenced Draper's decision not to print the Chainbreaker narrative.

The manuscript practices visible in the responses of Hendrick Aupaumut and Chainbreaker to the diplomatic events of the Ohio River Valley in the 1790s open to our view an emerging, often intertribal, conception of an Indian public that supplements our present understanding of eighteenth-century Indian Country. The material properties of the Aupaumut and Chainbreaker texts are not merely mimetic, not simply reports of performative practices, but are constitutive of political orientation within an emerging cross-cultural public sphere. They constitute one-half of the equation for indigenous subject-formation emerging in the 1790s for key American Indian players in the drama of the Ohio River Valley. The other half of the story emerges from the practices of the people neither Aupaumut nor Chainbreaker could convince to come to terms with the Americans. These tribal communities were centered in profoundly Nativist encampments like the Glaize, a village on the Maumee River near present-day Defiance, Ohio. Here prophets preached the abolition of white ways, and the saplings for hundreds of yards in every direction were painted with "red hieroglyphics" that defiantly invoked the superiority of traditional semiotic systems over those the missionaries and government agents proffered in exchange for traditional hunting grounds and homelands.[51]

Revitalization Publics

The nativist Indian publics that began taking shape in the 1790s Ohio Valley reached their apotheosis in the period from 1811 to 1814. These dates bracket Tecumseh's Rebellion, an intertribal war against the United States that was also the flash point for a series of revitalization movements across Indian Country. Such movements viewed the increasing prominence of manuscripts, books, and print as symptoms of the larger "contagion" that was European culture. The ambiguous relationship between Native peoples and European books became a centerpiece of the Native revivalist movements that flourished in Indian Country during the period. Gregory Dowd recounts how, from the 1750s forward, books — for good or ill — appear in the prophecies of nativists across Indian communities. They are one among many signs of cultural difference and cultural contamination, but also one among many sources of cultural revitalization. "Since God gave no such book to the Indian or negro," one prophet reasoned, "it could not be right for [Indians] to have a book."[52] Nevertheless, Neolin, the Delaware prophet, was reported to have constructed an "Indian Bible" that was a "Book of Pickters he Maid him Self."[53] In 1762, an American traveler to the Western Nations noted that Neolin used "a certain parchment marked with hieroglyphics," and, in 1767, Native religious leader Wangomen was seen using a similar "bible."[54]

Native-produced books like these were significant vehicles for revitalization well into the nineteenth century. During the 1813–14 Red Stick War among the Muskogee, for example, spiritual leader Hillis Hadjo announced he had attained literacy and a power over books in a spiritual vision. In this way, Joel Martin argues, Hadjo "symbolically assimilated all the powers of literacy and the Book. Though his people had no printed and bound books, he announced that the Breathmaker had personally instructed him in all 'the branches of writing and languages perfect enough to converse write and do his own business.'"[55] Like the Red Stick of justice from which the Muskogee revivalist movement takes it name, writing and print were "icon[s] of the enemy that Creek prophets appropriated for their own symbolic and practical purposes."[56]

On the Columbia Plateau, as Elizabeth Vibert has detailed, prophetic movements that featured revitalization of Native communities had existed since before contact with non-Indians. During the nineteenth century, however, these movements often turned toward whites as sources of contagion, specifically singling out their books and presses as agents of spiritual unrest. A measles outbreak among the Wishram tribe in 1847 threw suspicion on the Lapwai Mission press and was one of the causes that led to the murder of the local missionaries, Marcus and Narcissa Whitman. Many Spokane people on the Columbia Plateau would come to associate the coming of whites and books with the end of the world. Vibert documents an oral history related by a man named Cornelius to the Wilkes Survey for the U.S. government: "Soon," said he, "there will come from the rising sun a different kind of man from any you have yet seen, who will bring with them a book, and will teach you everything, and after that the world will fall to pieces."[57]

Between 1842 and 1843, among the Cree-speaking Omushkegowak people of Lake Winnipeg, a prophetic movement emerged that significantly featured a "generative role played . . . by a Cree syllabic writing system that had just been introduced in the region by a Methodist missionary."[58] The missionary, James Evans, produced printed hymns and Bible texts in a special Cree syllabary he invented for use on his mission press. The results were unexpected. Two Native men—Abishabis (Small Eyes) and Wasitay (The Light)—interpreted the missionary books in nativist terms, arguing that the complex syllabary characters spelled out more than the missionary realized. Abishabis and Wasitay claimed they could discern in the characters admonitions from the spirit world urging the Omushkegowak to purify themselves. The spirits further exhorted the community to recognize the pair as prophetic leaders and to forsake the Christian mission books in favor of books they created. As anthropologist Jennifer S. H. Brown suggests, these book prophets made perfect sense at this particular moment in Omushkegowak history, when pressures from Hudson Bay Company traders and the challenges posed by the new Christian religion were straining the traditional social fabric. Abishabis and Wasitay emerged as "plausible leaders" because they brought with them a blend of new ideas and practices and a new sign system (the Cree syllabary) that promised empowerment. Eventually, the prophets' demands revealed that they were more interested in self-enrichment than in spiritual revitalization. They were executed by former followers, "who symbolically began giving up or destroying their [homemade] 'books' and other materials." As Brown points out, "Written texts and the 'painting' of books" were at the core of this movement to revivify Omushkegowak in the 1840s.[59]

Alphabets, written manuscripts, and printed books played an undeniable role in these and other revitalization movements across Indian Country in the nineteenth century. This fact demands that any book history of Native America must come to terms with the profoundly ambiguous, on-again, off-again, public sphere such movements engage. It also highlights the impossibility of our appreciating the material meaning of even the most canonical nineteenth-century American Indian texts without considering their resonances within these emerging revitalizationist Indian publics, in which books were at once the cause of and the solution for many a community's despair.

Take the case, for example, of Sarah Winnemucca Hopkins's autobiography, *Life among the Paiutes* (1883). In the midst of a conventional retelling of the ominous incursion of non-Indian peoples into the Great Basin, the author's grandfather unveils the most "wonderful thing" the whites had recently given him: "It was a paper, which he said could talk to him. He took it out and he would talk to it, and talk with it. He said, 'This can talk to all our white brothers, and our white sisters and their children.' . . . He also said the paper can travel like the wind, and it can go and talk with their fathers and brothers and sisters, and come back to tell what they are doing."[60] It has been common to treat scenes such as this, found in so many Indian texts, as one among many "signs taken as wonders." Scholars then follow postcolonial theorist Homi Bhabha into a reading based on the hybridity, mimicry, and ventriloquism of the text. Winnemucca's next sentence does indeed seem to point in that direction. "After my grandfather told us this," she writes, "our doctors and doctresses said,—'If they can do this wonderful thing, they are not truly human, but pure spirits.'"[61]

Read within the context of the broader emergence of nineteenth-century Indian publics, however, Winnemucca's words may be understood to mean something quite different. From the standpoint of Native revitalization, the passage speaks to a society anxious about its future and contemplating how the supernatural powers of a major technology of the potential colonizer may be harnessed in such a way as to revivify the Paiutes' own cultural values. For although Winnemucca's grandfather may be temporarily entranced by the Europeans' *technological* achievements, the medicine people have a longer and grimmer view. "We are afraid your white brothers will yet make your people's hearts bleed," says one leader; "you see if they don't, for we can see it." "Their blood is all around us," another says, "and the dead are lying all about us, and we cannot escape it, it will come." The tribal leaders see millennial doom in the sheets of paper that so captivated Winnemucca's grandfather. In the bleak tone of so many of the revitalization movements occurring across North America, they predict that the old ceremonial ways cannot fend off a malignant future: "Dance, sing, play, it will do no good; we cannot drive it away. They have already done the mischief."[62]

Michael Harkin's introduction to *Reassessing Revitalization Movements* (2004) allows us to hear Winnemucca's story in a new way because it reminds us of the important fact that ideologies of Native revitalization may be "inflected with specific technologies that appear to be useful in coping with disruptions: ghost shirts, means of obtaining cargo, or, indeed, missionary-brought literacy and numeracy."[63] In other words, the very paper and books that presage the Paiutes' doom may be marshaled to help control it. It is equally significant that the spiritual leaders of the Paiute community see those who have produced these papers as "spirits." In the terms of revitalization theory, the white creators of those documents were "the dead," unwelcome and restless visitors from the Paiutes' own spirit world who represent an imbalance in the cosmos. The community will likely require ceremonies of mimetic performance to be rid of them.

Unlike conventional postcolonial theory, which reads material practices like the reading and writing of books by non-Western peoples as part of the discursive adoption (no matter how potentially resistant) of technologies imposed from *outside*, revitalization theory attempts to understand such adoption (or rejection) of new communicative material practices from within a Native culture. In the words of Elizabeth Vibert, it represents the attempt "to understand indigenous religious movements on their own terms and not merely as reactions to external forces."[64] As Russell Thornton observes, "Revitalization movements may thus be defined as internal, spiritually based efforts deliberately organized to create a better social and/or cultural system while reviving or reaffirming selected features."[65] Thus, revitalization movements can be seen as a response to colonialism carried out in local cultural terms. Colonialism is thereby generalized into a common human challenge, much like epidemics and environmental catastrophe—a profound rupture in the order of things, an aporia. Though colonialism's negative effects are profoundly spiritual in nature, they remain "inflected by specific cultural and historical forms."[66]

With these theories in mind, this discussion of the rise of Indian publics in the period from 1790 to 1830 concludes with attention to the works of two Native writers who were no friends to nativism in their communities. Nevertheless, revitalizationist Indian publics were potent enough to warp the shape of their scribal and print practices. The first, George Stiggins's eighty-eight-page manuscript history of the Red Stick War, "A Historical Narration of the Geneology Traditions and Downfall of the Ispocaga or Creek Tribe," was written between 1831 and 1844. Stiggins wrote it at the behest of Lyman Draper. As such, this manuscript shares much with Benjamin Williams's Chainbreaker narrative. Stiggins was born at Talladega (now in Alabama) in 1788 to a European father and a Natchez mother. He rose to the position of Indian agent to the Creek Nation in 1830. Although not completely fluent in the Muskogee language, he speaks with some nationalistic pride of his "woe-worn and pitiable country" (the Muskogee Nation). The manuscript's title promises a "history of the genealogy traditions of the . . . Creek tribe and its downfall, by a member of the tribe," underscoring its author's tribal membership and the narrative's grounding in clan relations. Part of a large body of work written during the period to "explain" the Red Stick War and Tecumseh's Rebellion, Stiggins's work differs from its Euro-American counterparts in its rootedness in Muskogee orature and storytelling practice, in its insistence that even in rebellion the Muskogee had a civil polity, and in its anxiety over whether written narrative is even capable of conveying the events it recounts.[67]

The manuscript's opening disclaimer specifically highlights Stiggins's concern about the nature of narration and chronology, suggesting that it partakes of the "aporia" of time and narrative that is characteristic of revitalization movements. In retrospect, Stiggins feels he has been "hoodwinked" into a narrative project beyond his skills. Casting his mind back to the Red Stick War, he claims he does not "see any materials to form or produce a narrative from." Unlike Euro-American authors who deal with "well known subjects" and "extract from approved and studied history," Stiggins is a writer working in "a labyrinth of paradoxes" made up of "fable and tradition" that have been "handed down through preceding generations more as a moral instruction than as information to elucidate the inquiring mind."[68] In the end, Stiggins wrote a lengthy and informative history of both the Red Stick War and the origins of the Muskogee Nation. Although he treated the prophetic leaders of the movement with disdain (calling them physically "ugly" and their beliefs "frenzied delusion"), he spent several pages of his narrative defending and contextualizing the actions of one of the mixed-blood Red Stick warriors, William Weatherford. It is both an example of special pleading, for Weatherford was his brother-in-law, and an attempt to create a more complex picture of the Indian public that animated the Muskogee war, in much the same way that Aupaumut and Chainbreaker frankly narrated their own nation's political divisions.

The second text, William Warren's *History of the Ojibway People* (written in 1851–52 but not published until 1885), exhibits similar signs of stress centered on narrative and chronology. It too was written by a man somewhat on the margins of the society whose history he recounts, although Warren was fluent in Ojibwe. It too is an example of Native nonfiction written at the urging of a non-Indian cultural entrepreneur. The work initially appeared as installments in a local newspaper, the *Minnesota Democrat*. Finally, it too is a book very much worried about its pretensions to Euro-American narrative and chronology—two categories of human experience that anthropologists see as fundamental to the structural stresses being worked through in revitalization movements.

As in the Stiggins narrative, Warren's assimilationist biases are apparent everywhere in his text, from the first sentence of the book ("The red race of North America is fast disappearing") to its underlying structural framework, which measures the lodge stories it recounts against "evidence" he has collected from the Christian Bible. In Warren's book, the Bible appears not just as a symbol or article of faith but as the surface-level sign of a deep-structural ideology of "the codex," valorizing the ideology of the book as a technology of colonization. As in the Winnemucca and Stiggins texts, however, the codex is constantly under scrutiny and pressure in Warren's work. When Warren recites Ojibwe oral "mythological traditions," he says they "may be termed the 'Indian Bible,'" thus subsuming Native discourse beneath the European codex. But in his chapter on the origins of the Ojibwe Nation, Warren acknowledges his discomfort with the totalizing nature of this ideology of the book. Sounding a bit like Stiggins here, he argues for his rhetorical authority even as his retold stories are found to be "clashing with the received opinion of more learned writers." At one moment Warren might intone, "Throw down the testimony of the Bible, annul in your mind its sacred truths, and we are at once thrown into a perfect chaos of confusion and ignorance." The next moment, he will make the case that the Ojibwe have the advantage of the "book of nature" to guide them. His narrative is avowedly comparative. Ever since he could first read the Bible, Warren reports, he would compare its truths with "the lodge stories and legends of my Indian grandfathers, around whose lodge fires I have passed many a winter evening, listening with parted lips and open ears to their interesting and most forcibly told tales." In the dialogic space between Euro-American and Ojibwe cultures, Warren opens up a conversation, "sometimes interpret[ing] to [the] old men, portions of Bible history." Their response was invariable in its generosity: "The book must be true, for our ancestors have told us similar stories, generation after generation since the earth was new."[69]

In the process of creating this cross-cultural narrative, Warren is careful to register what folklorists like Richard Bauman call the "situated communicative practice" always present in storytelling. Folktales of all nations and languages are always already in constant flux, in a constant oscillation between "decontextualizing and recontextualizing practices."[70] Warren distinguishes tales he receives from "old traditionalist[s]" from those told by "old half-breeds and traders" and is constantly pointing out the ironies of the supposedly "unlettered" culture of the Ojibwe. He cites approvingly those aspects of Ojibwe culture that are in fact "lettered," such as the midewiwin society scrolls. Meanwhile, he knowingly comments several times that books are produced for a marketplace and are therefore by their very nature lying, publicity-seeking technologies.[71]

Even though George Stiggins and William Warren are outliers to the Native revitalization movements they describe, they produced books that express cultural anxieties over narrative and writing that are surprisingly similar to those voiced by the prophets from the more activist or radical wings of their nations. Telling a tribal story in the nineteenth-century American public sphere did not mean casting aside one's faith in the "genealogical" clan sources of what William Warren calls Native "civil polities," nor did it mean completely acquiescing to the supposedly superior colonial technologies of print or the operational strategies of narrative chronology. It meant picking and choosing which aspects of the new technologies best fit an individual author's sense of his or her community's needs.

WITH THE INDIAN REMOVAL ACT of 1830, however, the communicative relationship between the Indian nations and the United States was forever transformed. The act that President Andrew Jackson pushed through both houses of Congress authorized the president to grant Native peoples "unsettled lands" west of the Mississippi in exchange for Indian lands within existing state borders. To Jackson and many other Euro-Americans, the Removal Act was the consummation of a "benevolent policy of the Government, steadily pursued for thirty years" (since the Jefferson administration) for the "removal of the Indians beyond the white settlements."[72] To Native people like Stockbridge sachem John Quinney, however, Jackson's policy was just one more in a series of government policies of "intrigues, bargains, corruption and logrolling" that left American Indians "in the tortures of starvation . . . [and] miserable existence."[73]

A few eastern tribes went peacefully, but most resisted relocation. Resistance was especially pronounced among the southeastern tribes. The Cherokee Nation litigated several important challenges to state and federal removal policies, including the landmark Supreme Court decision *Cherokee Nation v. Georgia* (1831), in which Chief Justice John Marshall ultimately ruled that Indian tribes were "domestic dependant nations." Despite this ruling and others that favored the Indian nations' rights against state authority, the courts allowed federally mandated removals to continue. During the 1830s, tribal communities faced the tough choice of either signing treaties of removal on their own terms or being forcibly removed to the West by federal troops. The first removal treaty signed after the act passed was the Treaty of Dancing Rabbit Creek. On September 27, 1830, the Choctaws in Mississippi ceded land east of the river in exchange for payment and land in the West. The Treaty of New Echota (signed in 1835) resulted in the removal of the Cherokee along a route now known as the Trail of Tears. Approximately 4,000 Cherokees died on this forced march. The next chapter examines the experiences of the Cherokee Nation in detail, providing a case study of the dominant shape of Indian publics as they emerged in the period from 1830 to 1880.

Five

The Cherokee, a "Reading and Intellectual People"

OF ALL THE NATIVE COMMUNITIES affected by the coming of print and alphabetic literacy to Indian Country, perhaps none has garnered more notoriety than the Cherokee. This is for good reason. Unique among indigenous nations, the Cherokee developed in 1821 a syllabic written form of the Cherokee spoken language not derived from the Roman alphabet. Not long after, the Cherokee tribal government mandated the establishment of a Cherokee national printing press, to be operated at the nation's center in New Echota, Georgia. It would produce works in both the new syllabary and English. Thus, not only were the Cherokee leaders involved in the establishment of a very sophisticated indigenous scribal and print system, but also, because of increasing pressure from American land speculators backed by the State of Georgia, they found themselves at the center of a print culture debate over the legal status of Native nations residing in the United States. Their unusual historical position as a tribal community that had adopted a written national language led to their participation in two groundbreaking Supreme Court decisions that forever changed the nature of federal Indian policy in America. The Cherokees' spirited and literate battle for sovereignty during the 1820s and 1830s was so impressive that non-Indians were forced to acknowledge them as a "civilized" tribe. And yet, under U.S. law, they remained a "domestic dependant nation" and "an unlettered people."[1]

Although there was a profound irony in the public perception of the Cherokee in the nineteenth century—considered simultaneously the most civilized Native society in America and yet "unlettered" and "dependant"—at the time, most non-Indians simply thought of the Cherokee as the leaders of the Five Civilized Tribes (Cherokee, Choctaw, Chickasaw, Muskogee, Seminole). If they had heard of Sequoyah—the man who invented the Cherokee syllabary—at all, they thought of him as "the American Cadmus."[2] Yet all contemporary figurations of Cherokee society essentially erased traditional and ceremonial practices, as well as substantial Cherokee oral tradition. In their place was erected a progressive model of literacy civilizing the Indian. As early as 1825, Elias Boudinot, a literate Cherokee leader, would take pains to differentiate his nation from other Native communities. Claiming that "traditions are becoming unpopular," he took issue with newspaper accounts that "associat[ed] the Cherokees . . . [with] the . . . 'Southern Indians.'" Boudinot felt that, unlike the Cherokee, southern nations like the Muskogee were in "rapid decline."[3] However, as the following chapter will demonstrate, despite their admittedly special standing in the history of the book in Indian Country, the Cherokee were no less susceptible than any other Native nation to the social strains produced by the uncomfortable yoking of traditional cultural practices with new, alphabetic ones. The Cherokee, like the peoples of the Columbia Plateau, the Seneca under Handsome Lake, the Shawnee and Delaware led by Tenskwatiwa and Tecumseh, and the Muskogee during the Red Stick War, experienced periods of intense factionalism, nativism, and revitalization that went hand in hand with battles over the proper uses of scribal and print literacies.

In order to better focus our attention on this aspect of Cherokee public writing, I first compare the lives of two Cherokee leaders from very distinct factions within the broader development of Cherokee literacy during the 1820s—Sequoyah (ca. 1767–1843) and Elias Boudinot (1804–39). I then move on to explore how the different forms of literacies these two men enabled and advocated in the Cherokee Nation contributed to the formation of a highly contested "Cherokee public." The political rifts erupted into full-blown civil war during the 1830s. But in the 1840s, the Cherokee Nation rose again in the Indian Territory west of the Mississippi within a complex public sphere that embraced a range of literacy practices, from print constitutionalism to manuscript coteries.

The Two Faces of the Cherokee Public

The Cherokee public sphere took shape, as did so many in Indian Country, within the contexts of colonial warfare and missionary evangelization. Like the mission presses on the Plains, in the Columbia Plateau, and in the Indian Territory, those established in the 1820s in the Native Southeast would have unintended consequences for the Cherokee Nation and its language. In 1817, the American Board of Commissioners for Foreign Missions (ABCFM) established its first station in the Southeast at Brainerd, not far from Chattanooga, Tennessee. The mission post was headed by the Reverend Daniel S. Buttrick (1817–47), who produced a Roman type syllabic system for the school there and eventually printed *Tsvlvki sqclvclv A Cherokee Spelling Book* (1819).[4]

At the same time that some Cherokee were coming to alphabetic literacy (in both the Roman orthography versions of syllabic Cherokee and in English) through the efforts of the ABCFM, a non-Christian tribal member named Sequoyah (known to whites as George Gist) had started working on an alternate form of writing that he felt was better suited to the Cherokee tongue and temperament. Although many parts of Sequoyah's life remain shrouded in mystery, there is enough extant biographical evidence about his activities and continued Cherokee cultural practice surrounding the syllabary he invented to provide us with an important key into one axis of the Cherokee pubic culture as it developed in the period from 1809 to 1838.

Sequoyah was born in the Cherokee town of Tuskegee in Tennessee, fought in the Muskogee Red Stick War against the nativist faction, and eventually emigrated to the Arkansas territory after American settlers pressured him and some 300 members of his community to trade in their homelands for land out west. His life was an itinerant one. He moved constantly back and forth across the Mississippi River whenever events in the traditional Cherokee land base in North Carolina, Tennessee, and Georgia seemed to warrant his return.

Sequoyah appears to have begun work on the syllabary even before his move west. His earliest biographers have dated his initial foray into writing to the year 1809.[5] If this date is accurate, it is the first among many facts in Sequoyah's life that point to his role in Cherokee society as a revitalizationist prophet whose ritual paraphernalia would come to include the written language he would invent. The date 1809 is especially significant in Cherokee history because it was then that the Cherokee people, who had previously been divided between "Upper Towns," which made peace with the Americans after the Revolution, and "Lower Towns," which waged guerrilla war against the new nation, began to meet in a unified national council. The meetings took place in the town of Ustanali, near the Chattahoochee River in Georgia. There, according to sociologist Duane Champagne, they established an increasingly "rationalized" system of national government that "rejected both removal and assimilation and adopted a strategy of national unification, government centralization, and economic change as a way of preserving their homeland."[6] In 1808, the national council produced the Cherokee's first written law, providing for a mounted police force. This was followed in 1810 by a statute prohibiting clan revenge.

It is also during this decade that the Cherokee briefly experienced their version of the revitalization movements that had inspired Tecumseh's Rebellion in the Ohio River Valley and the nearby Red Stick War of the Muskogee. A prophet named Charley emerged among the Cherokee and described "a dream or vision" in which the Great Spirit expressed his anger with the Cherokee "because they had departed from the customs and religious practices of their ancestors and were adopting the ways of the Whitemen."[7] To appease the Great Spirit, Charley argued, "the Cherokee must give up everything they had acquired from the Whites (clothing, cattle, plows, spinning wheels, featherbeds, cars, books)."[8] At the time Charley was making these pronouncements, the Cherokee were experiencing unprecedented economic and population growth, as well as a widening gap between rich and poor.[9] By 1811, Moravian missionaries were working daily to evangelize the unconverted villagers of many Cherokee townships, and the ABCFM was planning to launch a full-scale evangelical assault on the region. Then Black Fox, the principal chief of the newly unified Cherokee, died, leaving a momentary power vacuum. The confluence of these events stoked revitalization fervor in several communities. As in other Native nations that underwent revitalization movements, literacy, books, and print became the focus of Cherokee anxieties and prophecies. That same year, Cherokee leader Big Bear rebutted Moravian claims about the relevance of the Bible to the Cherokee, saying, "The white people know God from the book, . . . we know him from other things."[10]

It was from within this social upheaval that Sequoyah emerged to create his syllabary. Cherokee accounts of his creative process confirm anthropologist Margaret Bender's assertion that Sequoyah was not an assimilationist and that "he disliked the changes whites and some Cherokees were trying to make in Cherokee society."[11] Bender, who has worked extensively with modern Cherokee who still use the syllabary, also offers us a very useful label for Sequoyah, one that helps us comprehend the complex role literacy would play in forming a Cherokee public in the nineteenth century. Bender calls the inventor of the Cherokee syllabary "a progress-oriented separatist pagan."[12]

This characterization jibes with one of the earliest accounts of Sequoyah's invention, a manuscript version of his biography written in his syllabary and performed by Second Chief George Lowery verbally before a Cherokee council in 1835. New York journalist-turned-ethnographer John Howard Payne (1791–1852) happened to be in the audience and took down a record of the biography in English. The manuscript itself was based on oral traditions that had grown up in Cherokee country around Sequoyah and his symbol system. Although there are many written accounts of Sequoyah's life and his method — as well as many oral traditions still circulating in Cherokee country today — Lowery's version has much to offer our exploration of the emergence of a Cherokee public sphere.[13] It tells Sequoyah's story from a Cherokee point of view, in the words of Cherokee who knew the man, and (because Payne so carefully transcribed the scene of Lowery's performance) it provides us with a window into the public sphere in which the syllabary operated. Lowery's account provides the details that the Cherokee themselves felt were significant about Sequoyah's life — about how they viewed him personally, how they reacted when recollecting his actions, and how they felt his biography meshed with the larger story of their community as a whole.

After briefly reciting the circumstances of Sequoyah's birth and early years helping his mother farm and barter for pelts, Lowery focuses on the young man's first occupation and how it informed his later alphabetic work. In 1809, Lowery recalls for his audience, "it was the fashion of the Cherokee to decorate themselves with ornaments of silver, such as ear-rings, nose bobs, armlets, gorgets and fine chains." Sequoyah "took it into his head that he would make . . . such things. He became very ready in the business, and was thought to execute it in a very finished manner." This led to a desire to sign his work, so he called upon Charles R. Hicks, a literate Cherokee leader educated by the Moravians, "to write his name on paper in English." Having learned this technique from Hicks, Sequoyah "would engrave [his name] . . . upon the gorgets and arm bands that they might be known as his work." "With a piece of pointed brimstone he imitated the writing of Mr. Hicks on the silver and then cut it with a sharp instrument," Lowery recalled, and, as a result, he "became very famous." Sequoyah by 1809 was already a success story, tracing a trajectory from subsistence farmer to celebrity craftsman. With his fame as a silversmith established, Sequoyah moved on to "sketching upon paper" and painting.[14]

When Lowery comes to the crucial point in his recitation of the narrative of Sequoyah's great invention, however, there is an interesting disruption. Payne interjects that the page of the manuscript with the key passage is missing. Lowery exclaims, "No matter, . . . it was only what the Bark told me, and the Bark is hereabout."[15] Within minutes, a Cherokee named "the Bark" is summoned and quickly relates the central part of the tale—how Sequoyah was inspired to invent the Cherokee syllabary out of national pride:

> [Sequoyah] showed the Bark how to sketch horses, cows, sheep, and even men; and often, when thus employed, they would enter into conversation about the works of the white men. The Bark thought the most wonderful thing they did was the writing down of what was passing in their minds so that it would keep on paper after it had gone out of their minds. [Sequoyah] would often remark that he saw nothing in it so very wonderful and difficult. One day, he went so far as to declare that he was of the opinion he could detain and communicate their ideas just as well as the white people could. He said he had heard in former times there was a man named Moses, who was the first man that wrote, and he wrote by only making marks on stone, thus—upon which, [Sequoyah] would take a scrape [scrap] of paper, and draw lines on it with a pencil, to show how it was that Moses had written upon the stone.[16]

At this point, Payne recalls, Cherokees in the audience became "excited" and shouted out encouragement to the narrator in Cherokee: "Ha, now you're going to tell," a performative moment of intersubjectivity that harks back to formulaic interjections from Cherokee oral tradition, even as it appears in a written manuscript that mediates the process. Payne notes that when the missing manuscript page was eventually found it was a verbatim match of what the Bark recited. Thus, in a very significant way for the Cherokee, Sequoyah's story was bound up in a national contest with "the whiteman" and in oral tradition, performance, and consensual communal affirmation.

Sequoyah's life story takes on an even greater revitalizationist cast when Lowery reveals that during this early period of invention, while addressing groups of Cherokee assembled around kegs of rum he provided, Sequoyah would "good naturedly enter into huge discourses with his friends; and urge upon them that they should love one another, and treat one another as brother; and then he would sit himself down and sing songs for their amusement."[17] Although the Sequoyah narrative lacks the calls for sobriety that often accompanied prophetic movements in Indian Country, such scenes of him holding forth are revealing, especially taken together with the recurring theme of his determination to beat the whites at their own game.

As Sequoyah proceeded to develop his system, Native companions derided him as a fool for working on something that would not provide him "bread." During this period of the syllabary's development, Sequoyah's wife, who feared that the symbols contained a potent form of witchcraft, burned one version of the alphabet. Sequoyah apparently experimented for months, first with word-based symbols, before finally settling on a syllable-based system very close to the one still used in Cherokee country today. By 1821, he was ready to demonstrate the usefulness of his project to the community. At first, Chief Lowery expressed skepticism about whether the syllabary could actually be used to record events effectively, or if it was that its inventor merely had a good memory. Sequoyah responded, "When I have heard anything, I can write it down, and lay it by, and take it up some future day." Lowery remained unconvinced. "It may be," he suggested, that "the marks you have made bring up certain associations, as poles or heaps of stones call back all the events connected with particular places, or as a knot in a handkerchief reminds you of an engagement." The next day, in Lowery's presence, Sequoyah asks his five- or six-year-old daughter to "say over my alphabet by heart as I hold up the characters."[18] The girl's performance makes Lowery burst out in an enthusiastic Cherokee exclamation, "Yah." From this moment, this leader of the nation was convinced that the Cherokee had a written language of their own.

The final scene of Lowery's account reveals one further "national" dimension to the invention and adoption of the Sequoyah syllabary, one overlooked by those who focus exclusively on the syllabary's "civilized" printed form in the *Cherokee Phoenix* newspaper. "In order to show [ordinary Cherokee] the power of his invention," Lowery recalls, Sequoyah returned from a trip to the western country carrying "letters from Arkansas, written by Cherokee whom he had taught in the native character; and when he emigrated to Arkansas, he took back answers of the same description." Sequoyah's invention had the practical effect of holding together a nation experiencing removal in stages. It provided a way, as the narrative recounts, for the Cherokee "to talk from a distance," and it effectively worked to knit the community back together.[19]

To most Cherokee, then, Sequoyah was the face of a new, literate Cherokee nationalism, a traditionalist who co-opted the imperial concept of literacy and invented a homegrown version to outsmart the whites and to provide a much-needed medium for cultural persistence during a period of extreme social stress. To white missionaries, the syllabary initially smacked of "witchcraft," and they forbade its use precisely because it *was* native and associated with traditional medicine practices, which threatened their evangelization projects. Cherokee medicine people were the most fervent users of the syllabary in the 1820s. Many kept personal manuscript notebooks filled with formulas and ceremonial practices frowned upon by white Christians.[20]

By 1826, however, the missionaries were forced to relent under pressure from Cherokee leaders, who pointed out the superiority of Sequoyah's syllabary over the Roman type forms the missionaries had previously employed.[21] In 1828, the newly established Cherokee constitution mandated the syllabary's use in government publications. The Sequoyah syllabary also became a print culture medium in 1828, when the Cherokee Nation and the ABCFM joined forces to raise money to have special sets of type cast at a foundry in New England. In this print manifestation, the Sequoyah syllabary took on a distinctly nationalist cast. The Cherokee tribal council "made the move to obtain a printing press and types in the Sequoyah syllabary and to establish a national academy" before its constitution was even ratified.[22] Despite its unique roots in a Native-produced syllabary and nationalist movement, however, the actual running of the Cherokee Nation press, like its missionary counterparts throughout Indian Country, required the bicultural cooperation of American missionaries and Native converts. David Brown, a Cherokee convert, completed a manuscript translation of the New Testament into the new Cherokee syllabary in 1825. Then, in 1828, transplanted New England minister Samuel A. Worcester became one of the founders of the *Cherokee Phoenix*, the first *national* Indian newspaper. Yet the syllabary, even in this missionary-sponsored print form, never lost its semiotic value to everyday Cherokee as a sign of national identity.

Elias Boudinot (1804–39), a mission-educated Christian convert who edited the *Cherokee Phoenix* from 1828 to 1832, was from the opposite end of the Cherokee social spectrum as Sequoyah. Boudinot, whose Cherokee name was Gallegina (Buck), could trace his lineage to important leaders like his uncle, The Ridge, and his father, Oo-Waite. These men were members of the first generation of Cherokee to live on the individual land allotments that would soon blossom into full-blown plantations. Diverging from Cherokee matrilineal traditions, the Waite family took the father's surname as the source of their lineage. Unlike Sequoyah, who was a monolingual speaker of Cherokee and a non-Christian, Boudinot had attended the Moravian Mission School at Spring Place (1811) and the American Board School in Cornwall, Connecticut (1817). Adopting the name of the Anglo-American founder of the American Bible Society, Boudinot quickly became a civic leader among the young Christian Cherokee of his generation. In 1826, he married a non-Indian woman, Harriet Gold, whom he had met in Connecticut. White missionaries praised him as a young man who had been "raised to an equality with the polished sons of Europe," a man "whose learning, wisdom, virtue, and honor, deservedly place him in the first circles of civilized life."[23]

In 1825, he helped to found the Moral and Literary Society of the Cherokee Nation. Significantly, it was Boudinot's idea that the society should have a "Library of good books . . . attached to it. Books on Travels, Histories, both ancient and modern, maps, and in fine, books of all descriptions."[24] When the "fledging National Council of the Republic made the move to obtain a printing press and types in the Sequoyah syllabary,"[25] they chose Boudinot to travel the country to solicit donations. Part of the effort to drum up contributions included regular public lectures in which Boudinot strove to demonstrate that Cherokee progress deserved subsidizing. Boudinot published one of these lectures, the *Address to the Whites Delivered in the First Presbyterian Church* (1826). Like George Lowery's narrative of Sequoyah's discovery, Boudinot's *Address* offers a window into the segment of the emerging Cherokee public that he represented.

The *Address* made what Boudinot called "a powerful argument in favor of Indian improvement."[26] As evidence of his claims, Boudinot offered listeners "two statistical tables" listing startling material evidence of the Cherokee Nation's civility: "22,000 cattle; 7,600 horses . . . 2,488 spinning wheels, . . . upwards of 1000 volumes of good books, and 11 different periodical papers both religious and political."[27] The statistics were convincing enough to rally financial support for the purchase of a press and the production of the special types needed to reproduce the syllabary in print. Boudinot himself had been ignorant of the existence of the Sequoyah system for three years after its invention. It was only with the prompting of the Cherokee national council and Samuel Worcester that he investigated and eventually embraced it for use in the newspaper and other publications. "In return for the board's financial support," historian Theda Perdue reports, Boudinot promised to produce in the syllabary "published religious matter including the New Testament, a Cherokee hymnal, and a tract, *Poor Sarah*."[28]

Yet there was more to Elias Boudinot than progressivism and assimilation. As Perdue points out in her social historical interpretation of Boudinot's published works, he was a man profoundly conflicted about what exactly it meant to be a "civilized" Indian. He had personally experienced the racism that was an inescapable part of white/Native interaction. When non-Indian Cornwall, Connecticut, villagers discovered that he was engaged to a white woman, in 1825, they burned him in effigy.[29] Between that time and when he took over the reins of the newspaper in 1828, Boudinot seems to have developed his own version of "separate but equal" social ideals for the developing Cherokee Nation. Deciding that the Cherokee "would develop their own separate 'civilized' institutions," Boudinot's "encounter with and perhaps subconscious acceptance of white racism reduced to an afterthought the idea of Indian assimilation."[30] If Sequoyah was "a progress-oriented separatist pagan," then Boudinot was a Christian separatist assimilationist who would eventually embrace the removal of his nation to the Indian Territory (as would Sequoyah) as a way of keeping it distinct and untainted by white intrusion. Because of his fiercely held belief that the survival of the Cherokee Nation lay in its removal west, Boudinot was assassinated in 1839 by antiremoval Cherokee. Sequoyah, for his part, kept drifting farther south and west, seeking out remnant bands of Cherokee who had been dispersed by years of removal and trying to bring them back into the fold. He died mysteriously, either in Old or in New Mexico, ending his life in the manner of all prophets, on a mythic journey of cultural revitalization.

"A Reading and Intellectual People"

That the Cherokee were among the Native nations to hold out longest against removal is in part a testament to their early decision to harness print literacy to the service of their emerging sense of national identity. Thus, October 1828—the date of the first publication of the *Cherokee Phoenix*—represents a watershed moment in the history of American Indian public writing. The newspaper itself would be short-lived, running from 1828 to 1834, with frequent suspensions.[31] It nonetheless marked the beginning of a process by which the five southeastern tribes (Cherokee, Muskogee, Choctaw, Chickasaw, and Seminole) engaged in serious print culture interventions within the dominant public sphere. This process began with newspapers and evolved to include printed memorials addressed to the U.S. Congress and eventually national constitutions and statute law. In the *Cherokee Phoenix*, the two faces of Cherokee sovereignty represented by Sequoyah and Elias Boudinot (that is, non-Christian revitalization and separatist assimilation, respectively) came together to create a public voice for the separatist civility that both men shared. Boudinot had suggested in his 1825 *Address* that somehow political sovereignty and the Sequoyah syllabary would need to be merged for the Cherokee to achieve true independence. Among the signs of Cherokee civility that Boudinot included were "First. The invention of letters. Second. The translation of the New Testament into Cherokee. Third. The organization of a Government."[32] Most histories of the Cherokee have focused on the first two instances of "improvement" when discussing the importance of books and print to the Cherokee Nation. Boudinot's comments about "the organization of government," however, are especially revealing about his conception of the public sphere the Cherokee would occupy in the American nineteenth century.

Boudinot saw the relationship between print and government as a matter of giving voice to Cherokee experience within the dominant public sphere. In his own way, he was proposing a counterpublic discursive space from which to enunciate an emerging Cherokee nationhood. The publication of the *Phoenix*, he argued, would offer whites the opportunity "to obtain a correct and complete knowledge of these people." "There must exist a vehicle of Indian intelligence," he asserted, and then he asked, "Will not a paper [be] published in an Indian country?"[33] The paper's name and its impressive masthead image (a phoenix rising from a cluster of flames) are themselves powerful bicultural signs, which have long served as figures for Cherokee survival through books and print. Boudinot put it this way: "The Indians must rise like the Phoenix, after having wallowed for ages in ignorance and barbarity."[34] Unfortunately, the borrowed Euro-American symbol of the phoenix has often been interpreted by outsiders as indicating the fundamentally "assimilated" (and therefore "inauthentic") nature of Cherokee literary production. Taken in either its classical or its Christian manifestation, this reading goes, the phoenix is a firmly Euro-Western sign. That the Cherokee selected it for their nation's newspaper masthead is thus little more than an unabashed acknowledgment of the wholesale adoption of European taste and values (figure 21).

In his recent study of Cherokee literature, *Our Fire Survives the Storm*, however, Cherokee literary critic Daniel Heath Justice strongly disagrees. He explicates this well-worn image anew, tempering it in the sacred fire of the Cherokee origin story—a fire that Cherokee author Marilou Awiakta likens to "the spirit of the Creator, of the sun, of the people." By expounding on the specifically Cherokee context for the phoenix's fiery rebirth, Justice asks his readers to consider how "a historically rooted and culturally informed reading of the Cherokee literary tradition helps us to better understand Cherokee social history and vice versa."[35]

In his own 1829 Prospectus for the *Phoenix*, Boudinot set out the paper's goals, describing the "historically rooted and culturally informed" nature of the Cherokee press. The *Phoenix* would publish the "laws and public docu-

Figure 21. Front page of the *Cherokee Phoenix*, March 6, 1828. Courtesy of Edward E. Ayer Collection, Newberry Library, Chicago.

ments of the Nation, account of the manners and customs of the Cherokees, ... [as well as] miscellaneous articles intended to promote Literature, civilization and Religion" among the Cherokee.[36] In pursuing these goals, Boudinot traded articles and "intelligence" with one hundred other American newspapers. He also translated letters and articles written in the Sequoyah syllabary for his English-speaking readers. Devoted to "national purposes," the *Phoenix* routinely printed laws, ethnographic descriptions, news of the day, and even "entire speeches of the Cherokees, the Secretary of War, and Gen. Washington."[37]

In order to accomplish this multifaceted mission, the Cherokee tribal council hired Isaac Harris, a Euro-American printer, for a salary of 400 dollars per year. The council made Boudinot editor, a job that required him to "translate matter into the Cherokee language, manage finances, and apprentice Cherokee youth." John Candy, one of these apprentices, would go on to become the primary printer of the nation's press, moving west to the Indian Territory after the Trail of Tears. From 1828, when the *Phoenix* first entered the public sphere, to 1835, when the press was confiscated by Georgia militia troops, the Cherokee press printed more than 200 copies of the national news weekly.[38] Boudinot's many editorials from the early days of the paper, however, reflect its tenuous economic and material circumstances. Paper was constantly running out, and issues were often suspended. He also apologized frequently for making the newspaper a higher priority than the printing of religious tracts: "We are sorry not to be in a condition to meet the [religious] demands upon our press. The publication of Scripture, Tracts and Hymn books, must depend entirely on the limited force now connected with the establishment; and as yet the paper has occupied the full attention of our printers."[39] Yet, he argued, the newspaper also served an important function as an organ of Christian textual transmission in syllabary: "Cherokee readers will obtain Hymns, and the Gospel of Matthew, thro' the medium of the *Phoenix*." In 1829, the paper's title was amended to become the *Cherokee Phoenix and Indian's Advocate*, perhaps to reflect its growing role as a political organ for airing Indian grievances. Boudinot was nevertheless dissatisfied with the "Indian" content of his print productions in these early years: "Since the commencement of our labors, we have not been able to insert as much Cherokee matter, as might have been expected, and desired."[40]

Throughout his tenure as editor, Boudinot addressed the burgeoning Cherokee Nation as "the public," often requesting "the public ... [to] consider our motives."[41] Initially, Boudinot's editorial commentary imagines this public to be constituted by two somewhat benignly divided groups, "home" and "distant" readers.[42] In one fairly early article, Boudinot suggests that his goal is to gently educate this "public" of outsiders about the Indian cause: "For the amusement of our English readers, the following translations of our Cherokee Correspondence inserted above are presented to the public. They will convey to the reader [a] pretty good idea of Cherokee composition." Here, Cherokee-language literacy performs cultural difference in an entertaining and unthreatening way to "benefit . . . the Cherokee Nation and . . . the cause of Indians."[43] At other times, the *Phoenix* attempts, like most missionary publications of the day, to elicit "sentiment" or "sympathy" from this distant white readership. One Cherokee correspondent, for example, offers a letter "to prove to your white readers, that, instead of the poorer class of our people being in servile chains and oppression, . . . they are in possession of religious and political freedom and rural happiness." This rhetorical strategy was often successful. In a letter to the *Phoenix*, German scientist Wilhelm von Humboldt put it succinctly: "My sympathy [was] increased by reading the *Indian's Advocate.*"[44]

Appealing to the "distant" (often) white public was a complex endeavor and required that Boudinot be sensitive to his readers' desire to see themselves reflected positively in the Cherokee paper. He was careful to run items submitted by these distant subscribers to show that the admiration was mutual. A productive dialogism emerged from this practice. For example, "J.D.S." of Green Bay sent the *Phoenix* a letter that enclosed a copy of "a pamphlet we have just published, relative to the New-York Indians," in the hope that Boudinot would print an excerpt. This letter, which Boudinot printed, concluded with a stirring apostrophe to fellow friends of the Indians: "O, that the Patriot, the Philanthropist, and the Christian, would speak out on this subject."[45] In this way, while Boudinot spoke of the white missionary's struggles in New York, the northern cleric read and discussed the Cherokee publication with his colleagues and congregation, to the benefit of both.

By 1831, the removal crisis took center stage at the paper, engendering a public discussion of the role of a free press in Indian Country. Tensions increased as the Cherokee faced military force from the Georgia militia and the U.S. government. Meanwhile, internal political upheavals devolved into a bitter factionalism that would eventually spark a tribal civil war. In the April 16, 1831, issue of the *Phoenix*, Boudinot collated "the views of intelligent editors and correspondents respecting the opinion of the Supreme Court on the Cherokee case [*Cherokee Nation v. Georgia*],"[46] making a forceful case for

Cherokee sovereignty through the assembled outsiders' opinions. Throughout 1831, however, he was hounded from without by "an invasion of the liberty of the press"[47] in the form of the Georgia Guard. There were also charges that he was not a "real" Indian. In these instances, Boudinot faced "attempt[s] to prove that I have only been a tool in the hands of the Missionaries" and "that [Samuel] Worcester was the real editor."[48] Attacks on his loyalty to the Cherokee cause from within his own community intensified when he began to argue that removal might be the only humane way out for his nation. As in so many cases of the history of the book in tribal communities, alphabetic literacy became a litmus test for political identity both within and without the Native nation.[49]

As the removal crisis heated up, Cherokee who preferred the traditional political model of rule by the consensus of established tribal elders increasingly challenged Boudinot's liberal model of a "free" press. Antiremoval Chief John Ross was vocal in his criticism of Boudinot. In response, Boudinot turned the focus of the paper more toward "home" readers and issues, publishing extracts from treaties and court decisions to educate the Cherokee public about removal. For example, Boudinot reprinted the written negotiations taking place in Washington between the United States and the Cherokee as a way of making present these far-away events of a "distant" public: "In our last we published the 8th Article of the new treaty between the Unites States and the Arkansas Cherokees. We have since had access to the entire treaty which we insert in our first page." Boudinot was less than optimistic about the chances of the distant public sphere where treaty negotiations were taking place being able to "read" the true situation of Native peoples in Georgia. "The present administration must be Lynx-eyed if they can see from Washington 'public interest' suffering in these woods,"[50] Boudinot wrote of Jackson's supposedly "benevolent" removal policy, trying hard to develop an appearance of traditional political consensus in the pages of the newspaper. The strategy appears to have worked for some readers. At least one correspondent reported that he was "not sorry to see the *Cherokee Phoenix* speak a decided language."[51] It is clear that the reader felt the *Phoenix*'s language was ethnically Cherokee, whether in English or the Sequoyah syllabary.

Paratextual cues in the *Phoenix* also suggest how the paper helped to instantiate local, consensual Cherokee "public opinion." The home readers' letters to the editor, sometimes in the Sequoyah syllabary but often in English, gave Cherokees a chance to "sign on" to the public sphere the *Phoenix* had constructed by allowing their signatures and pseudonyms to stand as markers of self-fashioning. Cherokees Waterhunter and John Huss, along with Choctaw leaders Pushmetahaw and Puckshunnubbee signed their contributions to the paper. So did Glass, a Cherokee whose signature and valediction to one printed letter epitomize the emerging importance of print "visibility" for tribal members just entering the public sphere: "I The Glass write this. I am well."[52] Other writers cloak their public identities in classically derived pseudonyms reminiscent of the American Revolution's pamphlet wars. Letters from "Scipio" and "A Friend" join that signed by "A Cherokee" to assert what the *Phoenix* came to signify to its Cherokee print public sphere: "In a liberal government every person has a right to his sentiments."[53] In the columns next to these Native opinions appeared publications from a Euro-American network of authors and texts: Thomas L. McKinney, C. S. Rafinesque, Timothy Pickering, the *Vermont Chronicle*, the *Missionary Herald*, the *Bunker Hill Aurora*, and the *New York Advertiser*. Taken together, the Cherokee signatories and the Anglo-American authorities created a bicultural public sphere out of which Boudinot hoped public opinion would be shaped to ensure that Cherokee rights were "defended and protected."[54]

Under mounting pressure from Cherokee political opponents and having made a permanent enemy of Principal Chief John Ross, Boudinot resigned his editorship in 1832. Charles Hicks, Ross's brother-in-law, replaced him. By 1834, things had gotten so bad in Cherokee country that leading council members Major Ridge, John Ridge, and David Vann were impeached and the new Ross government forcibly shut down the press. A heated debate between Ross and Boudinot's group — now known as the "treaty party" — exposed the deep divisions characteristic of communities facing the trauma of economic and social annihilation. Theda Perdue has observed that the dispute between Ross and Boudinot revealed social fissures along economic lines: "The signers of the treaty came primarily from a rising middle class, and they resented the economic power of Principal Chief John Ross, [and] Chief Justice John Martin." Each side "argued that its approach to removal was the more moral and humanitarian," but the terms of the debate were essentially conducted in the language of literacy. Boudinot denounced Ross, for example, for putting materialism above the Cherokee public good. Significantly, he claimed that he and "the treaty party alone understood the 'true situation' and could act legitimately on behalf of the 'ignorant' masses" because his side could wield literacy more fully to the nation's advantage.[55]

In the course of its brief, initial six-year run, the *Cherokee Phoenix* evolved from an assimilationist newspaper with ethnic, national aims sharply inflected by the Christian, evangelical designs of its editor and missionary underwriters into a forum to replace the failed U.S. justice system, a true "tribunal where [Cherokee] injured rights [could] be defended and protected."[56] In the process, Boudinot came to embrace a classical liberal stance toward the relationship between a free press and an enlightened public sphere. In one editorial, he proclaimed that "the press is the safe guard of liberty, civil and religious — the medium of intelligence, . . . and the protector of virtue. An experiment is now making among us, whether the press established in this place will have its ordinary effects. Let a fair trial be made — let the *Phoenix* be fostered with care by the inhabitants of this Nation, and encouraged and patronized by friends of Indians abroad."[57]

Boudinot's liberal model of the Cherokee public sphere was, however, doomed to failure. The Cherokee press was seized by the State of Georgia in 1835, and in 1838 the Cherokee Nation was forcibly removed by federal troops to the Indian Territory. Nevertheless, the press had a lasting impact on Cherokee society. According to the Cherokee census of 1835, 18 percent of tribal members could read English, while 43 percent could read Cherokee, suggesting that printing among the Cherokee, in addition to fostering syllabary literacy, may also have supported nascent forms of class identification and class struggle. Historians of the Cherokee Civil War (1830–39) have clearly discerned such factors at work within the Native community.[58] Thus, the history of the press in the Cherokee Nation mirrors that of other presses introduced into Indian Country in the period. Missionaries entered the community and founded a press intent on printing the gospels and tracts, only to have the local community take over and begin to use the printed word for its own, largely nonreligious purposes.

The strain between Ross and Boudinot reflected the growing pains of the Cherokee Nation's evolving sense of the meaning of a Native public sphere and a free Native press. Purdue explains the division: "In prohibiting dissent, Ross expressed the traditional Cherokee approach to political disputes. Originally, the Cherokee arrived at decisions through consensus . . . [but the Boudinot] minority met at New Echota in December 1835 to negotiate wholesale removal."[59] In the Indian Territory, after the removal, Boudinot paid for his position with his life. On June 22, 1839, he was stabbed to death by Cherokee assailants from Ross's party. His fellow "treaty party" members Major Ridge and John Ridge were also assassinated that day.

As the Boudinot and Ross factions battled it out in the pages of the *Cherokee Phoenix*, both groups also sought print publication outside the Cherokee Nation in order to sway public opinion and government policy in the broader Anglo-American public sphere. The print publications they produced are known as "memorials," a genre in U.S. law that refers to a statement of facts in the form of a petition to the government (often reprinted in the *Congressional Record*).[60] During the 1830s, this genre became perhaps the single most important printed form for the expression of Native sovereignty in the realm of Euro-American public opinion. In the memorial, Native American writers wove personal autobiography, tribal history, and documentary evidence into a transgressive discourse that at times begged (or "prayed," as Stockbridge writer John Quinney put it) for the paternal government's patronage while at the same time asserting sovereign authority over identity, culture, and land.[61]

When read together, the body of removal memorials produced by the Cherokee and other Native nations after 1830 exhibit several common features, both rhetorical and material, which open to our view the changing nature of Indian publics during the period. Native memorials were often corporately written texts that employed oral and written, Native and non-Native discursive practices. Yet they cannot comfortably be called "hybrid" or synthetic works that easily bridge the discursive gaps between the various genres they employ or the cultural understandings they traverse. Most Native memorials contain three fundamental rhetorical tensions that signal their performance of a political "Indian" public identity. These are the tension between individual and collective voices, between humble and defiant rhetorical postures, and between verbal and documentary evidence.

In order to examine how Native memorials reflect an emergent discourse of indigenous public writing, we must first uncover what Greg Sarris calls the "social contingencies" out of which they arose. In a published 1838 letter to a friend, Cherokee leader John Ross describes one aspect of the social context behind the memorials. Ross details how in 1837 the Cherokee delegation that Ross led attempted to meet personally with President Andrew Jackson. They were denied access. They next tried to speak with the secretary for Indian affairs. Again, they were rebuffed. Unsuccessful in all their efforts at oral confrontation, Ross reports, the Cherokee delegates "then memorialized the Senate."[62]

The actual process of "memorializing" U.S. legislators was complicated and usually involved various kinds of corporate authorship. Many Indian nations appointed non-Indian attorneys to write on their behalf. For example, a group of Shawnee hired James H. Abbott to write the *Memorial in Behalf of the "Black Bob" Band of Shawnee Indians* (1870), which they submitted to Congress. As their "duly authorized attorney," Abbot argued in defense of the nation's land claims. Aside from the historical facts of the case, Abbott's memorial is interesting for what it reveals about how he worked with the tribe. This was not a case of ventriloquism, "appropriation," or assimilation. According to Abbott, an alphabetically literate member of the band, Charles Blue Jacket, drew up the letter and interpreted it to the tribal council, who then agreed to its principles and signed it. In addition, Abbott includes a letter from Seneca leader (and Indian Affairs Commissioner) Ely S. Parker attesting to Abbott's authority to speak for the group. In an interesting reversal of what many scholars of American literature have found—that non-white writers were often forced to preface their material with Euro-American attestations of authenticity—here it is the non-Indian who must be vouched for by an Indian. Not all of the signatories to the memorial were literate in English; many signed with an "X." And women were among the signatories.

The Indian memorials engage a range of political issues and rhetorical stances—from "authenticity" to corporate authorship, translation, and the proper role of cultural go-betweens.[63] At one end of the spectrum, a memorial could speak for an individual tribal member who had been wronged and sought personal redress. This is the rhetorical situation of Stockbridger John Quinney. In the *Memorial of John W. Quinney* (1852), Quinney writes to the Senate asking for a stipend as compensation for his negotiating services over the years. Following a brief autobiography (in which he calls himself "a true Native American"), Quinney contextualizes his request within the larger legal and moral issues that prompted his service in the first place: "The policy which keeps the tribe in continual mutation—I mean, removals." Quinney's memorial thus simultaneously asserts his individual rights and demands the sovereign autonomy of his people against "the mutations" removal threatens. It reflects another tension as well. Quinney's appeal for personal compensation and tribal sovereignty is also derived from his and his community's "rights and privileges of citizenship," a claim that can be read as appeasing the government's desire for Native assimilation. Quinney's plea for a permanent land grant and a pension thus reflects the postremoval ironies of law and ideology that the Native American memorial genre attempts to negotiate. On the one hand, the petitioner desires only what he is due, but he never asks that his personal debt be paid at the expense of tribal sovereignty. At times, the Native petitioner might be willing to ask for U.S. citizenship (thereby relinquishing traditional nationhood) if that meant preserving the homeland. These ironies are perhaps best summed up in one of Quinney's most poignant comments on Stockbridge removal and his own unique place in it: "I feel I cannot go into the wilderness again and begin anew."[64]

A similar tension can be found in the *Memorial and Argument Submitted to the Cherokee Commissioners in the Claim of Nancy Reed and Children* (1846). Here, the autobiography of Nancy Reed is sketched in brief to authenticate her and her children's claim to land. After discussing early Cherokee treaties with Britain and the United States, the author explains: "Prior to the conclusion of those treaties, your memorialist, a native Cherokee, had, agreeably to the custom her tribe, became the wife of a white man by the name of William Reed, and by whom she had children, who for her, and in her right, on the third day of August 1819, entered his name with the Cherokee agent, for a reservation of 640 acres." Later, Reed declares, the state sold her land to its citizens. In a pointed autobiographical sentence, Reed shows how a single life story can mirror the situation of an entire tribal community: "The undersigned, being deserted by her husband, who abandoned her and took another wife . . . [and] surrounded by a white population whose language she did not understand, subject to laws which afflicted her and threatened personal violence . . . and finding the U.S. would not defend her title, being too poor to defend herself, was compelled to abandon her reservation, and, with her small children, remove to her mother's, in the Nation." She concludes: "Signed, Nancy Reed, for herself and children."[65]

Not everyone agreed that autobiography was the best method of demanding tribal sovereignty in memorials to Congress. Too often, in the hands of Euro-American legislators, stories like the one Nancy Reed told merely appeared to corroborate lawmakers' belief that what Indians needed was *more* private ownership and *more* individual land allotments. In the *Memorial of the Indian Delegates from the Indian Country* (1880), the authors put the tribal argument against individualism succinctly: "You will discover that we hold our lands as Nations and not as individuals."[66] Thus, even when an individual like Reed or Quinney memorialized Congress, they did so in a way that attempted to instantiate a corporate tribal voice and to situate their claim within communal tribal needs. The balancing of corporate and communal gestures usually began in the memorials' salutations, where the petitioners referred to themselves formally as "your memorialists." A typical example appears in the *Memorial of the Muscogee or Creek Nation of Indians* (1852). Here the corporate authors, with the help of Albert Pike, apparently a non-Indian attorney representing the group, open their petition to Congress with customary courtesy: "Your memorialists, the Chiefs, Headmen, and People of the League of the Muscogee or Creek Nation of Indians, most humbly pray that you will listen attentively to that which they desire to make known to you." Throughout this document and many others like it, the Native community walks a fine line between asserting the sovereignty they feel they rightly deserve and performing the submissiveness demanded of "domestic dependant nations." Calling themselves a "weak, unfortunate, and ruined people," the Muskogee nonetheless went on for several pages of historical exposition concerning their present state "in order to [offer] a full understanding of the whole of the matters." In contrast to what had come before, they concluded with a declaration of defiant authority: "It will be seen that the undersigned have not used the language of humble suppliant, but that of men who know their rights, however unable they may be to maintain them."[67]

The doubled, intertwined gestures—of defiant sovereignty and humble petition—were constantly counterpoised against references to Euro-American print culture and "verifiable" history. Most memorials enclosed "papers" (print culture documents often authored by whites) to verify their version of events. Native memorialists did not speak in a vacuum, nor did they attempt to have "oral" culture stand alone in the modern American public sphere. The Muskogee in the 1852 example cited above insisted that "the truth of these matters does not depend upon the statements and assertions of your memorialists. They are matters of History. Nothing will be stated in this memorial which is not so."[68] Later in the tract, they offer evidence taken from "the lips of a general" as especially validating of their claims. In addition to this rhetorical tightrope walk between dependency and sovereignty, the Muskogee memorial demonstrates another trait common to the genre: an ongoing tension between verbal agreements and written history that the Indian Nations attempt to negotiate via this discursive form. The Muskogee "most humbly pray that [Congress] will listen attentively." Similarly, John Quinney begins, "I pray your listening ear." The original manuscript of the Quinney memorial suggests that these were the first ideas he sketched out, the rhetorical posture of the speaking subject performing his verbal art before the assembled representatives.[69]

As was the case with their founding of a national newspaper, the Cherokee were at the forefront of these memorializing print practices. Perhaps one of the most important ones written in the immediate postremoval period, the *Memorial of John Ross and Others* (1846), presented the case of the Cherokee Nation by questioning the discursive validity of the government's methods of treaty negotiation. As the Ross delegation argued their side of the famous Cherokee Controversy (an intertribal disagreement about whether immediate removal was more humane to the average tribal member than protracted litigation), they began by questioning the government's method of collecting affidavits from the Cherokee people. The memorialists "cannot but express their astonishment that the Commissioner [of Indian Affairs] should have adopted this course upon no other evidence than ex parte affidavits, and information from unknown and irresponsible witnesses." They accuse the U.S. government of "working without any knowledge of the character of the witnesses, the circumstances under which the testimony was taken, and all those advantages of viva voce testimony, which are the greatest security in trials of questions of fact." Here is a reasonable juridical argument for viva voce testimony — that is, for a live witness testifying before a jury of peers. But it also signifies the Native petitioners' valuing of the verbal, spoken, and "landed" testimony over and against the printed and written word. For ten more pages, the Ross group hammers home the problematic nature of ex parte witnessing, pointing out "the impossibility of any one remote from the scene coming to a satisfactory conclusion as to the weight of the testimony."[70]

In the concluding paragraph of the *Memorial of John Ross*, the authors make pointed and cogent observations regarding the nature of evidence drawn from Indian Country: "It may be remarked that the signature or mark of Indians is easily obtained to papers of any description by persons of influence or authority, without the individual having any real knowledge of the contents or object of the paper he is signing; little if any regard is, therefore, to be paid to any document signed by these people generally, unless it is accompanied by satisfactory evidence that its contents were fully and satisfactorily explained to them, that their signature was a voluntary act. . . . Such evidence is usually supplied by the Agent of the tribes."[71] In fact, linguists have noted that the Muskogee language contains a part of speech known as "the hearsay affect," which signals to Native listeners whether something being reported is an eyewitness account or merely secondhand information.[72] It appears that the Cherokee memorialists, while adhering to many print conventions, still respected their own basic linguistic and cultural structures that sensitively parsed hearsay from fact.

The memorials produced by the Cherokee and other Native nations facing removal in the 1830s and 1840s were published in a large variety of formats within the Euro-American print public sphere. Many appeared in newspapers; others were printed as separate pamphlets. Most of the ones addressed to the U.S. Congress were printed by the government as part of the *Congressional Record*. Speaking to both allies and foes within the community, as well as to government outsiders who had a great deal of power over Indian politics, these texts construct uniquely Indian publics that simultaneously resist and defer to the Supreme Court's decision that America's Native peoples constituted "domestic dependant nations." The Seneca memorialists who opposed their tribe's removal in 1847 appealed to the government on the grounds of shared humanity: "We think it is the dictate of humanity, and we confidently believe that the voice of the whole country would approve this course."[73] The "voice" they speak of is the "public opinion" of the republic of letters. The place from whence they speak is a newly formulated Indian public space, a space constructed in printed newspapers and congressional reports in an attempt to reconstitute the landed spaces of traditional tribal utterance (the council house, the sacred clearing in the woods) in the public sphere. This reconstructed print tribal space at once pleaded for clemency and demanded sovereignty. It also honored the authority of oral tradition—which usually went unrecognized in the U.S. legal system—in such a way as to make present not only individuals and tribal communities but also the landed nature of their utterances.

Print Constitutional Publics

Although the Georgia militia destroyed the original press for the *Cherokee Phoenix* in 1835, the newspaper would, like its mythic masthead symbol, rise again from the ashes. In the late 1840s, the *Cherokee Phoenix* would be reconstituted in the Indian Territory as a more potent bicultural and consensus-based project. Other Indian newspapers soon joined the Cherokee press. The *Choctaw Intelligencer* was launched in 1852, printed in English and employing a Roman type orthography for Choctaw language articles.[74] The *Chickasaw and Choctaw Herald* appeared in 1858, along with numerous printed tribal constitutions and statute laws. But the reestablished press did much more than reconstitute a public sphere of newsprint "home" readers. It was instrumental in the rise of print constitutionalism among the southeastern tribes in the aftermath of removal and was thus, as Robert Warrior observes of Osage constitutionalism in particular, "an expression of the modern intellectual aspirations of a people confronting the need to transform themselves on their own terms."[75]

According to Lester Hargrett's *A Bibliography of the Constitutions and Laws of the American Indians* (1946), more than 200 such constitutionalist publications flowed from tribal, missionary, and job presses during the period from 1828 to 1906. The five southeastern nations produced about 90 percent of these documents. These printed works are, as Hargrett rightly notes, "the important record of an increasingly unified effort by a more or less concentrated group of Indian tribes to adjust themselves to changing conditions by means of self-government under constitutional forms."[76] Most of the printing occurred on the reestablished Cherokee press, under the guidance of John Candy, Boudinot's old protégé.

Print constitutionalism in the Indian Territory took the form of consensus building and grew out of the slow and steady negotiation of oral, manuscript, and print cultures into a full-blown Indian public. The "sociology" of the production of print constitutions in the Indian Territory after removal was especially intricate. Printed legal texts that originated in public councils were written first into manuscript forms that circulated for many years before being committed to print. Hargrett, for example, lists 1808 as the date when the Cherokee first began writing down laws. It took until 1821, however, for the first of these statutes to roll off a press. This first publication of the Cherokee laws was done on a job press at Knoxville, Tennessee, and was produced using a Roman alphabet syllabary. By 1827, when the Cherokee finally adopted a printed constitution, it was produced in a parallel-column bilingual edition that employed the Sequoyah syllabary.

Yet the story of the rise of printed constitutionalism in the Indian Territory is not a progressivist, Whig history. Manuscript syllabary texts continued to dominate other quarters of Native life in the Indian Territory (in medicine societies, for example, as the Swimmer Manuscript demonstrates), while printed materials appeared irregularly in both syllabary and English formats. When the Cherokee regrouped after the Trail of Tears and in 1839 assembled at Tah-le-quah in present-day Oklahoma to promote an "act of union," they chose the elderly Sequoyah himself to represent the western Cherokee, capitalizing on his cultural centrality as the syllabary's inventor and his traditionalist, nonconvert status to affirm the print constitution's roots in the old, consensual politics.

Print constitutionalism thus served not only to balance traditional consensus building and liberal "public opinion" in the Indian Territory but also to preserve the "landedness" of Native identity, in spite of the various nations' removals far from their traditional homelands. Robert Warrior insightfully points out that both the Cherokee and Osage constitutions, unlike the U.S. Constitution on which they are based, "needed to . . . declare their boundaries." "In adopting their constitution[s]," Warrior observes, the Native nations were thus "'moving to a new country.'" The social structures of these "new countries" to the west of the old homelands would be imbricated with literacy practices formed in the early days of the *Cherokee Phoenix*. In the Osage Nation, Warrior notes, a "new generation of leaders arose as the realities of reservation life unfolded." Many in this generation had been "educated in the Catholic mission school" and were "committed to accepting usable parts of white culture without conceding the traditional past as worthless."[77] Men like Joseph Paw-ne-no-pa-she, "whose name means 'Not Afraid of Long Hairs,'" and James Bigheart harnessed print public opinion to oral traditional consensus to form a new kind of Indian public in the Indian Territory.

By the outbreak of the Civil War (which would precipitate new factional violence within the Cherokee Nation in the Indian Territory), print and manuscript books had permeated many aspects of Cherokee life. The Sequoyah syllabary became such a fixture of Cherokee identity that to this day, Margaret Bender observes, it "has a continuing association not only with Christianity, progress, and written law, but with medicine, animals and nature, and Cherokee place names." Yet in both its manuscript and print formations, the syllabary that Sequoyah invented and Christian progressives like Boudinot disseminated continued to reflect the profound ironies inherent in the circulation of books in Indian Country. Anthropologists from James Mooney, who worked among the Cherokee in the 1880s, to Margaret Bender have noted the "simultaneous love for the syllabary as a source of Indianness and an alienation from it on the part of the mixed-blood, English-speaking elite." The syllabary has been such a "potent and polyvalent symbol since its invention," Bender argues, precisely because of its inherent doubleness, "because it has been taken to represent both adoption and rejection of the dominant society's values and practices."[78]

Two final examples will serve to illustrate where Cherokee public culture stood at the outbreak of the Civil War. Even after his death, Elias Boudinot continued to influence Cherokee public culture through his translations of materials ranging from the New Testament to works like *Poor Sarah* (1847). A "steady seller," *Poor Sarah* was a religious tract of the sort that David Paul Nord describes as "popular prose presented in a cheap, consumable format."[79]

ABCFM missionaries printed Boudinot's translation of *Poor Sarah* on the Spring Hill press they shared with the Cherokee and other nations in the Indian Territory. It was part of their method of using printed materials to foster not only "religious and political" improvements among their constituents but class distinctions as well. The title page of the Cherokee reissue is especially revealing in this regard. It features a woodcut illustration of the narrative's climactic scene.

Like Jabez Hyde's Seneca hymnal and Jotham Meeker's Shawanoe Mission publications, the Cherokee imprint of *Poor Sarah* shows all the marks of bilingual cultural production that epitomized mission publishing in Indian Country during the nineteenth century. But the illustrated title page reveals more. It shows that the Cherokee press was an active participant in what Isabel Lehuu has described as Jacksonian America's print cultural "carnival on the page." Its expressive woodcut and pull-quote caption suggest that, like popular printed media in the non-Indian world, it sought to express "a festive and somewhat transgressive quality." The reissued Boudinot tract was "a feast for the eye, as much as . . . food for the mind."[80] Thus, the Cherokee press in the Indian Territory of the 1840s, in addition to its many "national" imperatives, may be said to have imbibed broader aesthetic concerns that would be involved in the formation of class structures in post–Civil War America. It actively worked to create a middle-class, Christian, book-reading public in the newly established western Cherokee Nation.[81]

At the other end of the syllabary book spectrum in Civil War Indian Territory were the medicine notebooks of the many healers and spiritual leaders among the Cherokee who continued traditional practice by sheltering and preserving it in the manuscript pages of a book. Cherokee medicine practitioners like Inali, also known as Black Fox, recorded formulas for rituals and doctoring practices on paper, supplementing the traditional method of preserving such knowledge verbally in song and story (figure 22). Scraps of paper like the ones Inali filled with his various formulas featured a wide array of scribal practices. Some used a capital-letter script derived from printed forms of the syllabary as it appeared in the *Cherokee Phoenix* and the Cherokee New Testament. Most "handwriting in such texts," however, "was not iconically modeled after print but was as unique and unreadable as the author could make it."[82] The individualist script of these notebooks thus marked both "ownership" of certain medicine techniques and its "distance" from Christian, assimilationist uses of the syllabary. Over time, the notebooks from which many of these sheets of paper were taken themselves became "book objects"

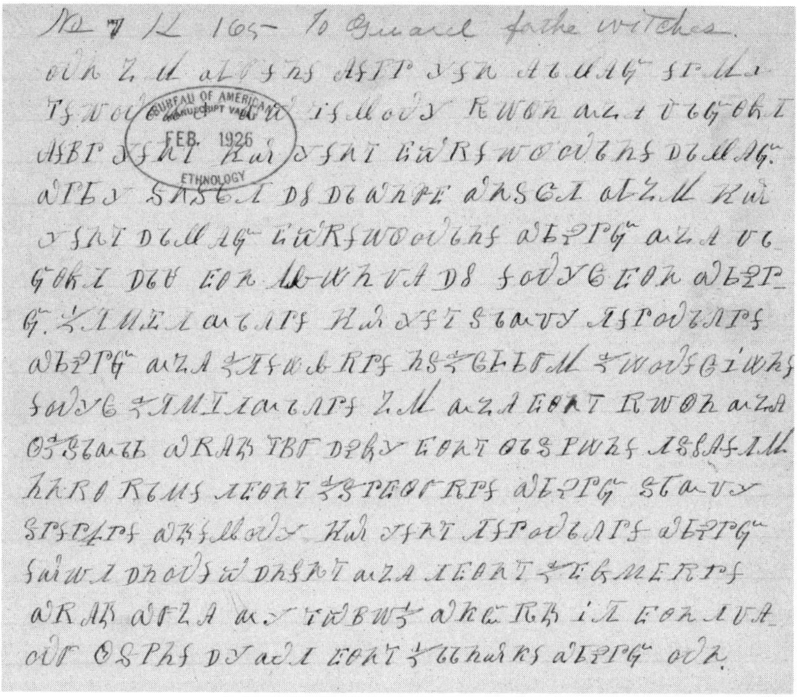

Figure 22. Inali (Black Fox), Cherokee syllabary formula. Courtesy of National Anthropological Archives, Smithsonian Institution (MS 2236).

of extreme sacredness. The bound form of these manuscript notebooks gave them "a certain tangibility that grew into reverence. The conjuror's notebook became imbued with some of the same holiness surrounding the white man's Bible."[83] Thus, to this day, the Cherokee public sphere is one marked by the axes of several sets of literacy practices—scribal and print, syllabary and Roman type—that continue to delineate the sacred and ethnic parameters of Cherokee life.

CHAPTER

Six

PROPRIETARY AUTHORSHIP

"PROPRIETARY AUTHORSHIP" is a term that describes a special, social category of writing in which the creator has secured copyright, becoming "visible" in the public sphere as a political entity given legal rights by statute law.[1] Such authorship emerged in America in the 1820s to offer "a radical redefinition of what it meant to communicate to a reading public."[2] In Indian Country, Tuscarora writer David Cusick was the first proprietary author of record. His book, *David Cusick's Sketches of Ancient History of the Six Nations* (1828), was the first Native-authored, Native-printed, and Native-copyrighted text. Its title page explicitly points out that this work is "owned" by its author. This is "David Cusick's History," no one else's. On the verso is the requisite paragraph from the New York district court that officially acknowledges Cusick's copyright. This declaration of legal identity and ownership and the title's forceful use of the possessive are counterpoised against Cusick's self-deprecatory introductory comments:

> I have long been waiting in hope that some of my people who have
> received an English education, would have undertaken a work as to
> give a Sketch of the Ancient History of the Six Nations; but found no
> one seemed to concur in the matter, after some hesitation I determined
> to commence the work; but found the history involved with fables,
> and besides, examining myself, finding so small educated that it was
> impossible for me to compose the work without much difficulty. . . . I,
> however, took up a resolution to continue the work, which I have taken
> much pains procuring the materials, and translating it into English
> language. I have endeavored to throw some light on the history of the

original population of the country, which I believe have never been recorded. I hope this little work will be acceptable to the public.[3]

The preface is signed—in capital letters—DAVID CUSICK. It also significantly locates its production site, date, and year as "Tuscarora Village, June 10th, 1825." The first edition of the work also notes that it was printed at "Lewiston, at the Tuscarora Village."

Within the context of this book, these introductory authorizing gestures may be construed to suggest the nation-centeredness of Cusick's work. It was not only copyrighted by a Tuscarora intellectual, but its type was set and its pages were printed by Tuscarora community members. The gestures may also reflect Cusick's wish for his book to be read as a local (and Indian) work. If this is indeed the case, then Cusick's preface, title, and decision to copyright his material all point toward what Robert Warrior has termed "intellectual sovereignty"—a form of "cultural criticism that is grounded in American Indian experiences" and is akin to the tribal sovereignty that Native peoples in the United States struggle to maintain each and every day.[4] Whatever the case, Cusick's preface speaks of the painstaking process of cultural preservation involved in this English translation of Haudenosaunee stories, which was compounded by struggles with assimilated intellectual categories like "fables." Yet the Six Nations remain Cusick's "people," and the second half of the preface emphasizes Cusick's search for sovereignty in print.

Evidence from later editions of Cusick's work points even more firmly toward sovereignty as the central issue in the book's production. In the second edition (which claimed a print run of 7,000 copies), Cusick added illustrations ("rude woodcuts," Francis Parkman later called them), which he probably carved himself. By including these illustrations, Cusick simultaneously engages more Native paratextual material than was available in the printed text and demonstrates his authorial prerogative by choosing for illustration those narrative moments he considered pivotal in the stories he gathered together as the precontact history of the Six Nations.

Other evidence, drawn from outside the physical properties of the two editions, suggests the broader American cultural context that may have influenced Cusick's decision to seek copyright and become a proprietary author. In *The Conspiracy of Pontiac* (1870), Francis Parkman digressed in a footnote on the physical properties of David Cusick's *History* to offer a revealing glimpse into Anglo-Americans' attitudes toward American Indian authors' efforts to master print culture. "Cusick," Parkman relates with typical anti-Indian condescension,

> was an old Tuscarora Indian, who, being disabled by an accident from active occupations, essayed to become the historian of his people, and produced a small pamphlet, written in a language almost unintelligible, and filled with a medley of traditions in which a few grains of truth are inextricably mixed with a tangled mass of absurdities. He relates the monstrous legends of his people with an air of implicit faith, and traces the presiding sachems of the confederacy in regular descent from the first Atotarho downwards. His work, which was printed at the Tuscarora village, near Lewiston, in 1828, is illustrated by several rude engravings representing the Stone Giants, the Flying Heads, and other traditional monsters.[5]

The demeaning tone regarding Indian authorship—characteristic of Anglo-American comments about Native writing since Occom's day—revolves around certain emerging Euro-American cultural assumptions about labor and genius. These were attributes that Native people, in Parkman's view, could not possibly hope to share. Inactive and disabled, the Tuscarora man has made a pitiful attempt at art, "rude" in its realization and "absurd" in its conception.

What Parkman viewed as an amusing anomaly, however, was in fact becoming the norm in Indian Country during the 1830s. There was a veritable rush to copyright by Native authors in the period. Over the next several decades, Pequot writers Paul Cuffe (1759–1817) and William Apess (1798–1838), Ojibwe autobiographer and historian George Copway (1818–69), and Paiute author Sarah Winnemucca Hopkins (1841–91) all followed Cusick's lead. Not only did these Native writers become proprietary authors, but they also made impressively shrewd print culture choices about which publishers to use and how their works should be laid out and marketed.[6]

A Son of the Forest

The writings of Pequot author and activist William Apess represent the most extensive early foray by a Native American into Anglo-American print culture. Yet among the many recent studies exploring Apess's work, none have focused on his role as proprietary author.[7] This omission is particularly striking in that William Apess himself worked diligently to secure copyrights for his books. Beginning in 1829, when he published his autobiography, *A Son of the Forest*, at his own expense, copyrighting it under his own name, Apess steadily and persistently pursued the legal and aesthetic advantages offered by proprietary authorship. Perhaps chief among these was what Grantland S. Rice has described as the proprietary author's unique "personhood through the construction of the law."[8] At a time when American Indians were being forcibly removed from their homelands, when the Supreme Court was redefining their position in American society, and when Indian writers were sensationalized either as "wild, unadulterated savage[s]"[9] or as "interesting convert[s] from heathenism,"[10] copyrighted authorship offered unique "rights and privileges" protected by the Constitution and sanctioned by the new social status being accorded professional authors.

An appreciation of the complex role that copyright and print culture played in Apess's textual production may help us to reconsider what it meant (politically and socially) to be a "public" Indian at the beginning of the nineteenth century. William Apess appropriated proprietary authorship at a moment in American history when four important social transformations converged to make print and copyright especially significant for Native Americans. As we have already seen, between 1823 and 1831 American Indians' relationship to the federal government was radically redefined and Native political identity was recast by Supreme Court rulings that paradoxically labeled Native people as both "sovereign" and "dependent." The 1830s also witnessed the "golden age of local publishing," out of which for the first time in America there emerged a "fluid and multilayered marketplace" for books.[11] Simultaneously, the very meaning of public writing was transformed, producing "new literary forms and aesthetic practices."[12] Finally, during the same period, American Protestantism began to undergo a fundamental shift in sensibility. Books, authors, and readers played a significant role in this shift, transmuting orthodox doctrine and traditional literacy into the civil religion that would underwrite Victorian sociability.

In order to understand how William Apess exploited the social possibilities of print authorship in early nineteenth-century American culture, it is first necessary to survey recent theories of authorship that view the creation of literature in the broadest sense as a social, rather than merely as a textual or linguistic, process. In the dominant culture of the early republic, the emergence of the social actor known as the "American author" coincided with the establishment of copyright law and mass publication. The new Constitution mandated that Congress "promote the progress of science and useful arts by securing to authors and inventors the exclusive right to their respective writings and inventions."[13] The resulting Copyright Law of 1790 established the legal and social category of "author," centered on an individual's creative "ownership" of the ideas that he or she published.

Historians have noted, however, that beneath the seeming security granted American authors by this law there lay several cultural tensions that soon adhered to the concept of authorship itself. During the Revolutionary period, the "author" had been conceived of as a cultural producer whose printed words were introduced freely into the public sphere for the good of the public at large. With the establishment of the copyright law, this egalitarian image was challenged and partly supplanted by a rival notion of authorship. In this version, the author became the "proprietor" of his or her words, a merchant of language. This liberal ideal of authorship as an independent enterprise rested uneasily alongside its republican counterpart in the first decades of the nineteenth century in England, America, and France. Some historians have even traced to this unease the seeds of the heroic self-representation of Romantic poets, which highlighted individual genius and inward subjectivity.

These scholars contend that the Romantic model of authorship worked to ease the tension created by the professionalization of authorship in two ways. First, idealizing the writer as an individual genius served to mystify "an activity which is of necessity rooted in tradition"[14] and thus erased the communal dimensions of literary production. Second, mystification of the traditional and corporate roots of literary production (by creating a hieratic genius, a receiver of inspiration unsullied by the marketplace) effectively cloaked the nastier forms of individualism involved in the notion of "writer-as-entrepreneur."

Calling oneself an author in 1829, when William Apess began publishing his works, thus involved negotiating cultural tensions that went deeper than the economic and legal ones apparent at first glance. Uncertain about their new social status within the proprietary model of authorship, many writers wondered how to prevent their words and ideas from becoming mere commodities. At least one theorist has traced the literary "crisis of the subject" during this period to writers' struggle to find textual and rhetorical features capable of converting "private meaning into social force." In this view, some forms of proprietary authorship became "pragmatic construction[s] and affirmation[s] of social and ideological authority." The social performance of authorship served to establish a much-needed connection between "the presumed 'inwardness' of a 'voice' and the social and authorial power of a text." Proprietary authorship emerged as a set of formal gestures intended to demonstrate both the writer's ownership of the ideas in the text and his or her shared social relationship with readers.[15]

These formal gestures consisted of legal and material efforts put forward by authors in the marketplace, as well as the rhetorical and physical properties of the books themselves. In the new proprietary literary marketplace, writers as seemingly unmaterialistic as William Wordsworth worked hard to maintain copyrights, to extend them beyond the usual fourteen years, and to cut special deals overseeing the publication and distribution of their works. Wordsworth once admitted to Gladstone that his groundbreaking *Lyrical Ballads* of 1798 had been published for money, and a recent critic has claimed that "Wordsworth's interests in the matter verged upon the excessive."[16]

Within their texts, proprietary authors like Wordsworth paid new attention to revision, patronage, allusion, and citation. The age-old labor of producing a credible ethos in print — something authors had struggled with since the Renaissance — became much more demanding in the new, entrepreneurial context of proprietary authorship. Under the proprietary system, for example, allusion and citation were strictly regulated by rules concerning plagiarism and intellectual property. Commercial associations now guided patronage, once primarily a function of customary social relations, so that authorial references to patrons and their sponsorship were increasingly colored by the ideology of possessive individualism.[17] Finally, revision itself was refracted by the exigencies of the market. Aside from the serial publication of works that were subsequently "revised" to form complete texts worthy of resale, there was also the possibility of revising works for posthumous publication. To many authors in the period, copyrighted print guaranteed immortality.[18]

In America during the 1830s, the formal gestures and ideological positioning involved in proprietary authorship reflected "a dynamic shift in not only the material conditions but also the very meaning of public writing." "The development of the legal fiction of 'literary property' in America," Grantland Rice has argued, "signaled a radical cultural attempt to reconfigure what it meant to communicate to a reading public in print, one that did not develop evenly nor result in an easy or clear verdict." Authorship was fraught with anxiety, and even successful writers like Washington Irving were "unsettled by the whole concept of literary property, especially in the way it entailed the legal transformation of a public and political activity into one that was private and productive."[19]

If Anglo-American authors were anxious about their position in the literary marketplace in 1830, American Indian writers were doubly so. Their situation was substantially different—socially, politically, and aesthetically. William Apess faced social uncertainties that few Anglo-American writers could have imagined. As a Pequot, New England's most maligned and oppressed Algonquian band, and for many years an indentured servant, Apess had enormous social hurdles to clear before he could even begin to entertain the luxurious notion of Romantic self-consciousness and the "inwardness" of genius. All of the steps toward social visibility that came "naturally" to Anglo-American writers represented hard-fought battles in Apess's life.

Reading and writing at the level necessary for published authorship were initially denied to Apess. When he was "sold" at eight years of age to Judge William Hillhouse, Apess was promised both an education and family membership. He was devastated when he learned that the judge was interested mainly in his labor and that the other conditions of his indenture would not be forthcoming. "To be sure, I had enough to eat," Apess reports, "but he did not send me to school as he had promised."[20]

His conversion to Christianity was fraught with racist obstacles, as were his later experiences preaching to mixed congregations. Not one of his masters or mentors ever mentioned or envisioned professional authorship as a suitable vocation for a Christianized Indian. "Friends of the Indians" made it clear that Native converts like Apess were expected to be ministers or teachers who could be "sent back to the several places of their nativity, to educate their own countrymen in return."[21] Despite good intentions, such policies promoted separate public spheres, hardly equal and certainly not productive of extensive social agency.

When, against all odds, Apess overcame these social impediments, he still faced racial political barriers that denied American Indians access to proprietary public writing. First among these was the U.S. Supreme Court's contradictory definitions of Native difference. Chief Justice John Marshall's Supreme Court recognized American Indians as "citizens," even as it sought to limit their rights under the Constitution to that of a "separate" people. It argued that "the relation of the Indians to the United States is marked by peculiar and cardinal distinctions which exist no where else."[22] Among the many "peculiarities" of this arrangement were the U.S. government's assumption of a "guardian" role toward Indian nations and its ongoing efforts to define Native people's relationship to the federal government by complex rules regarding bloodlines and tribal membership and the disenfranchisement of those who were presumed to have "abandoned their tribal relations voluntarily."

Given this legal and political context, how could an Indian writer ever presume to become a copyrighted author, that "original" and individuated social agent given legal identity by the very Constitution that Justice Marshall was using to exclude Native people from participation in the larger American society? Especially damaging to Native authors' chances of engaging in unmediated public writing was the Court's insistence on the Indians' need for guardians. The relationship of the United States to Native people was framed by the language of paternalism; its relationship to copyrighted authors, in contrast, focused on "exclusive right[s]" and "concrete labor." Yet American Indians also discovered that proprietary authorship underscored important questions about the relationship between "the author's ethical personality and the legal personality attributed to him or her by the law."[23] Such questions were intimately related to their larger political struggles in the American public sphere.

Jacksonian aesthetics, similarly hampered by racist assumptions of insurmountable difference, also threatened to rule out proprietary authorship for American Indians. Even white allies preferred Native Americans to not only "sound" like Indians but also to "act" in print like romantic savages. William Snelling's famous review of Black Hawk's 1833 autobiography exemplifies this bias. Snelling called Black Hawk's as-told-to autobiography "the only autobiography of an Indian extant," airily dismissing Apess's recently published autobiographical work, *A Son of the Forest*. "We do not consider Mr. Apes and a few other persons of unmixed Indian blood, who have written books, to be Indians," Snelling declares. The reason? In the Apess autobiography, Snelling could find no trace of the "wild, unadulterated savage, gall yet fermenting in his veins." The problem was not so much one of blood but of books. Apess was not really "Indian" because he had adapted so skillfully to print culture. "If he writes," Snelling continues, "it is in the *character* of a white man."[24]

Read within the context of contemporary debates about the nature of proprietary authors, Snelling's attack may be seen as an attempt to figure Apess's rhetorical ethos as totally conditioned by the materiality of print. To write in the "character" of a white man in 1830 was, quite literally, to find one's personhood embodied in type, in the mechanically printed, engraved, or inscribed text and thus devoid of spirituality or "genius."

Such attitudes toward Native writers survived well into the century. As late as 1883, Daniel Brinton's otherwise remarkable appreciation of Indian authorship, *Aboriginal American Authors and Their Productions*, continued to enforce "authenticity" as the standard by which Native utterance was to be judged as "literature." Oral production is celebrated over print production, and Brinton's subtitle emphasizes texts produced "in the Native languages." Native print authors like George Copway and David Cusick, however, are presented as mere collators of oral traditions, narrative historians whose works reflect their peoples' "desire of preserving the national history."[25] Their public writing thus becomes little more than a contribution to the memorialization of the noble savage undertaken by Euro-American culture throughout the nineteenth century.

Brinton reserves the terms "genius" and "author" for oral storytellers. He solicits his readers' admiration for their abilities as "raconteurs" and purveyors of "Goethe's *lust zu fabuliren*." At the end of an era that gave birth to the Romantic bard, the "true" Native writer is still being caricatured as figurative, metaphorical, and inventive to the point of fabulation. In discussing Cherokee writer and editor Elias Boudinot, who, we have seen, specifically employed print culture to extend American Indian political agency, Brinton pointedly remarks, "Whether [his works are] original or merely translated I do not know." William Apess receives only perfunctory mention in Brinton's account: "The Rev. William Apess (or Apes), a member of the Pequot tribe of Massachusetts, wrote and published five or six small books and pamphlets on questions relating to his people, between 1829 and 1837."[26]

The themes that swirled around Euro-American authorship in the 1830s — genius and originality, citizenship and literacy, exclusive rights and concrete labor — were thus intensely volatile issues for Native Americans, threatening to silence all but the most "savage" or pious forms of their utterance. Yet, despite the odds, William Apess made the remarkable and unlikely step into proprietary authorship. His insistence on being called "author" on the title page of many of his works and on holding copyright to them signals the profound importance that Apess attached to the institution of proprietary authorship. In 1831, Apess published and copyrighted *The Increase of the Kingdom of Christ and the Indians*. He followed this evangelical tract with a second edition of *Son of the Forest* (1831) and then produced *The Experiences of Five Christian Indians; or, An Indians' Looking-Glass for the White Man* (1833) and *Eulogy for King Philip* (1836). In 1837, he issued second editions of *Experiences* and the *Eulogy*.

What is even more extraordinary than the sheer number of copyrighted texts Apess produced is the social and political authority he seems to have expected as a result of having insisted that the copyrights be in his own name. It is also clear that Apess thought of autobiography in terms of print culture and

Figure 23. Frontispiece of William Apess, *A Son of the Forest* (1831). Courtesy of Ingham Collection, University of Iowa Libraries, Iowa City.

the physical properties of texts. In *The Experiences of Five Christian Indians,* he comments, "I intend publishing a book of 300 pages, 18 mo. in size, and there the reader will find particulars respecting my life."[27] Although Apess never produced a book of exactly that size and length, a close reading comparing the 1829 and 1831 editions of *A Son of the Forest* shows just how significant Apess believed the physical properties of texts and the proprietary-author function to be to his exploration of identity.[28] In the second edition, we can clearly trace the formal gestures of proprietary authorship Apess employed in an effort to position himself as a social actor in print culture. He worked carefully to revise not only the factual content of his life story but also his authorial presence.

The first of these gestures appears in the front matter to the 1831 edition (figure 23). Facing the title page, where the edition is defined as "revised and corrected" and "published by the author," there appears an engraving of "Mr. William Apes, a Native Missionary of the Pequot Tribe of Indians." In the engraving, Apess wears a coat and cravat, and his hair is cut short and styled like most Euro-Americans of the emerging middle class. Just behind his right shoulder, the reader can glimpse the settee that supports the sitter. It is note-worthy that the frontispiece engraving shades off at its edges, giving the bust a sketchlike quality, as though the daguerreotypic realism of its center were finished off with the rough cross hatchings of a pencil.

The illustration did not appear in the 1829 edition and thus seems to have held some significance for the establishment of the author function in the second edition. Such frontispiece illustrations had indeed become a conven-tion in print culture, helping to establish visually the "author figure," who would be fleshed out in the subsequent text. Apess's portrait is fairly standard in this regard. It is somewhat unusual, however, in that it does not contain direct references to spiritual inspiration or biblical literacy, like many frontis-pieces of non–Euro-American authors during the late eighteenth and early nineteenth centuries.[29] Instead, it taps into the developing "refinement of America," which placed portraiture at the center of bourgeois material iden-tity. At the same time that it asserts Apess's gentility, the portrait, with its rough edges, may also reflect an effort to represent authorship "as an act of labor." As Ed Folsom argues in his study of Whitman's frontispiece portrait for the 1855 edition of *Leaves of Grass*, such engravings, "with their empha-sis on the process of creating verisimilitude, their habit of incorporating in the same image various stages of composition . . . were more effective ve-hicles than photographs for representing identity as an act of labor."[30] Thus it would appear that Apess's frontispiece portrait served to ground his authorial identity firmly in middle-class respectability, concrete labor, and the physical properties of textual production.

But what about Apess's "Indian" identity? The frontispiece engraving also speaks to this aspect of his ethos, but more obliquely. When compared to the frontispiece portraits of two Native contemporaries, the Apess engraving ap-pears both less "traditional" and less sensationalized. The frontispiece engrav-ing accompanying George Copway's *Life, History, and Travels* (1847) depicts an Indian warrior, replete with bow and breechcloth, standing on a rocky outcropping over a river and gazing off into the forest (figure 24). The com-position and setting epitomize the romanticism of the Hudson River School, and the engraving's caption seals the image's meaning for the text: "I am one of Nature's Children."

In another depiction of "Indianness" on a title page, Black Hawk's portrait in the 1836 edition of his *Life* represents the Sac warrior in full regalia, with his blanket, peace medal, roach hairstyle, and jewelry clearly marking him not only as a leader but as a specific man known to whites as Black Hawk (figure

Figure 24. Frontispiece of George Copway, *Life, History, and Travels* (1847). Courtesy of Ingham Collection, University of Iowa Libraries, Iowa City.

25). This portrait underscores those elements of the composite narrative that William Snelling found most compelling—Black Hawk's honor and perhaps "the gall fermenting in his veins." He is the noble leader of a "defeated race." When viewed against these other frontispiece depictions of Indian authorship, Apess's image appears to steer a course between Copway's romantic, infantilized savage and Black Hawk's ennobled (and thus socially elevated) warrior.

In the 1831 edition of *A Son of the Forest*, the portrait and title page are followed by a letter from Fred J. Betts, clerk of the Southern District of New York, who verifies that Apess did indeed "deposit in their office" a copy of the autobiography on July 25, 1829, for copyright. Betts's letter cites the acts of Congress establishing the legal basis for copyright. This letter, which was also included in the first edition, appears here in a dialectical relation with the conventionality of the illustration and the sensationalism of the title ("Son of the Forest"). In 1831, the title page stands as a middle term between the polite portrait and the legal affidavit.

Again, a comparison with the Copway and Black Hawk texts bears out this

Figure 25. Frontispiece of Black Hawk, *Life of Ma-ka-tai-me-she-kia-kiak, or Black Hawk* (1836). Courtesy of Edward E. Ayer Collection, Newberry Library, Chicago.

BLACK HAWK.

inference. Like Apess, Copway sought and received copyright to his work, but his statement of copyright is largely undercut by the preceding engraving, which gives the "rights" an air of dependency. It is also undermined in the subsequent "A Word to the Reader," which cedes much of the text's print culture agency to a "friend" and to the printer. In Black Hawk's text, copyright is owned by J. B. Patterson, who is listed as "editor and proprietor" on the 1834 edition's title page.

Apess's opening matter stands in stark contrast to that of his contemporaries. Although the title page features the by-then conventional sensationalist subtitle for non–Euro-American texts ("written by himself"), Betts's note emphasizes something new — "the right whereof he claims as author." Apess's foray into proprietary authorship moves beyond simple self-assertion to demand a congressionally mandated "right." It is a political act. The title page further indicates that the text was "published by the author," emphasizing again the proprietary nature of his venture. Taken together, the frontispiece engraving, the county clerk's affidavit, and the title page perform a public, printed attestation of Indian identity quite distinct from most of Apess's Native contemporaries and quite different from that performed in the 1829 edition.[31] As Maureen Konkle has demonstrated, William Apess was not only an active participant in political debates about American Indian sovereignty but also a savvy rhetorician who mobilized the language of constitutional rights in many of his works. It is entirely consistent to view his approach to copyright authorship in the opening pages of his revised autobiography as part of this overall rhetorical effort.[32]

A new preface to the 1831 edition also foregrounds the activities of William Apess, proprietary author. Apess began the 1829 preface with self-deprecatory references to "this little volume" written "under many disadvantages" and confessing his "entire want of education." The later version, in contrast, refers confidently to Apess as "the author," and gives thanks for the "liberal patronage" of unnamed benefactors. As authorial proprietor of his own life, Apess remarks in the opening page of his revised autobiography that "the present edition [is] . . . greatly improved, as well in the printing as in the arrangement of the work and the style."[33] The "poor little Indian boy" of the autobiography's early chapters has grown into a man of print cultural taste and authorial presence. The transformation is subtle but revealing. By designating the relationship between his (presumably white) backers and himself as "patronage," Apess converts his social position from dependent participant in what Arnold Krupat calls a "composite composition" (like Black Hawk's as-told-to narrative) to full-fledged partner in the alliances between proprietary authors, publishers, and subscribers.

Apess then demonstrates his rights and powers as proprietary author. In the 1831 preface, instead of ignoring or eliding his decision to edit out an unpleasant episode in his life in which he was denied full membership in the Methodist Episcopal fellowship, Apess deliberately draws attention to those things he has "stricken out." Hearing that readers of the previous edition had found these passages "objectionable," he reports, he has decided to remove them. Such self-conscious revision allows him to perform in public print his awareness of the "social contract" between authors and readers.

These are the actions of a proprietary author, a writer whose choices are made with an eye toward how they will play in the marketplace. Apess employs them to create a new figure in the 1831 text, one that shadows the romantic "son of the forest" in his progress toward Christian redemption. That figure is the "author," a metanarrative voice produced through dialogue between writer and readers in the marketplace they both inhabit. In the 1831 edition of *A Son of the Forest*, the life history and the formal properties of the text come together, the latter qualifying the sentimentality and pathos of the "poor Indian" boy's struggle to come of age with shrewd and unsentimental editorial choices. Apess's apostrophes to his readers, like those of his sentimental novelist contemporaries, serve to establish a shared moral field with his audience. They also serve to reinforce his presence as a fully realized, political self in the text. William Apess, author, becomes a site of intersubjectivity whose commentary on and arrangement of the autobiography's events foreground "the specific social contingencies of . . . exchange," which Greg Sarris has described as being central to American Indian autobiography.[34]

The "specific social contingencies" foregrounded by the author function in *A Son of the Forest* include those previously outlined—anxieties about property and the exact nature of public writing and its relationship to private production. Over and above these, however, there emerges a tension between Apess's rhetorical ethos and his legal status, the same tension that permeated all Indian-white discourse in the period of the removal. In the 1831 edition, Apess seems careful to avoid playing his story to the fullest extent for its pathetic appeal, a common moral (and even political) effect in nineteenth-century sentimental fiction. His revisions work to temper sentimentality by portraying the "author" of the text as an empirical reporter of the facts. Apess assures his readers that he is telling his story "without any embellishment or exaggeration, to show the reader how we were treated."[35] It is more as reliable author than as a character in the narrative that Apess seeks and eventually finds his rhetorical ethos. The struggling boy in the text is merely pitiable; the author of the tale is worthy of attention and respect because he has established himself as part of the circle of print culture authors in Anglo-America.

But truth telling in nineteenth-century Indian-white discourse was a tricky thing. William Snelling's *North American Review* essay on Black Hawk's autobiography praised the composite text as "an anomaly in literature" because it was so truthful. For Snelling, its truthfulness derived from the assumed transparency inherent in its corporate mode of production. He considered it more believable than *A Son of the Forest* because of "the respected testimony of Antoine LeClaire" (the book's translator) and because of "the intrinsic evidence of the work itself." This last proof is the most slippery, for Snelling asserts that authenticity resides not so much in the details of the text as in Black Hawk's honor as a warrior. Indians will, Snelling argues, lie, steal, and cheat, but when put upon their honor—as Black Hawk was in the present case—their word is as "good . . . as the white man's oath." The communal production of truth that Snelling presents here harks back to a precommercial age. The nobility of the savage utterance is itself conditioned by the oral, gentlemanly, unwritten agreement that Black Hawk made with his captor, interpreter, and editor.[36]

For William Apess, truth is also inextricably bound up in the means of production, but he realizes that the fantasy of transparency Snelling rehearses for the Black Hawk text may do more harm than good to an Indian activist seeking social agency through printed words. As part of his life history, Apess thematizes the "specific social contingencies" that frame "Indian" utterance, in the process dramatizing why composite composition held little appeal for the Pequot writer. Early in the narrative, Apess takes up with a young white companion and runs away to New York to get rich. He is tired of being constantly accused of lying by his white masters and wants to make a fortune. When questioned by adults along the way, Apess leaves the talking to his friend: "Now, John was a great liar. He was brought up by dissipated parents and accustomed in the way of the world to all kinds of company. He had a good memory, and having been where he heard war songs and tales of blood and carnage, he treasured them up. He therefore agreed to be spokesman, and I assure my dear reader that I was perfectly willing, for abandoned as I was I could not lie without feeling my conscience smite me."[37] In this scene, Apess maps the discursive field of Indian-white relations at the beginning of the nineteenth century. First, their appearance in the public sphere is itself conditioned by economic forces. Intolerable servitude leads the boy on a quest for entrepreneurial freedom. Second, and most important, white intermediaries fundamentally mediate Indian public utterance. John functions as Apess's spokesman, or, if you will, as his "editor." He recites "war songs" and "tales of blood and carnage"—the traditional stuff of composite "Indian" stories. He acts as a go-between for oral, Native discourse and white, market speech.

In one of the autobiography's most famous passages, Apess points out that the word "Indian" is itself a signifier whose meaning is inextricably tied to the means of discursive production: "[At times] I thought it disgraceful to be called an Indian; it was considered as a slur upon an oppressed and scattered nation. . . . At other times I thought it was derived from the term *in-gen-uity*." Apess quickly moves on from this joke to state that "the proper term that ought to be applied to our nation . . . is that of Native."[38] But the middle term he has considered is interesting for the way it engages the "romantic" and entrepreneurial tensions present in both the Anglo-American literary marketplace and the white stereotypes of Native authorship. To be an "Indian" in Apess's world is either to be thought a "liar" or to be praised as "ingenious," "imaginative" in the sense of irrational, or "subtle," a partaker of the *Lust zu fabulieren.* The 1831 edition of *A Son of the Forest,* with its conscious marshaling of proprietary gestures, seems directed at reclaiming "genius" for the Indian writer, but on political, social, and legal terms that allow his text to have impact in the public sphere. The 1790 Congress, after all, conceived of copyright as "the most proper means of cherishing genius and useful arts."[39]

Copyrighted authorship offered Apess, like his European and American contemporaries, a way to establish a much-needed connection between "the presumed 'inwardness' of a 'voice' and the social and authorial power of a text."[40] And, indeed, making a direct connection between voice and text, cutting out the interpreter, the editorial middleman, seems to have been one of William Apess's main goals in 1831. But what exactly was the "inward voice" Apess was trying to project in print? Most readers of *A Son of the Forest* believe it was the voice of Apess's awakened Christian conscience. In the passage quoted above, Apess escapes the discursive colonization imposed by John's lying with the aid of his developing moral compass. "I could not lie," Apess reports, "without feeling my conscience smite me." When the autobiography is read as a conversion narrative, "the self as such is validated only in its social-collective (Christian) personhood."[41]

Yet the 1831 edition of Apess's life history actually downplays Christian personhood—partly by cutting his conversion from the story altogether and partly by underscoring how romanticized (and apolitical and impotent) Christian preaching had become for the Indian missionary. When Apess as a mature preacher finally gets a chance to speak in public, his fellow Christians, "who had come out to hear the Indian preach," are simply hateful. "One threw an old hat in my face, and this example was followed by others, who threw sticks at me," he relates. The church provides him with little protection against appearing freakish or like a rhetorical huckster: "I held meetings in Albany, and crowds flocked out, some to *hear* the truth and others to *see* the 'Indian.'" The public sphere of the city, of ministerial utterance and community activism, offer Apess some social agency, but at a steep price. He becomes a sensationalized commodity, "a gazing stock" and a spectacle. In moments like these, Apess reminds us that being a Christianized Indian preacher (especially when ordination and church membership were denied) means being seen predominantly as an "Indian," with all the negative connotations the word suggested to 1830s white America.[42]

By the conclusion of the 1831 narrative, it becomes clear that William Apess was seeking to remedy the Indian convert's untenable discursive situation through recourse to a form of proprietary authorship and print culture that marked his Christian ethos as a hybrid form of civil religion. In the revised autobiography's final paragraph, the reader is made aware that Apess's editorial efforts have been directed at moving away from Methodism's oral and affective preaching and prophecy and toward a print-based civil Christianity more suitable to his political needs as an American Indian. As with many of the rhetorical gestures in the 1831 edition, there is more than a touch of irony in Apess's remarks:

> Now, my dear reader, I have endeavored to give you a short but correct statement of the leading features of my life. When I think of what I am, and how wonderfully the Lord has led me, I am dumb before him. When I contrast my situation with that of the rest of my family, and many of my tribe, I am led to adore the goodness of God. When I reflect upon my many misdeeds and wanderings, and the dangers to which I was consequently exposed, I am lost in astonishment at the long forbearance and the unmerited mercy of God. I stand before you as a monument of his unfailing goodness. May that same mercy which has upheld me still be my portion — and may author and reader be preserved until the perfect day and dwell forever in the paradise of God.
> William Apess.[43]

The Christian subject of the conversion narrative speaks from within the authorial presence established in the 1831 edition. The signature confirms the conversion identity (it was a common feature of documents such as temperance pledges) at the same time that it mimics the attestations of Native sovereignty found in treaties and letters to the *Cherokee Phoenix*. The concluding prayer and celebration of the Lord's goodness is bracketed between a sentimental address to the reader and a specifically print culture figuration of the afterlife: "May author and reader be preserved until the perfect day."

Coming at the close of the book and at the end of the substantial editorial revisions of the 1831 edition, this concluding paragraph bears considerable moral and narrative weight. It monumentalizes Apess in an echo of the practices of European and American proprietary authors, while doing rather conventional duty as Christian apology.[44] Yet when read within the context of Apess's evolving authorial persona — a print culture mask that is concerned with specifically Native American political and discursive issues — it brings larger questions to the fore. These have to do with individualism and collectivism, ingenuity and entrepreneurialism. The closing comments about the author's being "dumb" and alienated from "the rest of my family and many of my tribe" set the stage for an appendix that reconciles the newly established Indian author to society through his powerful management of dominant culture materials.

Both versions of *A Son of the Forest* end with a long appendix that consists of an almost verbatim transcription of large sections of Elias Boudinot's *A Star in the West* (1816). The 1831 edition, however, shapes the citations and themes toward ownership, sovereignty, and agency. In his revised version, Apess self-consciously reimagines the post–life-history materials as a way to enunciate a new source of identity and agency.[45] Using space gained from editing out the story of his failed church membership, Apess adds a new introduction to the end matter in which he explains how the reader should approach the appendix. He thus specifically marks it as a place where he will perform a new sort of Christian Indian political agency in the gap left by his real-world failed attempts to gain religious community and political voice.

Apess introduces his appendix by stating that "the subscriber has somewhat abridged 'his life' to make room for this Appendix." By deliberately directing the reader's attention toward authorship and away from Christian ordination, Apess again tempers the passive mood of the narrative's concluding paragraph with the active voice of the author (here called the "subscriber" to highlight the marketplace nature of his social agency). In a move that heightens the authorial persona and ethos that Apess has forged through his editorial choices, he notes that, in the appendix, "the reader will find some 'general observations' touching his brethren." "General observations" on Indian life suggest the sober and factual reporting of the objective author. Apess's reference to "his brethren" recalls the Indian community that is coming to replace Anglo-American Methodism as the touchstone for the author's social-collective personhood.

At first glance, the appendix that follows seems little more than a blatant "imitation" of white materials that relies on the discourse of the dominant culture so heavily that it dilutes whatever counternarrative Apess had produced in the preceding pages of his life story. Indeed, some critics have lamented that the appendix is simply "a tissue of quotations" that fails to "rescript" the "dominant discourses of [Apess's] world."[46] Barry O'Connell's comments on the appendix, however, are worth noting. O'Connell points out that "were the Appendix not there, the rhetoric and the design of [this] spiritual autobiography [would] identify [Apess's] struggles in becoming an Indian [exclusively] with those entailed in becoming a Methodist."[47]

The 1831 edition underscores this point. Framed by the new introduction and the curtailed conversion narrative, the 1831 appendix highlights Apess's identity as compiler and commentator, not—as some readers have claimed— as imitator.[48] To be a compiler of authorities was a time-honored role in the European tradition, harking back at least to the time of St. Bonaventure, who had listed it as one of the highest goals of the "auctor."[49] By 1831, the production of appendixes had become a respectable and common technique, as proprietary authorship made citation a more self-conscious activity than it had been in the past.[50]

In addition, as a print cultural convention, the appendix offered Apess yet another way to emphasize his story's printedness, thus foregrounding his position as social agent rather than ethereal genius. Finally, the appendix allowed Apess to pay homage to a cultural figure (in this case, Anglo-American Bible society leader Elias Boudinot) through forthright emulation and thus to partake of his reflected glory. Creating an appendix was an acceptable way to borrow from the cultural productions of other geniuses, citation and quotation being viewed as forms of sociability rather than as plagiarism (the print culture version of lying and a specter that hovered over all Indian/white discursive relationships).

This final formal gesture thus allows Apess both to circumvent romantic stereotypes of Indian utterance and to avoid the materialistic pitfalls of professional authorship. It provides him recourse to an ethos of authorship that highlights the communal nature of his literary production without giving over agency of it to those with whom he participates. Apess turns the tables on white authorities and becomes *their* transcriber and editor. The appendix serves to highlight a practice of quotation Apess employs throughout the autobiography, where he collates and edits the work of many white writers and intellectuals—DeWitt Clinton (1769–1828), senator from New York and mayor of New York City; William Cullen Bryant (1794–1878); and Isaac Watts (1674–1748)—to name but a few. Sociologist Pierre Bourdieu points out that a pattern of citation such as this may be viewed as a strategy "in a game in which the conquest for cultural legitimacy and of the concomitant power of legitimate symbolic violence is at stake." From this perspective, Apess's citations become "so many landmarks circumscribing, within the common battlefield, the small network of privileged allies and adversaries proper to each category of producer." Constructing his authorial self through this pattern of formal gestures, Apess is able to forge a network to connect his otherwise sui generis "ingenuity" to a community of what Bourdieu has termed "those *privileged interlocutors* implicit in the writings of every producer."[51]

Foremost among these "privileged interlocutors" is the Anglo-American Elias Boudinot (1740–1821), a member of the Continental Congress from New Jersey and the first president of the American Bible Society. Apess, however, may have chosen his authorial mentor for reasons beyond the purely pious content of his work, for during his tenure in Congress, Boudinot was instrumental in passing the copyright law.[52] As a member of the American Bible Society, he was also representative of a new approach to print piety. Established in 1816 by a group of fifty-six delegates at the South Reformed Church in New York City, the American Bible Society was created to promote the "wider circulation of the scriptures without note or comment." It was committed to technological innovation in printing, establishing its own printing department in 1845 and its own bindery in 1848. In short, Boudinot was not merely a "friend to the Indian" but also a potent exponent of the Protestant vernacular's transformation into popular print in the early nineteenth century.

Finally, the appendix, with its rich pattern of citations, positions Apess as a commentator on the central problem of Indian/white relations in the 1830s, namely land ownership and forced expulsion. The appendix approaches these issues by exploring questions about the ownership of ideas and the recitation of history (particularly when that history is not one's own) in the literary marketplace. Ideas about copyright and proprietary authorship were inextricably bound up with ongoing discussions of property rights, especially as they were related to real estate and land law.[53] By foregrounding the act of recompiling the white historian's compilation, Apess draws attention to the complexities and ironies surrounding "ownership" and "proprietary privileges" in the arena of Indian/white relations in general. The question of who owns Indian history, Indian utterance, and Indian land is in some ways answered by the figure of the Indian proprietor-as-author that Apess sets up in his text. It is no coincidence that Apess's reconfiguring of the 1831 edition draws attention to questions of ownership and that the final pages of the autobiography are given over to a proprietary reappropriation of the historical materials of Indian land tenure and dispossession.

William Apess's performance of proprietary authorship extended beyond his 1831 revision of *A Son of the Forest*, making him an active participant in the public sphere. His role in self-publishing *A Son of the Forest* and several other works points to his recognition of the great opportunity for social agency that proprietary authorship represented in the broader public sphere, outside the margins of a text. Apess personally circulated in the New York neighborhoods where printing, bookbinding, and bookselling took place. Remarkable for a

Native American in the 1830s, he did so alone, without the authorization or sponsorship of a white editor or a Christian missionary society.

But Apess's efforts to turn print culture to political advantage went further still. Barry O'Connell, his modern editor, believes that Apess may have had the 1831 appendix to *A Son of the Forest* printed and bound separately to hand out after sermons.[54] This tantalizing bit of speculation suggests that Apess may have attempted marketplace manipulations of print culture and proprietary authorship that went beyond editorial gestures. Giving sermons as gifts was a venerable tradition in New England, but one generally restricted to orthodox elites. Cotton Mather, for example, is known to have given away about 600 books in one year. It is possible Apess emulated this print culture activity to supplement the authorial identity he established through copyrighting his texts. He certainly was well on the way to becoming a public figure.[55]

There remain many puzzling aspects about William Apess's decision to seek the political authority of proprietary authorship as an avenue to social agency. Why, for example, did he include Elias Boudinot's egregiously racialized dialect poem "Indian Hymn" in the second edition of *A Son of the Forest*? Placed after the appendix, it provides the autobiography's last word, and it is unclear whether Apess's goal was irony, pathos, or sentimentality.

A brief look at the physical properties and publishing histories of Apess's last three copyrighted texts — *Indian Nullification* (1835), *The Experiences of Five Christian Indians* (1837), and the *Eulogy for King Philip* (1837) — raises further questions about his proprietary motivations. *Indian Nullification* is an extended compilation of white editorial materials, Mashpee history and commentary, abolitionist editorials, and letters. The way communal authorship can work to mirror and supplement a communal identity seems to be a powerful subtext in this work, underpinning the overt arguments made for Mashpee political rights and land-tenure sovereignty.[56] The last two works that Apess republished, *Experiences* and *Eulogy*, contain what Barry O'Connell has called "critical and unexplained changes," as well as edits apparently designed to address market expectations. In the case of *Experiences*, O'Connell notes that Apess inexplicably chose to replace the powerful "An Indian's Looking-Glass for the White Man" with a "brief and bland" piece called "An Indian's Thought."[57] In the reprint of the *Eulogy*, Apess appears to have condensed the earlier version to match a shortened one he delivered publicly in January 1837, perhaps in an attempt to deploy the social power of ministerial sermon gifting and publication one last time.

Hovering over all of these questions about Apess's motives at the end of his career are the few known facts about his social position in the years following the second edition of his autobiography. By 1837 Apess was an economic casualty. He disappears from the historical record in 1838 when the Barnstable Court of Common Pleas attached his household goods and estate for debt. His last appearance in the public sphere is as the owner of a tiny lot of personal effects that are listed in the estate inventory. It may have been that Apess published his last works in a desperate attempt to stave off financial ruin.[58]

Regardless of scholars' ultimate verdict on the editorial choices he made during his final years, it seems clear from the second edition of *A Son of the Forest* that William Apess sought and defended the identity of proprietary author for reasons beyond that of its economic rewards. He was one of the first Native writers to realize that it offered one way out of the political corner Native Americans had been painted into by Supreme Court rulings and popular culture fantasies about the disappearing Indian. Proprietary authorship afforded all writers in the 1830s a venue for exploring their vexed relationship to the marketplace. Over and above this, it granted William Apess a way of avoiding the pitfalls of passivity and entrepreneurialism that seemed to be the only choices for Native American people in that period.

Although proprietary authorship in the 1830s provided William Apess a space within the public sphere in which to be both enterprising and Indian, during the middle decades of the nineteenth century Euro-American cultural entrepreneurs engaged in a concerted program of reprinting Indian texts for their own personal and ideological advantage. In this emergent "culture of reprinting," the long-fought battles over Indian sovereignty on the land moved into the rarefied world of cultural artifacts and oral traditions. Here again, it took great resourcefulness for Native communities to wrest print authority for reproducing their cultural heritage from the hands of non-Indian entrepreneurs. By the last decades of the nineteenth century, however, several communities had done just that, producing what amounted to "authorized" tribal histories grounded in distinctly local perspectives.

CHAPTER

Seven

THE CULTURE OF REPRINTING

PROPRIETARY AUTHORSHIP, though an essential tool for American Indian writers seeking intellectual sovereignty, was itself not a foundational structure in nineteenth-century American print culture. That honor went to the ad hoc local publishing practices of reprinting. Print historian Meredith McGill argues that such practices were fundamentally shaped by an "antebellum commitment to the circulation of unauthorized reprints" embodied in a decentralized system of publishing.[1] This culture of unauthorized reprints served as a counterweight to property-based paradigms of authorship (like those we examined in the previous chapter) and provided American literary culture with a republican model of textual dissemination. At the level of local publishing, reprinting books was viewed as the circulation of public property for the pubic good. Thus, the trends we observed in chapter 3 concerning missionary and tract society publication, in which mass-produced works emanated from centralized distribution centers, were counterbalanced by local, ad hoc publishing practices, especially reprints of already established works.

As I have argued in earlier chapters, books functioned as objects in Indian Country. As such, they flowed along the same imperial mercantile circuits as other material goods. As material objects imbued with intellectual property rights, they were subject to copyright, and thus a kind of legal protection as well as a form of social visibility. When Indian books were reprinted by non-Indians, however, it raised important questions about cultural sovereignty. These questions would remain largely unanswered during the nineteenth century. In fact, they continued to be unresolved until the late twentieth century, when Congress passed the Native American Graves Preservation and Repatriation Act, in 1992. In this legislation, Euro-American collectors and archaeologists were forced to confront a question that had basically been ig-

nored for 200 years: Who "owned" the human remains and ceremonial artifacts in the collections of Euro-American museums? In literary studies, such
questions also led to a reconsideration of cultural and intellectual property
rights in textual settings, and Native literary critics began to view non-Indian
reprinting and editing of Indian materials as a similar infringement on tribal
sovereignty.[2]

The marketplace afterlife of Samson Occom's *Sermon, Preached at the
Execution of Moses Paul* illustrates how reprinting by non-Natives co-opted
Indian intellectual sovereignty early on in the history of the production of
Native books. Occom's *Sermon* was reprinted many times during his life and
long after his death. Each of the nineteen editions produced from 1772 to
1827 offered publishers and booksellers a new opportunity to exploit Occom's
popularity for their own purposes. The substantive changes made between
editions had a significant impact on the meaning of the death of Moses Paul
and, more broadly, on American Indian identity as a whole. For example, in
1789 an edition of the *Sermon* printed by a New Haven publisher appended
the treatise on Indian languages of Jonathan Edwards Jr. to Occom's work. Instead of the grim death's-head and the black-letter "murder" motif of the original title page, this one featured a monolithic body of staid, crowded Roman
type, befitting the "scientific" nature of Edward's linguistic observations. In
this reprinting, Occom's work seems to function primarily as a supplement to
Edwards, granting the white-authored work "Indian" authenticity by virtue of
proximity.

In 1810, another reprint of Occom's *Sermon* appeared in Bennington, Vermont, with a title page illustration that undercut the authority of the Mohegan
author by employing the parodic image of a mountebank—that festive and
theatrical, jesterlike character who, as Patricia Crain notes, "descends from
the commedia dell'arte *zanni*, the artful scheming and bumbling clown" (figure 26).[3] It is not clear from the engraving whether Moses Paul or Occom is
the intended object of ridicule. Since Crain observes, however, that "scholars
and pedagogues" are generally the target of the zany's antics in nineteenth-
century children's primers, it seems likely that the Bennington edition was
attempting to belittle Occom's learning and literacy.

These two examples of the ways Occom's groundbreaking text was repackaged serve to remind us that Indian books were often pirated and exploited
to further non-Native publishers' particular agendas, intellectual sovereignty
notwithstanding. This chapter thus continues the previous chapter's exploration of the issues surrounding intellectual sovereignty, but from a slightly

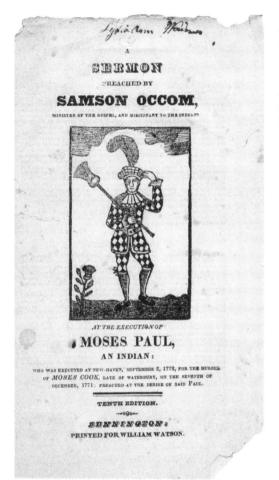

Figure 26. Title page of Samson Occom, *Sermon, Preached at the Execution of Moses Paul* (1810). Courtesy of Houghton Library, Harvard University.

different perspective—by examining the dramatic increase in the reprinting of Indian books during the nineteenth century. Following the lead of American Indian literary nationalists Jace Weaver (Cherokee), Craig Womack (Muskogee), and Robert Warrior (Osage), this chapter views "Native American literary output as separate and distinct from other national literatures." It is considered as a body of literary expression that "proceeds from different assumptions and embodies different values from American literature" as a whole.[4] This approach challenges Meredith McGill's claim that "the system of reprinting can be seen as a peculiar kind of advantage for writers who were marked by race and gender, providing access to print while suspending or deferring the question of authorial identity."[5] Although it is true that reprinting offered Indian authors the opportunity to reach a wider audience, reprinted

Indian materials were often co-opted by a white publisher or editor, thereby eroding Indian intellectual sovereignty. From the 1770s, when pirated editions of Samson Occom's *Sermon, Preached at the Death of Moses Paul* began to circulate, to the 1890s, when New York antiquarian W. M. Beauchamp reprinted David Cusick's *History* under the title *The Iroquois Trail, or Footprints of the Six Nations*, the nineteenth-century American culture of reprinting exposes fundamental questions about Native peoples' right to intellectual property that are still being debated today.

In the case of nineteenth-century Native print, manuscript, and oral works, ownership of Native intellectual property was pursued in one of two ways. Either Indian authors and tribal communities republished their own cultural productions, or, alternatively, "unauthorized" reproductions of Indian works were introduced into the marketplace by non-Indian printers, editors, and publishers. This struggle between two very different approaches to intellectual property rights encapsulated a set of underlying political questions that have continued to trouble recent histories of the book in nineteenth-century America. Was the republication of Native works merely part of the nationwide process of "decentralizing" print that enabled a "republican" democratization of print culture? Or was republication a conscious co-optation of Native intellectual property, an extension of the land-grabbing and removal policies pursued by the federal and state governments that were busy building a fantasy of nationalistic American history in which real, living Native peoples had no part to play?

Certainly the canon of non-Indian works published in America during the 1830s and 1840s is replete with books on Indian subjects. Many relied on Indian "informers" (as one work calls them) or on material culture objects "collected" to produce histories of the "disappearance" of a "doomed" people. Indian Affairs Commissioner Thomas McKenney and James Hall produced the *History of the Indian Tribes of North America* (1837–44) by printing materials gleaned from years of negotiating with Native peoples. They also put on a display in a Washington, D.C., museum that was called "The Archives of the American Indian."[6] Henry Rowe Schoolcraft made a whole career out of appropriating Native texts, garnering financial support from the federal government for his *Historical and Statistical Information Regarding the History, Conditions, and Prospects of the Indian Tribes* (1851–57).

These works stood in opposition to a growing body of Native-authored and -published works (like the 1831 second edition of *A Son of the Forest*) that self-consciously mobilized the economic, legal, and political authority of proprietary authorship to the maintenance of both personal and tribal intellectual sovereignty. This chapter thus charts the dialogic relation between the competing material print practices underlying the production of two rival print archives—the first characterized by non-Indian appropriation of cultural materials for "national" interests, and the other a Native-produced body of work centered on the furtherance of intellectual sovereignty. My argument seeks to establish a model of the field of cultural production in the United States at mid-century as a contested arena. By the 1850s, an "archive of the American Indian" compiled by Euro-American Indian agents and ethnographers competed for authority against the "separate form of discourse" that arose from the various tribal communities' very different "assumptions" and "values," articulated in modes structured by very distinct methods of social organization.[7]

"Very Happy to Make a Business of It"

Like all authors in nineteenth-century America, Native writers sought to publish their works for both polemical effect and financial gain. As we have already seen, American Indian authors like George Copway and William Apess often first entered the print culture field under the auspices of a missionary press.[8] Copway's *Life, Letters, and Speeches* (1847) was brought out by J. Harmstead, a publisher who specialized in religious tracts and was agent to the Methodist Sunday School Union of Philadelphia. William Apess chose James B. Dow of Boston to publish *The Experiences of Five Christian Indians* (1833). Dow was known almost exclusively for religious publications, such as the *Christian Witness and Church Advocate*, an organ of the Massachusetts Episcopal Convocation.

Yet, as we have also seen, missionary presses were not the only sources of print in Indian Country during the nineteenth century. David Cusick sought out a local press that was not affiliated with any missionary enterprise for his history of the Six Nations in 1827. In 1828, his book was reissued by a secular press in Lewiston, New York. Finally, *Sketches of the Ancient History of the Six Nations* was reprinted by a newspaper and job press (the *Democrat*) in Lockport, New York, in 1848. Significantly, when William Apess decided to re-issue his autobiography in 1831, he seems to have consciously chosen a printer whose list would not mark his life history as a Christian conversion narrative. For this later edition, Apess selected G. F. Bunce, a small New York printer who flourished during the period from 1830 to 1860. Apess's choice may have been influenced by cost considerations or by the fact that Bunce was open to a wide variety of publications. Several rather obscure and independent writers published mostly nonreligious works with the company. Apess's important autobiography issued from the same press that produced now-forgotten texts, such as Paul Abadie's *The Fireman, and Other Poems* (1852). George Copway issued editions of *Life, Letters, and Speeches* and *Traditional History of the Ojibwe* (1858) not only through the auspices of a Methodist-affiliated printer but also by employing Weed and Parsons of Albany, New York, a publisher that worked with the New York state government and that published a great deal of legal literature.

Native authors like Cusick, Apess, and Copway strategically placed their works in both religious and nonreligious settings and then reissued them with broader economic motives in mind. David Cusick quickly followed the original edition of *Sketches of the Ancient History of the Six Nations* with a version two years later that included woodcuts of his own making. In chapter 8, we will consider these woodcuts from the point of view of theories of book illustration and intellectual sovereignty, but here it is sufficient to note that Cusick's inclusion of illustrations in the later edition of *Sketches* may have been an attempt to widen the book's circulation. William Apess reprinted most of his works, most likely for both economic and political motives. We noted in the last chapter that Apess's twentieth-century editor was at a loss to explain his curious replacement of the powerful "An Indian's Looking-Glass for the White Man" with "An Indian's Thought" in the newer version of *Experiences of Five Christian Indians*. Viewed from the perspective of the culture of reprinting, we might postulate that the change was intended to blunt the political stridency of the first edition in order to broaden its appeal. The reprinted version of the *Eulogy on King Philip* is shorter and might reflect Apess's effort to produce a cheap pamphlet that could be circulated after his public performances. George Copway's *Life, Letters, and Speeches* went through seven printings from 1847 to 1848, with later editions appending commendatory letters and reviews that praised the work.[9] Copway reissued the volume again in 1850 under two separate titles: *Life, Letters, and Speeches* (New York) and *Recollections of a Forest Life* (London). A known commodity in American and Canadian print culture by 1850, it is possible Copway sought to enliven his London edition with a new title that underscored the romantic elements of his autobiography, thus "playing Indian" in European print, as he had done in person during his European tour that same year.[10]

Hovering at the fringes of these scenes of Native-authorized reprinting, however, were shadowy Euro-American figures. Their roles in nineteenth-century American publishing were akin to the "cultural entrepreneurs" Pierre Bourdieu has discerned in nineteenth-century French bourgeois society. Bourdieu argues that the creation of works of art in this period—drama, literature, painting, music—produced symbolic economies whose activities were characterized by a "collective repression of narrowly economic interests." For Bourdieu, cultural entrepreneurs were essential social actors in this emerging culture industry. They became "cultural businessmen" who symbolically "consecrated" cultural productions they claimed to have "discovered" and "which would otherwise [have] remain[ed] a mere natural resource." "For the author, the critic, the art dealer, the publisher," Bourdieu argues, "the only legitimate accumulation consists in making a name for oneself, a known, recognized name, a capital of consecration implying a power to consecrate objects (with a trademark or signature) or persons (through publication or exhibition)."[11]

For every Native author discussed in this book, there existed a corresponding series of Euro-American cultural entrepreneurs who sought to "consecrate" Indian printed works, "which would otherwise [have remained] a mere natural resource." Like Indian land, Indian books were ripe for exploitation. Several cultural entrepreneurs, for example, would "discover" David Cusick's work after his death. The first was Henry Rowe Schoolcraft, census marshal of the Indian tribes of western New York at the time Cusick produced his woodcuts for *Sketches*. Schoolcraft eventually reprinted the whole of Cusick's book as an appendix to one of his own. In 1892, Cusick would yet again be "rediscovered," this time by New York antiquarian William Beauchamp. He too reprinted Cusick's entire work within the covers of his own copyrighted text. William Apess had to deal with William Snelling, with whom he shared authorial and editorial duties on *Indian Nullification* (1837). Like most cultural entrepreneurs, Snelling was an ambivalent agent for Native cultural productions. In addition to submitting a critical review of *A Son of the Forest* to the *North American Review*, he seems to have done little to quash persistent rumors that he, not Apess, was the "real" author of *Indian Nullification*. George Copway's authorial experience was no different in this regard. He initially relied on patronage drawn from the highest echelons of America's literary elites, Washington Irving and Henry Wadsworth Longfellow. They would later turn on him, with Longfellow calling the Ojibwe author "Pau-Puk-Keewis," the name of the Indian troublemaker in his epic poem *Hiawatha*.[12]

Paiute author Sarah Winnemucca Hopkins was ushered into print and polite society by Bostonians Elizabeth Palmer Peabody and Mary Mann. The title page of *Life among the Paiutes* (1883) acknowledges Mann's patronage, announcing that the work was "edited by Mrs. Horace Mann and printed for the author." Using the political cover of Horace Mann, one of nineteenth-century America's most beloved education reformers, the two women carved out a space in the field of cultural production for a work that its editor claimed was as "extraordinary" as it was "colloquial." Mann's introduction to the book sets up Winnemucca's polemic against American encroachment on Paiute land in terms of the non-Indian's cultural entrepreneurship: "My editing has consisted in copying the original manuscript in correct orthography and punctuation, with occasional emendations by the author." Calling the book "an heroic act on the part of the writer," Mann includes an afterword and appendix clearly meant to frame the Native author's intellectual property within Mann's own social space, allegedly in order to protect it from "agents who wish to discredit" Winnemucca.[13]

Like their counterparts in the political public sphere (the "friends of the Indians"), these cultural patrons of Indian printed arts sometimes had reform in mind when they reprinted Native texts. Reprinting Indian works provided them with an opportunity to showcase an "extraordinary piece of Indian penmanship" they had discovered or to exhibit an example of the "progress" Native peoples were making on the road to civilization. Lyman Draper (1815–91) was typical of this nineteenth-century generation of non-Indian cultural entrepreneurs. Standing at only five feet, one inch, Draper was, in the words of his biographer, "ill-suited for heavy physical labor or sports, so he spent much of his time reading and hearing stories about his father's captivity by the British during the War of 1812."[14] With his interest in historical narrative thus whetted, Draper began a systematic project of recovering his father's (and nation's) past by circulating letters across the old backcountry settlements seeking "reminiscences from pioneers" and other primary historical materials. In 1854, Draper's avocation became a vocation when the newly established State Historical Society of Wisconsin made him its corresponding secretary. Like many of the century's cultural entrepreneurs, Draper moved from amateur "antiquarian" to government-sponsored agent. His collecting enterprise grew to include materials produced by Native peoples at the same time that Indian cultural productions were falling under the control of the government authorities for whom Draper worked.[15] The trajectory of Draper's life—his early casting about for a profession, his transition from antiquarian to government-sponsored authority—is in many respects typical of cultural entrepreneurs operating across America in the period.[16]

As noted in chapter 4, Draper collected the manuscript titled "Life of Governor Blacksnake" from the Seneca writer Benjamin Williams in the 1840s. Draper also compiled a sheaf of correspondence relating to his acquisition of the Chainbreaker documents. These letters shed a harsh light on the entrepreneurial practices of cultural "friends of the Indians." In a letter dated March 18, 1846, Williams, responding to one of the general calls for documents the antiquarian had been circulating across the former American frontier, offered Draper the Chainbreaker narrative. Williams carefully negotiated the print patronage system in this missive, dropping names of well-known Euro-Americans where appropriate and highlighting the marketable dimensions of his work. It was the "Editor of the Catt[arragus] Whig Ellicottville, ...NY," who had passed on the antiquarian's inquiry to Williams, he reported. Williams wrote that Draper's interests meshed well with his own "preparation of ... Gov. Blacksnake['s] history of his life," and he wondered if Draper "wished to have a copy of it, when completed it, and also Cornplanter son Charles history of his life." Sizing up his audience, Williams then emphasized the ethnographic scope of his manuscript. It described not only the old chief's life, Williams wrote to Draper, but also "our forefather's traditions, in their way of worshiping and the Division of the 9 tribes [clans] among the Seneca nation ... [and] the account of the beginning of the creation and the foundation of the world." Williams also played the authenticity card, assuring Draper that the manuscript was "written by my own hand."[17]

Having worked to hook this potential patron, Williams then floated the idea of print publication: "I should be very happy to send you any part of these.... You may have it the work and also the labor to prepare for the press whatever I may be able to furnish you any part of the abovementioned, I could finished with Gov. Blacksnake history within a few months if I had any means for to support my work because I shall have to pay them something for their time and for their addresses—indeed very hard times with me for money at the present, if you see fit to send me a small some of money ... twenty-five dollars to begin with." Williams is not only up front about his wish to be paid but also informative about how the symbolic and monetary exchange network surrounding Native intellectual property was beginning to crystallize in nineteenth-century Indian Country. Blacksnake wants a cut of any advance; so do the other informants. Since Williams employs the words "work" and "labor" to describe the project, it seems only fair to talk about fees and payment. Williams concludes with an appropriately submissive, yet optimistic, postscript: "I would be very happy to make business of it—if published made up into Books The Chief Blacksnake wished to have it so." He also cagily pressures Draper with hints that there may be competition for the manuscript. He and "Mr. Blacksnake partly made a bargain with W. P. Angole Esq. Dist. Attny. And R. Johnson land agent to have . . . the copy . . . Published."[18]

Despite his best efforts, Benjamin Williams's book was never published. Draper did acquire two copies of the manuscript for fifty or sixty dollars, but he never ushered the aspiring Native author's work through to press. Other letters between Draper and locals familiar with the Allegany Reservation provide the back story for the manuscript's failure to reach print. Abraham Casler, writing to Draper as the "adopted son" of Governor Blacksnake, provided a fairly upbeat assessment of the manuscript: "The Life of the Gov. Blacksnake Ben. Williams did undertake to get and has got the principal part of it in his own way but it wants revising. I have looked it through. It is good and entertaining and I can get it if wished."[19] Draper responded with caution, warning of his "inability to pay anything for such mss" and pointing out that he "should have risks enough . . . in the publishing the work."[20] C. Aldrich, another of Draper's correspondents on the matter, was much more critical of both Williams and his work, and his view may have carried the day. "I have seen the Benjamin Williams mss," Aldrich reported, and "I must say that I think it would be of but trifling use to you. Aside from such detailed facts as giving Indian names and significances." He continued: "Benj. was an intelligent Indian, but has become a bloated sot. You will see an awful example of rum's doings if you visit Cold Springs."[21] By 1852, Williams had lost his house, library, and manuscripts to a fire and Lyman Draper had moved on to Madison to take up his position as the director of the Wisconsin Historical Society. Yet Draper ended up with the Blacksnake manuscripts. We will never know if they were not printed because of the vagaries of the marketplace, as Draper claimed, or because of the slanders of enemies like Aldrich.

Whatever the case, judging from the magnitude of Draper's manuscript collection (it takes up more than 130 rolls of microfilm), his methods of cultural entrepreneurship were quite successful. Other cultural entrepreneurs would go even further to secure Indian materials for both national and personal gain. These culture brokers laid claim to Native "natural" cultural resources—in the form of oral stories, manuscript narratives and songs, and printed autobiographies and history—using copyright to safeguard their claim to these materials in the name of the preservation of a soon-to-be extinct people.

"A Continent Has Been Appropriated"

When Euro-Americans began the wholesale alienation of Indian lands in earnest in the 1830s, they simultaneously embarked upon a project of appropriating American Indian cultural materials for their own uses. George Copway remarked on this fact while touring Boston in 1839. The craze for collecting American Indian ceremonial articles and personal regalia infected even the august American Board for Foreign Missions. At the Missionary Rooms of the board, where Copway had called to pick up religious books to circulate in Indian Country, he noted "some articles, wrought by our people in the west, such as bead work, porcupine quills, moccasins, war clubs, etc. I thought that if Brother Green had seen as much of war clubs as I had, (for I have seen them stained with blood and notched according to the number of individuals they had slain) he would conceal them from every eye."[22] Although Copway was quite accommodating to the Christian missions and their literacy projects, he here expresses both the comic irony and the personal outrage that such collections ignited in the Native viewer. Pilfered from their rightful Ojibwe cultural contexts, the war clubs and moccasins served the urban missionaries as mute emblems of cultural conquest. Coming for Bibles and tracts, Copway left with the uneasy feeling that books were being exchanged for blood on the frontier.

When the appropriative practices that Copway witnessed at the American Board for Foreign Missions in Boston were applied to the material culture of Native textual production, a similar logic of colonial exchange held sway. As we saw in the introduction, Henry Rowe Schoolcraft's *Bibliographical Catalogue* (1849) underscored the geopolitical dimensions of his cultural entrepreneurship. Collecting and reprinting Indian books helped the U.S. government "group and classify" Native peoples. The information was then used to inform a removal policy so that peoples could "be removed or colonized in reference to this relationship, and foreign groups not be commingled with cognate tribes."[23] In his later work, *Historical and Statistical Information Regarding the History, Conditions, and Prospects of the Indian Tribes of the United States* (1851–57), Schoolcraft smugly summed up his collecting efforts: "A continent has been appropriated."[24]

Scholars have routinely used terms like "appropriation" and "representation" to describe the ideological formations underpinning Euro-American collecting practices in Indian Country, but my focus here is on the material consequences of these strategies.[25] Specifically, I am concerned with the social

Figure 27. Frontispiece of Black Hawk, *Life of Ma-ka-tai-me-she-kia-kiak, or Black Hawk* (1834). Courtesy of Ingham Collection, University of Iowa Libraries, Iowa City.

BLACK HAWK

Pendleton, Boston.

horizon within which appropriated material productions signified, and especially with the intellectual property issues that were ultimately engaged by these practices. In the context of book studies, the appropriative strategy most frequently applied to Indian written work was the practice of reprinting.

A vivid example of what was at stake in such republishing practices appears in the title page vignette from the 1834 Boston edition of Black Hawk's *Life* (figure 27). Unlike the many editions that featured an engraved portrait of the Sac leader in full regalia, this one represents him in a U.S. military coat with high collar and brass buttons.[26] His hair is closely cropped and most of the portrait is given over to pencil hatchings. In other words, although a prisoner of war, he appears totally assimilated into the system that imprisons him. Although the authorial frontispiece makes the politics of this reprint especially obvious, even those editions that featured Black Hawk in traditional dress and roach hairstyle contain traces of the whole complex web of non-Indian cultural influences at work in such productions. The mix of entrepreneurship, collaboration, and circulation practices (what D. F. McKenzie calls "the sociology of the text") that inhere in any published work when it appears as a material object in a capital marketplace are on display here in such a way as to highlight their explicitly political dimensions.

Originally, Black Hawk's autobiography was prepared by Antoine Le-Claire, an army interpreter whose mother was Potawatomie, and John B. Patterson, the non-Native editor of the *Oquawka Spectator*, a small weekly printed in Galena, Illinois. As we observed in the previous chapter, the material properties of the 1832 edition of Black Hawk's life story suggest the care with which these two men went about authenticating the as-told-to narrative. But the evidence of the 1834 Boston frontispiece also makes clear that such authenticity was never immune to editorial commentary and revision. For example, in 1882, late in his own life, Patterson reissued the autobiography, making substantial changes to the diction and adding new events and details.

Because Patterson, not Black Hawk or LeClaire, had copyrighted the original version, the Euro-American newspaperman was free to embellish the Native warrior's story in ways that better fit his perceived 1882 market. When the 1833 edition came out, some readers questioned the truth of Black Hawk's narrative, pointing out that Patterson appeared more interested in producing a "catch-penny publication" than a historical or literary text of real merit. In the 1882 version, these "catch-penny" goals are more glaringly obvious.[27] Patterson inserted a captivity narrative to pique the interest of a new readership for whom the issues of the removal-era Indian "problem" were no longer salient. He also included more "romantic" landscape description, lavishing attention on Black Hawk's "watch tower" on the Mississippi. Such aspects of reprinting were rarely simply matters of aesthetics or marketing, however, as the Sauk and Fox Nations discovered to their detriment when they faced the Indian Claims Commission in 1953. When they tried to use Black Hawk's memoir as evidence of their original land claims, the tribe found the commission unconvinced. It declared that Patterson's 1882 edition had cast so much doubt on Black Hawk's story that they were inclined to disregard any claims the two tribal communities made based on a book "which history had already discredited."[28]

Patterson was, however, only following accepted practice in American reprinting during the second half of the nineteenth century. By the 1840s, the appropriation of American Indian storytelling and printed materials had become official U.S. government policy. Some of the government's earliest and most significant forays into publishing took the form of reports and statistical surveys of Native peoples. Historian Oz Frankel has recently charted the rise of the federal government "as an energetic gatherer of facts about . . . social, economic, and other aspects of national affairs, and . . . prolific publisher of policy reports and official documents."[29] Calling this intertwining of federal policy and publishing "print statism," Frankel describes the 1840s' rise of "modern public culture" in America as a function of the production of the government-sponsored "factual report." For Frankel, "print statism flourished in a new cultural order and served differently conceived states, publics, authors, and readers."[30] At the center of this activity were the Indian nations and Indian authors of the United States.

Henry Rowe Schoolcraft took the lead in the establishment of print statism in Indian Country. Having been made Indian agent at Sault Ste. Marie in 1822, by 1836 Schoolcraft had risen to become superintendent of Indian affairs in Michigan. His marriage to Jane Johnston (1800–1842), daughter of Ozhaguscodaywayquay, an Ojibwe woman of distinguished Anishinaabe lineage, and John Johnston, an Irish-born fur trader, offered him unique access to Ojibwe storytelling traditions and linguistic materials. He began to parlay this into an authorial career in 1839 with the publication of *Algic Researches*. In 1845, Schoolcraft was appointed census marshal for the Indian tribes of western New York. He used this position to embark on an elaborate print culture scheme, circulating a printed pamphlet containing more than sixty-seven questions among the Native families under his jurisdiction. The tabulated answers to these questions, he believed, would lead to improved removal and colonization practices. Although he found local people less than enthusiastic about responding, Schoolcraft built on his New York experience and produced another printed circular of some 348 questions designed for national distribution. Titled "Inquiries, Respecting the History, Present Condition, and Future Prospects of the Indian Tribes of the United States," the pamphlet began circulating to Indian agents and missionaries across Indian Country in 1847.[31] Schoolcraft gathered enough information through these circulars to successfully petition Congress to publish his findings as *Historical and Statistical Information* (1851–57). The cost to the government for what would turn out to be a lavishly illustrated six-volume set was over $125,000.[32]

In one sense, Schoolcraft's project was coextensive with his larger strategy of "classifying" tribal peoples to facilitate their removal. It effectively gathered the cultural and intellectual properties of many Indian nations and published them at federal expense to help the American nation manage its new colonial subjects. In another sense, however, Schoolcraft's cultural entrepreneurship was pure self-aggrandizement. In 1859, Frankel observes, Schoolcraft's second wife "secured the passage of a private act under which Congress granted her husband an exclusive fourteen-year copyright for his Indian history," including "the use of the engraved plates."[33] This was a substantial coup for

Schoolcraft's authorial property rights. As Meredith McGill notes, "The culture of reprinting conferred a new kind of value on illustrations. While type could be easily reset, engravings were more difficult and expensive to reproduce, enabling publishers to secure property in their texts by investing heavily in ornamental plates, a practice that Hugh Amory has called 'proprietary Illustration.'"[34]

Given Schoolcraft's scrupulous maintenance of his own intellectual property rights and his project's patently colonialist aims, it not surprising that the majority of the articles in the book concerning Native scribal and storytelling materials are "authored" by Euro-Americans. Men like Schoolcraft and Samuel Worcester are given authorial credit, while their Indian "informers" rate only offhand mention. As motivation for producing the work, Schoolcraft cites a two-part agenda, typical of the "salvage ethnography" produced during the period. Schoolcraft wishes "to rescue the topic" of Indian cultural history "from a class of hasty and imaginative tourists and writers." Time is short, and this must be accomplished "while the tribes are yet on the stage of action."[35] Given the allegedly rapid disappearance of the tribes and the precarious nature of their cultural productions (Schoolcraft speaks of "the slender thread of their oral traditions"), *Historical and Statistical Information* constructs an elaborate scaffold of printed non-Indian authoritative materials to shore up the supposedly disappearing Native verbal and pictorial arts. This imperial framework includes a veritable who's who of nineteenth-century Euro-American authorities on Indian Country and Indian mythology. Schoolcraft cites Alexander MacKenzie and Lewis Henry Morgan, along with Indian agents and local authorities like Nathaniel Wyeth, New Mexico governor Charles Bent, and Thomas Williamson, a physician and translator of many texts into Dakota.

Yet it would be misleading to represent Schoolcraft's work as entirely the product of Euro-American fantasy, for the book relies on the intellectual property of many Indian authors (both storytellers and writers), without whom the *Historical and Statistical Information* would not have been possible. One series of narratives, for example, was drawn "from the lips of Se-ko-pe-chi" (Muskogee). They were "taken down from his narration, by Mr. D. W. Eakins," Schoolcraft reports, "in reply to the printed inquiries issued in 1847." Other "informers" who worked offstage, in the margins of the text, included "Chusco, an aged Ottawa of Michilimackinac," Dakota leaders Little Crow, Bad Hail, Good Road, Louis Rodger (Shawnee), Wabashaw from Drummond Island, Tenskwatawa (the Shawnee Prophet), and Ba-bahm-wa-wa-gezhig-egue, an Ojibwe storyteller Schoolcraft got to know during his time at the Michigan agency. The Native speakers Schoolcraft cites range from Abraham Le Fort, "an Onondaga Chief . . . believed [to be] a graduate of Geneva College," to Catherine Wabose, an Ojibwe spiritual leader, who receives perhaps the most extended treatment of any Native person in the book. Schoolcraft allots over ten pages to Wabose's religious beliefs and hymns, including a beautiful illustration that he captions "the Gods of Catherine Wabose, as drawn by herself."[36]

The only Native-printed source material in the *Historical and Statistical Information* is David Cusick's *Sketches of the Ancient History of the Six Nations.* Schoolcraft had already included excerpts from Cusick's book in the notes to an earlier work, *Notes on the Iroquois, or Contributions to American History, Antiquities, and General Ethnology* (1847), in which Schoolcraft called Cusick's book a "curious publication" but observed approvingly that "as the work of a full blooded Indian, of the Tuscarora tribe, it is remarkable." In the *Historical and Statistical Information,* Schoolcraft decided to print Cusick's book in its entirety as an appendix to the first volume of his work. A short biography accompanies the appendix, mentioning that "Cusick had received a common school education, and could read and write the English language." Schoolcraft notes that he has not edited the text, having instead left it "in the literary garb in which it came from [Cusick's] hands." It is, he claims, an "extraordinary piece of Indian penmanship." For Schoolcraft, David Cusick's book was little more than a curiosity, "a mere excursion of the North American Indian into the fields of the imagination."[37]

As Schoolcraft's reprinting of Cusick's book, Ba-bahm-wa-wa-gezhig-egue's stories, and Catherine Wabose's pictographic vision demonstrate, when Indian materials entered the field of cultural production through the auspices of Euro-American cultural entrepreneurs, the creators lost all claim to their intellectual property rights. Their work was absorbed into that of the non-Indian compiler and woven into a broader archive of non-Native historical, literary, and ethnographic work. Native texts were, moreover, framed by specifically print culture material practices that paradoxically marginalized them even as they affirmed their authenticity. Schoolcraft printed Cusick's complete book only as an appendix to his own. He would allow Se-ko-pe-chi's memories to appear in his work only within the pages of a letter authorized by an Indian agent. Schoolcraft himself pointedly drew attention to the central role print culture played in making Indian materials legible within the Euro-American cultural field. Early on in *Historical and Statistical Informa-*

tion he noted that the book's "system of pictography which is for the first time exhibited, imposes a degree of critical care in the typography which is not ordinarily expected."[38] Thus technology and aesthetics trump the "mere excursion into the field of the imagination" that was supposed to characterize Indian works.

David Cusick's *Sketches* was reprinted one final time. New York antiquarian William Beauchamp released a slender volume titled *The Iroquois Trail, or Footprints of the Six Nations in Customs, Tradition, and History in Which Are Included David Cusick's Sketches of the Ancient History of the Six Nations* (1892). Although in many ways Beauchamp's reprint gives its Native author his due, the appropriative practices established by Schoolcraft remain. The subtitle, *Footprints of the Iroquois*, inscribes Cusick's work within the trope of the vanishing Indian. Although Beauchamp cites the stories of many living Six Nations leaders as context for Cusick's work, both storytellers and book are presented as mere traces of a once-substantial people.[39] Despite the fact that Beauchamp claims that "Cusick's history has been largely quoted in recent years, with too much deference to its authority," he nevertheless goes on to argue that copies of it have "become so scarce that a reissue seemed desirable." So desirable, in fact, that Beauchamp retained copyright on the work.

Beauchamp's intellectual property rights thus take center stage even as he reprints the Tuscarora author's work in its entirety. Declaring that "it seemed well to add a few explanatory notes," he added contextualizing materials that in the end were about three times as long as Cusick's entire book. To position himself as authoritative cultural entrepreneur, Beauchamp claims he "has enjoyed the advantage of long personal acquaintance with the Onondaga" and twice underscores the fact that he is a Fellow of the American Society of the Advancement of Science. His brief biography of Cusick benefited significantly from his conversations with living Six Nations tribal members. Thanks to them, the New York antiquarian was able to locate Cusick within his family lineage ("his father was Nicholas Cusick, an important interpreter who lived until 1840, about 82 years old") and to cite local authorities as to the fact that Cusick was "thought a good doctor by both whites and Indians."[40]

Like Schoolcraft and other cultural entrepreneurs who shepherded Indian materials into the field of cultural production in the United States, Beauchamp wove Cusick's book into a fabric of non-Indian authorities, ranging from Charles Miner's *History of Wyoming* (1845) and Horatio Hale's *Iroquois Book of Rites* (1883), to Charlevoix, Adrien Van der Donck, Thomas Jefferson, Roger Williams, and Sir William Johnston. To authenticate these authorities,

Beauchamp added the comments of tribal leader Albert Cusick, Beauchamp's contemporary and lineal descendant of the Tuscarora author. Beauchamp also provided Albert Cusick's biography, a gesture that went far beyond what Schoolcraft deemed necessary for his "informers," perhaps a reflection of the improved state of late-century non-Indian ethnographic practice in the United States.[41] We learn that Albert Cusick's Onondaga name was Sa-go-na-qu-der and that he was a member of the Eel clan on his mother's side. For our purposes, Albert Cusick's biography is especially interesting in that Beauchamp mentions that he was a tribal leader for ten years before he became a Christian in 1864. Although Beauchamp sometimes buried Cusick's agency in the text's production, this comment makes it clear that Albert Cusick facilitated his great-uncle's reentry into print for reasons more complex than assimilation or missionization. Albert Cusick was Tuscarora-Onondaga first and Christian Indian second.

Autoethnography and the Culture of Reprinting

Albert Cusick was not alone in his desire to regain control over Native intellectual property. By the 1870s, American Indian intellectuals were beginning to wrest power back from their non-Indian overseers, republishing tribal literature on their own terms. In the current critical climate, such reappropriations are commonly labeled "transculturations." As such, they are read as Native North American "autoethnographies." In *Imperial Eyes*, Mary Louise Pratt points to the genre as the epitome of the decolonizing writing practices that arose across indigenous communities in Africa and the Western Hemisphere.[42] Indeed, Hilary Wyss employs this formulation quite effectively in *Writing Indians* to explicate bicultural production in the seventeenth-century Northeast. In her work, Wyss focuses on the ways Native people adapted and modified alphabetic literacy in order to construct new personal and communal identities with which to negotiate the new colonial context. Yet in her study and in others, the material properties of printed and manuscript texts have received little scrutiny. If, however, the works produced by alphabetically literate Native peoples (often Christian converts) were indeed "bicultural products," then it seems reasonable to assume that their hybrid textual performances of resistance might have included manipulating and transforming the formal properties of print texts, communities of the book, epistolary networks, and scribal communities.[43]

A classic example of the material practice of autoethnography in print appears in Tuscarora author Elias Johnson's *Legends, Traditions, and Laws of the Iroquois or Six Nations and History of the Tuscarora Indians* (1881). Johnson's book, a collection of reprinted oral, print, and manuscript sources, was printed only in a single edition.[44] Like David Cusick's *Sketches*, it was produced on a job press at Lockport, New York, not far from the Tuscarora settlement, thus suggesting a degree of material continuity with the earlier work. Johnson's opening expostulation casts the whole book as a dialogic engagement with the Euro-American world of reprinting that had flourished in the earlier decades of the century: "A book about Indians!—who cares anything about them?" It is an interjection framed as a non-Indian reader's response to the prospect of yet another text on Native peoples. Johnson's preface thus takes the form of an extended justification for his imposition on the literary marketplace. Having "longed to see refuted the slanders" common in most non-Indian books about indigenous peoples, Johnson promises "a truer knowledge of our civil and domestic life" and "our capabilities for future elevation" as the "inheritors of many wrongs," in order to raise "public estimation of the Indians."[45]

Johnson makes his case with a keen awareness of the print culture context within which his book will be read. "I might have covered many pages with 'Indian Atrocities,'" he tells his readers, "but these have been detailed in other histories, till they are familiar to every ear and I had neither the room nor inclination for even a glance at war and its dark records."[46] He thus locates his book within the established "archive"—the term Michel Foucault employs to describe a discursive practice that collates and validates all material traces (such as real books in real libraries) as well as the more evanescent structuring principles of the discursive field that enables certain utterances and publications (in this case, those surrounding American Indians) and forbids or stigmatizes others.[47] At the same time, he employs a counterpublic discourse designed to resist it. Significantly, Johnson signs this preface as "The Author." In doing so, he adopts and affirms the social and economic implications of the "unique personhood" of proprietary authorship discussed in the previous chapter.

Johnson's prefatory comments are clearly reappropriative and hence constitute a discursive form of autoethnography. *Legends, Traditions, and Laws of the Iroquois*, however, performs its reappropriative agency as much on the material level of the physical properties of the book as it does on the more ephemeral levels of colonial "mimicry" and carnivalesque troping. Throughout the opening pages, Johnson underscores how print culture constitutes the primary source and material "shape" of the misinformation he intends to refute.

Print culture also constitutes the material practice by which he will perform his rebuttal. Johnson thus follows his attention-getting opener by focusing on his work's bookishness: "I can say that the Indians are a very interesting people, whether I have made an interesting book about them or not."[48] Johnson's emphasis here is on authorship and bookmaking agency, not on the performance of affective sentiment or assimilative literacy. The process of making an "Indian" book is fraught with complexities, especially when white editors like Schoolcraft have condemned one's sources as "slender" and purely imaginative.[49]

Yet Johnson faces the issue head on, arguing that although his book is "based upon authorities" he is its sole author. As such, he is a "witness" whose "credibility . . . is known to depend upon his means of knowledge." For Johnson, authorial agency resides not so much in copyright as on the particularly nativist grounds of family, land, and clan. "For this reason," Johnson explains, "I deem it important to state, that I was born and brought up by Tuscarora Indian parents in the town of Lewiston, New York. From my childhood up was naturally inquisitive and delighted in thrilling stories, which led me to frequent the old people of my childhood's days, and solicited them to relate the Old legends and their Traditions, which they always delighted to do."[50] Drawing on childhood storytelling experiences and input from contemporary tribal elders like John Mt. Pleasant, Johnson compiled a comparative historiography that read non-Native "Indian history" against "*our* Legends and Traditions."[51]

The overall shape of the book follows that established by the Euro-American archive of print statism and is guided by received ethnographic categories. Johnson considers "National Traits," "Customs and Individual Traits of Character," "Creation," "Missionary Work," and "Iroquois Laws of Descent," among other topics. However, the materials he "reprints" to flesh out these ethnographic subjects, and the way he handles that reprinting, highlight his differences from cultural entrepreneurs like Schoolcraft and Beauchamp. Although he does provide some context by using the work of non-Native ethnographers, he primarily emphasizes Native-produced works, paraphrasing and glossing them with tribal knowledge when appropriate. In addition to oral tradition, Johnson draws on Mary Jemison's life story, a biography told as a captivity narrative in James E. Seaver's best-selling print edition, *A Narrative of the Life of Mrs. Mary Jemison* (1823). He also uses David Cusick's *Sketches* as the source for his chapter "Creations," reprinting the woodcuts of the second edition. He edits Cusick's story so as to both flesh out many details and silently smooth over the "grammatical" errors that Schoolcraft had derided. Most significant, Johnson reprints treaties in their entirety, thus presenting Indian ethnography as a living, political project and establishing what we might now term a practice of American Indian "literary separatism."[52]

Johnson's first chapter, "A Captive's Life," represents his opening foray into Native separatist reprinting practices. Drawing directly on Seaver's *Narrative*, Johnson effectively "reprints" the white-authored work, shaping Seaver's materials from the Indian perspective he advocated in his preface. Seaver had characterized Jemison's story as a titillating classic captivity narrative, tempting his audience with the sensational subtitle, "An Account of the Murder of Her Father and His Family; Her Sufferings; Her Marriage to Two Indians; [and Other] . . . Barbarities of the Indians." In contrast, Johnson frames it as an autobiography whose context is the "provocation given by white people" for her capture. Johnson carefully classifies Jemison's captivity as an "adoption" and shows proper respect for the solemnity of the adoption ceremony she experienced. He continually emphasizes the civility of the Seneca, pointing out that Jemison was never raped and "was 80 years a resident among the Senecas." Her "formal name," he tells the reader, was not Mary Jemison, but De-he-wa-mis.[53]

As he retells and paraphrases the published account of Jemison's captivity, Johnson is selective in the details he highlights, again focusing on the human dimension of the story and the civil context for Jemison's life among the Indians. When, at the age of ninety, Mary Jemison is visited by a group of white ladies concerned for the condition of her immortal soul, she is unable to remember the Christian prayer her mother had taught her so many years before. Yet Johnson does not treat this as a "tragic" moment in the narrative. Rather, it is seen as a vindication of the Seneca social system. In Johnson's view, Jemison's soul is in no danger despite forgotten Christian prayers: "She had not been in the midst of corruption, therefore [her soul] had not been destroyed." Jemison's final words serve as gloss on the technique of reprinting Johnson has employed: "I love the Indians."[54] Tribal membership, figured as human bonds of affection, is the narrative fabric from which Johnson represents Jemison's story.

Two chapters later, in "Creation," Johnson embarks on his second foray into reprinting, this time paraphrasing and literally reprinting parts of *Sketches* of fellow Tuscarora author David Cusick. Unlike Schoolcraft's handling of *Sketches*, Johnson's method is akin to the revitalized practices of tribal narrative that Anishinaabe literary theorist Gerald Vizenor advocates in his groundbreaking study, *Manifest Manners* (1993). The problem for the Native storyteller in a print world, as Vizenor sees it, is that "oral stories" have been virtually erased by Euro-American reprints that are "translated, published, and read at unnamed distances." Over and against the preemptive silencing and distancing of tribal narrative by appropriative reprinting, Vizenor posits literary/print practices that combine survival and resistance in what he terms "survivance." To print tribal narratives on Native terms means performing new "simulations" of oral tradition that in turn "mediate and undermine the literature of dominance." For Vizenor, Native peoples in the nineteenth century began practices like those exhibited by Elias Johnson's *Legends* as a form of "postindian" resistance to dominant culture appropriation, creating a "new tribal presence in stories."[55]

Johnson's paraphrase of Cusick is a fine example of the kind of "retelling" Vizenor advocates for the re-empowerment of tribal narratives after a century of appropriation by outsiders. Johnson's practice shifts attention away from the focus on Cusick's tale as an excellent example of "Indian penmanship" to highlight its urtext status as a kind of cosmological underpinning for the nation's experience in 1881 America. It also assumes the unspoken ground of most storytelling traditions in Indian Country. That is, the most ceremonial and sacred stories were "given" to certain clan elders and could be told only at certain occasions and for authorized audiences. Stories told to outsiders are always already assumed to contain the proviso that "this is just my version."[56]

In "Treaties of the New York Indians," Johnson reprints the 1833 Treaty of Buffalo Creek in its entirety, including addenda that contextualize the Six Nations removal controversy of the mid-1840s. He follows the treaty documents with a narration about the disastrous westward emigration of May 1846, during which, out of "about forty of the Tuscarora" who emigrated to Indian Territory, "about one-third . . . died." Johnson describes how the emigrants "were destitute of everything" and blames the situation on the "misconduct of [emigration agent] Hogeboom." It is clear that Johnson makes these accusations not as an interested party but as a historian whose interpretation is authorized by "reference to official documents in the Indian department."[57]

It is significant, however, that Johnson does not base all of his authorial agency on government-produced texts. Native-produced genres like condolence speeches delivered in the longhouse and memorials circulated to the press and Congress are also included to validate his version of events. One of the most powerful sections of the book recounts Israel Jemison's 1846 speech in council. "Brothers!" Jemison begins, "I believe [the removal] has been irregularly conducted [and] . . . great efforts were made to hurry off the emigrants." In the face of his vocal opposition to government officials, Jemison tells the council, "I was desired to be silent."[58] Johnson's book creates a space for Jemison's voice where the public sphere of 1846 would not. Johnson also reprints a Seneca memorial requesting that the emigrants be returned to their eastern villages at government expense. Again, the reprinting not only gives new voice and agency to the tribal members involved but also reaffirms the viability of a nation presumed "vanished" by Euro-Americans. The memorial itself is a riveting document. This is partly due to the fact that it employs "the illusion of mimesis," which historian Natalie Zemon Davis has described in another context as a rhetorical technique that gives credibility and voice to social groups disenfranchised by Euro-Western legal and bureaucratic power.[59] While describing the haphazard flight of the removal families from the Seneca homelands in 1847, the narrator pauses to offer his governmental audience a quotidian detail that lends a vivid immediacy to the whole memorial: "One family were hurried away from their table, leaving everything upon it just as it was when they arose from their dinner."[60]

Just as important as this "present-making" practice of mimetic storytelling is Johnson's inclusion of the signatories to the treaties and memorials. The 1880s descendants of the treaty signers could invoke these documents to assert their continued historical presence since removal. Among the names are several men who also wrote printed tracts and manuscript histories in the 1840s. This again suggests that Johnson viewed the tribal history he was writing to be an important means of sustaining Six Nations tradition in the present. Many of the treaty signers were themselves active in the revitalization of Six Nations tradition in the modern forms of print and manuscript publication. Benjamin Williams, author of the "Life of Governor Blacksnake" manuscript, appears here. So does Governor Blacksnake himself. N. T. Strong, author of *Appeal to the Christian Community* (1841), signed the document, along with Maris Pierce, author of *Address on the Present Condition and Prospects of the Aboriginal Inhabitants of North America* (1839).

In subsequent chapters, Johnson walks an empowering line between time immemorial traditions and "new" cultural activities that have been woven into the material practices of Six Nations life in the nineteenth century. Along with two chapters on missionization and schooling, Johnson includes two on the Handsome Lake prophecies, reading them very differently from non-Indian anthropologists like Lewis Henry Morgan and Horatio Hale. For

Johnson, "the new religion" of Handsome Lake was all about temperance. His first mention of the Seneca prophet comes in a chapter celebrating his community's triumph over alcoholism through its syncretic adoption of Handsome Lake's code and the Washingtonian Temperance Society pledge system. As in the chapter on treaties, Johnson is careful to list the signatories to the temperance pledges, giving tribal members both agency and history and their descendants some continuity with the past.[61] Among the signers of the many pledges Johnson describes are members of the traditional leadership of the Six Nations bands, men like Nicolas Cusick, William Mt. Pleasant, James Cusick, Chief William Chew, William and John Printup, and John Fox. At one point, Elias Johnson himself appears as a historical actor. "The author of this book" delivers a speech to the Oneida, welcoming them into the circle of temperance observance, which is now intertwined with the great covenant chain.

In the chapter titled "The New Religion," Johnson details the endurance of Handsome Lake's code in Six Nations life by splicing together condolence speeches given in the 1840s by Abraham La Fort (Onondaga) and Sase-ha-wa (known to whites as Jimmy Johnson) of Tonawanda. The latter had been "raised up" to fill Handsome Lake's preaching role after the prophet's death. Sase-ha-wa's and La Fort's speeches are in and of themselves interesting examples of Six Nations voices speaking the history of their own tribal communities. But Elias Johnson's material practice of copying council preaching verbatim goes beyond this to signal the "new" cultural practices that his book as a whole engages. Where outsiders had attributed Handsome Lake's prophecies and ensuing political power to motives of self-aggrandizement, Elias Johnson quotes Abraham La Fort to affirm that Handsome Lake's vision served "no more than to confirm [the Six Nations] ancient belief that they were entitled to a different religion [from the whites]—a religion adapted to their customs, manners, and ways of thinking." Sase-ha-wa's condolence speech contains powerful admonitions against drunkenness, child abuse, and interracial marriage and emphasizes the central importance of maintaining the physical homeland: "Whoever sells land offends the Great Spirit." Equally significant is Johnson's decision to include all of the formal rhetorical devices that Sase-ha-wa employed over his several days of speech making to adhere to the protocols of the longhouse. Sase-ha-wa opens each meeting with a long prayer of thanks, asking his audience to prepare themselves to hear the truth (to "uncover now your heads") in phrasing similar to that used by Six Nations negotiators in the Ohio River Valley a century before. When finished, he concludes with formulaic phrasing as old as the confederacy it-self: "I have done. This is all."[62] These rhetorical performances hark back to those Hendrick Aupaumut recorded in his journal nearly a century earlier and clearly represent Elias Johnson's desire to make his book a continuation of ancient material practice.

Johnson was aware that his readership might in fact be mostly white "friends of the Indians." He thus follows up this chapter of deeply Native-based discourse with a reprinting of a white-centered account of a condolence council written by "Mr. G. S. Riley of Rochester" in October 1842. Johnson re-prints Riley's observations without comment, even when it comes to a rather embarrassing peroration with which the non-Indian reporter rallied his white readership: "In view of . . . the known fact that the Indian race is everywhere gradually diminishing in numbers, the writer cannot close without evoking for this unfortunate people renewed kindness, sympathy, and benevolent at-tention." If Johnson's book had ended here, little could have been said of his reprinting practices in *Legends* other than that they were geared toward (in his words) encouraging the "philanthropist to stretch forth his hand for the protection" of the Indians.[63]

The book's final pages, however, belie this simplistic formulation. They completely undercut Johnson's occasional assimilationist comments on con-temporary Indian Country to expose their fundamental irony. In what are perhaps his two most conventional chapters, "Legendary" and "Osteological Remains," Johnson, in titles and subject matter, invokes the long-standing materials of non-Indian ethnological cultural entrepreneurs. But his seem-ingly straightforward recitation of three lodge tales is framed by a powerfully cautionary preface: "It is very difficult for a stranger to rightly understand the morals of [Tuscarora] stories, though it is said by those who know them best, that to them the story is always an illustration of some moral or principle." "To strangers," Johnson confides, "[the Six Nations] afford all the rites of hospitality, but do not open their hearts. If you ask them they will tell you a story, but it will not be such a story as they tell when alone. They will fear your ridicule and suppress their humor and pathos; so thoroughly have they learned to distrust pale faces, that when they know that he who is present is a friend, they will still shrink from admitting him within the secret portals of their heart." Perhaps thinking of his own book and its reception in the print public sphere, Johnson concludes: "And when you have learned all that language can convey, there are still a thousand images, suggestions and asso-ciations recurring to the Indian, which can strike no chord in your heart. The myriad voices of nature are dumb to you, but to them they are full of life and power."[64]

The book's final chapter is even more unsparing in its assertion of the gulf that separates Native "tradition" from Euro-American print practices like history and ethnography. Posing as a brief recitation of the 1824 discovery of a mass burial near the town of Cambria, six miles west of Lockport, "Osteological Remains" first appears to be just another example of preconquest Indian "barbarism." That is certainly how Henry Rowe Schoolcraft presented it, for Elias Johnson takes his initial version of events "from the writings of Mr. Schoolcraft."[65] Schoolcraft and other Euro-American antiquarians viewed these human remains as yet more evidence of Indian-on-Indian violence, a "massacre."

Yet Tuscarora oral tradition offers a very different explanation for the mass grave. Johnson relates how locals recalled that men dressed as priests lured the Indian community into a hastily constructed shelter for worship, only to trap them inside and burn them alive. The evidence of blunt-force trauma on some of the bones was, according to local lore, the result of burning timbers falling on the trapped victims. Although non-Indian archaeologists claimed to have found a skull with two arrowheads embedded in it—thus proving the massacre interpretation—Johnson and the local Tuscarora did not buy it: "How easy for the artifice of the white men that accomplished this massacre," Johnson asserts, "to have sunk these two flint arrows into one of those skulls, to leave the conjecture in after times to have been done by an Indian war." The book thus ends with Johnson's condemnation of the whole non-Indian historical print enterprise: "All historians are very cautious to leave out or omit from the pages of their history, any circumstance in the nature of the above tradition."[66]

For all of his efforts to reclaim intellectual sovereignty for his people, however, Elias Johnson's book remains a materially bicultural and conflicted object. On its leather cover shines a gold-embossed image of a Native man in traditional regalia, hair flowing with beads and feathers (figure 28). The following title page vignette, on the other hand, features a lithographic portrait of the author, in European dress, sporting a mustache and gazing confidently toward his reader. The tension between the stereotyped representation of a Native man and the true-to-life portrait reflects the conflicted cultural position of books and print in Indian Country during the 1800s in tribal communities across America. Within the space created by the two images, Elias Johnson battled for a stake in the archive of Indianness produced in prints

Figure 28. Cover and frontispiece of Elias Johnson, *Legends, Traditions, and Laws of the Iroquois or Six Nations and History of the Tuscarora Indians* (1881). Courtesy of Edward E. Ayer Collection, Newberry Library, Chicago.

and reprints throughout the nineteenth century. At issue was "image" and illustration—how best to represent pictorially the disposition of the Indian archive.

During the second half of the nineteenth century, pictorial illustration became increasingly common in Indian Country, due in large measure to its growing role in the development of the American print culture market as a whole. Yet, as was the case with movable type, printed illustrations entered Native communities freighted with the baggage of the ideology of book conquest. Illustrations bore another burden, unique to their status as images. For both Euro-Americans and Native peoples, pictures occupied an especially significant place in communicative culture before contact, and with the collision of cultures in the nineteenth century these often competing visions of how images should be used, their status in relation to the printed word, and the very different representational practices that obtained between non-Western and European pictorial traditions new kinds of illustrated books emerged. They once again offered Indian communities the chance to establish meaning on their own terms.

The Culture of Reprinting (199)

Eight

INDIGENOUS ILLUSTRATION

PICTORIAL ILLUSTRATION — a central feature of the printing revolution in nineteenth-century America — came more slowly to Indian Country than to the rest of North America. Its gradual and uneven dispersal in tribal communities was due in part to the complex technologies involved in producing steel plate engravings and chromolithographs, those techniques of illustration that turned American weeklies into a "a carnival on the page."[1] But pictures had always been on the minds of missionary publishers, whose spellers and primers were amply illustrated with woodcuts, a less expensive and simpler form of illustration (figure 29). Indian literacy texts (like ones made for Anglo-American children) had traditionally been accompanied by some form of pictorial illustration. Many Indian spellers, however, appear to have sometimes included pictures because of the general assumption that if Native Americans had anything like writing at all, it was "picture writing" — to borrow a phrase from Garrick Mallery's influential nineteenth-century study of pictographic systems in the Western Hemisphere. Even the spoken forms of Native semiotic production, early ethnographers theorized, were based on object, metaphor, and image.[2]

The convergence of type and image in Indian Country also derived from the fact that during the period that Native communities were establishing printing presses Euro-American periodical and book illustration was reaching its high point. Lithographic firms like Currier and Ives were churning out hundreds of thousands of cheap reproductions of genre paintings and historical scenes. Brian Le Beau has argued that such images "were the leading source of popular culture in America."[3] Woodcuts also made a significant contribution to this popular culture of images. Sue Rainey points out that "prints made from woodblocks were a popular feature of the inexpensive,

PÁPATAMOEWOAGAN EWEGET AUWEN GETA ACHKINDAN}
PATAMAWOS WTAPTONAGAN.

Figure 29. "Prayer after Reading," in Abraham Luckenbach, *Forty-six Select Scripture Narratives from the Old Testament* (1848). Courtesy of Edward E. Ayer Collection, Newberry Library, Chicago.

large-circulation newspapers and magazines . . . and their wide distribution made possible a common cultural experience that bridged class divisions."[4]

Like movable type, pictorial illustration did eventually become a fairly common material practice in Native communities that had adopted some form of alphabetic literacy by the 1880s. We have already seen how Elias Boudinot quickly harnessed the power of printed illustration to the Cherokee press's more general project of printing "laws and public documents of the Nation." The illustrated editions of *Poor Sarah* (1846) and *The Dairyman's Daughter* (1847) that he published were cheap steady sellers from the Euro-American popular religious canon translated into the Sequoyah syllabary. Boudinot was not alone in recognizing the power of this new technology available to printers in mid-nineteenth-century America. In chapter 6, we saw how Native authors like William Apess and George Copway deployed authorial frontispiece illustrations to influence how their readers approached Indian life stories.

By 1891, on the Great Plains, pictorial illustration had begun to permeate even the everyday life of leaders on the reservations. A photograph from the period—captioned "The Bed Room of American Horse"—graphically illustrates how some Native people had begun to incorporate lithographs,

Figure 30. "The Bed Room of American Horse" (1891). Courtesy of
Western History Collection, Denver Public Library (x-31435).

postcards, and photography into the decor of their dwelling places (figure
30). The pictured house belonged to the Oglala warrior Wasechum Tashunka
(American Horse). He had come to prominence in 1866 during the Bozeman
Trail War and had signed the 1887 treaty that ceded half the Dakota Territory
to the United States, finalizing the settlement of the Pine Ridge Reservation. By 1891, when the photograph was taken, American Horse had moved
from a traditional Plains tepee into a Euro-American–style cabin, complete
with woodstove, trunk, and bed. This type of dwelling was becoming more
common among the Lakota settled at Pine Ridge, and there is evidence that
another prominent leader, Red Cloud, had a similar home adorned with pictorial illustrations, as well as a prominently displayed American flag.[5]

These photographs of image-decorated walls, cast-iron stoves, and
European-style beds were often taken to show evidence of the rise of "civilization" at Pine Ridge, but in some ways they reflect continuity with traditional
Lakota practice. In the days before the reservation, although American Horse
and Red Cloud would have lived in tepees, they would still have inhabited a
world of vivid pictorial images. From the Kiowa in the south to the Blackfeet

and Gros Ventre of the northwestern border, prominent Plains leaders resided in dwellings whose protective buffalo hide covers were brightly painted with pictographic narratives detailing the heroic exploits and important life events of those within.

Much more than mere "decoration," these hide paintings were often based in imagery drawn from sacred vision quests of the tepees' occupants. In visions, warriors and medicine people were "given" images of the power they would wield for the good of the tribal community. The materiality of this Native semiosis — largely without alphabetic signs but powerfully filled with meaning — is dramatically exemplified by the medicine visions of Bull Lodge (1802–86), Gros Ventre keeper of the Feathered Pipe, one of that nation's most sacred objects. Bull Lodge told his daughter Garter Snake how in his vision the design for his shield "hung suspended before [him] as if giving him plenty of time to examine it and to imprint its features on his mind." He would later describe it to Garter Snake as a "surface . . . painted half red and half dark blue. A painted rainbow went all around the edge. In the center a black bird was painted, and from each side of the bird's head, green streaks of lightning, ending at the rainbow's inside rim." A voice from near the shield told Bull Lodge, "My child look at this thing. I am giving it to you from above. It is for your living." "For your living" — a powerful description of how material signs perform their meaning in the Native world.[6]

White overhunting of the Great Plains buffalo herds put an end to such hide painting. Faced with this daunting loss, Plains artists improvised, turning to paper and colored pencils for their work. With the help of this new technology, they continued and extended their traditional representational practices. As we saw in the prologue, many artists worked on the pages of lined ledger books designed for the recording of business transactions and military activities. The book that the band of Cheyenne leader Dull Knife acquired in the 1870s is an example of this mode of syncretic artistic expression, known as the Plains Pictorial Tradition. The abundance of printed pictorial illustrations on American Horse's walls (perhaps cut from the *Dakota Friend*, an illustrated weekly that circulated on the reservation), the appearance of ledger books, and even the increased use of the American flag in Lakota regalia all point to the fact that the last decades of the nineteenth century witnessed a profound reorientation of the technologies of pictorial representation in Indian Country.[7]

It was not until the 1880s, however, with the forced relocation of hundreds of Indian children to boarding schools, that Indian Country produced a body of professional illustrators trained in the representational techniques and print technologies that dominated Euro-American publishing. Students like Ho-Chunk (Winnebago) artist Angel DeCora, who began her career as a twelve-year-old student at the Carlisle Indian School, would emerge as professional illustrators in the twentieth century.[8] In 1904, DeCora collaborated with Dakota writer Zitkala Sâ to produce an illustrated work, *Old Indian Legends*. In 1907, she was enlisted by Euro-American ethnographer Natalie Curtis Burlin to create *The Indian's Book*, a work that features a visual tour through Indian Country. DeCora provided the traditional decorative artwork of each of the tribes considered. By the 1930s, Six Nations artist Jesse Cornplanter had published two illustrated works on Seneca ceremonial life, *Iroquois Indian Games and Dances* (1903) and *Legends of the Longhouse* (1938). Meanwhile, Hopi artist Fred Kabotie had become one of the founders of the Native American Fine Arts Movement. He was joined by many other artists who, like himself, had been trained at the Santa Fe Indian School.[9] Like movable type, steel engraving, woodcuts, and lithographs soon became constitutive of the new cultural formations that the Indian nations deployed for cultural survival at the end of the nineteenth century.

In this final chapter, I examine two of the illustrated books produced by Native peoples in North America during the nineteenth century. I focus on the woodcut illustrations David Cusick produced to accompany his *Ancient History* (1827) and the 1890s Target Record Book that contains the ledger art drawings of Kiowa artist Silver Horn (Haw-Gone). In examining Cusick's and Haw-Gone's work, I offer a provisional exploration of the relationship between images and texts that are written/printed versions of what would ordinarily have taken the form of oral performances. I conclude this chapter with a theorization of "indigenous illustration" that underscores how late-century print pictorialism began to serve Native cultural values and political objectives. I believe that many Native American printed illustrations from the nineteenth century represent bicultural representational practices emerging out of a desire to preserve oral and pictographic traditions and extend them into the new world of print culture in the United States. Printed pictures offered Native storytellers the opportunity to *re-create* traditional stories — instead of merely *repeating* them — with new technologies that enacted what Gerald Vizenor calls "a righteous paracolonial presence" in performances that otherwise might have been misunderstood as simply nostalgic imitations of the past.[10]

Although professional illustration (in the book history sense) is quite recent in Indian Country, its origins stretch back to European contact, when Native American graphic systems initially found their way into European print. Works like Thomas Harriot's *A Brief and True Report* (1590), briefly discussed in the introduction, depicted the graphic semiotic systems of the Powhatan confederacy in elaborately engraved plates. In the early days of the Anglo-American colonies, printers also found it necessary to accommodate the conventions of European print practice to Native discourse. They soon devised methods of reproducing Indian pictographs and name glyphs in reproductions of treaties and the like. Thomas Fleet's 1726 Boston edition of Samuel Penhallow's *History of the Wars of New England with the Eastern Indians*, for example, reproduces the name glyphs of several Native leaders as an integral part of its semantic gestures toward veracity and truth telling (figure 31). As with movable type, however, Euro-American printers and publishers often carefully erased the Native production and labor behind such illustrations. This was especially true in printed cartography. The ideology of conquest demanded a Eurocentric authorship of "discovery," even as the information gathered for the maps came from Native sources. Nicholas King's (1771–1812) manuscript, "A Map of Part of the Continent of North America" (1805), for example, relied on Native cartographic drawings for its detailed rendering of the American interior. The manuscript map of the Pacific Northwest found in William Clark's field notebook carried the following caption: "This sketch was given to me by Shaddot, a Choppunish and a Shillute at the Falls of Columbia, 18 April, 1806." One of the more celebrated examples of such collaboration, which was essential to the mapping of early America, is Thomas Kitchin's "A New Map of the Cherokee Nation" (1760), said to be "engraved from an Indian draught."[11]

Even during the several-centuries-long practice of printing Indian treaties, Euro-American printers often silently elided Native visual material practices that were an integral part of the diplomacy taking place in the American "woods." We have seen how Native writers and storytellers like Hendrick Aupaumut and Chainbreaker attempted to find ways of representing these essential Native material practices of diplomacy in writing. We even witnessed Samson Occom "reading" wampum belts from an Oneida treaty. What we have not seen, however, are these material practices integrated into printed

Figure 31. Page from Samuel Penhallow, *History of the Wars of New England with the Eastern Indians* (1726). Courtesy of Edward E. Ayer Collection, Newberry Library, Chicago.

treaties in pictorial form. That process was initially left to the cultural entrepreneurs, like Henry Rowe Schoolcraft. Men such as he insisted on reducing these material practices of Native public writing to "curious" art forms, rather than rhetorical necessities. One example of just such a petition from the Ojibwe that Schoolcraft included in his *Historical and Statistical Information* will serve to represent the hundreds of such pictorial documents that accompanied the treaty records of tribal communities across Indian Country in the nineteenth century (figure 32).

The Ojibwe petitioners who produced this pictorial "memorial" conceived of its communicative power from within their own culture's material practices. They may not have expected it to replace the Euro-Americans' alphabetic literacy, but they insisted that it rest side by side with printed and written treaties as a Native supplement to the discourse of diplomacy. The same logic held true for most of the significant Native revivalist movements of the nineteenth century. As we observed earlier in this study, Neolin, the Delaware prophet, created his "Indian Bible" as "a Book of Pickters he Maid him Self."[12]

The supplementary role of pictorial materials underwent a dramatic change in the 1830s when Native communities began to employ printing presses for political and cultural ends. Missionary newsletters were a particularly important engine for the circulation of printed illustrations in Indian Country. The Dakota-language newspapers, *Dakota Tawaxiku Kin, or, The Dakota Friend,*

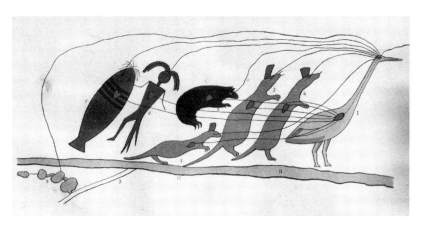

Figure 32. "Ojibwe Petition," in Henry Rowe Schoolcraft,
Historical and Statistical Information (1851–57). Courtesy of Ingham
Collection, University of Iowa Libraries, Iowa City.

and *Iapi Oaye, the Word Carrier*, which we have examined for their role in creating and sustaining a written form of the Dakota language that survived into the twentieth century, were also important for their role in supplying printed pictures of the sort seen on the walls of American Horse's bedroom.[13] The *Word Carrier*, especially, fashioned itself as an illustrated monthly, much like Frank Leslie's *Illustrated Newspaper* or *Harper's Weekly*. Its title pages were graced by sophisticated woodcuts of genre scenes produced for Anglo-American publications and then re-sold to the mission press. Local scenes and Native peoples were rarely depicted, but one important exception was the illustration of a Dakota Christian meeting produced for the *Word Carrier* by Alfred R. Waud (figure 33), an English illustrator who had supplied illustrations for Appleton's *Picturesque America*. Waud had earned his reputation drawing Civil War scenes. It is likely that Waud executed this picture while traveling in 1872 to the Dakota Territory for *Picturesque America*.[14] By the second half of the nineteenth century, Native peoples from the Great Plains to the western coast of Greenland were beginning to collect and display in their dwelling places pictorial illustrations and photographs like those in the *Word Carrier*.[15] These are the images we see on the walls of American Horse's cabin.

While print and pictorial illustrations were flowing into Native marketplaces from New Echota to St. Paul, non-Native printers and publishers were proliferating negative images of American Indians. These print representations of Native peoples constitute an important impetus for Native appro-

Figure 33. Alfred R. Waud, title page, *Word Carrier* (January 1875).
Courtesy of Edward E. Ayer Collection, Newberry Library, Chicago.

Figure 34. Cover detail, Henry Rowe Schoolcraft, *Historical and Statistical Information* (1851–57). Courtesy of Ingham Collection, University of Iowa Libraries, Iowa City.

priations of print illustration practices. When considered in tandem with "traditional" tribal artistic techniques, they outline the cultural field within which nineteenth-century Native illustrators and artists worked. The literature discussing imagery of Native savagery in the nineteenth century is too involved and prolific to engage fully here, but suffice it to say that America was flooded with images of Native peoples that Indians found objectionable and wished to counter. Henry Rowe Schoolcraft's influential *Historical and Statistical Information* infamously promulgated this kind of imagery. In fact, the cover itself featured a gold-embossed illustration of a Native man scalping a Euro-American settler (figure 34).[16]

William Apess summed up the feeling of many American Indians in the 1830s when he noted that Native peoples were surrounded by "monument[s] of the cruelty of those [who] came to improve the [Native] race and correct [its] errors."[17] In his introduction to the *Eulogy for King Philip*, Apess articulates the rage of a whole generation of Native Americans who had grown up beleaguered by images of their own supposed inhumanity. "My image is of God," Apess declares; "I am not a beast." Much indigenous illustration was no doubt produced in the same spirit as Apess's remarks and represents a counterpoint to such Euro-American representational practices.

Taken together, the emergence of Native presses and print markets and the flood of mass-produced Euro-American images of Indians provided a fertile ground for new kinds of indigenous representational practices. These practices merged traditional media and messages with newfound forms like lithography and woodcuts. In the two case studies that follow, I will highlight

Indigenous Illustration (209)

the relationship between text and image, recalling that, as J. Hillis Miller has pointed out, in the European book illustration tradition, "a picture must plainly illustrate a story." Yet, as Miller also observed, that relationship can be very slippery. Rejecting the traditional hermeneutics of book illustration, Miller cogently inquires whether "the interpretation of pictures [has] been illicitly invaded by models of reading based too narrowly on the kind of meaning written words have." "Is there a mode of meaning specific to the graphic image," Miller asks, "exceeding, supplementing, or lying beside any meaning that can be expressed in words?"[18] This question is especially relevant for my attempt to come to terms with Native illustrations that may not be referring to written context at all. It is the bicultural, "supplementary" role of indigenous images that I explore here.

David Cusick "Sketches" Ancient History

One of the earliest examples of Native illustration occurs in the second, 1827 edition of *David Cusick's Sketches of the Ancient History of the Six Nations*. Now recognized as a "neglected classic," Cusick's thirty-five-page reprint of his narration of the Iroquois mythical and historical past significantly added four plates produced by the author himself. Art historian Sharry Brydon notes that Cusick was as well known to his contemporaries for his art as for his writing. Thomas McKenney, director of the Bureau of Indian Affairs, bought works of art from Cusick when he visited him in 1826. Cusick's narrative and woodcuts were not only locally known but were nationally influential. They provided source material for many nineteenth-century accounts of the Iroquois, including Elias Johnson's *Legends, Traditions, and Laws of the Iroquois* (1881) and—sometimes with substantial modification—Henry Rowe Schoolcraft's *Historical and Statistical Information* (1851–57).

In his short pamphlet history, Cusick recounts some 2,800 years of Iroquois life, using what anthropologists call a "time-linear-sequence" method of narration. Readers familiar with Iroquois creation and migration stories regard Cusick's book as a very significant primary document in the ethnography. Even though it "translates story materials from the oral to the literary domain," it also significantly employs "the power of traditional Iroquois symbolic imagery." Its "sketch" format, popular in nineteenth-century Anglo-American storytelling, is also "in keeping with the Iroquois symbolic economy of tales."[19] Cusick's book physically parses Haudenosaunee history into three recognizable epochs—mirroring the more complex partitions of the Iroquois mythic canon that Christopher Vecsey outlines in *Imagining Ourselves Richly*.[20] Cusick's stories are shaped by the inflections of a nonstandard dialect into a complex weave in which tenses float and referents drift. By stylistic and structural standards, then, the book is clearly a hybrid bicultural production, with correspondingly complex bicultural rhetorical goals. In chapter 5, we examined how the book's physical properties, its title page, and its preface reveal its fundamental cultural hybridity (both copyrighted intellectual property and communal tradition). There, I suggested that Cusick's printed volume was a reflection of what Robert Warrior has termed "intellectual sovereignty."

Its illustrations offer further confirmation of this thesis. Added to the second and third editions of the text, in 1827 and 1848, these illustrations, Sharry Brydon speculates, may have been made possible by revenues generated by the first edition. They are thus quite possibly a tangible product of Cusick's attempt to maintain proprietary control over his work, at the same time that they represent his giving back to the community more of its own stories in the form of pictures that could be "read" by nonliterate members. Brydon also argues that Cusick's woodcuts allowed him greater intellectual reach by enabling him to communicate the narrative "visually and to reproduce his art on a large scale."[21] Nineteenth-century New England historian Francis Parkman dismissed both Cusick's narrative and his illustrations as "rude." Closer examination, however, reveals that these cuts are neither unskilled nor without ethnographic merit. They must be judged according to the standards of the text itself, as "a statement of nineteenth-century Iroquois collective experience, constructed by an Iroquois intellect,"[22] much like the prophecies of Handsome Lake. I also agree with Russell Judkins that "the inclusion of the four illustrations, adding as it does the pictorial element, appeals simultaneously to both Iroquois and Euro-American audiences, and thus extends the bicultural character and appeal of the work."[23] Exactly how Cusick achieves this bicultural semiotic bears closer scrutiny.

The first illustration in Cusick's *Ancient History*, "The Flying Head Put to Flight by a Woman Parching Acorns," portrays a monster that descended upon the newly established Five Nations of the Iroquois by night and devoured random villagers (figure 35). The scene Cusick chooses to illustrate comes from the section of his narrative in which an intrepid Iroquois woman foils this demon. The old woman, "who resided at Onondaga," was abandoned by her frightened community. Cusick depicts her "setting near the fire parching acorns" as the monster approaches. When it sees that she appears able to "eat the coals of fire," the monster flees in terror.

THE FLYING HEAD PUT TO FLIGHT BY A WOMAN PARCHING ACORNS.

Figure 35. David Cusick, "The Flying Head Put to Flight by a Woman Parching Acorns," in *David Cusick's Sketches of Ancient History of the Six Nations* (1848). Courtesy of Edward E. Ayer Collection, Newberry Library, Chicago.

That Cusick emphasizes this part of the story by selecting it for illustration prompts the reader to explore its significance. Perhaps its importance lies in the fact that it features a strong woman. Strong women are a point of particular cultural pride for the Haudenosaunee. Or perhaps it is noteworthy because it underscores how an everyday Iroquois practice—eating parched acorns—can prove a powerful deterrent to outside threats. The "Flying Head Put to Flight" caption seems designed to clear up any ambiguity that the somewhat nontraditional images might elicit in a reader. As Hillis Miller would say, "Words are necessary to indicate what story it is."[24]

In addition, this illustration establishes representational practices that will be continued throughout the book. The perceived "rudeness" of the image, about which both Horatio Hale and Francis Parkman complained, can probably be attributed to the minimal background embellishment and lack of perspective. Cusick employs a "ground line" to anchor his figures in pictorial space. All the woodcuts in the volume feature figures in simple profile, although some include more narrative "action" than this one. The uniquely Iroquoian elements in the woodcut, aside from narrative context itself, may be seen most prominently in the face of the Flying Head, which appears to be modeled on Iroquois False Face carving traditions.[25]

The most commonly reproduced illustration in Cusick's *History* is entitled

ATOTARHO, A FAMOUS WAR CHIEF, RESIDED AT ONONDAGA.

Figure 36. David Cusick, "Atotarho, a Famous War Chief, Resided at Onondaga," in *David Cusick's Sketches of Ancient History of the Six Nations* (1848). Courtesy of Edward E. Ayer Collection, Newberry Library, Chicago.

"Atotarho, a Famous War Chief, Resided at Onondaga" (figure 36). The caption is decidedly terse, for Atotarho, the leader whose head is teeming with writhing snakes, is a pivotal figure in Iroquois stories recounting the founding of the Longhouse.[26] His transformation from a wantonly cruel and manifestly evil figure into a supporter of peace and the confederacy is central to the creation story of the nation. Yet Cusick's illustration does not depict the moment of transformation, in which the Holder of the Heavens "combs the snakes" out of Atotarho's hair. Instead, the somewhat static scene sensationalizes the medusa-like figure, while balancing the overall composition with an everyday image, the playful—or menacing?—dog on the right.

It is in the tension between the marvelous hair and the ordinary dog that we gain some understanding of what Cusick's illustrative efforts are all about. Unlike many traditional oral and ethnographic print renditions of the origins of the Longhouse, Cusick's narrative and woodcuts do not emphasize politics. They instead highlight the commonplace—parching acorns, a frisking dog. Taken together, these elements of the figures challenge the notion of Cusick's detractors that his work is marginal or insignificant because it is full of "fables." In fact, the way Cusick gingerly uses the word "fables" in his preface suggests that he himself was acutely aware of how outsiders were likely to misunderstand traditional storytelling practice. This inference is reinforced by the way Tuscarora author Elias Johnson handled Cusick's work. We must remember that even though Johnson included some of Cusick's illustrations in his paraphrased and expanded version of the creation story, he added the significant cautionary note: "When you have learned all that language can convey, there are still a thousand images, suggestions and associations recurring to the Indian, which can strike no chord in your heart."[27] Perhaps Cusick had hoped his illustrations for the second edition of his work could help to bridge this gap.

Russell Judkins has commented that Cusick's woodcuts recall traditional Iroquois pictographic representational practices, found on canes, war posts, wampum belts, and beadwork. Cusick most likely deliberately echoed False Face Society carving practices in his illustrations to transform a traditional medicine practice, transferring the ancient art of carving to a two-dimensional paper surface for printing, and to the sequencing technology of the codex. Yet we should be careful not to overemphasize this aspect of his work. Henry Rowe Schoolcraft viewed Cusick's illustrations as "a *slightly* modified form of pictography."[28] The whole tale of what an indigenous craftsman and storyteller like Cusick was doing when he committed his images to print and his narrative to copyright is obscured by Schoolcraft's elision of Cusick's unique modification of traditional practices.

Cusick's "slight modifications" include important moments of agency: deciding which scenes to illustrate, carving the woodblocks from which the cuts were printed, and providing descriptive captions. These activities were also "new." None, with the possible exception of carving, were part of traditional Iroquois pictographic practice. Yet Cusick's representational practices also differed in important ways from contemporary Anglo-American techniques. If we compare Cusick's illustration of the Atotarho story with a chromolithograph based on Seth Eastman's (color) redrawing of Cusick's original that appears in Schoolcraft's *Historical and Statistical Information*, the differences are readily apparent (figure 37). What Eastman's image gains in raw color, it loses in the sinuous line of the original. Brydon has called Eastman's figures "bulky," and I agree. Without the dog, there is a different emphasis and order to the image, and the figure nearest Atotarho now seems to be crowding him. Moreover, the caption no longer locates Atotarho in a specific location (Onondaga) or identifies him with an honorific. He is here an ethnographic curiosity, an example, not a presence. In addition, the fine print below the illustration gives credit and proprietary privilege to Eastman and the Lippencott Company, without mention of Cusick or the Six Nations.[29]

Figure 37. Seth Eastman, "Atotarho," in Henry Rowe Schoolcraft, *Historical and Statistical Information* (1851–57). Courtesy of Ingham Collection, University of Iowa Libraries, Iowa City.

It is possible, too, that Cusick was exploiting the power of illustration that J. Hillis Miller calls "parabasis," the power "to detach a moment from its temporal sequence and make it stand there in a perpetual non-present representational present, without a past or future." In the context of indigenous illustration, however, we might wish to amend Miller's comment to read: "a perpetual representational present that is *full* of both the past and the future."[30]

David Cusick's illustrations flow from a specific social location within the emerging Tuscarora public culture of the 1820s and 1830s. Cusick was a member of a high-status family, one that had been associated with biculturalism and translation since his father's day. It is interesting to reflect on the artistic practices of Dennis Cusick, David's brother, in this regard. Also schooled at the Buffalo Creek Mission, Dennis chose to pursue a much more Western form of artistic representation. Several of his best-known images appear on a mission collection box depicting Indian children at their lessons. He was perhaps the first easel painter among the Six Nations, but Dennis Cusick's career was cut short by an early death. His small body of work nevertheless indicates that he was guided by very different aesthetic practices and goals than those of his brother. Much more interested in "modeling" his figures, Dennis Cusick also sometimes captioned his images with Bible verse. David Cusick, on the other hand, appears to have taken up his "Ancient History" project during a prolonged illness that prevented him from participating in other labor for the community. It may be, then, that the translation of Six Nations stories he produced served as a personal recuperative practice and that his later addition of illustrations similarly worked within a local system of healing that involved Iroquois representational practices associated with medicine societies reaching back to the time before European contact.[31]

Cusick was perhaps motivated by other competing outside forces. Since he could not work, it is possible he needed money. The title of his book—*David Cusick's History*—invokes the emerging capitalistic prerogative of authorship. Perhaps the illustrations added to later editions also served a market function, adding the allure of sensational images to an already sensational set of texts. We do not have as complete a record of David Cusick's artistic endeavors as we do of Silver Horn's, but we know that he worked in other media and produced at least one other version of Stonish Giants, a woodcut from the *Ancient History*. When compared, the two versions of the Stonish Giant offer us a glimpse of other possible motivations for Cusick's printed illustrations. The illustration of the Stonish Giant from the *History* follows the same style of the other illustrations in that text, but the version of this image included in Erminnie Smith's *Myths of the Iroquois* (1883) provides much more narrative action and landscape detail.

Unfortunately, Cusick receives no attribution and Smith provides no provenance for the image. The addition of more ethnographic detail in this illustration and in another called "Returning the Thanks to the Great Spirit" attributed to Cusick in Smith's collection invites us to consider whether Cusick produced these images for outsiders, community members, or a mixed readership. As more contextual clues come to light, we will be able to sharpen our appreciation of the kind of bicultural representational strategies Cusick engaged throughout his lifetime. Certainly even the scant information currently available suggests that Cusick was capable of adapting his illustration practices to suit different needs and that foremost among them was Tuscarora sovereignty.

Print Illustration and the Plains Pictorial Tradition

To conclude this discussion of indigenous illustration practices and their relationship to nineteenth-century U.S. print culture, I now consider a body of work drawn from perhaps the best-documented Native artistic tradition of the nineteenth century—Plains Indians ledger drawings. In the works of Haw-Gone (Silver Horn), the Kiowa artist who illustrated most of James Mooney's ethnographic reporting on his tribe, we find yet another example of bicultural representational practices emerging out of a desire to preserve oral and pictographic traditions and extend them into the new world of U.S. print culture.

Approximately 1,000 of Silver Horn's drawings have come down to us. Their subject matter reflects the three basic genres of Plains pictorial art: "narrative art, visionary art, [and] record keeping."[32] Candace Greene's groundbreaking book, *Silver Horn: Master Illustrator of the Kiowas*, has shown that a Kiowa-centered interpretive practice must be used in order to appreciate the range of Haw-Gone's innovations. This approach is also necessary to interpret their meaning in light of the broader changes then going on in Kiowa society. Greene's careful reading of Silver Horn's work provides us with a useful method for evaluating the illustration practices of other nineteenth-century Native artists who worked to mediate between traditional and printed images.

Greene's first and most important point is that we must treat these artists as "professionals." Her title gives its subject due respect; Silver Horn is both a "master" and an "illustrator." It is also necessary to locate the artist within the specific local traditions within which he or she worked. Silver Horn was an inheritor of the original Plains pictorial tradition, which embodied several artistic conventions. One important convention is that the blank space of the buffalo hide, tepee cover, shield, or page should contain no horizon or "setting" beyond what is necessary to its specific story. The Plains pictorial tradition also demands that a great deal of specific personal and historical detail be compressed into the representations of leggings, robes, coiffure, shields, and lances. The tradition encompasses profoundly narrative forms, employing representational conventions—such as the pattern of hoof marks—to denote the movement or direction of the story.

Greene emphasizes that the Native artist's personal life is also important. She firmly locates Silver Horn's pictorial work in what Pierre Bourdieu would call his "habitus"—the local Kiowa circumstances in which he produced his pictures. Like Cusick, Silver Horn was a member of a high-status family, a descendant of Tohausen, principal chief of the Kiowa from 1833 to 1864. Silver Horn was a keeper of several important cultural items, including the "Tipi with Battle Pictures" and one of the Tsaidetalyi medicine bundles. Art was central to the family's social duties within the Kiowa community and included such things as maintaining the artwork on the "Tipi with Battle Pictures." With these important contexts in mind, we are much better able to envision Sliver Horn's artistry as a mingling of communal and personal vision.

Greene expands her reading of Silver Horn's artistic context from traditional practices and personal history outward toward the popular culture of America at large. She demonstrates how Silver Horn transformed the Plains graphic art traditions he inherited in response to external circumstances. When warfare ceased to be the center of Kiowa life on the reservation, Silver Horn altered the focus of his own coup pictures, reflecting "a fundamental shift that was occurring in the Kiowa warrior art during the reservation period." Silver Horn's warrior art "became an illustration of war rather than an integral part of the war system." When he met Euro-American artist Edward Ayer Burbank in 1897, Silver Horn studied and adopted some of his naturalistic portraiture practices, but he used them only occasionally and selectively. In response to the many opportunities posed by the new medium of an Army Target Record Book, or of Euro-American blank ledger books in general, Silver Horn experimented with allowing the pages of the codex to provide narrative sequencing, sometimes filling many pages with events that occurred in a storytelling series. Greene believes that some of Silver Horn's earliest experiments in ledger books, now housed at the Field Museum in Chicago, indicate that he was "fascinated with exploring concepts of sequential illustration."[33]

When offered money for his work, Silver Horn changed tactics yet again. To increase output, he began to reduce the number of illustrations in each ledger book, using only one side of the page. He also adopted more naturalistic techniques of illustration if his patron demanded them. It is possible that the sequential nature of the Euro-America codex encouraged these improvisations, but it is also true that in Plains ledger art of the period, the codex is itself reimagined in new, often horizontal and nonsequential ways.

An examination of Silver Horn's illustration of Kiowa folktales demonstrates adaptive practices similar to those we saw in David Cusick's woodcuts. In the Target Record Book, filled with images between 1891 and 1894 at Fort Sill, Silver Horn illustrated some scenes from the Kiowa "Saynday" trickster story cycle (figure 38). This image combines traditional Plains pictorial conventions (note how the footprints denote narrative movement) with the pictorial sequencing made possible by the Euro-American codex. Saynday

Figure 38. Silver Horn, "Saynday Escapes from Sapoul,"
in Target Record Book (1890s). Courtesy of National
Anthropological Archives, Smithsonian Institution (MS 4252).

stories had never been illustrated before, but Silver Horn experimented with
ways to make his pictures "supplements" to the oral stories his children remembered him telling them when they were young.[34] Perhaps they functioned, as J. Hillis Miller says of European book illustration, as an "icono-
graphic countertext" to the oral story.

If Silver Horn's watercolor illustrations of the Saynday stories provided
a countertext, however, they did so within a broader context of "publication"
that stretched from a small manuscript reading circle to a potential national
print audience. In 1897, General Hugh Scott commissioned Silver Horn to
produce more pictures like the ones he had done of Saynday in the Target
Record Book, but this time for more general circulation. Under Scott's influence, Greene believes, Silver Horn "produced . . . more complex illustration[s]
by depicting several stages in the story in a single image." Silver Horn even
produced a set of illustrations on plain paper, the kind "suitable for photo-
mechanical reproduction." Greene feels these works are less like Plains traditional pictorial productions than any others in Silver Horn's immense oeuvre,
and she suggests that he was trying to adapt "a Western mode of illustration
to the traditional Kiowa stories."[35] Although these images were never printed,
the way in which they were prepared for print—the role of Scott, the use of

plain paper, the Western representational practices employed—all point to the many new choices and contexts available to Native artists in the nineteenth century.

Silver Horn was but one among hundreds of Plains craftsmen who took up colored pencils and ledger books in the 1880s to replace the hide painting they were no longer able to do. In previous sections of this study we have seen the ledger book used by Cheyenne artist Samson Kelley and Arapaho painter Carl Sweezy, as well as the "Winter Count" calendar that Battiste Good produced on paper, describing the year 1880 as the "sent-the-boys-and-girls-to-school-winter." To these we could add the significant works of Cheyenne ledger pictorialist Howling Wolf, Lakota artist Amos Bad Heart Bull, and even the great Oglala holy man, Sitting Bull himself. And beyond the Plains, similar adaptations of traditional pictorial practices were being pursued by different artists in different Native communities who worked to transfer techniques derived from various tribal media to paper and print. Fred Kabotie, the great Hopi artist of the early twentieth century, may have learned easel painting from the Santa Fe Indian School, but he went on to adapt a traditional mural painting practice from within his community to paper and paint. The same is true for Western Greenlandic (Kalaallit) bone and stone carvers who transferred traditional representational practices to woodcuts and engravings when Danish missionaries encouraged them to produce printed works in the nineteenth century. Illustrations by Aron from Kangeq, Jens Kreutzman, and Rasmus Bertelson adorn the pages of the Greenlandic-language newspaper, *Atuagagdliutit* (1861–52). Perhaps one of the most beautiful (Native/non-Native) collaborative printings was the work of Western Greenlandic carvers. They contributed extensive woodcut illustrations for a bilingual (Danish/Greenlandic) narrative collection of history and traditional storytelling, titled *Kaladlit Okalluktualliait* (1859).[36]

The illustrations of traditional stories produced by Silver Horn, David Cusick, and other Native illustrators demonstrate many things about how different indigenous artists, engaging in diverse indigenous representational practices at different points in the nineteenth century, met the challenges of print. In each case, both contemporary observers and recent critics note something "new" in the artists' works. Yet, as we have seen, the *new* could itself serve tradition. Following Dennis Tedlock, I argue that indigenous illustration, like indigenous storytelling, involved "a recreation of a text, rather than a recitation."[37] It was also "constitutive rather than . . . merely representational."[38] These works of indigenous illustration, in fact, bear witness to their immediate circumstances of production. Through them we may view the many acts of cultural improvisation that Native communities were undertaking in adapting all facets of print to their national use. These "circumstances of production" were often frankly commercial. Yet they partook of "intellectual sovereignty." Rarely assimilationist gestures, these works of art are examples of "survivance"—embodying that complex mixture of survival and resistance that is central to Native American life.[39]

These modes of survivance are articulated, however, within the interpenetration of specific local concerns, local cultural practices, and the increasingly invasive popular culture of Euro-American print. In the case of Cusick's illustrations, the woodcuts may enact survivance by countering the distorting effect of English translation on the Longhouse origin stories. As his preface makes clear, Cusick was concerned whether his mastery of English was sufficient to the task of translating Iroquois histories. As Gerald Vizenor has observed, printed versions of oral traditions often "silence" stories by wresting them from their performative and participatory contexts and flattening out the resonance of tribal memories heard in Native language performance. Cusick's pictures offer a way around this problem, providing allusive depth and what Vizenor describes as both the "shadow" and "echo" necessary to the survivance of traditional folktales in print.[40]

For Silver Horn, the Saynday illustrations may tap into a specifically local and Kiowa version of what Vizenor has called "trickster hermeneutics." The Saynday stories, full as they are of "the ironies of descent and racialism, transmutation, third gender, and themes of transformation," offer the Kiowa artist a way out of the silencing translations of the literature of dominance. The most visceral proof of the supplementary and recuperative power of Silver Horn's folktale drawings comes from the captions provided for them at the National Anthropological Archive. In the case of one illustration in the Target Record Book (NAA MS 4252), for example, the archivist offers a cryptic caption: "Indian flying through the air." Yet Candace Greene explains that the oral tale actually recounts that "Saynday is blown into the air by the force of his flatulence after eating a root that he has been warned against."[41]

By thus reimagining nineteenth-century indigenous illustrations on their own terms, we may not only contextualize local practices but also critique the prevailing interpretive paradigm by which Native printed illustrations are judged. Walter Benjamin's description of the function of art in the modern era of rapid technological reproduction has been rather indiscriminately applied to all printed artwork. At one point in his famous essay, Benjamin makes an especially startling and unsettling claim in this regard, particularly in the context of Native American practice: "Technological reproducibility emancipates the work of art from its parasitic subservience to ritual." Liberated from this subservience, "art is revolutionized[,] . . . based on a different practice: politics."[42] The foregoing discussion of Native illustrators demonstrates, however, that Benjamin's easy equation of mechanical reproduction and demythologizing may not always apply. As I think even these few examples demonstrate, it really is not quite that simple. There is a great deal of both politics and spirituality in Native illustration, mechanically produced or otherwise. Neither "primitive" nor "modern," nineteenth-century indigenous illustration embodied a complex political stand both within and without Native communities. Outsiders might judge them as "rude," but these illustrations were life sustaining to the artists themselves and the communities they served.

Extending this argument a bit further, we can also better understand how the situation of print illustration in Indian Country dramatizes the broader "bibliography and sociology" of American Indian texts throughout the nineteenth century. First, as we have seen with the Benjamin argument, our current theoretical assumptions about the relationship of mechanical reproduction (in this case, movable type) to the so-called primitive state of Native societies in North America carries within it a reinscribed, and yet no less debilitating, articulation of the ideology of book conquest. Second, as the previous chapters have demonstrated, when examined from local, Native points of view, the many choices indigenous artists and authors made regarding alphabetic literacy, copyright, and pictorial illustration reflect the specific concerns of individuals and tribal communities who, more often than not, cautiously appropriated new technologies for the express purpose of revitalizing their societies, safeguarding their homelands, preserving their languages, and litigating their rights.

Epilogue

THE VIEW FROM RED CLOUD'S GRAVE

THE PRECEDING CHAPTERS have argued that books and writing played constitutive roles in eighteenth- and nineteenth-century tribal communities. From the northeastern woodlands to the Great Plains, alphabetic literacy and printed books became integral elements in emergent, transitional cultural formations for indigenous nations threatened by European imperialism. From the 1660s, when John Eliot successfully petitioned the English government to support a Native-language literacy enterprise in New England, through the development of modern publishing practices such as stereotype printing, proprietary authorship, and reprinting, Native peoples approached the coming of books as both opportunity and threat, engaging them in countless different ways.

I have arrived at this conclusion by applying interpretive techniques drawn from American Indian literary nationalist criticism and book studies to the manuscript and print practices of tribal communities across Indian Country during the eighteenth and nineteenth centuries. From the perspective of the history of the book, the book practices I have uncovered reaffirm that Native textuality "cannot be understood except as a phenomenal event." Although books were material objects in the imperial nexus, they entailed a "set of events, a point in time (or a moment in space) where certain communicative interchanges [were] being practiced."[1] Such events are understandable only within the context of the Native communities where they were produced and consumed and thus where they gained meaning. However much the subscribers to missionary journals like the *Panoplist* wished to believe in the ideology of book conquest, Native peoples clearly had other ideas. Thus my study of the production of alphabetic literacy and book objects in Indian Country has reaffirmed a central premise of book studies—that reading is fundamentally a culturally specific "act of construction."[2]

From the point of view of tribally centered, "nationalist" literary studies, print and manuscript books have provided essential "opportunities" for many Native peoples. The "acts of construction" that these texts have involved have never replaced cultural traditions but have merely supplemented them. In the process, they enabled many tribal communities to establish new kinds of "publics," discursive spaces made up of communicative practices and modes of social governance that helped them resist and regroup after forced removal, prohibition of religious practices, erasure of language, and genocidal warfare. Yet, as we have seen in the many case studies outlined above, each of these book practices imposed its own set of stresses on the community. More often than not, Native nations were brought to the brink of civil war by the factionalism involved in the construction of new public cultures.

My study concludes in the 1880s because that was the decade that saw both the infrastructure and the ideology of print culture established in enough tribal communities to support a new generation of Native writers and alphabetically literate activists. In their interactions with the federal government and the Euro-American literary establishment, these writers and activists would engage in the cultural formations and material practices that have been handed down to the American Indian intellectuals of today. By the end of the nineteenth century, a Native-run printing press operating on the Ojibwe reservation near Hagersville, Ontario, proudly printed an ad in its newspaper, the *Indian*: "Job printing on the reserves!"[3] In 1918, Garnett Mosley, a Chickasaw student from Bromide, Oklahoma, wrote a valedictory essay for the *Indian School Journal*, the official publication of the Chilocco Indian School, entitled "Why I Am a Printer." Mosley celebrates his "important vocation" as ranking "fifth in the United States" for an emerging middle class. Printing gave Mosley not only a lucrative career but also an art. "I am proud to be called a printer," Mosley wrote, "because I believe it is the greatest mechanical art of the age." Sounding very much like Elias Boudinot nearly a century earlier, Mosley invoked the powerful liberalizing influence of print in the public sphere: "The truths that pass through the printing press can almost never be lost."[4]

At the 1893 Columbian Exposition in Chicago, Potawatomi storyteller Simon Pokegon famously distributed a birch-bark codex, *The Red Man's Rebuke*, to interested attendees. The book's contents, a scathing critique of the "disappearing Indian" motif so common in American literature and even in some of the Exposition's exhibits, was tempered by its birch-bark covers, which seemed to hark back to earlier times, and marked the book as both keepsake and curiosity.[5] Around 1896, on the Pine Ridge Reservation in South Dakota, Lakota elder George Sword began compiling a ledger book manuscript of ceremonial practices, storytelling, and cosmology. Dr. James Walker, local government physician and amateur ethnographer, had engaged Sword in question-and-answer sessions concerning tribal traditions in the hope of producing his own monograph on "Sioux" life. Rather than accept the role of static "informant," however, Sword became an active tribal chronicler, writing his work in a Roman alphabet orthography whose style was not quite the spoken Lakota of the pre-reservation period but not entirely "inauthentic." It was simply a "new genre of Native writing." Sword's use of the codex format and his employment and modification of missionary-introduced orthography point to a set of Lakota-centered material practices that mirror so many of the bookmaking activities I have described across Indian Country in the pages above.

Yet book practices like George Sword's went largely unrecognized as "literature." It was not until 1968, the year that Kiowa author N. Scott Momaday was awarded the Pulitzer Prize for his novel *House Made of Dawn*, that the critical establishment in the United States officially acknowledged Indian authorship. Momaday's achievement, and the subsequent rapid publication of a series of well-received books by his Native contemporaries, led literary critic Kenneth Lincoln to christen the period the "Native American Renaissance."[6] Yet, as we have seen, behind this "rebirth" of imaginative literature in Indian Country lay a complex material culture of bookmaking that stretched back more than two hundred years. Laguna Pueblo author Leslie Silko, a prominent member of that "renaissance" generation, has throughout her career shown an intense interest in the materiality of books. Her major work, *Storyteller*, is, among other things, a book whose unique horizontal format recalls the ledger drawings of the Plains artists of a century before. Silko's privately printed *Sacred Water* (1993) goes even further in making the materiality of the book part of its message. The very paper it is printed on incorporates blue corn, sacred to the Laguna for its life-sustaining power.

Some critics in Indian Country, however, have questioned whether imaginative literature written by contemporary American Indians is really any different from books written by non-Indians. If all that makes Indian books "Indian" is "the ethnicity of [their] producers," then I would agree with Ojibwe writer and critic David Treuer that it is "crucial to make a distinction between reading books *as* culture and seeing books as *suggesting* culture."[7] In that case, as Treuer rightly observes, we would be forced to focus exclusively on the style of Native American fiction, insisting that and realizing that "style is culture; style creates the convincing semblance of culture on the page. Then the real question becomes: what traditions and habits of thought have been mobilized and by what means in Native American fiction?"[8]

This is a provocative question and one worthy of the debate Treuer's book has caused, but the activities I have traced in my own study lead us to a very different sense of "tradition" from the one Treuer espouses. Instead of "habits of thought," we have encountered traditions of corporately produced nonfiction that engaged bicultural practices to further the aims of local tribal communities. This study has demonstrated, in fact, that for the period from 1663 to 1880, despite the fact that, as Treuer notes, Native "books are constructed of the same materials available to anyone else," they were most often formed from material practices—methods of composition and printing, paratextual editing, prefacing, and appending—unique to American Indian peoples. I close with one final case study of Native textual production in the twentieth century whose material practices reflect the centrality of this "tradition" down to the present day.

The Seven Visions of Bull Lodge first appeared in bookstores in 1980, the direct result of the effect of the Red Power Movement on activists in the Gros Ventre Nation. The book recounts the life of Bull Lodge (ca. 1802 to 1886), Gros Ventre pipe carrier, warrior, and healer. As George Horse Capture, the book's editor, notes in his introduction, *The Seven Visions of Bull Lodge* was printed "as part of a larger effort of tribal cultural restoration." Horse Capture felt that many in the Gros Ventre community had "become lost, without direction or goal." The remedy, he believed, was for the community to "live from its own history." Knowledge of Bull Lodge's life, his visions, quests, and sacred powers, might point the way to communal and personal redemption. Making explicit the implicit practices of many Native writers and editors we have examined in this study, George Horse Capture also argued that publishing the healer's story was—by the *very act* of printing—a defiant gesture of cultural sovereignty: "This material belongs to the tribe, not to any individual. In order to commemorate this, the proceeds from this project will be used to establish a tribal education scholarship fund. Our present tribal structure precludes copyrighting this work in the name of the tribe. I have copyrighted it in my name on its behalf. This material must always be part of the White Clay People."[9]

Horse Capture's comments encapsulate the reasons why I have chosen to make a brief exploration of the material properties of *The Seven Visions of Bull Lodge* a coda to the preceding overview of the history of books in Indian Country. His introduction frankly acknowledges the work as a "composite composition" in which all the major players were tribal members. Bull Lodge told the stories in the book to his daughter Garter Snake just prior to his death in 1886. She, in turn, retold the tales to tribal member Frederick Peter Gone, who, as the "reservation field worker" in charge of collecting Native stories on the Fort Belknap Reservation in northern Montana for the Works Progress Administration, translated and inscribed the narrative in written English in 1942. As Joseph Gone, great-great-grandson of Frederick Gone, explains, the Garter Snake narratives were copied into a notebook "of roughly 170 pages of longhand script constituting 'Bull Lodge's Life' . . . [and] four brief commentaries external to the actual life narrative, as well as intermittent asides within the narrative proper."[10]

In Joseph Gone's locally centered and nuanced reading of this composite composition, the "meaning" of the Bull Lodge stories is inflected at every turn by the different motivations of each of its compilers. When Bull Lodge told his story to Garter Snake, he did so to "actively harness, circulate, and redistribute power." That is, Bull Lodge recited his visions and ascension to healer and pipe carrier not to assert his individual achievements but to share the power he was given with his community and to show how that power was meant to circulate after he was gone. For her part, Garter Snake repeated her father's words to Frederick Gone out of a profound sense of "duty, obligation, [and] responsibility owed." Her actions were part of "an outstanding kinship obligation" that came with her own role in the community as her father's chosen successor in certain medicine practices. Frederick Gone's motivations were twofold: "to salvage a range of declining knowledge and fading experi- ence" and to "explicate the 'supernatural powers' associated with the sacred Feathered Pipe." Because he and his contemporaries had "little (if any) first- hand experience with the ancient Pipe rituals," he used the opportunity af- forded him by his Works Progress Administration employers to collect and preserve tribal knowledge that was in danger of being lost forever. George Horse Capture committed Gone's manuscript to print in a similar gesture of preservation, with the added goal of establishing Gros Ventre intellectual sovereignty by copyrighting the material.[11]

The Bull Lodge, Garter Snake, Frederick Gone, and George Horse Cap- ture collaboration is also paradigmatic of the larger story of how oral traditions and tribal material practices became books in Indian Country from contact through the twenty-first century. The way that Frederick Gone recorded the story contains almost as much meaning as many of the story's details. He employed what Joseph Gone calls "judicious entextualization of Garter Snake's stylized narrative" in order to make her story available to twentieth-century Gros Ventre people. "From Gone's own account," Joseph Gone reports, "it seems evident that he sought to render an authoritative and reliable text that forever preserved a narrative explication of the meaning of 'supernatural powers' in pre-reservation Gros Ventre life." Like countless Native authors, editors, compilers, and press workers before him, Frederick Gone "purposely recontextualized and redeployed" Garter Snake's oral rendition into a narrative format and manuscript codex of his own making. Gone translated from Gros Ventre into English as he went (much as Benjamin Williams did with Chainbreaker's story), expressing full confidence in the transparency of his translation. He also provided marginal asides that contextualized the elder's statements and explored their meaning for his contemporaries on the reservation. For his part, George Horse Capture took a role somewhat akin to that of Elias Johnson. He "tidied up" Gone's manuscript, shaping it into a more conventional autobiography, writing a defiant introduction to assert the text's sovereignty, and securing copyright for his and his kinsmen's labors.[12]

Like so many Native codices that went before it, *Seven Visions of Bull Lodge* emerged into print through a series of "gradualist" tribal practices that were neither completely new nor especially nontraditional. Such practices certainly were not new to the hundreds of Native American writers who came of age in the twentieth century trying to reconcile the printed word to the oral traditions and material practices of their grandparents' generation.

At the conclusion of *Bead on an Anthill*, Delphine Red Shirt's memoir of growing up at Pine Ridge in the 1960s, the Lakota author finds herself, a girl of sixteen, at the site of Red Cloud's grave. On the "old side" of the reservation cemetery, where students from her Catholic boarding school went "on slow afternoons," a three-foot-high block of cement marks the resting place of the Lakota leader most responsible for bringing books and print to his nation. From that vantage point, at the end of her story, poised to graduate from high school and eventually embark on a writing career, the narrator ponders Red Cloud's meaning for contemporary Lakota people.

The view from Red Cloud's grave shows Red Shirt that literacy implies a kind of freedom, and she acknowledges the "foresight" of this leader in a time of great turmoil for his nation. Without her hard-won literacy, Red Shirt reflects, "I would not have known that Red Cloud was buried here, and that he, too, understood these things: how hard it was to be Lakota in a world where Lakota is not the language of choice." Inspired by Red Cloud's leadership, she writes a poem in the voice of the great leader:

> Walk frontward and learn of the white man's ways, of his writings,
>   his books, and his language.
> But most important, learn to walk side by side with him, as a friend.
> Perhaps his books will tell you what you wish to know.

In Delphine Red Shirt's view, Red Cloud chose alphabetic literacy not to escape his culture but to preserve it. Although he followed the Catholic teachings of the fathers who brought writing and books to Pine Ridge, late in life "he said that when we Lakota relied only on our relationship with T'unkasila and lived according to the old beliefs . . . that we would live happily and die satisfied. He looked at what the wasicu (non-Indians) brought to us, after they put us on the reservation, and he saw how inadequate it was for the Lakota, how insufficient." Books do not replace Lakota tradition. They can only supplement it. The author concludes her memoir by pondering whether she, sitting on Red Cloud's grave, is "a young sapling grafted onto an ancient tree, whether I absorbed some nourishment from him, my ancestor whose spirit remains firmly planted there."[13]

Notes

Prologue

1. In the following discussion, I use the English translation of this manuscript, as it appears in Tac, "Indian Life and Customs," 94.

2. Ibid.

3. In *Kiowa Humanity*, Jacki Rand discusses Pratt's assimilation plans for the Fort Marion prisoners and how one Kiowa artist he enlisted to produce ledger drawings, Wo-haw, probably employed the art form to "express experiences and observations that radically challenged the discussions and patterns of the colonizers" (102).

Introduction

1. Apess, *On Our Own Ground*, 120. Barry O'Connell argues that even though *Experiences* was not published until 1835, this passage "seems unambiguously a reference to *A Son of the Forest*, not an entirely new second autobiography, and thus suggests that some, if not most of *Experiences* was drafted before the writing of *A Son of the Forest* in 1828/29" (120n1). If O'Connell is right, then Apess had conceived of his entire career as a writer (and perhaps his whole public self-presentation) in terms of a broader culture of the book.

2. In 1653, Eliot had produced a combined primer and catechism in the Algonquian language. Between 1653 and 1663, he released portions of the Bible as they became available in translation. His efforts culminated in the 1663 Bible, with its complete Old and New Testaments all in one volume. See Eliot, *Eliot Tracts* (13–14), for more detail on the chronology of these texts.

3. Rice, *Transformation of Authorship*, 3.

4. Crain, *Story of A*, 4.

5. Gilmore, *Reading Becomes a Necessity*, title page.

6. Hall, *Cultures of Print*, 43, 51.

7. See also Willard B. Walker, "Native Writing Systems," 158–86; and Warkentin, "In Search of 'the Word,'" 16.

8. DeMallie and Parks, "Plains Indian Native Literatures," 126. Discussing the Lakota language manuscripts of George Sword (1847–1910), DeMallie has argued that such texts "are not . . . simply written versions of oral narratives but are instead a new type of written narrative" (126).

9. 18 U.S. Code, Section 1151.

10. My point here is not that oral traditions reached their perfection in printed versions, but merely that they entered into printed texts at this time, at the instigation of both Native and non-Native writers. This book will explore the vexed relationships that

obtained among the printed, oral, and semasiographic sign systems throughout Indian Country in the nineteenth century.

11. Gilroy, *Black Atlantic*, 3, 11.

12. Elmer, "Black Atlantic Archive," 161. In a similar way, historian Richard White has described a specific geographical location, the *Pays d'en Haut* (the Great Lakes region), during the seventeenth and eighteenth centuries as having given rise to an analogous field of cultural production he calls the "middle ground," "the place in between: in between cultures, peoples, and in between empires and the nonstate world of villages" (*Middle Ground*, x). Philip Deloria's recent reappraisal of White's work focuses on "new cultural production within the frame of encounter" ("What Is the Middle Ground?" 23). Only by underscoring the *new* cultural productions of Native peoples as they appear within the frame of encounters with Europeans, Deloria argues, can we move beyond failed narratives of the American Indian colonial experience that ignore "critical points of relation between Indians and non-Indians that lie outside military conflict, political negotiation, and economic exchange" (23).

13. Young Bear, *Black Eagle Child*, 78.

14. Womack, *Red on Red*, 60.

15. Cheyfitz, "(Post)Colonial Construction of Indian Country," 55.

16. Womack, *Red on Red*, 11, 76. Alyssa Mt. Pleasant has articulated the situation that scholars now face: "How do historians understand alternating periods of plenty and times of deprivation; the regular, disruptive role alcohol played in American Indian lives; the impact of colonial encroachment, manifest in religious, economic, and territorial challenges? Do we see devastation and decline, adaptation and persistence, some combination of the two?" ("After the Whirlwind," 52).

17. Donaldson, "Writing the Talking Stick," 47, 2.

18. Axtell, "Power of Print," 304.

19. Wogan, "Perceptions of European Literacy," 408.

20. On the many "literacies" present in early New England, for example, see Wyss and Bross, introduction, *Early Native Literacies*: "Recent scholarship has worked to complicate [a] neat division between oral and literate culture. . . . Material objects played — and continue to play a significant role in Algonquian communicative practices. Burial goods, basket patterns, pictographs, mats that line the interiors of wigwams, and even utensils reinforce oral exchanges with physical inscriptions" (4).

21. Harriot, *Brief and True Report*, 27.

22. Ibid.

23. Dowd, *Spirited Resistance*, 106–7.

24. Galland, *Chronicles*, 9. Germaine Warkentin comments, "Most difficult to understand in terms of the history of the book, is the semasiographic or sign-oriented level of [Native] discourse, in the material form of wampums" and other material signifying practices ("In Search of 'the Word,'" 3).

25. Lisa Brooks, *Common Pot*, 8, 12. In a similar way, Robert Warrior's *People and the Word* explores the "intellectual trade routes" through which Native nonfiction traveled (181–87).

26. Mignolo, *Darker Side of the Renaissance*, 76; Darnton, "What Is the History of Books," 22. Of their extratextual nature, Darnton explains, "Books also refuse to be contained within a single discipline when treated as objects of study. Neither history nor literature nor economics nor sociology nor bibliography can do justice to all aspects of the life of a book" (22).

27. Mignolo, *Darker Side of the Renaissance*, 76, 83 (emphasis added).

28. Timothy Alden, *Account of Sundry Missions*, 74.

29. Kirkland, *Journals*, 24.

30. Saunt, *New Order of Things*, 201.

31. Womack, *Red on Red*, 15, 16.

32. Henry Rowe Schoolcraft, *Bibliographical Catalogue*, unpaginated preface.

33. McKenzie, *Bibliography and the Sociology of Texts*, 1, 5.

34. Krupat, "Native American Autobiography," 184. The critical discourse surrounding Native texts produced prior to the twentieth century is often framed by recourse to binomial categories (oral/written; center/margin; white/Indian; assimilation/authenticity; Christian/traditional), which, as David Murray has shown in *Forked Tongues*, do little more than essentialize difference and efface the diversity of Native American textual expression in the first three centuries after European contact.

35. McKenzie, *Bibliography and the Sociology of Texts*, 130. As Sidonie Smith and Julia Watson have observed, "The language of writing, the means of publication — publishing house, editor, distribution markets . . . are associated with the colonizer's domination" (*Women, Autobiography*, 47). Indian books and manuscripts (and autobiographies in particular) find themselves immersed in what Philippe Lejeune has succinctly described as "the vicious circle imposed by the market of cultural goods" (*On Autobiography*, 197).

36. Warkentin, "In Search of 'the Word,'" 3 (italic in original).

37. McKenzie, *Bibliography and the Sociology of Texts*, 13, 15.

38. Basso, "Ethnography of Writing," 432.

39. Erdrich, *Books and Islands*, 99.

Chapter 1

1. Bartlett, *Historical Sketch of the Missions*, 1.

2. Ibid., 10.

3. Mignolo, *Darker Side of the Renaissance*, 77.

4. Bross, *Dry Bones*, 2.

5. Thatcher, *Brief Account*, 4. See also Laura Stevens's excellent study of the missionary movements in America, *Poor Indians*. Rather "than asking what missionary writings tell us about Indians and their responses to the colonial presence," however, Stevens's "book asks how these texts encouraged their readers to think about their own emotional responses . . . [and] to untangle the knot of ambivalent benevolence" (4).

6. Matthew Brown, *Pilgrim and the Bee*, 179, 180.

7. Increase Mather, *A Brief History* (1676), in Slotkin and Folsom, *So Dreadful a Judgment*, 84.

8. Quoted in Round, *By Nature and by Custom Cursed*, 256.

9. John Eliot, quoted in Matthew Brown, *Pilgrim and the Bee*, 185.

10. See David Murray, *Forked Tongues*, whose aim "is to demonstrate the complex and various ways in which the process of translation, cultural as well as linguistic[,] is obscured or effaced in a wide variety of texts which claim to be representing or describing Indians, and what cultural and ideological assumptions underlie such effacement" (1).

11. Matthew Brown, *Pilgrim and the Bee*, 180–81.

12. *Clear Sunshine*, in Eliot, *Eliot Tracts*, 118.

13. Anonymous, *Day Breaking If Not the Sun Rising of the Gospel* (1640), in Eliot, *Eliot Tracts*, 85. Joshua Bellin argues that scenes of "Indian play" in John Eliot missionary writings offer us a unique opportunity to "acknowledge the unequal yet joint context

within which early American literature and culture arose . . . through encountering, contesting, performing . . . Others" ("John Eliot's Playing Indian," 29).

14. Matthew Brown comments, "The educative role of the written word only partially explains its function in the New England missionary context, especially given the relative failure of the English Protestants to convert native peoples. . . . Another appeal relied on the extraverbal symbolism of monumentality, and appeal embedded in Eliot's *tabula abrasa* trope . . . where the linguistic codes of imaginative expression and the bibliographic codes of documentary materials built a sensory aesthetic that justified Anglo superiority" (*Pilgrim and the Bee*, 194).

15. Matthew Brown describes the process as follows: "Eliot invented a visible language, wherein literacy was to be cultivated through a system of meaning new to both Amerindians and Europeans" (ibid., 195).

16. These and the following statistics on the Eliot tracts are derived from Eliot, *Eliot Tracts*, 13.

17. Matthew Brown, *Pilgrim and the Bee*, 182.

18. Bross, *Dry Bones*, 54.

19. For this comparison, I have used *Holy Bible Containing the Old Testament and the New: Newly Translated Out of the Originall Tongues, and with the Former Translations Diligently Compared and Revised*, a commonly reproduced Bible of the period. The quotation on typography is from Gutjahr and Benton, *Illuminating Letters*, 2.

20. For Algonquian translation, I rely on John Trumbull's *Natick Dictionary* (1909). David Silverman argues that there is evidence in the Algonquian Bible's diction that early on the Native translators and compilers were shading the print work toward local meaning, as when "the advice of these Indians convinced Eliot to title the Gospels 'Wun-aun-chemok-aonk' drawing on the native word, 'Wun-nam-moo-waonk,' meaning truth" ("Indians, Missionaries," 22).

21. The quotation is from John Sergeant, missionary to the Housatonic. Although he is speaking about translation of English words in general in an eighteenth-century mission, it reflects a widely held opinion in Eliot's day (quoted in Hopkins, *Historical Memoirs*, 154–55).

22. Ibid., 155.

23. Matthew Brown, *Pilgrim and the Bee*, 179.

24. Bross, *Dry Bones*, 68.

25. Wyss, *Writing Indians*, 50.

26. Ibid., 11.

27. Bragdon and Goddard, *Native Writings in Massachusett*, xvii.

28. Ibid., 439.

29. Silverman, "Indians, Missionaries," 5.

30. Quoted in Matthew Brown, *Pilgrim and the Bee*, 195. Silverman tallies 119 question-and-answer sessions that Cotton held during a twenty-month period ("Indians, Missionaries," 21).

31. Eliot to Baxter, 1696, Eliot, *Eliot Tracts*, 430.

32. Matthew Brown, *Pilgrim and the Bee*, 3.

33. Eliot to Baxter, 1696, Eliot, *Eliot Tracts*, 430.

34. The use of the term "steady seller" to describe seventeenth-century New England's prolific devotional literature is explored by David D. Hall in *Worlds of Wonder*, 55–57. Matthew Brown, *Pilgrim and the Bee*, expands this discussion to include the "phenom-

enology" of the devotional reading practices instantiated by these steady sellers in New England.

35. Chartier, *Order of Books*, 13, 14.

36. Ibid., 13.

37. Trumbull, *Natick Dictionary*, 120–21.

38. Kristina Bross argues that Eliot's specifically millenarian representation of Native peoples as the "dry bones" mentioned in the book of Ezekial must be read in the context of a transatlantic cultural field where Eliot participated in an ongoing debate among English men and women as to the nature and timing of the last days. As Bross notes, the "propagation of the gospels was elevated to part of the providential design" (*Dry Bones*, 9).

39. Book dissemination could rely on a large body of literate Native ministers and lay leaders. Jean O'Brien lists over twelve Native preachers and deacons operating in New England during the period from 1650 to 1720, including Waban, John Speen, Nishohkou, Wuttasukoopauin, Anthony, Piambouhou, Tuckapawillin, Daniel Takawampbait, John Neesumin, John Thomas, Josiah Shonks, and Joseph Ephrraim (*Dispossession by Degrees*, 57–58, 119–20).

40. Eliot to Baxter, 1696, Eliot, *Eliot Tracts*, 430.

41. Ibid.

42. Matthew Brown observes that Hiacoombe's Bible was treated as an "amulet" (*Pilgrim and the Bee*, 199); and Electa F. Jones notes that the "good Book" was buried with a Native parishioner at Stockbridge (*Stockbridge, Past and Present*, 29). David Silverman, however, argues that these beliefs in the "magic" of books were not "much different from English 'horse-shed' Christians, as [David] Hall calls them, who professed Christianity . . . but dabbled in the occult in private" ("Indians, Missionaries," 27).

43. Quoted in Lepore, *Name of War*, 31.

44. Chartier, *Order of Books*, 3, 8.

45. Crain, *Story of A*, 42.

46. Monaghan, "She Loved to Read," 505.

47. In *Dispossession by Degrees*, Jean O'Brien terms the descendants of these literate families "proprietary lineages" (126) and charts the course of nineteen such lineages in the Praying Town of Natick throughout the eighteenth century.

48. Monaghan discusses parental roles and concludes that "Indian girls taught to read, whether at home or school, were not also taught to write" ("She Loved to Read," 507).

49. Bragdon, "Interstices of Literacy," 123.

50. Winslow, *Glorious Progress*, in Eliot, *Eliot Tracts*, 152.

51. O'Brien, *Dispossession by Degrees*, 4.

52. Anthropologists David Schmidt and Murdena Marshall describe the many uses of manuscript books written in a nonalphabetic script called *komqwejwi'kasikl* in Mi'kmaq communities from the seventeenth century to the present day. See especially their diagram on page 13 of a prayer book with facing pages written for reading in opposite directions (*Mi'kmaq Hieroglyphic Prayers*, 1–15).

53. Lepore, *Name of War*, 52.

54. Wyss, *Writing Indians*, 31.

55. Dwight, *Travels in New England*, 351.

56. Quoted in Szasz, *Indian Education*, 118. I have compiled James Printer's biography from Szasz and from Wyss.

57. Wyss, *Writing Indians*, 38.

58. Ibid., 43.

59. Rowlandson, *Sovereignty and Goodness of God*, 76.

60. Ibid., 86.

61. Lepore argues that "although the shape and size of the possibilities" for Sassamon's motives vary, "behind each of them lies the specter of John Sassamon's position as a cultural mediator . . . and for Sassamon, the ability to hold this mediating position was predicated on his bilingualism and literacy" (*Name of War*, 25).

62. Quoted in Wyss, *Writing Indians*, 175.

63. Lepore believes that "what the colonists moved toward (but never fully embraced) in their writings about King Philip's War, was the idea that Indians were not, in fact, human, or else were humans of such a vastly different race as to be . . . biologically inferior to Europeans" (*Name of War*, 167).

64. Quoted in O'Brien, *Dispossession by Degrees*, 88. O'Brien notes the rapid depopulation of Praying Towns, commenting that when "Grindall Rawson and Samuel Danforth visited the plantation in 1698," they found "only 10 church members, out of 110 adults and 70 children under the age of sixteen who were living there" (ibid.).

65. Monaghan notes that the "striking lack of commitment to presenting the Bible in Massachusett, along with the new insistence after 1700 on bilingual texts . . . is symptomatic of a change in the official attitude toward native Americans" and that "the 1720 version of the *Primer* fairly oozed with anti-Indian sentiment" (*Learning to Read and Write*, 78–79).

66. The phrase "proprietary lineages" is from O'Brien, *Dispossession by Degrees*, 126.

67. Wheelock, *Plain and Faithful Narrative*, 11.

68. Ibid.

Chapter 2

1. Joseph Johnson, *To Do Good*, 179.

2. Gustafson, *Eloquence Is Power*, xvi.

3. Shields, *Civil Tongues*, xviii.

4. On "unlettered" Native peoples, see MacLean, "Concurring Opinion."

5. Lisa Brooks explains that seventeenth- and eighteenth-century Algonquians, Wabanaki, and Haudenosaunee (with some tribal differences) viewed the landscape they inhabited and their political autonomy as coterminous, conceiving of "Native space as a network of villages connected by rivers and relations" that made them "an independent people" (*Common Pot*, 137–38).

6. Ibid., 43.

7. Ibid., 67.

8. Joanna Brooks, "This Indian World," 4.

9. O'Brien, *Dispossession by Degrees*, 63, 45.

10. Ibid., 67, 68.

11. Ibid., 75. For more on Wompas, see Pulsipher, "Subjects unto the Same King."

12. O'Brien notes, for example, that the process began "in 1715 . . . [with the] dramatic reconfiguration of their land management and distribution practices" (*Dispossession by Degrees*, 101), and thus "the English proprietary system created different classes of individuals with greater and lesser community rights. Proprietorship carries the privilege of future rights to the remaining undivided land" (104). Yet, despite the increasing "bureaucratization of inheritance" (114) and other colonizing practices, Natick Native

peoples continued to be culturally and linguistically "Indian" throughout the eighteenth century.

13. Gustafson, *Eloquence Is Power*, 75.

14. Ibid., 91.

15. Joseph Johnson, *To Do Good*, 185.

16. Gustafson, *Eloquence Is Power*, xvii.

17. Fish, *Old Light on Separate Ways*, 5.

18. Ibid., 29, 52, 40. The struggle over different forms of literacy that these scenes from the Narragansett community illustrate was replicated across the Native spaces of the Northeast. At the Moravian missions on the Muskingum River led by David Zeisberger, local people were divided over the efficacy of literacy in Christian and other forms of spirituality. See Wellenreuther and Wessel, *Moravian Missionary Diaries*, 37–41.

19. "Protestant vernacular" is David Hall's term for the "distinctive mode of literacy" that held sway in New England in the seventeenth century (*Worlds of Wonder*, 18).

20. Occom, *Collected Writings*, 74.

21. Ibid., 51.

22. Samuel Penhallow comments in his *History*, "God has made them a terrible Scourge for the punishment of . . . that very Sin of ours in neglecting the welfare of their souls" (in the nonpaginated introduction).

23. Occom, *Collected Writings*, 53.

24. Sergeant, *Letter*, 3, 5, 7.

25. See Timothy Dwight's comments in *Travels in New England* (76) and Titus Smith's observations in Wheelock's *Brief Narrative*. Laura Stevens has provided a fine analysis of how these tropes of husbandry entered into missionary literature, in *Poor Indians*, 34–61.

26. Wheelock, *Brief Narrative*, 43.

27. Joseph Johnson, *To Do Good*, 164.

28. Sir William Johnson was made a civil leader by the Haudenosaunee in 1760 and participated in many of their councils.

29. Stiles, *Literary Diary of Ezra Stiles*, 25.

30. Kirkland, *Journals*, 157.

31. Occom represented his community in its grievances against schoolmaster Robert Clelland. His 1764 petition to missionary authorities offers a telling view of the educational priorities of the Native community. The Mohegan petitioners, Occom wrote, felt that Clelland had taken too many English children into his classroom, who "take room from Indian Children." Parents particularly resented Clelland's practice of keeping Indian children from the fire in winter, presumably to make room for the English children. He also angered the community by taking "Indian horses without asking leave of the owners" and because he had "no government or authority . . . neither does he hear his Schollars carefully." In addition, Clelland "does not Pray in his School Neither does he teach the Indian Children English Manners" (*Collected Writings*, 145–46).

32. Ibid., 56.

33. Ibid.

34. Chartier, *Order of Books*, 8.

35. Ibid.

36. See note 31 above.

37. McCallum, *Letters*, 268.

38. Shields, *Civil Tongues*, xviii.

39. Occom, *Collected Writings*, 101.

40. Kaestle, *Literacy in the United States*, 53.

41. Joseph Johnson, *To Do Good*, 120.

42. Ibid., 109, 163.

43. Occom, *Collected Writings*, 130.

44. Quoted in Kelsay, *Joseph Brant*, 84.

45. Stiles, *Literary Diary of Ezra Stiles*, 134.

46. Occom, *Collected Writings*, 57, 53.

47. Chartier, *Order of Books*, 8.

48. The quotation is from Richardson, *Indian Preacher*, 74. Stephanie Fitzgerald reminds us that to "consider early native [material culture] as texts is to decenter or problematize current critical conceptions of early Native literacies and textualities. What would a history of native print culture look like if it included three-dimensional texts such as baskets or tipis?" ("Cultural Work," 88).

49. Occom, *Collected Writings*, 95, 101.

50. Manuscript autobiography, in Eleazar Williams Papers, Box 2, Newberry Library, Chicago.

51. Occom, *Collected Writings*, 42, 95.

52. Thatcher, *Brief Account*, 3, lists over 300 books circulated in the northeast backcountry during this period. Not all were for Native converts, but many spellers and primers were specifically set aside for this group.

53. Occom, *Collected Writings*, 83, 150.

54. Love, *Samson Occom*, 47.

55. For a discussion of the singular popularity of writing manuals like *The Universal Penman* (1735), from which practice aphorisms likes these were copied, see Monaghan, *Learning to Read and Write*, 279.

56. Lisa Brooks does concede, however, that many Native communities began to cover themselves by demanding that written versions of their oral transactions be recorded, as the Housatonic sachem Konkapot did at the Deerfield Conference in 1735 (*Common Pot*, 47).

57. Monaghan discusses parental roles and concludes that "Indian girls taught to read, whether at home or school, were not also taught to write" ("She Loved to Read," 507).

58. Joseph Johnson, *To Do Good*, 156.

59. Love, *Samson Occom*, 46.

60. Joseph Johnson, *To Do Good*, 108, 254.

61. Laura Murray describes Johnson's methods of producing these manuscript books in some detail, in "Joseph Johnson's Diary," 79–80.

62. Missionary Charles Barclay, for example, noted that Native converts in the Mohawk Valley in 1737 "write as good a hand as myself" (quoted in Lisa Brooks, *Common Pot*, 48).

63. Manuscript autobiography, in Eleazar Williams Papers, Box 2, Newberry Library, Chicago.

64. Joseph Johnson, *To Do Good*, 256.

65. Laura Murray, "Pray Sir, Consider a Little," 21, 20.

66. Occom, *Collected Writings*, 104.

67. John Parrish, "Book Relative to Indian Affairs," 235, Newberry Library, Chicago; Joseph Johnson, *To Do Good*, 232; John Alden, "Cherokee Archive," 240. For an exhaustive list of the appearance of such papers in eighteenth-century reports from Indian Country, see Shoemaker, *Strange Likeness*, 160n32.

68. The edition of the sermon that contains this autograph and marginalia is part of the Ayer Collection at the Newberry Library in Chicago.

69. Joseph Johnson, *To Do Good*, 151, 187.

70. Joanna Brooks, "Six Hymns," 70.

71. Ibid., 70, 81, 78. Brooks also discusses the way in which Occom's hymnal served as both a "template" and a source for later Anglo-American songbooks like *Divine Hymns* (1791) of Joshua Smith (1760–95) and how Occom's own text was printed several times, in 1785, 1787, and 1792.

72. In 1771, Ezra Stiles commented that he "commonly [wrote] two sermons a Week; tho some are only heads and leading sentiments" (Stiles, *Literary Diary of Ezra Stiles*, 166).

73. Occom, *Collected Writings*, 24.

74. Similarly, Occom took advantage of his marginal social position in a 1787 exposition of Luke 10:27, in which his authority as an explicator of texts turns ironically on whether his audience believes *anything* he says: "Now I either understand this Text or I do not, I have either given Some thing of the Sense of our text or I am in a misstate about it—But let it be as it will. I have given my opinion upon the Text and it is either a false Doctrine, or it is a true one,—and as I have given my opinion upon it, So I shall now draw some Infrences from it." In yet another sermon, Occom combines tribal rhetorical protocols with Pauline epistolary discourse to engage his Indian listeners: "To all the Indians in this Boundless Continent,—I am an Indian also, your Brother and you are my Brethren the Bone of my Bone and Flesh of my Flesh" ("To All the Indians in This Boundless Continent" (1784), in Occom, *Collected Writings*, 196).

75. Ibid., 291. There are many other examples.

76. Although Wheelock's educational system was not the only one in British North America, it was in many ways the most influential. For a discussion of Anglican teaching among the Mohawk during the period, see Monaghan, *Learning to Read and Write*, 166–89. The Moravians were also fairly successful, producing several printed primers in Delaware and offering education at Stockbridge to influential Mahican sachem Hendrick Aupaumut. For the latest discussion of the Moravians' mission in this period, see the introduction to Wellenreuther and Wessel, *Moravian Missionary Diaries*, 1–88.

77. For a literary anthology that follows the literacy production of the Wheelock complex from the Northeast to Wisconsin, see Tigerman, *Wisconsin Indian Literature*.

Chapter 3

1. *Panoplist* 14, no. 5 (May 1818): 211.

2. McMurtrie, *Jotham Meeker*, 55.

3. *Baptist Missionary Magazine* 29 (1849): 403.

4. Conn, *History's Shadow*, 32.

5. See Gustafson, "Nations of Israelites," 31–53; Conn, *History's Shadow*, 5, 119–44; and Galland, *Chronicles*, 9.

6. See David Oestreicher's debunking of the Walam Olum, a birch-bark scroll thought in the nineteenth century to be the historical record of the Delaware Nation ("Unmaking the Walam Olum," 14–20). Steven Conn discusses William Pidgeon's *Traditions of Decodah* (1858) as an example of the mound builder myth (*History's Shadow*, 130), but Pidgeon's work also makes the commonplace argument that the Indians' "book" was the landscape itself, thus displacing the codex from a real to a mythical presence in the backcountry.

7. Mitchell, *Missionary Pioneer*, 33.

8. This quotation comes from the typescript of Riggs's manuscript history, "Sketches of the Dakota Mission," 41, in Stephen R. Riggs and Family Papers, Minnesota Historical Society, St. Paul. "Heretofore," Riggs observed, "the *wowape* had consisted of rude paintings or hieroglyphs. . . . So when the hieroglyphs of language were first introduced among them, and arbitrary signs made in the ashes with a stick, or drawn with chalk on a board, spelled out words that they had been accustomed to speak and hear, that also they called *wowape*" (ibid., 41).

9. Ibid., 43.

10. Quoted in Berkhofer, *Salvation and the Savage*, 109, 18.

11. See Hawkins, *Historical Notices*, 28.

12. *Baptist Missionary Magazine* 21, no. 7 (1841): 234. Publication numbers for each of the individual mission presses are included in the final pages of the missionary societies' yearly reports.

13. Nord, *Faith in Reading*, 66.

14. Riggs, "Sketches of the Dakota Mission," in Stephen R. Riggs and Family Papers, Minnesota Historical Society, St. Paul, 43.

15. Nord, *Faith in Reading*, 48, 84, 115.

16. White, *Middle Ground*, x.

17. Merrell, *Into the American Woods*, 51. Stephen Riggs described his Dakota Mission as "our miniature Babel" to one of his correspondents. See Stephen R. Riggs and Family Papers, Correspondence, August 23, 1838, Minnesota Historical Society, St. Paul.

18. Merrell, *Into the American Woods*, 55. As I noted in the introduction, Philip Deloria argues that "middle ground" remains important as a term in early American studies because it continues to focus our attention on "new cultural production within the frame of encounter" ("What Is the Middle Ground?" 23). Print was one such critical "new cultural production" that emerged from the middle ground of nineteenth-century Indian Country.

19. Saunt, *New Order of Things*, 154. On the backcountry, see Hinderaker and Mancall, *At the Edge of Empire*, in which the authors define the region as the vast territories beyond "core settlements" where Euro-American immigrants encountered existing Native American settlements.

20. Saunt, *New Order of Things*, 6.

21. Martin, *Sacred Revolt*, 110. The term "points of contact" draws upon Berkhofer, *Salvation and the Savage*; Teute, *Contact Points*; and Pratt, *Imperial Eyes*. Pratt defines these "contact zones" as "social spaces where disparate cultures meet, clash, and grapple with each other, often in highly asymmetrical relations of domination and subordination" (4).

22. The journals of the Brainerd Mission in Cherokee country report that the Cherokee were especially disturbed by their mission's participation in U.S. government plans to build a road through the heart of Cherokee country (Phillips and Phillips, *Brainerd Journal*, 10). Comments like this one from a missionary to the Ojibwe are common in the missionary publications of the period: "We are becoming rich by impoverishing them, and they are as sensible of it as we are" (*Baptist Missionary Magazine* 24, no. 5 (May 1844): 108.

23. Severance, *Narratives of Early Mission Work*, 133, 141.

24. Phillips and Phillips, *Brainerd Journal*, 136, 200.

25. Severance, *Narratives of Early Mission Work*, 159.

26. See Schoenberg, *Lapwai Mission Press*, 39. The journal of the Cherokee Mission at Brainerd notes: "Dr. Worcester was with us [and] he thought it highly important that we should have a set of maps, and globes, especially a territorial globe" (Phillips and Phillips, *Brainerd Journal*, 232). It records in great detail the effort to "convert" one Cherokee man's traditional method of keeping time to the missionaries' system (ibid., 312).

27. William Gilmore has argued that the period between 1780 and 1835 in America is marked by "a series of profound but subtle material and cultural changes [that] altered the way life was lived in rural society" (*Reading Becomes a Necessity*, 17). One of the main factors responsible for this change was "the creation of a new regional communications environment . . . based on printed and written forms" (ibid.). Gilmore defines this "printed and written culture as a form of knowledge about self and the world received and transmitted by means of the alphabet on paper in print or handwriting" (ibid., 20).

28. Martin, *Sacred Revolt*, 115.

29. Mitchell, *Missionary Pioneer*, 26.

30. Ibid., 27–28.

31. Williams to John Taylor, March 28, 1822, in Eleazar Williams Papers, Newberry Library, Chicago.

32. The journals of the Brainerd School complain of itinerant "sham school masters" (Phillips and Phillips, *Brainerd Journal*, 123) who take advantage of the frontier literacy gap. Mitchell, *Missionary Pioneer*, frames John Stewart's mission among the Wyandot as a morality tale in which traders work against the missionary, using their influence with Native leaders to spread false rumors about his motives. Ojibwe writer William Warren turns this trope on its head in his *History of the Ojibway People*, presenting the *coureurs du bois* as "honest" if illiterate. See Warren, *History*, 108, 123, 225.

33. For an interesting interpretation of the culturally centrifugal power of the mass production of print in the nineteenth-century American literary marketplace, see Loughran, *Republic in Print*, 303–69.

34. Cincinnati's growth as one such regional publishing center, as well as its role in distributing books printed from stereotype plates produced in the East, is described in Sutton, *Western Book Trade*, 73–81. In addition to the records of the mission presses discussed below, see Finley, *Life among the Indians*: "If they do not sufficiently understand what they read, it is for want of suitable books in their own tongue" (353). The Detroit-based Episcopal missionary Frederick O'Meara comments both on the power of print to forestall mistakes made by translators of missionary discourse (25) and on the dangers of "Romanism" as a nonscriptural and nonprint theology (35), in his *Report*.

35. Warkentin, "In Search of 'the Word,'" 3. See also Willard B. Walker, "Native Writing Systems," 158–86.

36. Pickering's work is the apotheosis of antebellum ethnology centered at the American Philosophical Society in Philadelphia. Students of indigenous language like Stephen DuPonceau (1760–1844) and Albert Gallatin (1761–1849) began to explore the "national" meaning of Native languages. A founding member of the American Ethnological Society, Gallatin was secretary of the treasury under both Jefferson and Madison and an avid student of American Indian languages. His *A Table of the Indian Languages of the United States* (1826), as Robert Bieder observes, "accepted several givens: all mankind constituted a single species; man progressed from savagery through barbarism to civilization" (*Science Encounters the Indian*, 32).

37. Pickering, *Essay on a Uniform Orthography*, 8–9.

38. Ibid., 3. Popular writers echoed Pickering's beliefs that "our tongue has been en-

riched by them, and they will doubtless ever remain as part and parcel of our vocabulary." The author of "Indebtedness of the English to the Indian Languages of America," for example, found it "a pleasing thought; for the vestiges of the original occupants of this country are rapidly passing away; such indistinct landmarks as they had are soon to be obliterated. . . . But the language is imperishable. In this the Indian still lives; in this he enters into the academies of science and the halls of art; in this he speaks with our statesmen and sings with our poets; he sits at our firesides; he lives in our life . . . [as] a benefactor to our literature and our race" (Nason, "Indebtedness of the English," 309).

39. For an interesting description of how haphazard the production of books for the Six Nations had been in the eighteenth century, see O'Callaghan, "Papers Relating to the Six Nations," 292–396. Sir William Johnson initially contracted the Reverend Barclay to print an edition of a Mohawk prayer book in 1762, but when Barclay contacted "Mr. Weyman, the printer," he was told, "We are put to prodigioys Difficulty to print such language (in form) in North America, where we have not the command of a Letter-maker's founding house to suit ourselves in the particular Sorts required, such as—g's, k's, y's &c. &c—when it had been in the Engllish tongue, we could make much greater dispatch—but at present, 'tis absolutely impossible—I have been obliged to borrow sundry letters from my brother Printers even to complete this present half sheet" (ibid., 334). Weyman died in 1768, and the unfinished book was found in individual sheets lying about his printing office.

40. John Norton Papers, Newberry Library, Chicago.

41. Rayman, "Joseph Lancaster's Monitorial System," 398.

42. The New York Missionary Society also sponsored Thompson S. Harris, *Gospel of Luke in the Seneca Language* (1829).

43. Mt. Pleasant, "After the Whirlwind," 101.

44. Alfred, *Peace, Power, and Righteousness*, 52. Before the breaking up of the Six Nations by the Treaty of Fort Stanwix, the Native bands involved (Oneida, Mohawk, Onondaga, Cayuga, Seneca, and Tuscarora) considered themselves bound into what Europeans later called the Iroquois League or Confederacy. To most Haudenosaunee people, this bond was conceived of as a kind of kinship organization between the bands and was derived from an origin story in which the Onondaga culture hero, Deganawidah, received the gift of the Two-Row wampum from the spirit world as a guide to bringing peace to the constantly warring bands. Historian Daniel K. Richter observes: "In my view, the Iroquois Great League of Peace and Power was not . . . a device for nation-state–style central political authority. . . . Instead, it existed merely (or, better, sublimely) to keep the peace and preserve a spiritual unity among the many autonomous villages of the [Six] Nations" (*Ordeal of the Longhouse*, 7). Still, as Haudenosaunee historians from David Cusick to Taiaiakee Alfred have observed, the power of the story of the Two-Row wampum knit together the people long after Europeans had deemed them "vanquished." The "Longhouse" is a shorthand way of expressing this bond, referring to the idealized dwelling place shared by all the Six Nations when in council.

45. Mt. Pleasant, "After the Whirlwind," 143.

46. Quoted in ibid., 157.

47. Thomas Abler, in "Protestant Missionaries," offers a sensitive and nuanced reading of the role both missionaries and literacy played in Haudenosaunee society during the first decades of the nineteenth century. Focusing on Asher Wright's work on behalf of Seneca who opposed the land secession treaty of 1838 (he translated many English

language legal materials into Seneca), Abler concludes that "since the Chiefs under the traditional system were more likely to be Christian than the warriors who supported the new republican government, Wright, in the limited support he lent the supporters of the new government, turned his back on a large portion of his own congregation and allied himself with practitioners of the traditional religion" (29).

48. Severance, *Narratives of Early Mission Work*, 158. After issue no. 10, the *Mental Elevator* was transferred to the Cattaragus Reservation.

49. Mt. Pleasant, "After the Whirlwind," 173–74.

50. Ibid., 14.

51. See Jackett, "Words to the Ganoda Chant."

52. McMurtrie, "Pioneer Printing," 4.

53. Data on Native apprentices appears in *Baptist Missionary Magazine* 20, no. 11 (1840): 262; and in McMurtrie, *Jotham Meeker*, 49, 67. Meeker's journal also records his work with several Native ministers and interpreters, including Samson Birch (Choctaw), Solomon Davis (Muskogee), and Deshane, possibly a métis who spoke Shawnee.

54. Quoted in McMurtrie, *Jotham Meeker*, 27–28. Most "books" in Indian Country began as handwritten manuscripts. See George Copway's description of his father's conversion, where he reports, "On Sabbath mornings, I read a chapter in the New Testament, which had been translated for my father, before we went to meeting" (Copway, *Life, History, and Travels*, 102).

55. McMurtrie, *Jotham Meeker*, 27–28.

56. A nonalphabetic syllabary devised in 1840 by Anglican missionary James Evans for the Cree proved more effective, and Willard Walker notes that for many tribal communities "syllabic literacy is a mark of ethnic identity . . . [and] is well-entrenched and ramified in the Cree and Ojibwe communities, but it has not been allowed to infringe on the role of the story teller or the value of the spoken word. The esteem with which syllabic writing is regarded as part of native culture is reflected in local traditions that the syllabary was a gift made directly to the native people by a deity or other supernatural being" ("Native Writing Systems," 176).

57. McMurtrie, *Jotham Meeker*, 49. Meeker's journal is full of entries that show the comings and going of Natives and missionaries who drop by the mission to read proofs and check text: "Br. Blanchard brings his Delaware book prepared for the press" (14); and "Ride to Br. Lykins to read proof" (14).

58. Buckner, *Gospel*, 11–13.

59. McMurtrie, *Jotham Meeker*, 5.

60. *Baptist Missionary Magazine* (January 1849): 28. Ojibwe missionary George Copway describes how his literacy education at the hand of missionary James Evans was itself a powerful spiritual and consecrating activity: "Memory, like an angel, will still hover over the sacred spot, where first you taught me the letters of the alphabet" (Copway, *Life, History, and Travels*, 95).

61. Caldwell, *Annals of the Shawnee Mission*, 17–18.

62. McMurtrie, *Jotham Meeker*, 5. At Highland, in the northeast corner of Kansas, a similar process of Native-language missionary printing was going on at the same time that Meeker worked at the Shawanoe press. Missionaries Samuel Irvin and William Hamilton were sent a small press by the Presbyterian Board of Foreign Missions, with which they published the *Elementary Book of the Ioway Language* (1843) and *Original Hymns in the Ioway Language* (1843). In their preface to the hymnal, the two missionaries-turned-printers apologized for their imprint's rudimentary typography, explaining that

it was produced "with only two kinds of type, and that experience in the art has been acquired entirely in the Indian Country, and without any instructor."

63. On the Lapwai Mission press, see Schoenberg, *Lapwai Mission Press.*

64. Furtwangler notes that the Hudson Bay Company required church attendance of all: "It . . . instituted Sunday service as a matter of policy, and required every man, woman, and child to attend, including Indians" (*Bringing Indians*, 16).

65. Ibid. Furtwangler observes that "the people had been greatly influenced" by Spokane Garry's recent teaching (18), but he also acknowledges that many Native leaders remained unconvinced of the utility of print culture for their communities. In 1827, one Okanagan leader reportedly told a missionary: "[We] smoak Tobacco from a much different and better motive . . . than that which moves the white people to look in the Great Fathers Book: for the moment he takes his Pipe, he cannot help thinking of the Great Creation of the world" (17).

66. Ibid., 59.

67. Quoted in ibid., 107. The actual printer, Edwin O. Hall, was sent to Idaho from Hawaii by the American Board of Commissioners for Foreign Missions in 1839. Spaulding's attitude toward Native peoples' approach to Roman typography was shared by others. In 1895, a writer for the *American Bookmaker* observed, "The Roman letters drive an Indian almost to distraction, and he rapidly forgets what he learns with so much trouble" (72). See "Type for Indian Books."

68. See Schoenberg, *Lapwai Mission Press,* 19–20.

69. In addition to the *Nez Perce First Book* (1839), the Lapwai Mission press produced *Etshiit* (1843); *Laws and Statues* (1842); *Talapusapaiain* [Hymns] (1843); *Matthewnim Taaiskt* [Book of Matthew] (1845); and *Shapahitamanash* [Vocabulary] (1845).

70. Schoenberg, *Lapwai Mission Press,* 46–47.

71. Ibid., 43.

72. For a bibliography of Native newspapers in North America, see Littlefield and Parins, *American Indian and Alaska Native Newspapers and Periodicals.*

73. DeMallie and Parks, "Plains Indian Native Literatures," 122, 126.

74. Cebula, *Plateau Indians,* 129.

Chapter 4

1. Quoted in Richardson, *Indian Preacher,* 28–29.

2. Lisa Brooks points out that many Mohegans were skeptical of the sincerity of Occom's apology. See *Common Pot,* 97.

3. Jean O'Brien's study of Natick, Massachusetts, *Dispossession by Degrees,* discusses the many kinds of texts and literacy practices that informed Native subject formation in that Praying Town during the first half of the eighteenth century. See the essays and documents in Bross and Wyss, *Early Native Literacies,* for more examples of intertwined literacy practices.

4. Habermas, *Structural Transformation,* 19, 16. For further discussion of the role of print in the development of the U.S. public sphere, see Warner, *Letters of the Republic,* especially 38–39.

5. Gustafson, "American Literature and the Public Sphere," 465.

6. Warner, *Publics and Counterpublics,* 56–57.

7. Warrior, *Tribal Secrets,* 115. In a more recent work, Warrior sharpens this definition to include "a process that highlights the production of meaning through the critical

interaction that occurs between a text as a writer has written it and a text as a reader understands it [in Indian Country]" (*People and the Word*, xiv).

8. Loughran's *Republic in Print*, for example, although it purportedly describes "the nation (and nation state) in the most materialist way possible" (xix), emphasizing the actual — rather than theorized — institutions through which information, argument, and identity flowed in the early republic, totally disregards the Indian Removal Act of 1830, a federal law that simultaneously (and forcibly) "cleared" the geographic national space of its indigenous inhabitants, produced a print culture explosion (in books like Black Hawk, *Life of Ma-ka-tai-me-she-kia-kiak, or Black Hawk* [1834]), and set in motion a set of very significant Supreme Court rulings with states' rights implications (*Cherokee Nation v. Georgia* [1831] and *Worcester v. Georgia* [1832]).

9. Elizabeth Dillon, for example, has observed that the Euro-American public sphere was based on a political liberalism that was a "structuring force" behind publication in America. She specifically describes how "gender is one of the categories through which liberalism scripts the interrelated public and private lives of citizens" (*Gender of Freedom*, 2). Following Dillon, I would argue that liberalism treated Native peoples in a way parallel to its treatment of women. Although "liberalism does not exclude" Native peoples entirely, it "reserves a discrete position" for them in society (3). This "position" was both rhetorical and material, with Indian territory and reservations serving as very real spaces for the sequestration of the indigenous presence in America. In a similar way, Ivy Schweitzer has argued that the emerging public sphere engendered discourses of affiliation and friendship that knit together not only Euro-American social groups but also those of "non-elites, people of color, and women" (*Perfecting Friendship*, 13). As we will see in the following discussion of Indian publics, the term "friend" would be a very contested one in the construction of Native voices and political actions in the public sphere.

10. Occom, *Collected Writings*, 177.

11. Ibid.

12. Ibid., 74.

13. See Heather Bouwman's account of Occom's "Temperance and Morality Sermon" (ca. 1768), in which she argues that "the Temperance and Morality Sermon, like the Moses Paul sermon, shows that Occom used his position as an Indian preacher to address various constituencies in his mixed audiences. . . . This was part of a larger pattern — evident throughout his sermons — of playing to multiple audiences and addressing white constituents as well as Indian constituents in complex and multilayered ways" ("Samson Occom and the Sermonic Tradition," 68).

14. These comments appear in the unpaginated preface to Commuck, *Indian Melodies*.

15. Alfred, *Peace, Power, and Righteousness*, xvi.

16. Ibid., 21, 25, 28.

17. Columbus, "Letter of Columbus on the Discovery of America" (1493), in Castillo and Schweitzer, *Literatures of Colonial America*, 25.

18. Round, "Neither Here nor There," traces the complex negotiations indigenous people of the New World engaged in with metropolitan colonial authorities through transatlantic letters (436–38).

19. See White, *Middle Ground*, xiv, where the author calls this performative space a "joint Indian-white creation."

20. Merrell, *Into the American Woods*, 51.

21. See John Alden, "Cherokee Archive," 240. For an exhaustive list of the appearance of such papers in eighteenth-century reports from Indian Country, see Shoemaker, *Strange Likeness*, 160n32.

22. Timberlake, *Memoirs*, 41.

23. See Schweitzer's discussion of the federal government's use of the distribution of peace medals in 1790 as a means of mobilization of a rhetoric of "friendship" with tribal communities that supported its national policies. Schweitzer reads these newly implemented material symbols of U.S./Indian diplomacy as "ritual objects in a complex performance of power and allegiance [that] . . . underscore[s] the close relationship of international diplomacy and friendship discourse" (*Perfecting Friendship*, 18).

24. In the following discussion, I rely on the manuscript version (in Aupaumut's hand) of the "Journal of a Mission to the Western Tribes" preserved at the Historical Society of Pennsylvania, in Philadelphia, and on a manuscript version of Chainbreaker's oral history housed in the Draper Manuscripts, Joseph Brant Papers, Wisconsin Historical Society, Madison. All quotations concerning Aupaumut's scribal practices refer to this manuscript, which has handwritten pagination in parentheses in the upper corner of each page. For quotations and discussions of thematic elements of the text, I use the only full printed version of the manuscript, the 1827 edition published in the *Pennsylvania Historical Society Memoirs*: Aupaumut, "A Narrative." All quotations from Chainbreaker are from Abler's modern edition, *Chainbreaker*, except those in which manuscript practices are at issue. These manuscript examples are taken from Williams, "Life of Governor Blacksnake," Draper Manuscripts 16-F-107-219, Joseph Brant Papers, Wisconsin Historical Society, Madison. The page numbers I use to describe Williams's scribal practice thus refer to the handwritten pagination Draper provides for the narrative. Draper does not begin his pagination of the "Life" on page one but rather numbers it cumulatively, as part of the larger collection he calls the Brant Papers.

25. Aupaumut, "A Narrative," 87; Chainbreaker, *Chainbreaker*, 52.

26. Aupaumut, "A Narrative," 78, 129, 86.

27. Chainbreaker, *Chainbreaker*, 75.

28. Ibid., 170, 163.

29. See Merrell, *Into the American Woods*, 215–19. Merrell finds "contention between the . . . media" of these Indian Country discourses, and "the weight each side accorded" the various communication technologies. For other descriptions of hybrid Native/Euro-American diplomatic discourses and materials, see Shoemaker, *Strange Likeness*, 65–68; and Saunt, *New Order of Things*, 190.

30. Aupaumut, "A Narrative," 76.

31. Ibid., 106.

32. Chainbreaker, *Chainbreaker*, 228. This comment appears at the head of the manuscript, but Abler has chosen to publish it as an appendix to the main body of the work. On the process of editing such texts, see Round, "Literature of the Middle Ground."

33. Williams, "Life of Governor Blacksnake," Draper Manuscripts 16-F-107-219, Joseph Brant Papers, Wisconsin Historical Society, Madison, 227–28.

34. Chainbreaker, *Chainbreaker*, 17.

35. Williams, "Life of Governor Blacksnake," Draper Manuscripts 16-F-107-219, Joseph Brant Papers, Wisconsin Historical Society, Madison, 227.

36. Ibid.

37. Ibid., 116, 113.

38. Sarris, *Keeping Slug Woman Alive*, 85; Aupaumut, "A Narrative," 95, 54.

39. Aupaumut, "A Narrative," 103, 130.

40. Williams, "Life of Governor Blacksnake," Draper Manuscripts 16-F-107-219, Joseph Brant Papers, Wisconsin Historical Society, Madison, 123.

41. Abler notes that Williams, in another manuscript he sent to Draper, "put the Seneca creation myth into a format resembling the English Bible, including chapter and verse" (Chainbreaker, *Chainbreaker*, 11).

42. Williams, "Life of Governor Blacksnake," Draper Manuscripts 16-F-107-219, Joseph Brant Papers, Wisconsin Historical Society, Madison, 129.

43. Lyons, "What Do American Indians Want," 450–51.

44. Aupaumut, "A Narrative," 95–96.

45. Ibid., 91.

46. Chainbreaker, *Chainbreaker*, 54.

47. Aupaumut, "A Narrative," 91, 93, 112.

48. Gustafson, "American Literature and the Public Sphere," 473, 475.

49. Aupaumut, "A Narrative," 122, 131.

50. Quoted in Chainbreaker, *Chainbreaker*, 12. Abler himself takes a more judicious stance toward Williams's nonstandard style, commenting, "Readers must be forewarned that Blacksnake's narrative is not elegant or lucid prose," but he too echoes Wallace, *Death and Rebirth of the Seneca*, in saying that "in some respects it is even worse than 'reservation English' . . . since one must add confusion about spelling and punctuation to the other non-standard aspects of English as spoken by Indians for whom it was neither a first language nor even one used in everyday communication" (Chainbreaker, *Chainbreaker*, 12).

51. See Dowd, *Spirited Resistance*, 106–7.

52. Quoted in ibid., 38.

53. Hunter, "Delaware Nativist Revival," 2.

54. Dowd, *Spirited Resistance*, 43. Not only were such revivalist "books" symbolic of the appropriation of Euro-American power and technology by the prophets but they were also a kind of economic empowerment as well, as is clear when we recall that "Neolin advised his hearers to obtain a copy of the 'bible' which he offered to reproduce at the fixed rate of one buckskin or two doe skins each" (ibid., 46). Gordon Sayre reproduces one European traveler's reproduction of an illustration from one such prophetic book, in *Indian Chief*, 149.

55. Martin, *Sacred Revolt*, 160.

56. Saunt, *New Order of Things*, 252.

57. Vibert, "Natives Were Strong to Live," 212.

58. Jennifer J. S. Brown, "Wasitay Religion," 105.

59. Ibid., 111.

60. Hopkins, *Life among the Paiutes*, 19.

61. Ibid.

62. Ibid.

63. Harkin, *Reassessing Revitalization Movements*, xxiv.

64. Vibert, "Natives Were Strong to Live," 203.

65. Thornton, "Boundary Dissolution," 362.

66. Harkin, *Reassessing Revitalization Movements*, xxiv.

67. Stiggins, "Historical Narration," 17.

68. Ibid., 18–19. On Stiggins's performance as an ethnographer and his defense of Weatherford, see Sayre, *Indian Chief*, 220–21, 259.

69. Warren, *History*, 27, 55, 59, 62, 71.

70. Bauman, "Nationalization," 248.

71. Warren, *History*, 108, 225, 115.

72. Jackson, "President's Message," ix.

73. Quinney, "Celebration of the Fourth," x.

Chapter 5

1. MacLean, "Concurring Opinion."

2. "American Cadmus" is the term used by George E. Foster to describe Sequoyah in his biography, *Sequoyah: The American Cadmus* (1885).

3. Quoted in Perdue, *Cherokee Editor*, 17.

4. In 1801, the Moravians began the Cherokee mission at Spring Place, Georgia, and in 1821 another at nearby Oothcaloga. Both missions were broken up by the State of Georgia in 1843. In 1804, Rev. Gideon Blackburn, for the Presbyterians, established a Cherokee mission school in east Tennessee.

5. Foreman, *Sequoyah*, 5.

6. Champagne, *Social Order*, 99.

7. McLoughlin, "New Angles of Vision," 318.

8. Ibid.

9. Champagne, *Social Order*, 321.

10. McLoughlin, "New Angles of Vision," 326.

11. Bender, *Signs of Cherokee Culture*, 35.

12. Ibid., 36.

13. Biographies include Foreman, *Sequoyah*; Foster, *Sequoyah: The American Cadmus*; and Lowery, "Notable Persons." Traveller Bird's *Tell Them They Lie*, by contrast, takes a decidedly nationalist approach to Sequoyah, arguing that the syllabary predates Sequoyah's invention and was a time-immemorial device in Cherokee culture.

14. Lowery, "Notable Persons," 386.

15. Ibid., 387.

16. Ibid.

17. Ibid., 387–88.

18. Ibid., 389.

19. Ibid., 390.

20. Examples include the Swimmer Manuscript, a collection of sacred Cherokee formulas written into a manuscript book by a medicine practitioner by the name of Swimmer. Anthropologist James Mooney published a description of this work, in *Sacred Formulas of the Cherokees* (1891). The manuscript was later reproduced in full in Mooney and Olbrechts, *Swimmer Manuscript* (1932). Louise Erdrich, among many others, believes that the birch-bark pictographic scrolls that accompany Ojibwe midewiwin sacred societies show that "Ojibwe people were great writers from way back and synthesized the oral and written traditions by keeping mnemonic scrolls of inscribed birchbark. The first paper, the first books" (*Books and Islands*, 10–11). The ledger books used by many Plains artists are another example of books being incorporated into traditional communicative practice in Indian Country. See chapter 8.

21. See Walker and Sarbaugh, "Early History of the Cherokee Syllabary," for a convincing defense of Sequoyah as the sole inventor of the system.

22. Perdue, *Cherokee Editor*, 12.

23. Quoted in Gaul, *To Marry an Indian*, 16.

24. Perdue, *Cherokee Editor*, 46.

25. Ibid., 12.

26. Ibid., 74.

27. Ibid., 72–73.

28. Ibid., 15.

29. Ibid., 74. See Gaul, *To Marry an Indian*, 3, 10–12.

30. Perdue, *Cherokee Editor*, 11.

31. For a detailed and focused study of the Cherokee press, see Brannon, *Cherokee Phoenix*. Brannon believes that the press the Cherokee Nation used was a Super Royal made by the Union Company of Boston.

32. Perdue, *Cherokee Editor*, 74.

33. Ibid., 77.

34. Boudinot, *Address to Whites*, in ibid., 78.

35. Justice, *Our Fire Survives*, 7 (quoted on p. 203).

36. Perdue, *Cherokee Editor*, 15.

37. *Cherokee Phoenix*, August 20, 1828, 2.

38. The publication numbers are drawn from Brannon, *Cherokee Phoenix*, 29.

39. *Cherokee Phoenix*, February 11, 1829, 3.

40. Ibid.

41. Ojibwe writer George Copway makes a similar observation in 1845: "When we have a press of our own, we shall, perhaps, be able to plead our own cause. Give us but the Bible, and the influence of a Press, and we ask no more" (Copway, *Life, History, and Travels*, 152).

42. A typical entry of this type states: "We have gained the sympathies and good wishes of some of our white readers, for the Aborigines of this Country, For the encouragement of our home readers, we have occasionally inserted in the Phoenix extracts from our private correspondence" (*Cherokee Phoenix*, June 3, 1829, 2).

43. *Cherokee Phoenix*, July 2, 1828, 2. Boudinot comments: "One thing we are pleased to notice in one of these pieces, & we hope our white readers will consider the sentiments here advanced [as] not only the sentiments of an individual, but of a majority of the Cherokees."

44. *Cherokee Phoenix*, June 10, 1829, 2. Humboldt's comments appear in *Cherokee Phoenix*, June 24, 1829, 2.

45. *Cherokee Phoenix*, March 4, 1829, 1.

46. Perdue, *Cherokee Editor*, 125.

47. Ibid., 169.

48. Ibid., 134, 136. The Cherokee were very sensitive about this issue of intellectual sovereignty from the beginning. Boudinot commented: "The font of type now used in this place was not procured by the general government, but at the public expense of the Cherokee Nation, though it is true the U. States have appropriated (not however altogether gratuitously) one thousand dollars, for the establishment of a press among the Cherokees of the Arkansas" (*Cherokee Phoenix*, July 29, 1829, 2).

49. Perdue, *Cherokee Editor*, 138. Boudinot had a running printed debate with Colonel

Nelson of the Georgia Guard about whether or not he had been a "tool in the hands of the missionaries" and whether he was actually literate. See ibid., 132–39. Later, he would have a similar running printed battle with John Ross, whom he criticized for having to use a translator to speak to his fellow Cherokee (ibid., 187).

50. "Post Office Reform," in ibid., 127.

51. *Cherokee Phoenix*, June 4, 1828, 2.

52. *Cherokee Phoenix*, October 29, 1828, 2.

53. *Cherokee Phoenix*, April 10, 1828, 3.

54. The pattern of citations suggested by the submissions and commentary in the *Cherokee Phoenix* from outsiders, along with the signatures of locals using their own names as well as pseudonyms, reminds us that such arrays, in the words of Pierre Bourdieu, "may nearly always be associated with such diverse functions as the manifestation of relations of allegiance or dependence, or strategies of affiliation, or annexation or of defence" (138) and suggest "those *privileged interlocutors* implicit in the writings of every producer" (*Field of Cultural Production*, 139).

55. Perdue, *Cherokee Editor*, 26, 29.

56. Ibid., 118n61.

57. *Cherokee Phoenix*, December 3, 1828, 2.

58. See above where I discuss Theda Perdue's thesis that "the signers of the treaty came primarily from a rising middle class, and they resented the economic power of Principal Chief John Ross, [and] Chief Justice John Martin" (Perdue, *Cherokee Editor*, 26). On the role of popular and sensational print in the establishment of class identification, see Lehuu, *Carnival on the Page*, 29.

59. Perdue, *Cherokee Editor*, 26.

60. As a recent government publication states, "The term memorial derives from the Latin, meaning literally 'to remember' . . . [and is a] request . . . that the Congress take some action or refrain from taking some action." Petersen, "Messages, Petitions, Communications."

61. Quinney, *Memorial*, x.

62. Ross, *Letter*, 15.

63. Although I do not discuss translation in the following pages, translation is a major issue for all Indian memorials. The Lake Superior Ojibwe in 1846 hedged their bets in this regard and submitted a bilingual petition to the commissioner of Indian affairs. See Nicols, "Statement by the Indians."

64. Quinney, *Memorial*, x.

65. Reed, *Memorial and Argument*, 1, 2.

66. *Memorial of the Indian Delegates*, 8.

67. Muskogee Nation, *Memorial of the Muscogee*, 1, 9.

68. Ibid., 7.

69. Quinney's handwritten draft is found in Stockbridge and Munsee Tribe Papers, Newberry Library, Chicago.

70. Ross, *Memorial*, 3, 12.

71. Ibid., 12.

72. Saunt, *New Order of Things*, 191.

73. Quoted in Elias Johnson, *Legends*, 129.

74. David Folsom's "Prospectus for the Choctaw Intelligencer" was published in the *Indian Advocate* in November 1848. Folsom claimed that his paper would be devoted to "the advocacy and dissemination of Morality, Education, Agriculture and General

Intelligence—one half in Choctaw, and the other in the English language." It would be, Folsom continued, "a Family newspaper, (neutral in Religion and Politics)." It would also provide a "full and correct account of the Markets" in agricultural commodities.

75. Warrior, *People and the Word*, 51.

76. Hargrett, *Bibliography of the Laws*.

77. Warrior, *People and the Word*, 77, 74, 72.

78. Bender, *Signs of Cherokee Culture*, 39, 41, 1.

79. Nord, *Faith in Reading*, 119.

80. Lehuu, *Carnival on the Page*, 3.

81. This was not the only steady seller the Cherokee press produced. It also printed Richmond, *Dairyman's Daughter*, which shows similar illustrations and adaptations intended to foster a "middle-class" print market in Cherokee country. Almanacs were another steady seller genre, with Christian and bourgeois socialization overtones. See *Holisso Hushi Holhtine . . . Chata Almanac for 1839*.

82. Bender, *Signs of Cherokee Culture*, 93. The Cherokee New Testament, originally published in 1860, has served the Cherokees for generations as the sourcebook for correct syllabary usage and language preservation. See ibid., x.

83. Ibid., 112. In *Sacred Formulas of the Cherokees*, Mooney reports that he found Inali's commission as a Methodist minister among these papers as well. I have decided to publish an image of this page of Inali's notebook because his daughter gave it to Mooney for public use (but kept some more sacred and personal materials) and because, as Jack and Anna Kirkpatrick observe, such syllabary formularies lose their sacredness (they are "dead, of no effectiveness") upon the death of the owner, unless preserved within a family or clan ("Notebook," 85).

Chapter 6

1. Martha Woodmansee defines the proprietary author as "an individual who is the sole creator of unique 'works' the originality of which warrants their protection under laws of intellectual property known as 'copyright' or 'author's rights'" ("On the Author Effect," 15).

2. Rice, *Transformation of Authorship*, 70.

3. Cusick, *David Cusick's Sketches of Ancient History*, 1.

4. Robert Warrior's *Tribal Secrets* purposely avoids offering a clear-cut definition of the term so that it can be conceived in terms of praxis rather than theory. Warrior does, however, make this case for how intellectual sovereignty operates, and it sounds very much like what we read in Cusick's preface: "We, as critics, can find within such a praxis a way of making ourselves vulnerable to the wide array of pain, joy, oppression, celebration of contemporary American Indian community existence. . . . Within that vulnerability we do not reduce intellectual production to mere aestheticism or functionalism. . . . We see that the process of sovereignty, whether in the political or intellectual sphere, is not a matter of removing ourselves and our communities from the influences of the world we live in" (Warrior, *Tribal Secrets*, 114). Cusick's move in this text, then, is into the "modern" contemporary space that Iroquois peoples inhabited in 1827. This world was significantly changed by the coming of print.

5. Parkman, *Oregon Trail*, 369.

6. Thomas Abler speculates that the emergence of other Native-authored works at the time of Benjamin Williams's emergence as a writer (most significantly, Cusick, *David Cusick's Sketches of Ancient History* [1827]) and increasing non-Indian interest in Indian

stories might have spurred the Williams/Chainbreaker collaboration. (Chainbreaker, *Chainbreaker*, 10–11.)

7. Warrior's *People and the Word* opens with a chapter on Apess that discusses the author at "a critical nexus in which his realities, reflected in his ideas . . . inform a broader discussion about the tasks and responsibilities of [Native] intellectuals" (2), but the materiality of his print choices is not the focus of Warrior's analysis.

8. Rice, *Transformation of Authorship*, 93.

9. Snelling, "Life of Black Hawk," 69.

10. Brown, *Memoir of Catherine Brown*, x.

11. Hall, *Cultures of Print*, 44, 51.

12. Rice, *Transformation of Authorship*, 3.

13. Quoted in ibid., 74.

14. Woodmansee, "On the Author Effect," 16.

15. Pfau, "Pragmatics of Genre," 134–35.

16. Eilenberg, "Mortal Pages," 352.

17. Rose, *Authors and Owners*, 15.

18. See Eilenberg, "Mortal Pages." Ojibwe writer George Copway explicitly engages this trope of Romantic authorship, in *Life, Letters, and Speeches* (1847): "If perchance I may yet speak; when my poor aching head lies low in the grave; when the hand that wrote these recollections shall have crumbled into dust; then these pages will not have been written in vain" (79).

19. Rice, *Transformation of Authorship*, 3, 7.

20. Apess, *A Son of the Forest*, included in Apess, *On Our Own Ground*, 16. All subsequent quotations from this work come from this edition, unless otherwise specified.

21. Morse, *Report*, 78.

22. The Marshall Court's attitude toward Native Americans is well summarized in Konkle, "Indian Literacy," 463.

23. Rice, *Transformation of Authorship*, 94.

24. Snelling, "Life of Black Hawk," 70 (emphasis added).

25. Brinton, *Aboriginal American Authors*, title page, 19.

26. Ibid., 13.

27. Apess, *Experiences*, in Apess, *On Our Own Ground*, 120. See note 1, introduction, for a discussion of Barry O'Connell's interpretation of this passage.

28. All of my observations about the physical properties of the second edition of *A Son of the Forest* (New York, 1831) are based on two original copies I have worked with, one in the Massachusetts Historical Society and another in the Special Collections of the University of Iowa Main Library.

29. The use of the frontispiece portrait to establish the "author figure" in the Anglo-American literary tradition has been fruitfully explored by Roger Chartier and others. See Chartier, *Order of Books*, 25–60. Examples of non–Euro-American authors' frontispieces, like those of Phyllis Wheatley and Olaudah Equiano, often show the author staring to the heavens for guidance (as in the case of Wheatley) or holding the Bible open to a relevant passage in the scriptures (as in the case of Equiano). An interesting counterexample appears in the portrait of Samson Occom, in which the American Indian evangelist is represented wearing his clerical collar seated before an impressive bookcase filled with fine volumes.

30. Ed Folsom, "Appearing in Print," 142. On Southern Algonquians' relationship to daguerreotypes and portraiture, see Turano, "Taken from Life."

31. A fruitful comparison can again be made with Black Hawk, *Life of Ma-ka-tai-me-she-kia-kiak, or Black Hawk* (1833), the work that William Snelling believed to be the more authentic Indian autobiography. Black Hawk's autobiography follows its title page with a letter of certification from Antoine LeClaire, the text's interpreter. The reader is then presented with an alphabetic transcription of the Sac language in the form of a dedicatory letter from Black Hawk to Brigadier General H. Atkinson. This letter is in turn followed by an "Advertisement," written by the text's editor and amanuensis.

32. Konkle reads Apess's *Eulogy on King Philip* "in light of several texts Apess would have known of, that he probably had read" ("Indian Literacy," 458), including Supreme Court decisions in the 1830s and Edward Everett's *Address at Bloody Brook* (1835). Konkle's reading is directed against critics like Snelling who believe that "writing obscures Indian identity." I here extend her argument while redefining the general term "writing" to include the physical properties of texts and their legal and marketplace meanings.

33. Apess, *Son of the Forest*, 1.

34. Sarris, *Keeping Slug Woman Alive*, 85. Sarris is speaking of "as-told-to" narratives in which later literary and ethnographic interpretations have elided the intersubjective contexts of such exchanges. I believe that a similar elision often occurs when we consider print culture texts produced by Native Americans without looking at the intersubjective (marketplace, collaborative, legal) contexts for their production. This intersubjectivity is specifically political, part of a dialogic relation between author and reader that is enforced not only by print conventions but also, in the case of American Indians, by non-Native assumptions of fundamental racial difference.

35. Apess, *Son of the Forest*, 5.

36. Rufus Anderson, non-Indian editor of the Cherokee conversion narrative *Memoir of Catherine Brown*, makes similar truth-telling claims in his preface: "The author is not conscious of having exaggerated a single fact, nor of having made a single statement not drawn from authentic documents. His object has been to give a plain and true exhibition of the life and character of a very interesting convert from heathenism."

37. Apess, *Son of the Forest*, 23.

38. Ibid., 10.

39. Quoted in Amory and Hall, *Colonial Book in the Atlantic World*, 478.

40. Pfau, "Pragmatics of Genre," 135.

41. See Krupat, "Native American Autobiography," 184.

42. Apess, *Son of the Forest*, 51. Ojibwe preacher Peter Jones recalled that while in England he was "gazed upon as if I were some strange animal" (quoted in Donald B. Smith, *Sacred Feathers*, 125).

43. Apess, *Son of the Forest*, 52.

44. Eilenberg, in "Mortal Pages," observes that, "in Wordsworth's mind, copyright had everything to do with epitaph, the writing due to the memory of the dead" (356) and that the formal properties of such texts highlight "the analogy between copyright and monumentality" (368) that held sway during the period.

45. I agree with Sandra Gustafson that Apess's writings "chart his journey away from a primarily Methodist identity and toward an ethnically defined identity, a transformation revealed in his shifting rhetorical emphases" ("Nations of Israelites," 33), but I locate this quest earlier in his career and within the physical properties of his texts, his economic relationship with the bookselling marketplace, and his editorial practices. Gustafson sees Apess's appropriation of Boudinot's *A Star of the West* as an example of his participation in Lost Tribes discourse, as a discourse that grounded "assertions of cultural indepen-

dence on native Hebraism," but I describe below how Apess cited Boudinot to assert his newfound independence in a print-based Protestant vernacular that Boudinot helped establish through the American Bible Society. See Gustafson, "Nations of Israelites," 31–53.

46. Sayre, "Defying Assimilation, Confounding Authenticity," 8. See also Moon, "William Apess and Writing White," 45–54. Moon comments, "I sense a political unease over Apess because he writes too much like a white person" (52).

47. Apess, *On Our Own Ground*, xlvii.

48. Of course, to be a "compiler" did not always give one the social status of the "genius" author, and Mark Rose quotes Lord Hailes's 1773 decision in *Hinton v. Donaldson* to demonstrate the animus some felt toward a copyright law that conferred "the name of *original author* on every *tasteless compiler*" (*Authors and Owners*, 136).

49. Quoted in Eisenstein, *Printing Press*, 122.

50. Jedidiah Morse, for example, makes these observations about the role of appendixes in his *Report*: "The nature of the *composition* of this report . . . is not intended to be original, but to consist of existing facts and materials, now scattered in many books and manuscripts, which it is important should be collected and arranged, for convenient use, under proper heads. To accomplish this, so far as it had been accomplished in this volume, has cost no small labor" (22). He goes on: "The body of the information collected in compliance with the part of my commission . . . I have, for obvious reasons, thrown into an *Appendix*, to which reference may be had for facts and information in detail, to establish and illustrate the different branches of this Report" (23).

51. Bourdieu, *Field of Cultural Production*, 137, 138, 139.

52. Boudinot was the recipient of a letter in 1783 from Joel Barlow urging the new Congress to develop copyright protection. Grantland Rice calls it "the most famous document in early American copyright history" (*Transformation of Authorship*, 81).

53. Mark Rose reminds us that "public domain" is "a concept that is itself an import from the realm of real estate" and that "the model for copyright is real property" (*Authors and Owners*, 133).

54. Apess, *On Our Own Ground*, xvii.

55. See Silver, "Financing the Publication," 163–78; and Amory, "Under the Exchange," 31–60. In addition to O'Connell's speculation, we have evidence of Apess's public celebrity in Samuel Drake's scrapbook ("The Indian Miscellany"), housed in the Newberry Library. Drake pasted an autographed ticket to Apess's public performance of *Eulogy* into his scrapbook. George Copway engaged in similar gestures of proprietary authorship. New Jersey Methodist missionary Alexander Winchell recorded in his diary that, after a public lecture, "[Copway] sold several books here containing his biography[.] I have also obtained his autograph" (quoted in Donald B. Smith, "Kahgegagahbowh," 35).

56. Lisa Brooks discusses Apess's other writings in *Common Pot*, 176–218.

57. Apess, *On Our Own Ground*, 311.

58. See Warrior's discussion of the circumstances surrounding Apess's death in New York and its implication for the project of Native American intellectuals as a group (*People and the Word*, 38–47).

Chapter 7

1. McGill, *American Literature and the Culture of Reprinting*, 4.

2. At the center of Jace Weaver's critique of non-Native treatment of indigenous texts

is "a defense against such co-optation and incorporation" that is inherent in the culture of reprinting ("Splitting the Earth," in Weaver, *American Indian Literary Nationalism*, 40).

3. Crain, *Story of A*, 76.

4. "Splitting the Earth," in Weaver, *American Indian Literary Nationalism*, 15, 17.

5. McGill, *American Literature and the Culture of Reprinting*, 41. Although McGill specifically cites women and African American writers, she never considers Native authors or Native texts.

6. See Conn, *History's Shadow*, 49–50.

7. See "Splitting the Earth," in Weaver, *American Indian Literary Nationalism*, 17. Pierre Bourdieu argues that European society in the nineteenth century reproduced its social and economic system in a "refracted" homologous system of cultural production (of which literature is a major component), but Weaver believes that a similar "refraction" takes place in Native communities. He cites Bill New, who argues that "whatever pattern emerges [in Native cultural production] . . . will spell out a society's social organization and — in a very general way — affect and contextualize its literary culture" (ibid.).

8. Other Native authors of note sought similar outlets in missionary and tract society presses. Pequot writer Paul Cuffee's *Memoir* was reprinted by a religious publisher in London in 1840. Peter Jacobs (1824–57) published his *Journal* in 1853 with the Toronto Wesleyan Conference. He also printed a Boston edition the same year.

9. Ruoff, "The Literary and Methodist Contexts of George Copway's *Life, Letters, and Speeches*," in Copway, *Life, Letters, and Speeches*, 5.

10. Donald B. Smith, "Kahgegagahbowh," 41. Comparing variants in the two texts, Smith observes that the later works exhibit "a finer gloss — evidence of outside collaboration . . . [and] at least one story, the story of his first bear hunt, returns from his *Life*, elaborated on in much greater detail" (ibid.). Verbatim excerpts in the history total about 100 pages of the 298 pages of the book.

11. Bourdieu, *Field of Cultural Production*, 74, 76, 75.

12. Longfellow made this comment in a letter to Ferdinand Freiligrath, in 1858 (quoted by Donald B. Smith, "Kahgegagahbowh," 46).

13. See Zanjani, *Sarah Winnemucca*, 236–54.

14. Draper's biography is taken from the Wisconsin Historical Society's website: ⟨www.wisconsinhistory.org/topics/draper/index.asp⟩.

15. In *History's Shadow*, Steven Conn traces the midcentury movement in American intellectuals' treatment of Native peoples from amateur antiquarianism to professional science. Americans institutionalized the discourse surrounding American Indian peoples by establishing Harvard's Peabody Museum in 1866, the Bureau of American Ethnology in 1879, and the University of Pennsylvania Museum in 1889.

16. See Oz Frankel's discussion of Schoolcraft (*States of Inquiry*, 248–66). See also Conn's description of Daniel Brinton (*History's Shadow*, 111).

17. Williams to Draper, March 18, 1846, Draper Manuscripts 16F-223, Joseph Brant Papers, Wisconsin Historical Society, Madison.

18. Ibid.

19. Casler to Draper, October 30, 1848, Draper Manuscripts 16F-224, ibid.

20. Draper to Casler, December 16, 1848, Draper Manuscripts 16F-225, ibid.

21. Aldrich to Draper, April 19, 1849, Draper Manuscripts 16F-229, ibid.

22. Copway, *Life, History, and Travels*, 123.

23. Henry Rowe Schoolcraft, *Bibliographical Catalogue*, unpaginated preface.

24. Henry Rowe Schoolcraft, *Historical and Statistical Information*, iv.

25. Jace Weaver's blistering attack on poststructural readings of Native literature contends that indigenous peoples "are being pushed into a postmodern boarding school, where instead of Christian conversion and vocational skills, assimilation requires that we all embrace our hybridity and mixed blood identities, and high theory replaces English as the language that must be spoken" ("Splitting the Earth," in Weaver, *American Indian Literary Nationalism*, 30).

26. Black Hawk's biography appeared in many editions during the 1830s. In chapter 6 we examined the frontispiece illustration from an 1836 London edition. There was also a very rough woodcut frontispiece portrait attached to the 1833 Cincinnati edition in which the warrior was virtually unrecognizable.

27. Donald Jackson, Black Hawk's twentieth-century editor, cites the several substantive changes Patterson made in the later edition (*Black Hawk*, 29–30). Jackson offers a two-column, side-by-side comparison of several emended passages on page 29.

28. Quoted in Jackson's introduction to the modern edition of *Black Hawk*, 25.

29. Frankel, *States of Inquiry*, 2.

30. Ibid., 2, 5, 9–10.

31. This pamphlet appears as an appendix to volume 1 of Henry Rowe Schoolcraft, *Historical and Statistical Information*.

32. Frankel, *States of Inquiry*, 260.

33. Ibid., 266.

34. McGill, *American Literature and the Culture of Reprinting*, 28.

35. Henry Rowe Schoolcraft, *Historical and Statistical Information*, v.

36. Ibid., 265, 319.

37. Henry Rowe Schoolcraft, *Notes on the Iroquois*, 631.

38. Henry Rowe Schoolcraft, *Historical and Statistical Information*, vi. In his earlier *Notes on the Iroquois*, Schoolcraft engages in a long digression about the print culture context for his ethnographic productions: "Some interesting topics of inquiry, bearing on Iroquois history, cannot be well pursued at this time, without access to European libraries. The state of the book trade, and the importation of books into this country, but a few years ago, were such as to present still more scanty advantages to the pursuit of historical letters. There were but few libraries deserving notice, and they were placed at remote points, spread over a very extensive geographical area" (284).

39. The most famous example of the footprint as the trace of the Other occurs in *Robinson Crusoe*, when Defoe's protagonist first sees Friday's tracks in the island's beach sand and stands "like one thunder-struck or as if I had seen an apparition."

40. Beauchamp, *Iroquois Trail, or Footprints*, 41.

41. See Conn, *History's Shadow*, 154–95.

42. Pratt defines "autoethnography" as a genre produced by colonized peoples in which they "engage with the colonizer's own terms . . . [by] partial collaboration with and appropriation of the idioms of the conqueror" (*Imperial Eyes*, 7).

43. Jace Weaver demands that literary interpretation of Native texts "reject a non-Native imposition of hybridity and Western theoretical discourse—to contend that Native American literature stands outside the American canon" ("Splitting the Earth," in Weaver, *American Indian Literary Nationalism*, 31).

44. I was unable to find the print run of this single edition.

45. Elias Johnson, *Legends*, 5, 7, 9.

46. Ibid., 6.

47. In *Archaeology of Knowledge*, Michel Foucault describes how statements come into being and thus become "history." Statements accrue to an "archive," which is itself a "general system of the formation and transformation of statements," the "law of what can be said, the system that governs the appearance of statements as unique events" (127, 129).

48. Elias Johnson, *Legends*, 5.

49. Johnson makes his "nativist" stance explicit when he comments, "I have written in somewhat of the spirit which will characterize a History, by an Indian, yet it does not deserve to be called Indian partiality" (19). This is akin to what Weaver, Womack, and Warrior call "American Indian literary nationalism." Quoting Taiaiake Alfred, Weaver points out that someone in Elias Johnson's position could be "nativist" while writing a book in English: "Experience has shown that cultural revival is not a matter of rejecting all Western influences, but of separating the good from the bad and fashioning a coherent set of ideas out of the traditional culture to guide whatever forms of political and social development . . . are appropriate to contemporary reality" ("Splitting the Earth," in Weaver, *American Indian Literary Nationalism*, 31).

50. Elias Johnson, *Legends*, 8. As Alfred points out, "The clan or the family is the basic unit" of any indigenous epistemology (*Peace, Power, and Righteousness*, 25).

51. Elias Johnson, *Legends*, 8 (emphasis added).

52. Weaver defines this central term, "literary separatism," in the first essay of the collection of the same name in terms of tribal sovereignty: "What is at stake is nothing less than Native identity . . . 'constituted by the historical continuity of relatively open-ended processes of self-definition by community members that relate to both what they take themselves to be and how they define their interests or ends over time'" ("Splitting the Earth," in Weaver, *American Indian Literary Nationalism*, 41). I believe this chapter's reading of Johnson's work allows his Tuscarora-grounded goals to orient our interpretation of his book's material practices.

53. Elias Johnson, *Legends*, 20, 26.

54. Ibid., 32–33.

55. Vizenor, *Manifest Manners*, 12.

56. In her autobiography, Kumeyaay narrator Delfina Cuero often explains to the ethnographer who is recording her recollections of early twentieth-century Kumeyaay life that "this is just my story." See Round, "There Is More to It," for a more detailed discussion.

57. Elias Johnson, *Legends*, 120–21.

58. Ibid., 126.

59. See Davis, *Fiction in the Archives*, especially p. 37. Craig Womack also emphasizes the "mimetic function, the link between literature and social realities that is a natural part of the oral traditions" of Native nations and perhaps a part of their memorials as well (*Red on Red*, 16).

60. Elias Johnson, *Legends*, 127.

61. See Augst, "Temperance, Mass Culture," which argues that the Washingtonian program of collecting signatures and confessions from its members "opened alternative spaces in the public sphere. . . . Their vernacular rhetoric was not just politics or religion by other means, but a populist challenge to official discourses claiming to represent the 'truth' about social welfare" (317). These goals would be refracted and amplified in nativist ways in the reservation contexts Johnson describes.

62. Elias Johnson, *Legends*, 189, 194.

63. Ibid., 216, 228.

64. Ibid., 220.

65. Ibid., 233.

66. Ibid., 234.

Chapter 8

1. Elizabeth Lehuu observes that the post–Civil War press was engaged in a concerted effort to produce a "feast for the eyes" in print publications (*Carnival on the Page*, 4).

2. See Mallery, *Picture-Writing of the American Indians*. Other typical spellers marketed for "Indian youth" that include illustrations are James, *O-jib-ue* (1835); and Stevens, *Sioux Spelling Book* (1836). The famous teacher of the hearing impaired, Thomas Gaulladet, also had one of his children's books translated into Choctaw, perhaps with the idea that Native students were like deaf students and more teachable via pictures. David Murray explains the implications of this sort of linguistic theorizing for Native/non-Native relations. Reducing Native expression to "object" or "image," Murray argues, does little more than essentialize difference and efface the "complex and various" nature of Native American textual expression in the first three centuries after European contact (*Forked Tongues*, 27). Gerald Vizenor echoes this critique in *Manifest Manners* and urges us to consider such "picture-writing" as "*pictomyths*" (100).

3. Le Beau, *Currier and Ives*, 2.

4. Rainey, *Creating Picturesque America*, 7.

5. The photograph of Red Cloud's home was also produced as a postcard and can be viewed in the collections of the Denver Public Library, Western History photos x-3/433.

6. Horse Capture, *Seven Visions of Bull Lodge*, 32.

7. See Schmittou and Logan, "Fluidity of Meaning," for a discussion of how the American flag became integrated into Lakota regalia.

8. Although Robert Warrior and Battiste Good offer two Native perspectives that support this periodization of American Indian history, the recent literature on the dangers of conflating the national and the local (along with the colonialist ramifications of such practices) is cautionary and instructive. For an excellent recent summary of the issues involved, see Philip Deloria, "Historiography," 6–24.

9. See Benes and Emerson, *Native American Picture Books*.

10. Vizenor, *Manifest Manners*, 77.

11. On the importance of indigenous cartography, see Warhus, *Another America*; and Lewis, *Cartographic Encounters*.

12. Dowd, *Spirited Resistance*, 43. Such revivalist "books" were not only symbolic of the appropriation of Euro-American power and technology by the prophets, but were also a kind of economic empowerment. This becomes evident when we read that "Neolin advised his hearers to obtain a copy of the 'bible' which he offered to reproduce at the fixed rate of one buckskin or two doe skins each" (ibid., 46).

13. For a bibliography of Native newspapers in North America, see Littlefield and Parins, *American Indian and Alaska Native Newspapers and Periodicals*.

14. Rainey, *Creating Picturesque America*, 307.

15. In addition to the Red Cloud photograph, see "Kaladlit," an illustration of a Native dwelling adorned with printed illustrations from the Western Greenland newspaper, *Atuagagdliutit* (published in Gothad, Greenland, in 1865).

16. See, for example, Berkhofer, *White Man's Indian*; Philip Deloria, *Playing Indian*;

and Bataille, *Native American Representations*. Alan Trachtenberg's recent *Shades of Hiawatha* also provides insights into the cultural purposes toward which Euro-Americans employed these images, offering 1880 as a significant period marker for the "modern" development of this practice.

17. Apess, *On Our Own Ground*, 277.

18. Miller, *Illustration*, 63.

19. Judkins, "*David Cusick's Ancient History of the Six Nations* as a Neglected Classic," 26–38.

20. Vecsey lists twenty-two separate sections common to all known versions of the Iroquois stories concerning the founding of the Iroquois Confederacy (*Imagining Ourselves Richly*, 99–106). Although Cusick's three-part breakdown is a greatly simplified version of the underlying story structures that Vecsey cites, Cusick includes stories concerning two of the three central figures of these stories — Deganawida and Tadadaho (Atotarho). The main point I wish to make here is that Cusick was, I think, self-consciously employing the physical properties of his text to mirror the structural complexities and protocols of the Iroquois story tradition but greatly simplifying it for practical as well as local cultural reasons. Few people know all the stories of their communities, and many stories are "owned" by clans. Perhaps this is also what Cusick means to imply by the possessive in his book's title — that this is just David Cusick's version of the story: *David Cusick's Sketches of Ancient History*.

21. Brydon cites as evidence of the illustrations' local value Schoolcraft's observations about a Seneca man he had met who held one of Cusick's drawings in great reverence and had kept it safe for many years in his dwelling place ("Ingenuity in Art," 63).

22. Judkins, "*David Cusick's Ancient History of the Six Nations* as a Neglected Classic," 32.

23. Ibid., 35–36.

24. Miller, *Illustration*, 63.

25. False Face Society carving traditions are directed to the medicinal role of the society in Iroquois communities, and thus have much more specific and ceremonial purposes than are indicated by Cusick's image. Stylistically, however, there seems to be a great deal of overlap in how the faces are represented in the carving of masks and how Cusick appears to have carved his woodcut face of the Flying Head. Another Cusick illustration, "Stonish Giants," reflects a similar practice.

26. Atotarho also serves as a more general figure of Iroquois identity. See, for example, James Thomas Stevens's poetry collection, *Combing the Snakes from His Hair* (Michigan State University Press, 2002).

27. Elias Johnson, *Legends*, 63.

28. Quoted in Brydon, "Ingenuity in Art," 65 (emphasis added).

29. Interestingly, Peter C. Marzio (*Democratic Art*, 29) cites the publication from which this image is taken — Henry Rowe Schoolcraft's *Historical and Statistical Information* — as both "a milestone in anthropology" and a watershed moment in the history of chromolithography in America. But not because the chromos were good. It was precisely the failure of later editions of this multivolume collection to live up to its sought-after illustrative use of chromolithography that Marzio cites as evidence of the early technical difficulties of the medium and the complexities of government publishing in the mid-nineteenth century.

30. Miller, *Illustration*, 66.

31. See Wallace, *Death and Rebirth of the Seneca*, 78–86. Fenton, *False Faces*, notes the

shared origin of the Stonish Giants and the False Faces in some Iroquois stories (pp. 487–88).

32. Greene, *Silver Horn*, 223.

33. Ibid., 17, 144.

34. Greene tells us that Silver Horn was respectful of the Kiowa protocol that these stories be told only in the winter, and she speculates that his copying of the images must have been a practice that lay outside this prescription (ibid.).

35. Ibid., 74, 158, 153.

36. Bertelsen, "Greenlandic Literature," 344–45.

37. Quoted in Ridington, "Narrative Technology," 794.

38. Miller, *Illustration*, 151.

39. Anne Ruggles Gere ("Art of Survivance") has argued that DeCora's art also exhibits Vizenor's "survivance." I wish to tease out some of the more subtle aspects of the term as Vizenor employs it in *Manifest Manners*, both because it is in danger of becoming a jargon word with little critical value and because not all Native illustrative practices engage survival and resistance in the same way.

40. Vizenor, *Manifest Manners*, 75.

41. Greene, *Silver Horn*, 151.

42. Benjamin, "Work of Art," 106.

Epilogue

1. McGann, *Textual Condition*, 4, 21.

2. Ibid., 104.

3. The advertisement in the *Indian* appears in the August 18, 1886, edition.

4. Mosley's essay appears in the *Indian School Journal*, 1918, 39.

5. Cheryl Walker, *Indian Nation*, 202, 210–11.

6. Lincoln, *Native American Renaissance*.

7. Treuer, *Native American Fiction*, 5.

8. Ibid.

9. Horse Capture, *Seven Visions of Bull Lodge*, 11, 20.

10. Gone, "As If Reviewing His Life," 72.

11. Ibid., 79, 75.

12. Ibid., 82, 68, 85n23.

13. Red Shirt, *Bead on an Anthill*, 144, 143, 145–46.

Bibliography

Manuscripts

Chicago, Ill.
  Newberry Library
    Samuel Drake, "The Indian Miscellany," [1836]
    John Jackett, "Words to the Ganoda Chant of the Little Water Society"
      (1849–70)
    John Norton Papers
    John Parrish, "Book Relative to Indian Affairs, 1791–1794"
    Stockbridge and Munsee Tribe Papers
    Eleazar Williams Papers
Hanover, N.H.
  Dartmouth College
    Eleazar Wheelock Papers
Madison, Wis.
  Wisconsin Historical Society
    Draper Manuscripts, Joseph Brant Papers, 1710–1879
      Benjamin Williams, "Life of Governor Blacksnake," Draper Mss.
        16-F-107-219
Philadelphia, Pa.
  Historical Society of Pennsylvania
    Hendrick Aupaumut, "Journal of a Mission to the Western Tribes of Indians"
      (1791), Indian Papers, Ms 310
St. Paul, Minn.
  Minnesota Historical Society
    Stephen R. Riggs and Family Papers, 1837–1958

Published Primary Works

Abbott, James H. *Memorial in Behalf of the "Black Bob" Band of Shawnee Indians.*
  Washington, D.C., 1870.
An Account of the Society for the Propagation of the Gospel in Foreign Parts. London:
  Printed by John Downing, 1706.
Alden, Timothy. *An Account of Sundry Missions Performed among the Senecas and
  Munsees in a Series of Letters and an Appendix.* New York: J. Seymour, 1827.
American Board of Foreign Missions. *A Catalogue of Books.* Boston, 1837.
Apess, William. *On Our Own Ground: The Complete Writings of William Apess, a Pequot.*
  Edited by Barry O'Connell. Amherst: University of Massachusetts Press, 1992.

————. *A Son of the Forest*. New York: By the author, 1829.

————. *A Son of the Forest*. New York, 1831.

Aupaumut, Hendrick. "A Narrative of an Embassy to the Western Indians [1791]." *Memoirs of the Historical Society of Pennsylvania* 2, pt. I (1827): 61–131.

Baptist Missionary Magazine. Boston: Board of Managers, Baptist Convention, 1836–49.

Bartlett, Samuel. *Historical Sketch of the Missions of the American Board among the North American Indians*. Boston: The Board, 1876.

Baxter, Richard. *A Call to the Unconverted*. London, 1652.

Beauchamp, William. *The Iroquois Trail, or Footprints of the Six Nations in Customs, Tradition, and History in Which Are Included David Cusick's Sketches of the Ancient History of the Six Nations*. Fayetteville, N.Y.: H. C. Beauchamp, Recorder Office, 1892.

Black Hawk. *Life of Ma-ka-tai-me-she-kia-kiak, or Black Hawk*. Boston, 1834.

————. *Life of Ma-ka-tai-me-she-kia-kiak, or Black Hawk*. London, 1836.

Brinton, Daniel G. *Aboriginal American Authors and Their Productions*. Philadelphia, 1883.

Brown, Catherine. *Memoir of Catherine Brown, a Christian Indian of the Cherokee Nation*. Edited by Rufus Anderson. Philadelphia, 1831.

Brown, P. H. *Poor Sarah*. Edited and translated by Elias Boudinot. Park Hill, Indian Territory: Mission Press, 1843.

Buckner, H. F. *The Gospel According to John*. Marion, Ark.: Domestic and Indian Mission Board of the Southern Baptist Convention, 1860.

Burlin, Natalie Curtis. *The Indian's Book*. New York: Harper, 1907.

Caldwell, Martha, ed. *Annals of the Shawnee Mission and Indian Manual Labor School*. Topeka: Kansas State Historical Society, 1939.

Chainbreaker [Governor Blacksnake]. *Chainbreaker: The Revolutionary War Memoirs of Governor Blacksnake as Told to Benjamin Williams*. Edited by Thomas S. Abler. Lincoln: University of Nebraska Press, 2005.

Cherokee Phoenix. New Echota, Ga., 1828–34.

Church of England. *Portions of the Book of Common Prayer, Psalms, and Hymns, and the First Epistle General of John, in Cree*. London: Church Missionary House, 1856.

Commuck, Thomas. *Indian Melodies*. Harmonized by Thos. Hastings, Esq. New York: Published by G. Lane and C. B. Tippett for the Methodist Episcopal Church, 1845.

Copway, George. *The Life, History, and Travels of Ka-ge-ga-gah-bowh*. Albany, N.Y.: Weed and Parsons, 1847.

————. *Life, Letters, and Speeches*. Edited by LaVonne Brown Ruoff and Donald B. Smith. Lincoln: University of Nebraska Press, 1997.

Cornplanter, Jesse. *Iroquois Indian Games and Dances*. N.p., 1903.

Cruden, Alexander. *A Complete Concordance to the Holy Scriptures of the Old and New Testament*. London: Printed for D. Midwinter, 1738.

Cuffee, Paul. *Memoir of Paul Cuffee*. London, 1840.

Cusick, David. *David Cusick's Sketches of Ancient History of the Six Nations*. Tuscarora Village, N.Y., 1827.

————. *David Cusick's Sketches of Ancient History of the Six Nations*. Lockport, N.Y.: Union and Democrat, 1848.

Drake, Samuel. *The Book of the Indians of North America*. Boston: Antiquarian Bookstore, 1833.

Dwight, Timothy. *Travels in New England and New York.* Edited by Barbara Miller Solomon, with the assistance of Patricia M. King. Vol. 1. Cambridge, Mass.: Belknap Press of Harvard University Press, 1969.

Eliot, John. *The Eliot Tracts: With Letters from John Eliot to Thomas Thorowgood and Richard Baxter.* Edited by Michael Clark. Westport, Conn.: Praeger, 2003.

———. *The Indian Primer.* Boston, 1720.

———. *Mamusse wunneetupanatamwe up biblum God.* Cambridge, Mass., 1663.

———. *Wehkomanonganoo Asquam Peantogig* [Call to the Unconverted]. Cambridge, Mass., 1664.

Everett, Edward. *An Address Delivered at Bloody Brook, in South Deerfield, September 30, 1835.* Boston: Russell, Shattuck & Williams, 1835.

Field, Thomas W. *An Essay towards an Indian Bibliography.* [1873.] Columbus, Ohio: Reprinted by Long's College Book Co., 1951.

Finley, James B. *Life among the Indians, or Personal Reminiscences and History.* Cincinnati: Methodist Book Concern, 1857.

Fish, Joseph. *Old Light on Separate Ways: The Narragansett Diary of Joseph Fish, 1765–1776.* Edited by William S. Simmons and Cheryl L. Simmons. Hanover, N.H.: University Press of New England, 1982.

Folsom, David. "Prospectus for the Choctaw Intelligencer." *Indian Advocate* (November 1848): 1.

Galland, Isaac, ed. *Chronicles of the North American Savages* 1, no. 1 (May 1835): 9.

Harriot, Thomas. *A Brief and True Report of the New Found Land of Virginia.* Francoforti ad Moenum, 1590.

Hawkins, Ernest. *Historical Notices of the Missions of the Church of England Previous to the Independence of the United States.* London: B. Fellowes, 1845.

Holisso Hushi Holhtine . . . Chata Almanac for 1839. Indian Territory: Park Hill Mission Press, 1839.

Holy Bible, Containing the Old Testament and the New. London: Evan Taylor for the Society of Stationers, 1653.

Hopkins, Samuel. *Historical Memoirs Relating to the Housatunnuk Indians . . . under the Ministry of the late Rev. Sargent.* Boston, 1753.

Hopkins, Sarah Winnemucca. *Life among the Paiutes: Their Wrongs and Claims.* [1883.] Reno: University of Nevada Press, 1994.

Horse Capture, George, ed. *The Seven Visions of Bull Lodge: As Told to His Daughter, Garter Snake.* Lincoln: University of Nebraska Press, 1992.

Irvin, Samuel, and William Hamilton. *Original Hymns in the Ioway Language.* Iowa Territory: Ioway and Sac Mission Press, 1843.

Jackson, Andrew. "President's Message." 21st Cong., 2nd sess.

Jacobs, Peter. *Journal of the Reverend Peter Jacobs, Indian Wesleyan Missionary.* Boston: Press of G. C. Rand, 1853.

James, Edwin. *O-jib-ue Spelling Book Designed for Native Learners.* Boston: Crocker and Brewster, 1835.

Jemison, Mary. *A Narrative of the Life of Mrs. Mary Jemison.* Edited by James E. Seaver. London: Longman, 1827.

Johnson, Elias. *Legends, Traditions, and Laws of the Iroquois or Six Nations and History of the Tuscarora Indians.* Lockport, N.Y.: Union Printing Co., 1881.

Johnson, Joseph. *To Do Good to My Indian Brethren: The Writings of Joseph Johnson, 1751–1776.* Edited by Laura J. Murray. Amherst: University of Massachusetts Press, 1998.

Jones, Electa F. *Stockbridge, Past and Present, or, Records of an Old Mission Station.* Springfield, Mass.: Sam. Bowles and Co., 1854.

Kirkland, Samuel. *The Journals of Samuel Kirkland.* Edited by Walter Pilkington. Clinton, N.Y.: Hamilton College, 1980.

Love, W. Deloss. *Samson Occom and the Christian Indians of New England.* [1899.] Syracuse, N.Y.: University of Syracuse Press, 2000.

Lowery, George. "Notable Persons in Cherokee History: Sequoyah or George Gist." Introduction and transcription by John Howard Payne. *Journal of Cherokee Studies* 2, no. 4 (Fall 1977): 385–93.

Luckenbach, Abraham. *Forty-six Select Scripture Narratives from the Old Testament. Embellished with Engravings, for the Use of Indian Youths.* New York: Daniel Fanshaw, 1848.

Maclean, John. "Concurring Opinion," *Worcester v. Georgia.* 31 U.S. 515 (1832).

Mallery, Garrick. *Picture-Writing of the American Indians.* Washington, D.C., 1894.

Marshall, John. "Majority Opinion," *Cherokee Nation v. State of Georgia.* 30 U.S. 1 (1831).

McCallum, James Dow, ed. *The Letters of Eleazar Wheelock's Indians.* Hanover, N.H.: Dartmouth College, 1932.

McKenney, Thomas, and James Hall. *History of the Indian Tribes of North America.* 1837–44.

Memorial of the Indian Delegates from the Indian Country . . . Washington, D.C., 1880.

Mitchell, Joseph. *The Missionary Pioneer, or, a Brief Memoir of the Life, Labours, and Death of John Stewart, (Man of Colour) Founder, under God, of the Mission among the Wyandotts at Upper Sandusky, Ohio.* New York: J. C. Totten, 1827.

Mooney, James. *The Sacred Formulas of the Cherokees.* 7th Annual Report, Bureau of American Ethnology. Washington, D.C.: Smithsonian Institution, 1891.

Mooney, James, and Frans Olbrechts. *The Swimmer Manuscript: Cherokee Sacred Formulas and Medicine Prescriptions.* Bureau of American Ethnology, Bulletin 99. Washington, D.C.: Government Printing Office, 1932.

Morse, Jedidiah. *A Report to the Secretary of War of the U.S. on Indian Affairs.* New Haven, Conn., 1832.

Mosely, Garrett. "Why I Am a Printer." *Indian School Journal* (Chilocco, Okla., June 1918): 38–41.

Muskogee Nation. *The Memorial of the Muscogee or Creek Nation of Indians.* Arksansas, 1852.

Nason, Elias. "Indebtedness of the English to the Indian Languages of America." *New England Genealogical and Historical Register* 20, no. 4 (October 1866): 309.

Norton, John. *The Journal of Major John Norton, 1816.* Edited by Carl F. Klinck. Toronto: Champlain Society, 1970.

O'Callaghan, E. B., ed. "Papers Relating to the Six Nations." In *The Documentary History of New-York.* Vol. 4. Albany: Weed, Parsons, 1851.

Occom, Samson. *A Choice Collection of Hymns* (1774).

———. *The Collected Writings of Samson Occom, Mohegan.* Edited by Joanna Brooks. New York: Oxford University Press, 2006.

———. *A Sermon, Preached at the Execution of Moses Paul.* New Haven, Conn.: Samuel Green, 1772.

———. *A Sermon, Preached at the Execution of Moses Paul.* New Haven, Conn., 1789.

———. *A Sermon, Preached at the Execution of Moses Paul.* Bennington, Vt., 1810.

O'Meara, Frederick. *Report of a Mission to the Ottahwahs and Ojibwas, on Lake Huron.* London: Society for the Propagation of the Gospel, 1846.

Panoplist.

Parkman, Francis. *The Oregon Trail: The Conspiracy of Pontiac.* [1870.] New York: American Library, 1991.

Penhallow, Samuel. *History of the Wars of New England with the Eastern Indians.* Boston, 1726.

Perdue, Theda, ed. *Cherokee Editor: The Writings of Elias Boudinot.* Athens: University of Georgia Press, 1983.

Phillips, Joyce B., and Paul Gary Phillips, eds. *The Brainerd Journal: A Mission to the Cherokees, 1817–1823.* Lincoln: University of Nebraska Press, 1998.

Pickering, John. *An Essay on a Uniform Orthography for the Indian Languages of North America, as Published in the Memoirs of the American Academy of Arts and Sciences.* Cambridge, Mass.: Hilliard and Metcalf, 1820.

Pidgeon, William. *Traditions of Decodah.* New York: Horace and Thayer, 1858.

Quinney, John. "Celebration of the Fourth of July at Reidsville, New York." 1859.

————. *Memorial of John W. Quinney.* Washington, D.C., 1852.

Reed, Nancy. *Memorial and Argument Submitted to the Cherokee Commissioners in the Claim of Nancy Reed and Children, Cherokee Indians of North Carolina.* Washington, D.C., 1846.

Richardson, Leon Burr. *An Indian Preacher in England.* Hanover, N.H.: Dartmouth, 1933.

Richmond, Legh. *The Dairyman's Daughter.* Edited and translated by Elias Boudinot. Park Hill, Indian Territory: Mission Press, 1847.

Riggs, Stephen. *Dakota abc wowapi kin Tamakoce kaga.* Chicago: Dean and Ottaway Steam Printers, 1866.

Riggs, Stephen R., and Gideon Pond. *The Dakota First Reading Book.* Cincinnati: Kendall and Henry Publishers, 1839.

Ross, John. *Letter from John Ross, Principal Chief of the Cherokee Nation, to a Gentleman in Philadelphia.* Philadelphia, 1838.

————. *Memorial of John Ross and Others, Representatives of the Cherokee Nation of Indians.* 29th Congress, 1st Session. Senate Document 331. Washington, D.C.: Ritchie and Heiss, 1846.

Rowlandson, Mary. *The Sovereignty and Goodness of God, Together with the Faithfulness of His Promises Displayed.* Edited with an introduction by Neal Salisbury. [1682.] New York: Bedford/St. Martin's, 1997.

Schoolcraft, Henry Rowe. *A Bibliographical Catalogue of Books, Translations of the Scriptures, and Other Publications in the Indian Tongues of the United States: With Brief Critical Notices.* Washington, D.C.: C. Alexander, 1849.

————. *Historical and Statistical Information Regarding the History, Conditions, and Prospects of the Indian Tribes of the United States.* 10 vols. Philadelphia: Lippencott and Grabo, 1851–57.

————. *Notes on the Iroquois, or Contributions to American History, Antiquities, and General Ethnology.* Albany, N.Y.: J. Munsell, 1847.

Schoolcraft, Jane Johnston. *The Sound the Stars Make Rushing Through the Sky: The Writings of Jane Johnston Schoolcraft.* Edited and with an introduction by Robert Dale Parker. Philadelphia: University of Pennsylvania Press, 2007.

Sergeant, John. *A Letter from the Revd. Mr. Sergeant of Stockbridge to Dr. Colman of Boston.* Boston, 1743.

Severance, Frank H., ed. *Narratives of Early Mission Work on the Niagra Frontier and Buffalo Creek.* Publications of the Buffalo Historical Society. Vol. 6. Buffalo, N.Y.: 1906.

Snelling, William Joseph. "Life of Black Hawk." *North American Review* 40, no. 86 (1835): 68–87.

Stevens, Jedidiah Dwight. *Sioux Spelling Book: Designed for the Use of Native Learners.* Boston: Crocker and Brewster, 1836.

Stiggins, George. "A Historical Narration of the Genealogy Traditions and Downfall of the Ispocaga or Creek Tribe." In "Creek Nativism and the Creek War of 1813–1814 (Parts 1–3)," edited by Theron B. Nunez Jr. *Ethnohistory* 5, no. 2 (1958): 131–75.

Stiles, Ezra. *The Literary Diary of Ezra Stiles.* Edited by Franklin Bowditch Dexter. New York: Scribner's, 1901.

Strong, Nathaniel T. *Appeal to the Christian Community on the Condition and Prospects of the New-York Indians.* New York: E. B. Clayton, 1841.

Tac, Pablo. "Indian Life and Customs at Mission San Luis Rey." Edited and translated by Mina Hewes and Gordon Hewes. *Americas* 9, no. 1 (July 1952): 87–106.

[Thatcher, Peter]. *Brief Account of the Society for Propagating the Gospel among the Indians and Others in North-America.* Boston: S. Hall, 1798.

Timberlake, Henry. *The Memoirs of Lt. Henry Timberlake: The Story of a Soldier, Adventurer, and Emissary to the Cherokees, 1756–1765.* Edited by Duane H. King. Cherokee, N.C.: Museum of the Cherokee Indian Press, 2007.

Trumbull, John. *Natick Dictionary.* Washington, D.C.: Government Printing Office, 1903.

"Type for Indian Books." *American Bookmaker* 21, no. 3. (September 1895): 71–72.

Warren, William W. *History of the Ojibway People.* [1885.] St. Paul: Minnesota Historical Society Press, 1984.

Wellenreuther, Herman, and Carola Wessel, eds. *The Moravian Missionary Diaries of David Zeisberger, 1772–1781.* Translated by Julie Tomberlin Weber. University Park: Pennsylvania State University Press, 2005.

Wheelock, Eleazar. *A Brief Narrative of the Indian Charity-School in Lebanon in Connecticut, New England.* London: Printed by J. and W. Oliver, 1767.

———. *A Plain and Faithful Narrative of the Indian Charity School at Lebanon in Connecticut.* Boston: Samuel and Richard Draper, 1763.

Williams, Eleazar. *Good News to the Iroquois Nation.* Burlington, Vt.: Printed by Samuel Mills, 1813.

Wright, Asher, ed. *Go' wana gwa ih sat hah yon de'. . . A Spelling Book in the Seneca Language.* Buffalo Creek, N.Y.: Seneca Mission House, 1842.

———, ed. *The Mental Elevator.* Buffalo Creek, N.Y.: Seneca Mission House, 1841.

Zitkala Sâ [Gertrude Bonin]. *Old Indian Legends.* Boston: Ginn, 19091.

Secondary Works

Abler, Thomas. "Protestant Missionaries and Native Culture: Parallel Careers of Asher Wright and Silas Rand." *American Indian Quarterly* 16, no. 1 (Winter 1992): 25–37.

Alden, John. "The Cherokee Archive." *American Archivist* 5 (1942): 240.

Alfred, Taiaiake. *Peace, Power, and Righteousness: An Indigenous Manifesto.* Ontario, Canada: Oxford University Press, 1999.

Amory, Hugh. "Under the Exchange, the Unprofitable Business of Michael Perry, a Seventeenth-Century Boston Bookseller." *American Antiquarian Society Proceedings* 103, no. 1 (1993): 31–60.

Amory, Hugh, and David D. Hall. *The Colonial Book in the Atlantic World.* Vol. 1 of *The History of the Book in America.* Cambridge, Mass.: American Antiquarian Society, 2000.

Augst, Thomas. "Temperance, Mass Culture, and the Romance of Experience." *American Literary History* 19, no. 2 (Summer 2007): 297–323.

Axtell, James. "The Power of Print in the Eastern Woodlands." *William and Mary Quarterly* 3rd ser., 44, no. 2 (April 1987): 300–309.

Basso, Keith. "The Ethnography of Writing." In *Explorations in the Ethnography of Speaking,* edited by Richard Bauman and Joel Sherzer, 425–32. Cambridge: Press Syndicate of the University of Cambridge, 1974.

Bataille, Gretchen, ed. *Native American Representations: First Encounters, Distorted Images, and Literary Appropriation.* Lincoln: University of Nebraska Press, 2001.

Bauman, Richard. "The Nationalization and Internationalization of Folklore: The Case of Schoolcraft's 'Gitzee Gauzine.'" *Western Folklore* 52, no. 2/4 (April–October 1993): 247–69.

Bellin, Joshua. "John Eliot's Playing Indian." *Early American Literature* 42, no. 1 (2007): 1–30.

Bender, Margaret. *Signs of Cherokee Culture: Sequoyah's Syllabary in Eastern Cherokee Life.* Chapel Hill: University of North Carolina Press, 2002.

Benes, Rebecca C., and Gloria Emerson. *Native American Picture Books of Change: The Art of Historic Children's Editions.* Albuquerque: University of New Mexico Press, 2004.

Benjamin, Walter. "The Work of Art in the Age of Its Technological Reproducibility." *Walter Benjamin: Selected Writings.* Vol. 3. Cambridge, Mass.: Harvard University Press, 2002.

Berkhofer, Robert F. *Salvation and the Savage: An Analysis of Protestant Missions and American Indian Responses, 1787–1862.* Lexington: University of Kentucky Press, 1965.

———. *The White Man's Indian: Images of the American Indian from Columbus to the Present.* New York: Knopf, 1978.

Bertelsen, Christian. "Greenlandic Literature." In *Arctic Languages: An Awakening,* edited by Dirmid R. F. Collis, 343–54. Paris: UNESCO, 1990.

Bieder, Robert E. *Science Encounters the Indian, 1820–1880.* Norman: University of Oklahoma Press, 2003.

Bourdieu, Pierre. *The Field of Cultural Production: Essays on Art and Literature.* New York: Columbia University Press, 1993.

Bouwman, Heather. "Samson Occom and the Sermonic Tradition." In *Early Native Literacies in Early New England: A Documentary and Critical Anthology,* edited by Kristina Bross and Hilary Wyss, 63–71. Amherst: University of Massachusetts Press, 2008.

Bragdon, Kathleen. "The Interstices of Literacy: Books and Writings and Their Use in Native American Southern New England." In *Anthropology, History, and American Indians,* edited by James Merrill and Ives Goddard, 121–30. Washington, D.C.: Smithsonian, 2002.

Bragdon, Kathleen, and Ives Goddard. *Native Writings in Massachusett.* Worcester, Mass.: American Philosophical Society, 1988.

Brannon, Frank. *Cherokee Phoenix, Advent of a Newspaper: The Print Shop of the Cherokee Nation, 1828–1834.* Tuscaloosa, Ala.: SpeakEasy Press, 2005.

Brooks, Joanna. "Six Hymns by Samson Occom." *Early American Literature* 38, no. 1 (2003): 67–87.

———. "This Indian World: An Introduction to the Writings of Samson Occom." In Samson Occom, *The Collected Writings of Samson Occom*, edited by Joanna Brooks, 3–43. New York: Oxford University Press, 2006.

Brooks, Lisa Tanya. *The Common Pot: The Recovery of Native Space in the Northeast.* Minneapolis: University of Minnesota Press, 2008.

Bross, Kristina. *Dry Bones and Indian Sermons: Praying Indians in Colonial America.* New York: Cornell University Press, 2004.

Bross, Kristina, and Hilary Wyss, eds. *Early Native Literacies in Early New England: A Documentary and Critical Anthology.* Amherst: University of Massachusetts Press, 2008.

Brown, Jennifer S. H. "The Wasitay Religion: Prophecy, Oral Literacy, and Belief on Hudson Bay." In *Reassessing Revitalization Movements: Perspectives from North America and the Pacific Islands*, edited by Michael Harkin, 104–23. Lincoln: University of Nebraska Press, 2004.

Brown, Matthew. *The Pilgrim and the Bee: Reading Rituals and Book Culture in Early New England.* Philadelphia: University of Pennsylvania Press, 2007.

Brydon, Sharry. "Ingenuity in Art: The Early 19th-Century Works of David and Dennis Cusick." *American Indian Art* (Spring 1995): 60–69.

Cebula, Larry. *Plateau Indians and the Quest for Spiritual Power, 1700–1850.* Lincoln: University of Nebraska Press, 2003.

Champagne, Duane. *Social Order and Political Change: Constitutional Governments among the Cherokee, the Choctaw, the Chicasaw, and the Creek.* Stanford, Calif.: Stanford University Press, 1992.

Chartier, Roger. *The Order of Books: Readers, Authors, and Libraries in Europe between the Fourteenth and Eighteenth Centuries.* Stanford, Calif.: Stanford University Press, 1994.

Cheyfitz, Eric. "The (Post)Colonial Construction of Indian Country: U.S. American Indian Literatures and Federal Indian Law." In *The Columbia Guide to the American Indian Literatures of the United States since 1945*, 28–108. New York: Columbia University Press, 2006.

Conn, Steven. *History's Shadow: Native Americans and Historical Consciousness in the Nineteenth Century.* Chicago: University of Chicago Press, 2004.

Crain, Patricia. *The Story of A: The Alphabetization of America from The New England Primer to The Scarlet Letter.* Stanford, Calif.: Stanford University Press, 2000.

Darnton, Robert. "What Is the History of Books?" In *The Book History Reader*, edited by David Finkelstein and Alistair Cleery, 9–26. London: Routledge, 2002.

Davis, Natalie Zemon. *Fiction in the Archives: Pardon Tales and Their Tellers in Sixteenth-Century France.* Stanford, Calif.: Stanford University Press, 1987.

Deloria, Philip. "Historiography." In *A Companion to American Indian History*, edited by Philip J. Deloria and Neal Salisbury, 6–24. London: Blackwell, 2002.

———. *Playing Indian.* New Haven: Yale University Press, 1998.

———. "What Is the Middle Ground, Anyway?" *William and Mary Quarterly* 3rd ser., 63, no. 1 (January 2006): 15–22.

Deloria, Vine. *Custer Died for Your Sins.* Toronto: Macmillan, 1969.

DeMallie, Raymond, ed. *The Sixth Grandfather: Black Elk's Teachings Given to John G. Neihardt*. Lincoln: University of Nebraska Press, 1984.

DeMallie, Raymond, and Douglas Parks. "Plains Indian Native Literatures." *boundary 2* 19, no. 3 (Autumn 1992): 105–47.

Dillon, Elizabeth. *The Gender of Freedom: Fictions of Liberalism and the Literary Public Sphere*. Stanford, Calif.: Stanford University Press, 2004.

Donaldson, Laura. "Writing the Talking Stick: Alphabetic Literacy as Colonial Technology and Postcolonial Appropriation." *American Indian Quarterly* 22 (Winter/Spring 1998): 46–63.

Dowd, Gregory. *A Spirited Resistance: The North American Indian Struggle for Unity, 1745–1815*. Baltimore: Johns Hopkins University Press, 1992.

Eilenberg, Susan. "Mortal Pages: Wordsworth and the Reformation of Copyright." *ELH* 56 (1989): 351–74.

Eisenstein, Elizabeth. *The Printing Press as an Agent of Change: Communications and Cultural Transformations in Early Modern Europe*. New York: Cambridge University Press, 1979.

Elmer, Jonathan. "The Black Atlantic Archive." *American Literary History* 17, no. 1 (Spring 2005): 160–70.

Erdrich, Louise. *Books and Islands in Ojibwe Country*. Washington, D.C.: National Geographic, 2003.

Fenton, William N. *The False Faces of the Iroquois*. Norman: University of Oklahoma Press, 1987.

Fitzgerald, Stephanie. "The Cultural Work of a Mohegan Painted Basket." In *Native Literacies in Early New England*, edited by Hilary Wyss and Kristin Bross, 51–61. Amherst: University of Massachusetts Press, 2008.

Folsom, Ed. "Appearing in Print: Illustrations of the Self in *Leaves of Grass*." In *The Cambridge Companion to Walt Whitman*. New York: Cambridge University Press, 1995.

Foreman, Grant. *Sequoyah*. Norman: University of Oklahoma Press, 1938.

Foster, George E. *Sequoyah: The American Cadmus*. 1885.

Foucault, Michel. *The Archaeology of Knowledge*. New York: Pantheon Books, 1972.

Frankel, Oz. *States of Inquiry: Social Investigations and Print Culture in Nineteenth-Century Britain and the United States*. Baltimore: Johns Hopkins University Press, 2006.

Furtwangler, Alfred. *Bringing Indians to the Book*. Seattle: University of Washington Press, 2005.

Gere, Ann Ruggles. "An Art of Survivance: Angel DeCora at Carlisle." *American Indian Quarterly* 28, nos. 3–4 (Summer/Fall 2004): 649–84.

Gilmore, William. *Reading Becomes a Necessity of Life: Material and Cultural Life in Rural New England, 1780–1835*. Knoxville: University of Tennessee Press, 1992.

Gilroy, Paul. *The Black Atlantic: Modernity and Double Consciousness*. Cambridge, Mass.: Harvard University Press, 1993.

Goddard, Ives, ed. *Languages*. Vol. 17 of *Handbook of North American Indians*. Washington, D.C.: Smithsonian Institution, 1996.

Gone, Joseph. "'As If Reviewing His Life': Bull Lodge's Narrative and the Mediation of Self-Representation." *American Indian Quarterly* 30, no. 1 (2006): 67–86.

Greene, Candace S. *Silver Horn: Master Illustrator of the Kiowas*. Norman: University of Oklahoma Press, 2001.

Gustafson, Sandra. "American Literature and the Public Sphere." *American Literary History* 20 (2008): 465–78.

———. *Eloquence Is Power: Oratory and Performance in Early America*. Chapel Hill: University of North Carolina Press, 2000.

———. "Nations of Israelites: Prophecy and Cultural Autonomy in the Writings of William Apess." *Religion and Literature* 26 (1994): 31–53.

Gutjahr, Paul, and Megan L. Benton, eds. *Illuminating Letters: Typography and Literary Interpretation*. Amherst: University of Massachusetts Press, 2001.

Habermas, Jürgen. *The Structural Transformation of the Public Sphere: An Inquiry into a Category of Bourgeois Society*. Translated by Thomas Burger. Cambridge, Mass.: MIT Press, 1991.

Hall, David D. *Cultures of Print: Essays in the History of the Book*. Amherst: University of Massachusetts, 1996.

———. *Worlds of Wonder, Days of Judgment: Popular Religious Belief in Early New England*. Cambridge, Mass.: Harvard University Press, 1990.

Hargrett, Lester. *A Bibliography of the Laws and Constitutions of the American Indians*. Cambridge, Mass.: Harvard University Press, 1947.

Harkin, Michael, ed. *Reassessing Revitalization Movements: Perspectives from North America and the Pacific Islands*. Lincoln: University of Nebraska Press, 2004.

Hesse, Carla. "Enlightenment Epistemology and the Laws of Authorship in Revolutionary France, 1777–1793." *Representations* 30 (Spring 1990): 109–37.

Hinderaker, Eric, and Peter Mancall. *At the Edge of Empire: The Backcountry in British North America*. Baltimore: Johns Hopkins University Press, 2003.

Hunter, Charles E. "The Delaware Nativist Revival of the Mid-eighteenth Century." *Ethnohistory* 18, no. 1 (Winter 1971): 39–49.

Jackson, Donald, ed. *Black Hawk: An Autobiography*. Champagne/Urbana: University of Illinois Press, 1965.

Judkins, Russell A. "*David Cusick's Ancient History of the Six Nations* as a Neglected Classic." In *Iroquois Studies: A Guide to Documentary and Ethnographic Resources from Western New York and the Genesee Valley*, edited by Russell A. Judkins. Geneseo: Department of Anthropology, State University of New York, 1987.

Justice, Daniel Heath. *Our Fire Survives the Storm: A Cherokee Literary History*. Minneapolis: University of Minnesota Press, 2006.

Kaestle, Carl. *Literacy in the United States: Readers and Reading since 1880*. New Haven, Conn.: Yale University Press, 1991.

Kelsay, Isabel Thompson. *Joseph Brant, 1743–1807, Man of Two Worlds*. Syracuse, N.Y.: Syracuse University Press, 1984.

Kirkpatrick, Jack F., and Anna G. Kirkpatrick. "Notebook of a Cherokee Shaman." Smithsonian Contributions to Anthropology, vol. 2, no. 6, 1–125. Washington, D.C.: Smithsonian Institution Press, 1970.

Konkle, Maureen. "Indian Literacy, U.S. Colonialism, and Literary Criticism." *American Literature* 69, no. 3 (1997): 458–86.

Krupat, Arnold. "Native American Autobiography and the Synecdochic Self." In *American Autobiography: Retrospect and Prospect*, edited by Paul John Eakin, 171–94. Madison: University of Wisconsin Press, 1991.

Le Beau, Brian F. *Currier and Ives: America Imagined*. Washington, D.C.: Smithsonian Institution Press, 2001.

Lehuu, Elizabeth. *Carnival on the Page: Popular Print Media in Antebellum America.* Chapel Hill: University of North Carolina Press, 2000.

Lejeune, Philippe. *On Autobiography.* Minneapolis: University of Minnesota Press, 1989.

Lepore, Jill. *The Name of War: King Philip's War and the Origins of American Identity.* New York: Knopf, 1998.

Lewis, G. Malcom, ed. *Cartographic Encounters: Perspectives on Native American Mapmaking and Map Use.* Chicago: University of Chicago Press, 1998.

Lincoln, Kenneth. *Native American Renaissance.* Berkeley: University of California Press, 1983.

Littlefield, Daniel, and James Parins, eds. *American Indian and Alaska Native Newspapers and Periodicals.* Westport, Conn.: Greenwood Press, 1984.

Loughran, Trish. *The Republic in Print: Print Culture in the Age of U.S. Nation Building, 1770–1870.* New York: Columbia University Press, 2007.

Lyons, Scott. "What Do American Indians Want from Writing?" *College Composition and Communication* 51, no. 3 (February 2000): 447–68.

Martin, Joel. *Sacred Revolt: The Muskogees' Struggle for a New World.* Boston: Beacon, 1991.

Marzio, Peter C. *The Democratic Art: Pictures for a 19th-Century America.* Boston: David R. Godine, 1979.

McGann, Jerome. *The Textual Condition.* Princeton, N.J.: Princeton University Press, 1991.

McGill, Meredith. *American Literature and the Culture of Reprinting, 1834–1853.* Philadelphia: University of Pennsylvania Press, 2003.

McKenzie, D. F. *Bibliography and the Sociology of Texts.* New York: Cambridge University Press, 1999.

McLoughlin, William. "New Angles of Vision on the Cherokee Ghost Dance Movement of 1811–1812." *American Indian Quarterly* 5, no. 4 (November 1979): 317–45.

McMurtrie, Douglas. *Jotham Meeker: Pioneer Printer of Kansas.* Chicago: Eyencourt Press, 1930.

———. "Pioneer Printing of Kansas, 1855–1850." *Kansas Historical Quarterly* 1, no. 1 (November 1931): 3–16.

———. "The Shawnee Sun: The First Indian-Language Periodical Published in the United States." *Kansas Historical Quarterly* 2, no. 4 (November 1933): 338–42.

Merrell, James. *Into the American Woods: Negotiators on the Pennsylvania Frontier.* New York: Norton, 1999.

Mignolo, Walter. *The Darker Side of the Renaissance: Literacy, Territoriality, and Colonization.* Ann Arbor: University of Michigan Press, 2003.

Miller, J. Hillis. *Illustration.* Cambridge, Mass.: Harvard University Press, 1992.

Monaghan, E. Jennifer. *Learning to Read and Write in Colonial America.* Amherst: University of Massachusetts Press, 2005.

———. "'She Loved to Read Good Books': Literacy and the Indians of Martha's Vineyard, 1643–1725." *History of Education Quarterly* 30, no. 4 (Winter 1990): 492–521.

Moon, Randall. "William Apess and Writing White." *Studies in American Indian Literature* 5, no. 4 (Winter 1993): 45–54.

Mt. Pleasant, Alyssa. "After the Whirlwind: Maintaining a Haudenosaunee Place at Buffalo Creek, 1780–1825." Ph.D. diss., Cornell University, 2007.

Murray, David. *Forked Tongues: Speech, Writing, and Representation in North American Indian Texts*. Bloomington: Indiana University Press, 1991.

Murray, Laura. "Joseph Johnson's Diary, Farmington, Connecticut." In *Early Native Literacies in Early New England: A Documentary and Critical Anthology*, edited by Kristina Bross and Hilary Wyss, 42–50. Amherst: University of Massachusetts Press, 2008.

———. "'Pray Sir, Consider a Little': Rituals of Subordination and Strategies of Resistance in the Letters of Hezekiah Calvin and David Fowler to Eleazar Wheelock." In *Early Native American Writing: New Critical Essays*, edited by Helen Jaskoski, 15–41. Cambridge: University of Cambridge Press, 1996.

Nord, David Paul. *Faith in Reading: Religious Publishing and the Birth of Mass Media in America*. London: Oxford University Press, 2004.

O'Brien, Jean. *Dispossession by Degrees: Indian Land and Identity in Natick, Massachusetts, 1650–1790*. New York: Cambridge University Press, 1997.

Oestreicher, David. "Unmasking the Walam Olum: A Nineteenth-Century Hoax." *Bulletin of the Archaeological Society of New Jersey* 49 (1994): 1–44.

Perdue, Theda, ed. *Cherokee Editor: The Writings of Elias Boudinot*. Athens: University of Georgia Press, 1983.

Petersen, R. Eric. "Messages, Petitions, Communications, and Memorials to Congress." ⟨www.rules.house.gov/Archives/98–839.pdf⟩.

Pfau, Thomas. "The Pragmatics of Genre: Moral Authority and Lyric Authorship in Hegel and Wordsworth." In *The Construction of Authorship: Textual Appropriation in Law and Literature*, edited by Martha Woodmansee and Peter Jaszi. Durham: Duke University Press, 1994.

Pratt, Mary Louise. *Imperial Eyes: Travel Writing and Transculturation*. London: Routledge, 1992.

Pulsipher, Jenny. "Subjects unto the Same King." *Massachusetts Historical Review* (2003): 29–57.

Rainey, Sue. *Creating Picturesque America: Monument to the Natural and Cultural Landscape*. Nashville, Tenn.: Vanderbilt University Press, 1994.

Rand, Jacki Thompson. *Kiowa Humanity and the Invasion of the State*. Lincoln: University of Nebraska Press, 2008.

Rayman, Ronald. "Joseph Lancaster's Monotorial System of Instruction and American Indian Education." *History of Education Quarterly* 21, no. 4 (Winter 1981): 295–409.

Rice, Grantland S. *The Transformation of Authorship in America*. Chicago: University of Chicago Press, 1997.

Richter, Daniel K. *The Ordeal of the Longhouse: The Peoples of the Iroquois League in the Era of European Colonization*. Chapel Hill: University of North Carolina Press, 1992.

Ridington, Robin. "Narrative Technology and Eskimo History." *Ethnohistory* 47, no. 3 (2000): 791–96.

Rose, Mark. *Authors and Owners: The Invention of Copyright*. Cambridge, Mass.: Harvard University Press, 1993.

Round, Phillip. *By Nature and by Custom Cursed: Transatlantic Civil Discourse and New England Cultural Production, 1620–1660*. Hanover, N.H.: University Press of New England, 1999.

————. "Neither Here nor There: Transatlantic Epistolarity in Early America." In *Companion to the Literatures of Colonial America*, edited by Susan Castillo and Ivy Schweitzer, 426–45. New York: Blackwell, 2005.

————. "'There Was More to It, but That Is All I Can Remember': The Persistence of History and the Autobiography of Delfina Cuero." *American Indian Quarterly* 21, no. 2 (Spring 1997): 1–22.

Ruoff, A. LaVonne Brown. *American Indian Literatures: An Introduction, Bibliographic Review, and Selected Bibliography*. New York: Modern Language Association, 1990.

Sarris, Greg. *Keeping Slug Woman Alive: A Holistic Approach to American Indian Texts*. Berkeley: University of California Press, 1993.

Saunt, Claudio. *A New Order of Things: Property, Power, and the Transformation of the Creek Indians, 1733–1816*. New York: Cambridge University Press, 1999.

Sayre, Gordon. "Defying Assimilation, Confounding Authenticity: The Case of William Apess." *a/b: Autobiography Studies* 11 (Spring 1996): 1–18.

————. *The Indian Chief as Tragic Hero*. Chapel Hill: University of North Carolina Press, 2007.

Schmidt, David L., and Murdena Marshall, eds. and trans. *Mi'kmaq Hieroglyphic Prayers: Readings in North America's First Indigenous Script*. Halifax, Nova Scotia: Nimbus Publishing, 1995.

Schmittou, Douglas, and Michael Logan. "Fluidity of Meaning: Flag Imagery in Plains Indian Art." *American Indian Quarterly* 26, no. 4 (Fall 2002): 559–604.

Schoenberg, Wilfred. *The Lapwai Mission Press*. Boise, Idaho: Center for the Book, 1994.

Schweitzer, Ivy. *Perfecting Friendship: Politics and Affiliation in Early American Literature*. Chapel Hill: University of North Carolina Press, 2006.

Shields, David. *Civil Tongues and Polite Letters*. Chapel Hill, N.C.: Published for the Institute of Early American History and Culture, 1997.

Shoemaker, Nancy. *A Strange Likeness: Becoming Red and White in Eighteenth-Century North America*. New York: Oxford University Press, 2004.

Silver, Rollo G. "Financing the Publication of Early New England Sermons." *Studies in Bibliography* 11 (1958): 163–78.

Silverman, David K. "Indians, Missionaries, and Religious Translation: Creating Wampanoag Christianity in Seventeenth-Century Martha's Vineyard." *William and Mary Quarterly* 3rd ser., 74, no. 4 (December 2001): 622–66.

Slotkin, Richard, and James K. Folsom, eds. *So Dreadfull a Judgment: Puritan Responses to King Philip's War, 1676–1677*. Middletown, Conn.: Wesleyan University Press, 1978.

Smith, Donald B. "Kahgegagahbowh." In *Life, Letters, and Speeches, George Copway*, edited by A. LaVonne Brown Ruoff, 1–22. Lincoln: University of Nebraska Press, 1997.

————. *Sacred Feathers: The Reverend Peter Jones (Kahkewaquonaby) and the Mississauga Indians*. Lincoln: University of Nebraska Press, 1987.

Smith, Sidonie, and Julia Watson, eds. *Women, Autobiography, Theory: A Reader*. Madison: University of Wisconsin Press, 1998.

Stevens, Laura. *The Poor Indians: British Missionaries, Native Americans, and Colonial Sensibility*. Philadelphia: University of Pennsylvania Press, 2004.

Sutton, Walter. *The Western Book Trade: Cincinnati as a Nineteenth-Century Publishing and Book Trade Center*. Columbus: Ohio State University Press, 1961.

Szasz, Margaret Connell. *Indian Education in the American Colonies, 1607–1783*. Albuquerque: University of New Mexico Press, 1988.

Teute, Fredrika, ed. *Contact Points: American Frontiers from the Mohawk Valley to the Mississippi, 1750–1830*. Chapel Hill: University of North Carolina Press, 1998.

Thornton, Russell. "Boundary Dissolution and Revitalization Movements: The Case of the Nineteenth-Century Cherokee." *Ethnohistory* 40, no. 3 (Summer 1993): 359–83.

Tigerman, Kathleen. *Wisconsin Indian Literature*. Madison: University of Wisconsin Press, 2007.

Trachtenberg, Alan. *Shades of Hiawatha: Staging Indians, Making Americans, 1880–1930*. New York: Hill and Wang, 2004.

Traveller Bird. *Tell Them They Lie: The Sequoyah Myth*. Los Angeles: Westerlore Press, 1971.

Treuer, David. *Native American Fiction: A User's Manual*. St. Paul, Minn.: Graywolf Press, 2006.

Turano, Jane Van Norman. "Taken from Life: Early Ethnographic Portraits of New England Algonkians, ca. 1845–1865." In *Algonkians of New England: Past and Present*, 121–43. Dublin Seminar for New England Folklife Annual Proceedings. Boston: Boston University Press, 1993.

Vecsey, Christopher. *Imagining Ourselves Richly: Mythic Narratives of North American Indians*. New York: Crossroad Publishing, 1988.

Vibert, Elizabeth. "'The Natives Were Strong to Live': Reinterpreting Early Nineteenth-Century Prophetic Movements." *Ethnohistory* 42, no. 2 (Spring 1995): 197–229.

Vizenor, Gerald. *Manifest Manners: Postindian Warriors of Survivance*. Hanover, N.H.: Wesleyan University Press, 1994.

Walker, Cheryl. *Indian Nation: Native American Literature and Nineteenth-Century Nationalisms*. Durham, N.C.: Duke University Press, 1997.

Walker, Willard B. "Native Writing Systems." In *Languages*. Vol. 17 of *Handbook of North American Indians*, edited by Ives Goddard, 158–86. Washington, D.C.: Smithsonian, 1996.

Walker, Willard B., and James Sarbaugh. "The Early History of the Cherokee Syllabary." *Ethnohistory* 40, no. 1 (Winter 1993): 70–94.

Wallace, Anthony F. C. *The Death and Rebirth of the Seneca*. New York: Vintage, 1972.

Warhus, Mark. *Another America: Native American Maps and the History of Our Land*. New York: St. Martin's Press, 1997.

Warkentin, Germaine. "In Search of 'the Word of the Other': Aboriginal Sign Systems and the History of the Book in Canada." *Book History* 2, no. 1 (1999): 1–27.

Warner, Michael. *The Letters of the Republic: Publication and the Public Sphere in Eighteenth-Century America*. Cambridge, Mass.: Harvard University Press, 1990.

———. *Publics and Counterpublics*. New York: Zone Books, 2005.

Warrior, Robert. *The People and the Word: Reading Native Nonfiction*. Minneapolis: University of Minnesota Press, 2005.

———. *Tribal Secrets: Recovering American Indian Intellectual Traditions*. Minneapolis: University of Minnesota Press, 1995.

Weaver, Jace. *American Indian Literary Nationalism*. Albuquerque: University of New Mexico Press, 2006.

White, Richard. *The Middle Ground: Indians, Empires, and Republics in the Great Lakes Region, 1650–1815*. New York: Cambridge University Press, 1991.

Wogan, Peter. "Perceptions of European Literacy in Early Contact Situations." *Ethnohistory* 41, no. 3 (Summer 1994): 407–29.

Womack, Craig. *Red on Red: Native American Literary Separatism*. Minneapolis: University of Minnesota Press, 1999.

Woodmansee, Martha. "On the Author Effect: Recovering Collectivity." In *The Construction of Authorship: Textual Appropriation in Law and Literature*, edited by Martha Woodmansee and Peter Jaszi. Durham, N.C.: Duke University Press, 1994.

Wyss, Hilary. *Writing Indians: Literacy, Christianity, and Native Community in Early America*. Amherst: University of Massachusetts Press, 2000.

Young Bear, Ray A. *Black Eagle Child: The Facepaint Narratives*. Iowa City: University of Iowa Press, 1992.

Index